Look to the Mountain

LeGrand Cannon, Jr.

The Countryman Press, Inc.
Woodstock, Vermont

LOOK TO THE MOUNTAIN

This edition published by The Countryman Press, Inc, Woodstock, Vermont, by arrangement with Henry Holt & Co., Inc.

PRINTING HISTORY
Holt edition published October 1942

2nd printing	October 1942	7th printing	May 1953
3rd printing	October 1942	8th printing	September 1956
4th printing	November 1942	9th printing	May 1958
5th printing	December 1942	10th printing	January 1961
6th printing	April 1943	11th printing	March 1963

12th printing February 1965
Book-of-the-Month Club edition published October 1942
Condensation published in Omnibook 1943
Sun Dial edition published October 1944
Armed Services edition published October 1944

Bantam edition October 1951

2nd printing	October 1951	3rd printing	January 1952

New Bantam edition November 1960

2nd printing	November 1960	8th printing	September 1974
3rd printing	April 1965	9th printing	December 1975
4th printing	June 1968	10th printing	June 1976
5th printing	June 1971	11th printing	May 1980
6th printing	November 1971	12th printing	July 1980
7th printing	April 1973	13th printing	January 1983

Countryman Press edition July 1991
2nd printing September 1994

All rights reserved.
Copyright 1942 by Henry Holt & Co., Inc.
Copyright © 1970 by LeGrand Cannon, Jr.

Cover and text design by Ann Aspell
Cover illustrations by Judy Jensen

ISBN 0-88150-215-4

PRINTED IN CANADA

23 22 21 20 19 18

Contents

Foreword

Look to the Mountain is one of the most enduring popular novels written in the United States during the past half century. Published first in 1942, it has remained in print, appearing in seven different editions with two dozen reprints, and has sold over a million copies. The book's history testifies to the continuing appeal of the novel.

It is not difficult to understand that appeal. LeGrand Cannon writes about a subject of widespread historical and romantic interest—the pioneering experience of America's early settlers. Whit Livingston and his young wife Melissa leave the growing village of Kettleford (Bedford) in colonial New Hampshire to homestead for themselves in the township of Tamworth nearly a hundred miles north. They become the first permanent inhabitants in the town. Through hard work, perseverance, and frugality the young couple turn a small portion of the wilderness into a virtually self-sufficient farm. They have children who adapt well to frontier living. They witness the arrival of other pioneers, watch the population of the township increase, and near the end of the novel take pride in Tamworth's first official town meeting. Americans are trained to think of their pioneering ancestors as "hardy" and "courageous," both as individuals and as community builders. Whit and Melissa fit the image perfectly.

The book is written in simple and direct language. At first one New York critic commented, the style "may seem bare and unadorned, but it quickly becomes obvious that (Cannon) uses words subtly and writes sensitively as well as selectively." The plot, although emphasizing the success of the Livingstons, contains enough near tragic events to make the reader anxious about the ultimate fate of the protagonists. Whit and Melissa swamp their canoe while traveling north in November's freezing temperatures; the Livingstons' close friend and benefactor, Jonas Moore, nearly dies of an infected hand; Whit has several close calls, including one while serving as a volunteer in the revolution. A compelling story well told provides an attractive menu item for the the reading public. "*Look to the Mountain*," wrote another critic shortly after the Book-of-the-Month Club selected it as its choice for November, 1942, "is a novel with a future. It is the kind of book individual readers fall in love with . . . and go on year after year recommending to their friends."

Finally, developments independent of the intrinsic quality of the book have helped to sustain its popularity. *Look to the Mountain* is a New Hampshire novel, and during the past forty years the state, along with the rest of northern New England, has become an increasingly attractive place for tourists and for Americans seeking permanent residence away from urban centers. Cannon summered for years in Tamworth and developed a deep personal love for north central New Hampshire. His novel reflects this "sense of place." It is so geographically specific that readers can easily trace the routes traveled by Whit and Melissa. They can also climb Mount Chocorua, which as Coruway Mountain provided Cannon with the central symbol of his novel.

Look to the Mountain, then, is a novel for everyone who cares about the Granite State, its history and its people. It remains "a novel with a future."

Jere Daniell
Dartmouth College

PART ONE

The Fields
1769

1

It was a hot, dry-feeling day early in August in the year 1769. Kettleford, in New Hampshire Province, was haying. Throughout the whole township—on the west bank of Merrimack below Amoskeag Falls and twenty miles north of the Bay Province line—there was nothing but haying. Politics, fishing, linen and flax, woodcutting, potatoes, the reaping of rye, speculating in land, the Presbyterian church, those things were forgotten, or at least put aside.

There wasn't much doing in politics anyway. Young Governor Wentworth—old Uncle Benning's nephew and successor—had been two years in the chair, and was doing well at it. John was as honest as his uncle was not. Kettleford liked him—whenever they thought of him.

Three weeks ago, the Kettleford men had finished their fishing up at the falls, and they'd made a fair catch of it. They'd taken more fish—salmon and shad—than the Indians ever did back in the old days. Three hundred pounds for a man in a night would go a long way toward paying expenses of setting a weir and tying a net, finding the rum, and mending the spears, buying the salt, all the various things that a man had to reckon.

The making of linen wouldn't come until later, and the flax wasn't pressing. Winter rye wasn't ready—though soon it would be—and no one would think of cutting wood in the summer. Digging potatoes and pressing out cider belonged to the autumn; churchgoing to Sabbath and maybe to Lecture Day; everything in its season. Right now it was haying.

Kettleford fields were pleasant to mow in. That is, some of them were, and they were pleasanter now than they had been. Thirty years had got rid of the stumps, and even in the western part of the town, back from the river, oxen had hauled away some of the boulders. True, there were weeds now, but there weren't any seedlings—poplar, witch hazel, and ironwood bushes; they'd stopped coming in. So had the Indians. And there weren't many steep places: either a field had been interval land, or level enough to warrant its clearing.

The land, of course, varied. The northwestern corner of Kettleford township lay near to the base of the low, round

Uncannunucs—twin, wooded hills that could be seen for some distance but that were not high enough to be called proper mountains. In the western part of the township, it was uneven and stony—more like New Boston, which was still farther west. The best land in Kettleford was along the bank of the river—fine, rolling meadows that lay in the sun, planted to rye and to Indian corn, flax in the low places, hay, and so on. Here the houses were stout and the barns were tremendous. In the southern part of the town, there was a good deal of clay.

Generally speaking, the hills were left wooded—four out of five acres in the town as a whole. But it didn't seem so—in summer, at any rate, because then a man would spend most of his time in his fields. Ever since Monday, every man in the town, a good many women, the oxen, and the boys had been hard at it haying. Go north up the river; it would be the same way—in Goffstown, and Hooksett, Bow, Pennacook, Boscawen—or southward in Londonderry, Brenton's and Nottingham. In all of New Hampshire, everybody was haying—except maybe in Portsmouth. Portsmouth was different. No doubt in Portsmouth—forty miles east and north—there'd be merchants and gentlemen, King's officers, sailors, and a varied assortment of ladies, who, at this time in the morning, were not doing a thing. But Kettleford lived by the field and the river. And when the sun shone in August—the first week in August—Kettleford mowed hay. They let it make in the field, and they raked it, they cocked it, and hauled it—and no man was exempt from doing his part.

Young Nathaniel Thett, for example—he was the schoolmaster—had been swinging a borrowed scythe since the sun was an hour high—and it now lacked but two hours to noon. The blister in the pocket of Thett's right thumb had broken, and there was a notable pain in his left shoulder muscle. But he was still swinging—not so smart as he had been, perhaps, but all the same keeping the heel of his scythe well down and avoiding such rocks as he could see.

Thett was working for Lawrence Murphy, the tailor, against a blue surtout that Murphy would fashion him in the fall. It was a deal of comfort to Thett to know that this winter he'd have a coat.

Down in a remote corner of the Governor lot, Mr. Gavin Gowan, the minister, was somberly cutting a little hay for himself. Mr. Gowan's contract with Kettleford provided for hay, but Mr. Gowan had learned that a cow can't eat contracts. A good

3

hand to mow, Mr. Gowan was, too. He was still on his third gill of rum, and he'd cut close on to three cocks since breakfast.

Even old David Gillmor was haying, but he couldn't mow or pitch this year; he was pulling a loafer rake. He was about the lamest this summer that he'd ever been. Twelve years ago, David had made the mistake of wearing his waistcoat as he'd come out of Fort William and Henry in the surrender. It was a lovely garment made out of loonnecks—and the first Indian who saw it had sought to hamstring David so as to get it. But David was short in the legs, and the blow had landed too high. Fleeing into the brush, David had not only kept his waistcoat but had carried along the tomahawk also, stuck in his backside. Lately, the wound had been full of pain, even in weather like this. But David still managed to hitch himself along somehow, and in the course of a day he'd rake his share of hay.

In the big handsome meadow that lay close to the river on Widow Karr's place, there were five men—all haying, all single men, two of them widowers. Nobody knew, yet, just how it was going to come out.

William Cauldwell, the cordwainer, had Ensign Lord working with him. Cauldwell had made Ensign a pair of pumps back in February. Tonight they'd be square. Lord was finding the rum for the haying, as against the sole leather Cauldwell had found for the pumps. It had been pretty poor leather, so Ensign had thought, and Cauldwell was now thinking the same of the rum.

Down back of Porter's place, Zebulon Porter was pitching to his wife, who was up on top making the load. She could make a load right, too—starting at the outside and then working in—and not lose hardly a wisp, except what was snatched off by a branch, maybe, between there and the barn. If she'd been strong enough to pitch off when they got to the barn, it would have been better yet. It was hard for Zeb to pitch off a load he hadn't made because he didn't know in what order each fork had been laid. They were doing all right, though; they'd hauled two jags already and would get in a third before dinner.

Joe Felipe hadn't had a fire in his forge since Saturday night, but he'd be done with his haying some time this forenoon. Joe had hayed Sunday. He was a Portygee, and they knew he was Popish. But still he'd been allowed to remain when he first came to town, and now they were used to him. About a year and a half ago Joe had showed up at Butler's tavern one morning in January after traveling all night on the crust. It was just after Captain Karr

4

died and the town was without any smith. Joe said that he was a worker in iron—which he had been at one time. He bid in the smithy when they held the vendue, and paid for it in gold. He had then moved the smithy, setting it up near the center of town, just down the road from the new meetinghouse, and not too far from the tavern. He turned out to be a fair smith when sober and a good one when drunk. But he wasn't as good as old Karr had been, and nobody made out to Joe that he was. He was a squat, bull of a man, dark-complected—as anyone might be, but as not many in Kettleford were—and he wore his black hair tied with a scarlet hair ribbon. He had little small ears that set tight to his head and made his neck look all the bigger. And he wore a knife like a sailor.

The reason the town didn't take to him better, Joe laid to Whit Livingston. It was Whit who kept the talk going about what a smith Karr had been—a far better smith than this Portygee Joe ever had been or would be. If it hadn't been for that kind of talk, Joe had an idea, they might forget his dark complexion even in winter and about his being Popish, as well. Joe couldn't see that these things were important. He hadn't a drop of black blood in his veins, and if his being born Popish wasn't important to him, Joe couldn't see why it should be to anyone else. He hated Whit Livingston.

This young Whit Livingston was the best hand to mow that there was in Kettleford. Aside from that, he was a joke. When Whit had been twelve years old—right on his birthday—his father, Tom Livingston, had treated the boy at the tavern—and Whit hadn't been able to drink it. Rum was new to Whit then, because old Tom had never seen fit to spare the boy any. It had stuck in Whit's throat. It was a comical thing for the men standing round, but it was all the more funny because old Tom himself was such a great drinking man. The joke was on Tom, and all of them laughed at it. Tom hadn't taken it kindly. He figured the boy was making game of him, too. So Tom stood his son up in the middle of the room and yanked the shirt off the boy's back. Then Tom laid it on him with the piece of rope that until then had held up the boy's pants. After a time, some of the men—although they hadn't yet finished laughing—had made Tom give over. The boy was still on his feet, to be sure, but Captain's daughter was there—Captain Eliphalet Butler, kept the tavern—and though she was only a little thing then, ten years old or so, maybe, still her being there didn't make it seem right.

5

Whit never did learn to drink rum. And it was a year or two after that before he'd go to the tavern when he was sent on an errand. He didn't seem to like to go about amongst people at all. He thought they were still laughing about what they remembered—and as often as not, probably, he was correct.

Old Captain Karr, though, had taken a liking to Whit. Whit would go over and hang round the smithy—more particularly times when there weren't any other boys there—and sometimes the captain would give him a task to do.

When Whit was sixteen and ready for it, Karr had told Whit that he was going to make him a scythe blade. He told Whit that he'd make him as pretty a blade as a man could wish for. And Captain Karr made it; he kept his word. Whit cut him twenty-one cords of rock maple for it, and Karr claimed that he'd hit the blade a lick with his hammer for every blow Whit had struck with the ax. It might be he had. She was a beauty. Whit didn't know how he was going to wait for the summer to come.

That blade was the last thing Karr ever made before he died.

By the end of that summer, a few men were saying already that young Whit Livingston, now, was the best hand to mow that there was in the town. And then they'd say that, if Tom Livingston's boy could mow that good, it *must* be the blade! Why, alongside of Karr, this dog of a Portygee couldn't hammer out a blade to cut mullen.

It was in that way that Whit kept the talk going. He didn't know that he did; he didn't hear it—but Joe Felipe heard it. Karr being gone, Whit stayed around home mostly, or he might go gunning somewhere off by himself. Karr had left him the gun in his will. The following winter, Whit ran a trap line. When he had need to go to the tavern to do any trading or to buy gear or the like, he'd go there in the morning. But he did go to the tavern, and lately he'd been there more often. He was nineteen now, tall, with a quiet face and slow-spoken. He went to the tavern because of Butler's daughter, Melissa.

For a long time Whit had been more afraid that he'd meet up with that girl on the road than he was that he'd meet up with the devil. If a man laughed at him, that was one thing. But she'd seen it, too—she'd seen him stripped and beaten because he couldn't drink rum—and Whit knew she was laughing. She might not show it—whenever he thought she was looking at him, he'd never been able to look back—but there was no reason why she shouldn't be laughing. Then somehow or other—this was the

6

strange thing—the temptation to see her got to be like the temptation to bite on a sore tooth. Whit bit on it often. It wasn't pain that he felt, but still it was a feeling that had some pain in it.

This morning, Whit was mowing in the sparse and dry grass that his father's fields always ran to. Besides Whit, there were three men: old Tom and Whit's half brother, who was younger than Whit was, and Whit's uncle, Rob Murdough. Rob had brought with him a pair of young oxen, yoked into a rick he had managed to borrow, and between Whit and the oxen they were getting in hay. In return for the oxen, old Tom had agreed to lend Whit to his uncle for four days next week—two days for each ox. Old Tom, as usual, had got the worst of the bargain.

Even in grass like this, thin and hard and the whole field sprinkled with rocks, Whit could mow clean and he could mow fast. He might not look to be fast, but that was because he mowed easy and gentle and the speed didn't show. He used a straight snath made out of white ash that had just the least little mite of a whip to it, and a piece of black oilstone for a rifle. The stone had been given him by a White Hills man he'd met trapping. The man said there was a lot of it in a place west of Great Ossipy Pond. It was a stone to put a nice edge on a blade—not wired, but sweet. Whit was having a pretty good time.

Old Tom stopped midway of a swath, wiped the sweat out of his eyes, dropped his scythe to the ground, and walked back to the keg. Other men used a jug mostly for haying, but not old Tom Livingston. When he hayed, he hayed right. There was a ten-gallon keg, all complete with a spigot, set under a beech tree and a gourd lying beside it.

Tom was tired—and looked it. He was a stringy kind of man, and when he was tired, he drooped. He looked like his farm.

Down on one knee, he picked up the gourd, held it under the spigot, and then turned the handle. Nothing happened. He tipped the keg forward slowly . . . and it seemed to take him a long time before he'd tipped it all the way forward—and the truth had come out. That was all that came out.

Tom stared at the keg for a while, and then he sat back and wondered if he was going to cry—but he found he'd been sweating so much that he was more sober than he'd thought he was. He tried to think what to do. They were clean out of rum at the house, and Rob wouldn't lend. Neither would anyone else. He guessed he'd have to send Whit to the tavern. If he sent Whit, Whit would come back.

It was four miles to Butler's, and while Whit was gone, they could all spell themselves.

The other boy came over for a drink, and Tom let him find out for himself what had happened. The boy cursed for a while and then Tom said, "Go get Whit." The boy stood there and bawled for Whit. Whit finished his swath, and then he came over.

"This here's dry," said Tom, touching the keg with his foot. "You go to Butler's and fetch some."

Whit knew about how much they'd work while he was gone.

"You ain't got to take the keg with you." His father's voice rose. "Get a yoke from the house and a couple of jugs. And get a move onto you! I'm too dry to wait long."

Whit was trying to figure if there wasn't some other way out of it. They hadn't any more than got started, and now Rob and the oxen would be going to waste all the time he was gone.

His father roared at him: "It ain't going t' kill you to go fetch some rum, is it?"

"No, I don't know as it is."

"Then fetch it!—and don't stand there like a sick shad thinkin' about it. Just because you're a unnatural freak ain't no sign that the rest of us want t' hay dry."

Whit hung his scythe on the highest branch he could reach.

"Leave that thing where I c'n git at it," his father said. "I got a gap in mine."

"Then you'll have t' grind it."

"You do as I tell you!"

Whit turned slowly round to him. He spoke straight into his father's face: "You touch that scythe, and I'll cut your throat with it." Then he bent down to pick up the keg.

Old Tom didn't say a word, and no more did the other two.

Whit took the loose bung out of the bunghole and put it into his shirt. Then he swung the keg up to his shoulder and started off across the field—not toward the house, toward the tavern.

His uncle called after him, speaking as gently as he could: "What about the yoke, Whit?"

"I ain't only bringin' one keg."

Rob leaned on a tree. "He'll have quite a lug," he remarked, "'fore he gets back."

Old Tom said, "God," and lay down.

The other boy went down to the house to fetch up some cider.

2

Captain Eliphalet Butler, taverner, storekeeper and Captain of the Train Band, had been putting in a bad morning. A dozen times he'd stepped out into the yard to look at the weather, and each time he'd shaken his bald little head because the weather was fine. Captain's small meadow was ready to cut—and he could get no man to work in it.

Captain had to have hay. He didn't own any oxen, but he did have three cows, and now and again he'd furnish hay to a teamster or to a traveler on horseback. There weren't many travelers. Captain Butler's small tavern was mainly a local affair: rum and provisions, gunpowder, nails. . . . Bed and board were available but were not often called for. Merrimack River was no longer the highway that it had been for Indians. The men using it now as a route north and south were trappers and hunters, and only occasionally settlers. Connecticut River carried the settlers. As for east and west traffic, there wasn't much anyway. There was a road to Portsmouth from Kettleford, and it ran past the tavern and on down to the river. But it brought little custom to Captain. A week on that road would shorten the life of a pair of oxen a year. In between towns it was full of brush and down trees, mudholes and boulders, and big hollow stumps. Any traveler who'd come over that road deserved to put up at an inn that was better than Captain's. There was an inn to the east of him the other side of the river, and there was one a few miles to the west in New Boston. That left Captain Butler to make what money he could out of Kettleford people—a course to which he applied himself with more greed than hard work.

Coming in from the yard now, he leaned on his counter, his chin in his hands, and wondered what he could do. The thing that graveled him most was that he was the town's biggest creditor— and yet he couldn't collect. If he were to try to force payment in labor from a man who could vote, they'd vote in somebody else to keep tavern. Same way with the men who were in the Train Band: they elected him Captain. Training Day, he had his headquarters here at the tavern, and even after deducting for enough treats to assure his election, he still made more money on

Training Day than he did any other day in the year. He couldn't risk losing that.

In resentful despair, he mixed himself a small brandy and water, and stood musing in front of the open shutters at one end of the room. From there, looking past a corner of the stable and the springhouse beyond, he could see away down in the distance one end of his meadow—with the breeze shifting the colors on the grass and the whole thing a fine picture of summer. But Captain saw nothing of beauty—only possible waste.

Something moved on the far side of the meadow—and the quick little eyes at the window made out a man come forth from the woods—a man carrying a load on his shoulder. Swiftly the figure came along the edge of the field—not running, not walking. Captain knew every gait in town: that was Whit Livingston . . . bringing a ten-gallon keg to be filled.

Captain's daughter came out of the springhouse to set one of her milk pans out in the sun. And she looked toward the meadow—and her hands flew to her hair. Then she smoothed out her apron. She gazed at the meadow—and then she darted back into the springhouse again.

Captain stood with his mouth hung open . . . and turned away from the window, shaking his head. His mouth shut, and he smiled. Whit Livingston, eh? Well, there couldn't be anyone safer!

Four years ago, being newly a widower, Captain had carefully reckoned that a daughter cost less than a wife, and had decided he wouldn't remarry. Since that time, Melissa had done as much work as a woman. It had agreed with her, though; she was rugged enough, even though she was small. But lately Captain had worried: he was afraid he might lose her. He could not see her beauty, but he did know that a girl who could do as much work as Melissa, and whose father was supposed to have money, couldn't fail of some suitors.

Melissa'd had them, all right. She could have married well at fourteen or at any time after that. It had been her own deciding—so she had supposed—that had kept her from marrying.

Captain knew better. Men are not at their best round a tavern—and he had seen to it that she wasn't spared very much. Melissa had witnessed more than one brawl—and with bucket and mop had set the place to rights afterward. Fighting, a good many times, followed singing. She had used to like ballads—but not any more. A gouged eye made her sicken. She had learnt, too, how to wrench free when they seized her. Melissa didn't much want to get married. She'd seen too many men in the morning, lying face down on the midden who'd been flung out there to sleep where it was warm.

But in those ways Whit Livingston was not like the others.

Captain—although he could see that—wasn't the least bit disturbed. Whit was next thing to a pauper. Melissa'd get over it promptly. After all, she was his daughter.

Melissa came in from the springhouse, and her father greeted her testily. "Where you been all this time?"

"Churnin'," she said.

"Settin' in the cool of the springhouse, more like it."

Melissa thought he looked sickly. "What's the matter with you, pa? You look out o' case."

"Hay."

"Your hay's good!" she exclaimed.

"'Tain't no good if 'tain't cut."

"You c'n git a crew to come mow it."

"Crew!" said Captain. "Can't get a man!" He explained his position.

Melissa said, "Joe Felipe don't belong to the Train Band. Maybe you could get him."

"I owe him!" said Captain. "Shut the eye of an ax a month ago for me, 'n two weeks ago he fixed a beal on the pot."

They were both silent—both thinking of Whit. When his knock came at the door, only Captain looked up.

Whit stood motionless in the doorway waiting for his eyes to get used to the dimness.

Melissa thought he was lovely.

In point of fact, he was clean, having washed himself in the brook the other side of the meadow—and his hair was neatly drawn back and secured. His clothes were the same as most men's: a loose gray linen shirt and a pair of breeches—Whit's were leather—that came just below his knees. He was carrying the keg with two fingers hooked into the bunghole.

"You ain't goin' t' lug that home *full*, are you?" Captain said hopefully.

Whit nodded.

"Set it there under the cask, then. Melissa, you draw."

Melissa got down the funnel, and Captain watched Whit.

With the keg slowly filling, Melissa turned her head and looked up. "Hayin'?"

11

Whit opened his mouth to answer, closed it, and nodded his head.

Whit, Captain concluded, was worse off than Melissa.

"Wish't I could get mine cut," Captain remarked.

"Looks prime," agreed Whit. "I come up through t' meadow."

"You're about done down to your place, I expect."

"Ain't hardly got started."

"Mowin' hadn't ought to take long. They tell me you're quite a hand."

"I got a good blade." It was always his answer.

"So I hear. Karr's, ain't it?"

"Yes."

"He was an awful good smith," Melissa put in.

"You're drawin' rum," her father reminded her. "How many is workin' down to your place now, Whit?"

"There's three there besides me, and my uncle Rob's oxen."

"You got a crew."

Whit thought of them as he knew they were now, lying under the beech tree.

Melissa rolled the keg gently to see how it was coming. "This here's going t' be wonderful heavy," she said.

Whit managed better this time. "I c'n lug it, I guess."

"There ain't many would want to."

"'Tain't a great ways."

"Four mile," said Melissa.

Captain judged the keg nearly full. "Whit," he demanded, "whyn't you take a day 'n come and cut mine for me?"

"Well—"

"I could rake," said Melissa.

Captain was proud of himself. It was what he had hoped for. He figured his field was as good as mowed now.

But Captain had counted his chickens a little soon.

Just himself and Melissa? Whit thought. All day alone in a field? It was so much more than he'd hoped for, that now he drew back. "Got to get our'n in first," he told Captain.

Melissa banged shut the spigot. She stood up and faced Whit. "Go git it in, then," she said. "We'll git a man to cut our'n."

Whit could say nothing. He felt his face flush—and at that moment Joe Felipe ambled in.

Captain greeted him.

Joe answered politely—and looked at the other two.

"We were talkin' 'bout hay," Captain explained.

12

Joe wondered what Whit could have said about hay to make Melissa look that way. The two or three times Joe had tried for Melissa, he'd not succeeded in so much as making her angry. Melissa had laughed at him. (It had sounded to her as though he called her "militia.") Envy rose up in Joe, and he hated Whit more than ever.

"Your'n in, Joe?" said Captain.

"My hay?" Reluctantly Joe turned to Captain. "I finish this morning."

"You done well. Have some brandy."

"Treat?" Joe inquired, scarcely believing.

"Treat," Captain assured him. "First man in the town t' get his hay in. Girl, set out t' brandy!"

Melissa, with a flourish, set out the stone bottle. She gave Joe a smile, but Whit failed to see it; he was down on one knee, with fumbling fingers trying to fit the bung into his keg.

Joe poured himself brandy in a quantity that suited his talents and the fact that the brandy was free—eying Melissa while he was drinking it. He set the heavy glass down on the counter. "T'at's a' right!" he exclaimed.

Whit began to rap with the bungstarter.

"Joe," proposed Captain loudly, "you're done up to your place—you mow for me the rest of the day, 'n you c'n have that brandy to mow on—what's left in the bottle."

Whit had left off his rapping.

"Mine now," Joe responded. "T' ax an' t' beal," he reminded Captain.

"I told Pa I'd rake," Melissa said coolly.

Joe's eyes went from one to the other—but he looked last at Whit. The boy was standing up, waiting. . . .

Joe turned back to Captain. "Done," he said—and he reached for the bottle. "I take a roun' of it now."

Whit came over and laid the bungstarter down on the counter. "That's a big meadow; you'll want two hands to mow that meadow."

Joe laughed aloud. "Too late, boy!" he said. "Here—" he held the bottle toward Whit—"have a drink of t' brandy 'n t'en you go home."

"You better drink it. It might be you'll need it."

"By God," Joe exclaimed happily, "maybe I will!"—he looked across to Melissa—"eh?" But she wouldn't promise.

Whit's not taking his eyes off of Joe for an instant made

13

Captain uneasy. Moreover, Whit was cold sober—there was no telling what he might do. Captain slid his hand toward the bungstarter. It was a very good bungstarter, with a square, ironwood head and a short, slim, withy handle.

Joe finished his drink, and banged the glass on the counter. "Go on home!" he told Whit. "I hear a'ready too much of your mowing."

"I can mow," Whit acknowledged.

"You and your Karr blade! Look! T'ey send you t' tote rum. T'at's how good you can mow! You, t'ey better yoke in wit' t'oxen—where you belong!"

Captain had the bungstarter now and felt better.

Melissa was perched up on one end of the counter. "Whit's a good hand to mow," she said.

"I got a good blade." Whit said it from habit.

"God damn your blade!" bellowed Joe, and whipped out his knife. He held the point of it, quivering, just under Whit's nose.

Whit stood his ground. He was scared, but stood quiet. Gently Captain moved into position.

There wasn't a sound from Melissa.

Joe's hand was trembling and so was his voice. "I c'n cut me more hay wit' t'is here little knife 'n what you c'n cut wit' your Karr blade! You come 'n mow! I show you t' man who c'n mow: José Felipe!"

"That's fair," Whit agreed.

"And t' best one to mow, she rake for him tomorrow. Si?"

Whit made no answer.

It was the girl's voice that came into the silence. She spoke low and even. "That's fair."

3

Joe, going back after his scythe, met a man on the road. The word spread pretty fast after that, and it didn't thin out in the spreading. Nathaniel Thett, for example, mowing along the wall, learned from a breathless youth that Whit and the Portygee were at that moment fighting a duel with scythes in the meadow down back of the tavern. Thett informed Murphy, and set off at a run. Murphy followed more leisurely.

Mr. Gowan heard it that Whit, coming on Joe and the girl under a haycock, had grabbed up Joe's scythe and gone at him.

14

Mr. Gowan didn't believe the whole of it, but still he thought he'd better go up there.

Down at Widow Karr's place, they understood the tavern was afire. They couldn't see any smoke, but they went all the same.

Those in Tom Livingston's field, being asleep, came as near to the truth as did any. Whit had arrived there with the keg about noontime. He hadn't waked anyone—he'd just left the keg, taken his scythe and his oilstone, and started back to the tavern. Later, when the men wakened, they concluded that Captain must have talked Whit into doing some mowing. They went to work on the keg.

Meantime, at the tavern, there was confusion and some disappointment. Joe had shrewdly bethought himself that, on the morrow, there might be more privacy down in the meadow if the whole town didn't know what was doing. Therefore, on his return from fetching his scythe, he'd denied his first story and had sworn to the earlier arrivals that what had occurred had been no more than high words between him and Whit over who had the best scythe blade. They would now mow it out.

Melissa, appealed to, had confirmed this, and so had Captain.

Some believed it; some didn't. No one was quite certain as to just how the girl did figure in it. But they were certain of one thing: they were here now, and they might as well make the best of it. A contest at mowing wasn't the same thing as a fire—and it wasn't a murder—but they'd been working hard haying and they had a mind now to make holiday. A mowing contest would serve . . . and they all started in drinking and swearing and wagering just as though they'd been gentlemen. They bet about even. Whit was the best hand to mow, but he'd likely be tuckered after lugging that keg home.

Mr. Gowan, the minister, drew apart from the crowd. Unless this thing were done properly, there'd be nothing but argument, and a fight to wind up with. He found a smooth place where the dirt was packed down, and fishing a nail out of his pocket, he squatted down on his haunches. He drew a rough outline of Captain's hay field—as near as he could remember it. It was a long narrow field and irregular enough so that there was no proper way to divide it in half—not without a compass and chain and take half a day to it . . . and even then the grass wasn't the same in all parts of the field. All right then: they'd have to mow round it. But that wouldn't work, either. The man on the inside would have too much advantage; his laps would be shorter.

Gowan puzzled and puzzled . . . and finally he got it. He was greatly relieved. They'd mow the field lengthwise. Between swaths, they'd cross over. That made it come out right.

Whit had taken the same way back to the tavern—the short way through the woods. The scythe seemed a light thing to carry after the keg, but it was pesky where there were bushes. Still, he made pretty good time. As he came up through the meadow, he figured he'd been gone from the tavern less than two hours.

The men in the yard saw him come round the corner of the stable, traveling at an earnest, shuffling lope, and bearing his scythe like a banner. When Whit saw them, he stopped. There were more than two score of them.

They gave him a cheer, with a good deal of laughter.

Whit stood stock-still, facing it out. Then he turned to go home—and he heard the roar at his back as they thought they were going to be cheated.

A man spoke close behind him and then laid hold on Whit's arm. The boy jerked free and swung round—to face Mr. Gowan. They looked at each other a moment, Mr. Gowan quiet and easy. "Now, Whit," he said, "you stay and go through with it."

"No!"—and because it boiled up within him, Whit gave the reason: "All that they're after is something to laugh at."

"That's correct," Gowan answered. "And you quit now, and they'll have it." He let this sink in, and then asked, "Can you wax him?"

The boy had calmed down some. "I got an awful good blade, sir."

"Are you spent?"

"I'm a little mite blowed, but I ain't anyways spent."

"That'll pass in a minute. We'll go down to the meadow." He turned round to the crowd. "How about it?—Joe ready?"

"He's ready!" they shouted. "Joe's prime!" Those that had bet on Joe had been getting him ready. Joe himself felt he could mow like a whirlwind. "José is a'ready!" he told Mr. Gowan.

The minister spoke to the crowd: "We shall adjourn to the meadow."

They gave a great shout and trooped away down the cart track, past the springhouse and stable, bound for the meadow. Someone asked Whit if he'd had his dinner. Whit said, "No, come to think of it," and two or three heard him.

Strung out, they made quite a procession: the small boys on ahead, then Joe and his backers, then two men who were carrying thirty gallon of rum on a hand barrow, followed by the Captain, fearfully watching the rum. Then some more men, and then Whit, walking alone, and last of all Mr. Gowan, stalking along in the rear, barefoot like the rest—just as he'd come from his haying—but having authority. Some ways back of them all, limped old David Gillmor. No one waited for David—but David would get there.

Melissa had stayed at the tavern.

They passed through a thicket of alder, crossed a small stream, and came up a rise into the meadow. The men in the lead turned round to see where to go now.

"Keep to the edge!" Captain begged them. "Don't trample the hay! Go round to the side, there, under them ash trees. That'll make a good place for this barrel."

Mr. Gowan called Ensign Lord back to him, and inquired, "You sober?"

"I ain't very far from it."

"Well, that's near enough probably. You stay about that way. I may need someone to help me."

Lord nodded. "I'll be here." He was disappointed a little, but at the same time he was flattered.

The barrel was rigged, and Captain, yielding to pressure, treated a round. Ensign held off. But Joe took his with the rest of them, and then fell to work at whetting his blade. He made her ring!

Whit, off to one side, was caressing his blade with the oilstone. It made a soft, slipping sound.

Mr. Gowan, looking over the meadow, found it to be about as he had remembered it. He called for silence—and got something approaching it; they seemed more than willing to have somebody run things. He told them what he had decided, and a few understood it. "Joe," he said, "will lead in."

A cheer stopped him. When a crew mowed, the best hand always was lead man. Joe's backers were cheering. When the noise had let up, Lawrence Murphy, the tailor and an old friend of Karr's—and who had bet on Whit Livingston, dinner or no dinner—called out clearly, "Why Joe?"

"Joe claims he's the best hand," Mr. Gowan explained. "Until Whit proves to the contrary, Joe's statement is good. Joe will lead in."

No one argued.

"Speed's not the only thing," he further explained; "they have to mow clean. I shall be judge of that. Joe, you all whetted?"

Joe said, "What?" and half a dozen men shouted, "You all whetted?"

Joe said proudly, "By God, she's a razor!—skin a mouse wit' her!"

"Whit?"

The boy nodded.

"Now, then, Joe, you'll strike in right here. You'll mow along the edge—keeping well clear of the bushes—to the south end of the field, understand?"

"Oh, I un'erstan' a'right."

"Then you pick up your scythe and walk across to the other side, and mow back along that."

"Sure!" said Joe. "Sure? I un'erstan'."

"Then you pick up your scythe and walk over to *this* side, and mow back to here."

"Sure, I mow round t' field, but I walk on t' ends."

"That's correct. When you get back to here, you'll move into the field a swath, and do the same thing again."

"Sure, sure! You don' need t' tell me. I mowed before, mister."

"Whoever is leading," Mr. Gowan explained to them both, "can mow as wide or as narrow as he's got a mind to. It's up to the other to match his swath to the lead man's. I'll be judge of that, too. You can both whet as it pleases you, or stop for anything else. If there's aught in your minds that I've not provided for, speak of it now."

The crowd murmured approval.

"First man to finish," Mr. Gowan said simply—"in the middle of the field and opposite here—is the best hand to mow." He stepped to one side. "All right, Joe . . ."

Joe spat on his hands and lightly hefted his scythe. It was a great heavy thing with a snath like a tree trunk.

"Strike in!" Gowan ordered.

Joe's eyes narrowed and his face changed. He was serious. He bent to his right and struck in—coming round with a great, long-armed stroke, and a hook onto the end of it. It was clean, too—clean as a whistle! He could mow, all right. Joe was a good one.

The men watched in silence as Joe took his two steps forward, and again the great swing. He was built right to mow, Joe was, short-legged, close to the ground—and those terrible arms on him! He was cutting a wide swath, too—half a yard wider than most men. Two steps and his third swing. Two steps more . . .

At the fifth stroke, Mr. Gowan said, "Whit—"

Whit bent and struck in. He'd had to move over some to his left hand because of the width of Joe's swath, and now, when he lengthened his own swing to match Joe's, Whit found it awkward. He began to lose ground. Joe reached the turn a good ten strokes ahead of him.

Mr. Gowan knew what the trouble was—and maybe some of the others. Whit, having to reach more than was natural at both ends of his stroke, was being pulled off his balance. It made him look clumsy. But there was nothing Mr. Gowan could do.

Joe kept on gaining all the way down the far side. He was a chain's length in the lead now. He walked very businesslike across the end of the field, and began to mow toward them. They began cheering him as he came nearer.

It was the first sound of approval that poor Joe had heard since he'd come to Kettleford. He grinned with delight; he was having a fine time. He stopped to whet in the shade, had a swallow, moved in across Whit's swath, and was all set to strike in again before Whit was come up to them. Joe stood up straight, resting easy, and called out to Whit, "Come on, boy! Get to mowin'!"

They liked that and laughed loudly.

Whit didn't know what Joe had said and he just kept on mowing. Noise was all he could hear; he didn't hear what they called to him. He got the tone of it, though: they were making rare game of him. Well, it wasn't the first time.

As he moved in across the beginning of Joe's second swath, he saw that his own swath was full wide enough. And as clean as Joe's, too. He struck in again without whetting . . . and before very long, he had to repeat several strokes and was forced to whet, then. Because he'd put it off, it took longer. By the time he had an edge fit to mow with, Joe was so far in the distance that that hair ribbon of his didn't look any bigger than the red on a blackbird. Whit fell to mowing again. The fresh edge was a help—but he was still awkward and clumsy.

He'd been trying to keep Melissa from coming into his mind. But that didn't work, either. He kept seeing her. And he heard her voice, too. "That's fair." He heard the low and cool sound of it. When he heard it, it made him mow furiously, like a wild man, with no thought to saving his strength any.

They made a dozen full crossings that way—counting a swath and a back-swath as a crossing—and Joe led now by half the length of the meadow.

Joe began to let up some—he could afford to. Moreover, Joe had a pain in his side. On top of that, Joe had taken to thinking. Hearing them cheer him had done something to Joe: he wanted more of it. Joe was thinking about after tomorrow. Maybe, he was thinking, after tomorrow he'd best let the story get round. If he didn't do that, they'd think Captain had tricked him into mowing this meadow for nothing. For nothing, eh? José Felipe chuckled. He was going to get paid! He was going to get paid for a lot of things. Tomorrow—right over there under them pine trees! Once the town had heard that story, they'd tell it a long time. José Felipe would be quite a fellow!

Joe swung happily on with his mowing—in spite of the stitch in his side and some shortness of breath. They had half the field to go yet.

Whit, men were saying, wouldn't last out. He looked pretty bad. "I'll wager anyone," a man said, "Whit'll fall flat on his face 'fore another five crossings. I'll bet two to one on it."

"Done," he was answered. "Pint to a gill. That's in Medford. Me, now, I figure he'll fall over backward."

All up and down the line, they repeated that. That was a good one!

Mr. Gowan, stalking and watching, finally thought he saw what he'd been looking for. Whit's swath seemed the wider. He paced them off carefully . . . Whit's showed a foot wider.

Mr. Gowan had made up his mind beforehand that, if this happened, he'd tell Whit only. That was proper—whichever man led fixed the width and the other man matched it.

He came up behind Whit and on his near side. "You're mowing too wide, Whit." The boy didn't hear him. Mr. Gowan tried him again, but Whit still didn't hear him. So Gowan reached out and put his hand on Whit's shoulder. The boy kept on mowing. Mr. Gowan took him by the two arms at the elbows—and Whit had to stop then. The boy swayed a little, and the older man held him.

Back under the ash trees, they were puzzled. Then a man said, "Mr. Gowan's showin' him mercy."

"Let him finish!" they shouted. "'Twon't hurt him none, Mr.

Gowan. Let the boy finish!"

"You listen to me, Whit. I'm Mr. Gowan."

Whit nodded.

"You're mowing too wide. Do you hear me? Cut down your swing some. You're about a foot wide. You hear me, now, do you?"

Whit nodded again. He'd heard it all right, but he had no impulse to answer. He tried to pull free, to go on with his mowing.

"Let him mow!" the men shouted. They began to move forward.

"Hold still," Gowan said to Whit. "Listen to me! When you get down to the end there, you go douse your head in the brook. Will you do that?"

Whit croaked out something.

"All right—" He released him.

The minister walked back toward the keg and the people. "He won't quit," he told them—and before they could answer: "I don't know but I'll have a drop. Hot out there in the open."

Melissa, up at the tavern, had held out about as long as she could now. From the window, she could see only the middle part of the field—the part they'd not mowed yet. She couldn't tell how things were going.

On a sudden, Melissa slipped out the back door, round the far side of the stable, and then picked up the cart track to the meadow. It was downhill and Melissa found herself running. She liked to run—just as a child does. Her yellow hair stood out behind her.

But she came cautiously up the side of the rise—and peered over the top of it into the meadow. She could see Whit and the Portygee mowing, but she couldn't tell as to which one had the best of it. It sounded to her as though Joe was ahead. She'd got to get closer—but she didn't want to join the men under the ash trees. Over there on the far side of the meadow there didn't seem to be anyone. From the pines over there, she could watch by herself. She stepped back into the woods and went around that way.

Whit hung his scythe over the first limb in front of his face, and then blundered his way into the woods. It was no more than a couple of rods to the stream and he got there without putting his eye out, lay down on his belly, and plunged his head into the water like a horse with a fever. Both his arms, too, right up to the shoulders. The shock went all through him. He sozzled his face in the water and then he drank some. When he raised up onto his knees, he felt like a new man. But when he looked up, the strength all went out of him. Melissa was standing there. Whit thought she was a vision.

"You done mowin'?" she asked.

Whit got to his feet before trying to answer. He looked at her—and it surprised him that he was able to think to himself that if she was a vision, he couldn't have asked for a better one. There was a smile just starting in round her eyes and she was smiling some round her mouth, too. It was a friendly smile, and yet more than that. It meant she was with him. Whit's strength came back to him. He squared his shoulders, and he gave a hitch to his breeches. "No—" he said, "I ain't started yet."

"Then you better get started—'stead of playin' here goin' swimmin'."

Whit wanted to stay there.

"Go on, now," she ordered. "You get on with your mowin'."

Whit said, "Yes, ma'am,"—and for the first time in his life smiled at her.

Melissa said desperately: "Don't stand there like a booby! Get out there and mow!"

Whit nodded. "I'm goin'." He turned away then—although he knew something was missing—and started back to his mowing. Joe, he took note as he came out of the woods, had pretty near the length of the field on him.

Whit took down his scythe. "Mowing too wide," Mr. Gowan had said. Well, that was easy fixed, certainly! He touched up the edge with a stroke or two, hefted his scythe, and struck in. *This felt like mowing!* Inside of ten strokes, he was humming, keeping time with his mowing. Melissa was probably watching him. All right, let her watch—he'd show her some mowing! He was a good hand to mow, he knew that; it wasn't all in his blade.

Mr. Gowan, standing then under the ash trees, moved over to Ensign and touched him on the elbow. Ensign followed him. A few steps from the crowd, Gowan said to Lord quietly, "Bet three pounds, Bay old tenor, for me on Whit, will you? Get the best

22

odds you can on two pounds of it; the other pound, bet with Captain. And remember: as far as they're concerned, it's you who are wagering."

Ensign said, "Yes, sir." He had to bet even with Captain in order to get him to bet. On the other two pounds, he got three to one. At the same odds, he also wagered ten shillings on his own account with Nathaniel Thett—although he doubted that Thett would ever be able to pay it. He didn't try to go any further: the rest of them knew too much about mowing. Odds were no longer available. They were peering at Whit and beginning to wonder and mutter . . . They'd be trying to copper their bets pretty soon. Ensign thought he was lucky: maybe, if Thett couldn't pay off in money, next winter he'd get Thett to teach him to read.

When Whit and Joe were come near to each other—Whit going one way and Joe going the other—Joe said, "Where you been, for God's sake, boy? You been sleepin'?"

"Dreamin', maybe," said Whit. "Joe, you look to me kinda blowed. Ain't that scythe a mite heavy?"

"God damn, boy, I c'n swing 'er!"

"You're swingin' too slow, Joe. I'm a-comin' up on you."

"You got a way to go yet, boy!" Joe answered truthfully. All the same, soon as Whit had his back to him, Joe began to swing faster. It didn't lengthen his swing any.

Whit, passing the crowd, had a good many things called to him. "What you got hid in the woods over there, Whit? Keg o' skim milk?" "You better wax him, Whit, or your pa'll give you a lickin'." "You're mowin' good, Whit. You c'n catch him. He ain't got more'n half a mile on you."

Lawrence Murphy called out to him, "You're doin' good, boy. You keep a-goin'."

Down at the end of the field, Whit stopped and whetted—where there was no one to bother him. He had gained enough now so that they could all see it. Joe didn't offer a word to him this time.

"Faster yet, Joe," said Whit, "I'm a-comin' up on you!" It didn't sound in his ears like his own voice at all.

Joe swore some in English, and he swore some in Portuguese. He knew Whit was coming!—and he tried to mow faster. He began to miss some, and that brought Mr. Gowan down on him. "Mow clean, Joe," Mr. Gowan said to him.

As Joe passed the middle, they shouted encouragement—they had bets riding on him. A man ran out from the crowd to him.

23

"Have some brandy and water, Joe—just a swallow." Joe took it gratefully. "He can't catch you, Joe. Keep a-goin'! Field's more'n half done now. How're you feelin'?" Joe, his ribs heaving, said he was fine.

The man turned away. "You look it," he said.

A boy with two musquash skins bet on Joe shouted an offer to whet his scythe for him. Joe shook his head. "Go on, Joe," said another boy—the one who'd bet with the first one. "Go on! Leave him whet it!" This was a subtle thrust. Even the victim enjoyed it. They began to wrestle each other, rolling over and over.

Joe whetted a moment after his drink and then fell to mowing. The pain in his side didn't trouble him now—he'd forgotten about it. He made a great show of mowing—while he was here in the middle where they could see him.

But what they saw was that Whit was then making his turn. A man didn't have to be sober to figure out what that meant: the Portygee's lead had been cut now to half what it had been. Those who had bet on Joe began to fall silent.

Ensign squeezed back a grin, spat, and decided that Mr. Gowan could have no objection—

By the keg, he met Murphy. "How's he look to you?" Lord asked.

"How does who look?"

"The young un."

"You bet on him?" asked Murphy.

"Some. So did you, didn't you?"

"Some. He looks all right."

"Mowin' smooth, ain't he?" offered Ensign.

"You mean clean?"

"No, smooth. Way he does it."

"Smooth, right enough," Murphy conceded. "Smoother'n whale ile runnin' out'n a spiggit. Question is: can he last?" That had been the question to start with. "Think Thett'll pay you?"

Trust a tailor to hear things! "One way or another."

"Well, you don't stand to lose much," Murphy said comfortably; "not compared to what you bet with Captain."

"You ain't hard of hearin', are you?"

"Not very, no." Murphy smiled faintly. "Thett goin' to pay you in Latin? He's got it to spare, I guess."

"Maybe. We ain't settled that part of it."

"You better let him. Be a handy thing for you, Latin would.

You 'n Mr. Gowan could talk it together."

"It's an idea, anyhow."

"That's all it is. Surely. It's a good one, though, ain't it? I guess you can say 'three pound' in Latin. I don't know, though."

Ensign said blandly, "No, you don't, do you?"

Murphy laughed with him.

They watched Whit coming toward them. Lord said, "He don't act none like a man missed his dinner."

"Maybe he don't miss it. He's a trapper—off 'n on, anyhow. They don't eat more'n once a week, trappers don't, generally."

"Still, Whit done better'n a day's work for most men this forenoon."

"I guess it won't be the first time for that either," said Murphy. "Now'n again, I sh'd think somebody'd have t' work down t' their place."

"Look at him mow, will you?"

"He's a-mowin'."

They watched raptly.

After some time, it was Murphy who tried to sum up for them both. "I d'know as I ever see anything prettier."

Lord moved his head from side to side in agreement.

Whit himself was clear in his own mind as to how things were going. He found it no trouble to reckon how many crossings were left, and how much he was gaining. If he could keep going this way, he would catch Joe—but without much to spare. That is, he would catch him if Joe didn't pick up any. And he doubted Joe would. Joe, from what Whit could see, was going about as tight as he could now—he looked to be, anyhow.

The thing that scared Whit was this very clearness. He'd felt it before, and he knew too well what it came from. It came from not eating. If he'd been traveling in the woods now, he'd have stopped for a spell—unless he was onto something—and had him a bite to eat. This was a false clearness; you couldn't trust it. Things seemed clear, he knew, only because there was a whole mess of things his brain wouldn't take any account of. Next thing in order, he'd be getting lightheaded. And pretty soon after that he wouldn't know what he was doing. He'd been through it before. He'd waked up in his lean-to once in the winter with no knowledge at all of how he had got there. A man couldn't expect to be that lucky twice.

He couldn't bate now, though. He'd got to keep going.

So he kept going. He told himself, "When he whets, you can

25

whet, but not until then. Your edge had ought to hold out longer'n his does."

Joe didn't stop to whet, and Whit didn't notice. Mr. Gowan did, though—and Mr. Gowan said nothing. They weren't mowing as clean as they had been, but one wasn't any worse than the other.

Whit had come up close enough now so that when he raised his eyes to it, he could see the red bow on Joe's pigtail waving and bobbing not far in front of him. The space between him and Joe, though, seemed to have got pretty solid. Whit had no sense of motion any more, no feeling of moving forward over the field. All he knew was that he was up hard against that solid space between him and Joe, trying somehow to get through it.

Now and again, he seemed to feel himself falling . . . but each time he'd recover. It was hard for him to get his breath into him. The pain in his arms and the way his back hurt him, he took for granted; he didn't mind that. What he did mind was that his body had quit on him. He couldn't make it do anything. It seemed to have gone dead—same as it does in a dream, when a man tries to run. He knew he could catch Joe and go past him—if only his body would do as it ought to. This made him angry. He wanted to cry—and he did cry a little. The space between him and Joe still was solid. He hacked away at it. . . .

The scarlet bow had grown bigger. It was close at hand, now, off to one side. Whit thought, "That's something that's happened . . . if I can think what it means . . . yes, I recollect: I've got to go past him. . . . All right, I'll go past him." He began to.

He passed him.

. . . Joe heard the shouts, too. All the men had swarmed out into the meadow and were on both sides of them and back of them. Joe couldn't mow any faster. He was doing the best that he could. He was right up against it. "Mow, you black Portygee, damn you! Mow, can't you?" Joe heard it. "You fat, Popish bastard! Mow, damn you!" Joe heard it. There was more, too, not so gentle. They didn't like to lose money.

Still, there were some who had bet on the Portygee who were cheering Whit on because they couldn't help it. Thett was, for one.

Joe saw that Whit was pulling away from him. Everything Joe had won, he saw Whit lugging off with him. It was hard on Joe.

He saw Whit's legs moving away, two steps . . . and two steps

. . . he saw the muscles working in the calves of them, just below where Whit's pants came to. . . .

"God damn you, Joe, you're no good!" a man shouted.

That bit into Joe. He stepped toward the legs—four steps—and swung his scythe at them.

Gowan jumped him. He'd been right behind Joe and in one leap he was on him and had struck down Joe's arm—his right one—just about at the elbow. The tip of Joe's scythe was raised up, so that it sliced across the back of Whit's legs between the knee and the seat of Whit's breeches, cutting the leather clean as a razor would and fetching Whit, too, but not deeply—not deep enough for a tendon.

Lord wasn't more than half a jump behind Mr. Gowan and the three of them went down in a heap. Mr. Gowan rolled off and stood up—and was followed by Ensign. Joe, as he got to his feet, reached for his knife. Ensign hit him. Joe seemed to fall, at first, slowly, in a puzzled way. He landed loosely, his head rolled—and he stayed there. Ensign stood over him, but there was no need to.

A voice said admiringly, "God, Ens'n, you hit him."

It was beginning to come to Ensign that he might have broken his hand. That was the way it felt, anyhow. He didn't answer.

The men had forgotten Whit for the moment, watching the scuffle.

Old David Gillmor's voice crowed like a rooster. "And Whit," David marveled, "Whit still a-mowin'!"

They looked round then. Whit was still mowing. He was finishing out his swath—with the blood running slowly down the backs of his legs to his heels. Whit, they guessed, didn't know that—they couldn't tell, even, if he knew he was mowing.

Then they saw the girl standing there at the finish—waiting—standing stock-still. She was standing at the place she had known Whit would come to.

It was a strange thing to see. No one spoke. Whit made his last swing, grounded the heel of his scythe, and with both hands clasped round the snath, stood there and leaned on it. His head was bowed forward and his knees ready to buckle. He swayed with his breathing.

The girl made no move.

Then Whit looked up at her. He didn't start any, so he must have known she was there—or at any rate been expecting her.

27

She didn't start either. She was waiting—gently, somehow—for him to say something. A breeze riffled her hair. Ensign, watching them, felt Joe stir under him; he kicked him to make him stay quiet.

"I guess," Whit said to her, "that'll—take care of the mowin'."

"Yes, Whit."

"I'll be over—tomorrow t'rake it."

"Yes," she told him, no one hearing her only Whit, if he did. Whit put his scythe to his shoulder and looked round for the place he must head for—saw it—and set off for home. He went down to the end of the meadow and then disappeared into the woods. It was the same way he'd come. No one spoke to him nor called after him.

David Gillmor said, "Where he's walked, t'wouldn't take no Injun to track him."

"That ain't a deep cut," a man said; "the blood didn't squirt out any."

"'Tain't so deep as your'n was, anyhow, is it, David?" said another. "He didn't lug no scythe off in it."

They all laughed at that. They felt better.

When they turned round to look at the girl again, she had gone.

There was still some rum left in the barrel, and they cleaned that up in jig time. Then some went up to the tavern, but more of them went home—they didn't want to pay Captain for supper. They felt pretty well satisfied, on the whole; they had something to talk about. And tomorrow, if this weather'd hold, they'd be all day again haying.

Mr. Gowan saw Joe safely started, and then he followed Whit through the woods until there weren't any more bloodstains. He decided Whit was all right, then, and didn't need him to look out for him. He lay down to rest himself for five or ten minutes, and then he got up and took a line for his own place. He was tired.

4

Whit had traveled more than a mile on his way home before he discovered the cut on his legs. It came about then only because, his scythe being such a bad thing in the low places where there was underbrush, he'd gone a little out of his way up

28

onto a horseback. It was steep climbing the side of the horseback and slippery with pine needles. When he got to the top, he felt faint. So he sat down to rest himself, and that was when he saw the blood on the backs of his legs. But his head was ringing so much he didn't want to try to figure out how the blood came to be there. It seemed like one thing too many; he let it go. He brushed aside the dry twigs with the flat of his hand and laid himself down in the hot smell of the pine needles.

For a time, his head swirled pretty badly, and then that was overlaid with a thin kind of sleep. When the sleep lifted, he knew where he was, and that he was thirsty; he made out that it was close on to sundown, remembered Melissa as he had last seen her, and even remembered something about a cut on his legs. He tried to think what he ought to do. Thirst pushed everything else aside. He thought about water, and he seemed to recollect that there was a stream on the south side of this horseback that might be dry, or it mightn't. That was all that was needed to get him up onto his knees, and then onto his feet. When his head cleared a little, he slid down the slope, and stumbled and pushed his way through to the stream. He might have missed it if he hadn't stepped in it.

He lay down and drank all he wanted to, made free with the water over his head and his arms, and then sat with his feet in the brook. He was all right now, he told himself—and he set about washing the blood off his legs. How in the world he'd come by that cut, he couldn't figure. Finally he got up and took off his breeches to see if he could tell what had done it . . . something with a good edge to it, anyhow. No, he couldn't remember the first thing about it. He looked at the cut itself, twisting his neck around, and decided to leave it alone—wash the blood off his legs and leave the cut as it was. It couldn't be deep or it would bother him more. "Sat down on a scythe blade, what it looks to me like." That amused him. He'd have to look at his own blade when he went up on the ridge again, see if it showed anything. Might be he had done it himself, somehow, coming through the brush back along earlier, and not mindful of what he was doing. Well, it was no matter. He'd have to mend up his breeches, though, before he could wear them—where Melissa was, any-how. That was tomorrow.

The thought of Melissa and of tomorrow took hold of him hard. He thought how she'd look—of what her voice would sound like—and that they'd be a good part of the day just the two of them there in the meadow. He found the thought more than he could take care of. To get hold of himself, he held his breeches up in front of him and looked at them ruefully. "Yes, sir," he said, "you're a properly stove-up pair of breeches. I'll have to mend you"—and he put them on and went up the ridge after his scythe. He'd like to get home before it was dark. He was hungry. Even after all the water he'd drunk, his mouth was still foul with hunger, and his belly was lame and sore with it, too. Well, he'd beaten Joe, anyway, that was one thing. And there was tomorrow. If he could get home now without getting a stub in his eye, he'd be all right. He was blundering along like a June bug. . . .

There was no one at all in the house when he got there. He didn't waste any time wondering where his stepmother was. As for the others, they must have decided to lie out in the field. Or what was more likely, they hadn't been up to deciding to lie there—they had just laid there.

He ate, first of all. He ate corn bread and cheese, and drank three pints of the good cider. This was one time he wasn't going to drink water-cider. When he'd had all he could hold, he threw down a bearskin in front of what was left of the fire, and went to sleep on it. He was ready to sleep.

5

It was light when he wakened. He made up the fire, and found himself a stout breakfast—cold samp and molasses, more bread and cheese, a piece of some beef she'd been soaking, and a quart measure of cider. He packed himself good and solid, and felt better for it. A man or a rifle, you got to load them up good before they can work right. He ate a couple of dried apples then—you might say as wadding. They weren't much to travel on, but they did keep a man feeling as though it wasn't so long as it really was since he'd eaten.

He went out to the barn, and with the awl and some rawhide he sewed up his breeches—turning them inside out first and getting most of the blood off. He made a good job of the sewing, laying the rawhide flat each time, over and over, and tying it off on the inside. After he'd turned them right side out again, a little dirt rubbed into the rawhide took away the new look. He was pleased with them.

He put some grease on his scythe blade and put that away, and then he went to the barrel and got a nice-looking piece of salt pork to take along for his dinner. Captain hadn't said anything about found, and it wouldn't do to take any chances. It wouldn't look right, for that matter. He hoped Melissa'd bring her own dinner down to the meadow. It would be a good sign if she did—there couldn't be any better. He knew, though, that if he did see her bringing it, his knees would feel funny. They were beginning to now.

It took him a few minutes to clean up his hair, grease it and tie it in place, and to wash his face carefully. Then he was ready to set out for Butler's. If he'd just come onto a moose yard, he couldn't have felt more excited.

The first stream he came to, he washed yesterday's sweat out of his shirt, wrung the shirt fairly dry, and put it back on again. It would be dry time he got there. He'd have done that before, if he hadn't forgotten it. It was a lovely morning—wind out of the west, and the clouds high as could be!

Thinking ahead, he came to the question of how they were going to haul the hay once it was cocked. Captain had a rick, he thought he remembered; one he'd taken in on a debt two or three years ago. But no oxen. Reason for that was, they said, Captain had always been scared there might come a day when he'd have no work for his oxen and yet have to feed them. Still, you can't hay without oxen, and yesterday Captain would have agreed with somebody for the loan of a yoke—young ones, he'd get, and not more than half broke: they'd come cheaper—and it wouldn't be Captain who'd have to drive them. Whit thought he'd like to see Captain driving a yoke of young oxen—say a pair hadn't ever been in together before. Oxen might not amount to much afterward, but aside from that it would be a fine thing to see. Not this morning, though. This morning, he—Whit—would be doing the driving himself. But you hold on a minute—now, would he? Man owned the oxen would bring them over to Captain's or else send a boy with them. Then what would the man or the boy do—stay and work, or go home?

Whit didn't like the looks of that question. While he was trying to answer it, a doe with a fawn hid down in a hollow blew three times, and Whit didn't choose to pay any attention. He passed within ten feet of a porcupine that had climbed up an oak tree about three weeks too early for acorns and was just sitting there waiting for the acorns to grow; Whit took no account of

31

him. In one place, he breathed bear-smell strong enough to have waked a man out of his sleep—and didn't turn his head even to look round for sign.

What it depends on, he told himself, is whether Melissa can build or not. If she can build a load, then there's no need for him to stay. Captain will know that, and won't agree with him *to* stay. But if she *can't* build a load, then Captain'll figure that to get the most out of the oxen, he's got to take the man, too. And he'll take him. I could teach her to do it in one or two loads—well enough, anyhow, so we wouldn't lose a great deal of it, that cart track ain't rough—because she's awful clever. But I don't know if Captain'll think that far into it. He might, there's no telling. Where there's expense, he can think a long ways; it don't tire him any. If he was to lose a pistareen sometime, he'd think all night on it—and then go look the wrong place in the morning. I don't know as I got any call to complain, though; I wouldn't have it to lose.

He ran onto a hen partridge had four of her chicks with her—thought for a minute he might take one of the chicks along to Melissa—and then decided he wouldn't. It wouldn't be much of a present. "A little small pa'tridge!" people would say. "If that ain't the kind of a thing he would give her!" After he'd gone on, though, he couldn't help thinking she might have liked it. She'd hold it in the cup of her hand up against her and stroke the back of its neck with her fingers. He wished now he had brought it.

About half a mile short of the meadow, he saw something that did stop him: blood—on the end of a brake, up better than knee-high, and about a day old or less than that. Came from a deer, he thought, being as high as it was—probably someone had shot at it. But when he parted the brakes, he didn't see any tracks. He thought then it might have come from something an owl had been carrying. Not until he saw a place looked like a footprint, did he remember. He put his hand to the back of his leg, and under the sewed place in his breeches he could feel it sore to the touch. He laughed right out loud. A minute ago, he'd been all ready to start right in tracking—hoping the blood would turn out to be a bear and that he could get a shot at it. But what he'd really been hoping was to get a shot at himself. That was a pretty thing, that was! Yes, sir, that was pretty.

He followed the blood clear into the meadow. It stopped about where he'd finished mowing. . . .

Whit stood thinking about it. It was before this place that he'd passed Joe. So when they got to here, of course, Joe was in back.

He thought of how the cut had looked in his breeches . . . and then he just wondered—standing there scratching his head—if Joe could have done it. "Yes," he said, not quite aloud, "he could a done it. He'd be upset over my passing him—and he let go with his scythe at my legs. Yes, sir, I'll be bound that was the way of it. Reason he didn't let go a second time, must have been somebody stopped him. Mr. Gowan, I expect, not wantin' trouble. The rest of them wouldn't have minded. I must have been too tuckered by that time and too busy mowin' to know aught about it. I *was* tuckered, too, from the looks of this mowin'. His is about as bad, for that matter. Then I lit out for home soon as I'd spoke to Melissa. I must have; I don't recollect anythin' else that went on." He moved toward the pine trees where he'd gone in to get water. And as she had been yesterday, he let himself see her . . . while in his eyes only there was the steady green of the branches. Very clearly, he saw her—and his lips parted and his eyes dimmed a trifle. He half smiled, and he winced. What he felt, went all through him. . . .

From close to the place where he was looking, Melissa herself stepped out into the meadow. She stepped lightly—on account of the hay stubble poking her feet at the base of her toes. She had her head up and was smiling. "Mornin'," she greeted him.

Whit came all abroad. Sudden things in the woods mightn't startle him—like a rocketing partridge or a loon's cry in the night. But this sight of Melissa, suddenly fresh and alive in the meadow on an August morning that looked like her, made his jaw drop and his eyes widen.

She waited, half smiling, while he collected himself—at least enough to say "Mornin'."

"Pa's lookin' for you," she informed him. "He sent me down here t' see if you'd come yet." This was almost true, anyhow; he would have sent her if he'd been awake.

"I slept awful heavy. I'm sorry. I didn't wake up until daylight."

Melissa felt a little put out; for her part, she hadn't slept any—or not much of any. "You didn't look to me more'n half awake yesterday, time you'd finished your mowin'."

"I wan't, I guess likely."

She forgave him. "You done better than Joe, though, at that. Joe, he went sound asleep 'fore he ever did finish."

"Did he?" said Whit, and by way of reminding her that he'd passed Joe, he added, "I couldn't see him."

"You'd seen enough of him, I guess, time you went by him. He'd been ahead of you all afternoon."

"That's true enough."

"You don't know yet what happened. Do you?"

"Not the whole of it, maybe. I been figurin' some."

"Turn round," she commanded.

"I mended 'em," he said promptly—and didn't turn round.

"What with?"

"Piece o' rawhide."

"Oh. Did he hurt you?"

"Who?"

"Joe."

"No. Not any."

"You bled awful."

"No . . . not all the way home, even." And then shyly, because he felt the strangeness of talking easily with her: "A funny thing happened."

"What?"—helpfully.

"Comin' over . . ." He told her about the blood on the brake back there. "A man thinkin' to get a shot at himself," he finished, "I thought that was a pretty thing."

Melissa laughed. "That *is* pretty, yes. I heard Schoolmaster tell of things ain't a mite prettier'n that."

Whit was flattered.

"It's pretty twice," said Melissa. "Supposin' you *had* treed yourself: you didn't have no gun to shoot you with, did you?"

Whit's face fell. "I never thought of that," he said—and both of them laughed.

"We got to go up now," she said, "Pa'll be waitin'." When he woke up, he'd be waiting loud enough to hear him clear down here in the meadow.

Whit nodded, and followed beside her.

They crossed the meadow in silence, each one of them thinking about the day now begun. Whit wanted to ask her if the man who'd brought the oxen was staying. But he was afraid she might think he was forward.

Melissa, in love with him, was thinking a thousand things. There wasn't one of them she could have said.

As they approached the stone bridge—three flat slabs of granite—over the brook in the alders, she walked very slowly. "Whit—"

"Ayuh?"

34

"What you goin' do to him?"

"Do to who?"

"Joe."

"Joe?" he said innocently. "Nothin'. Why should I?"

"You ain't?"

"No."

Melissa hung on to that; it was what she had hoped for. "He may to you, though."

"I don't think it. He was upset, was all, and so he tried to cut me. Joe wouldn't go to do that again."

"Not if Ensign was there. Whit, you wouldn't be walkin' if 'twasn't for Mr. Gowan. You wouldn't have nothin' to walk on—only stumps, maybe. Don't you know that?"

"Oh. Mr. Gowan? That's what I figured. Quick, wa'n't he?"

"Yes, he was quick. So was Ensign. But they can't follow you round the whole time. You know that."

"Ensign? How was he into it?"

She told him.

"Oh." Whit, on the bridge, was peering down into the water. "Prob'ly under the bridge," he said.

"What?"

"Trouts," he explained.

It was Melissa's turn to say "Oh."

"What's the matter?" He was thinking to toss a stick over his shoulder into the downstream side—and watch on the upstream.

"'Trouts'!" said Melissa. She reverted to Joe. "Whit, I saw him!"

Whit, searching the water, inquired, "How big was he?"

She stamped her foot and it hurt her. "Whit Livingston, you listen to me, will you!"—Whit turned round and listened—"I saw him!" she said again. "I seen his face, Whit, while they were cheerin' him. That's what you robbed him of, first time he's had it. That's what'll fester! I know, Whit! I saw him!"

Whit looked away. "I waxed him mowin', was all."

"No, that ain't all!"

"Well—maybe it ain't, then. But he won't come after you. I can see to that for you."

"No, I don't want you to. I can handle that part of it. He ain't any worse than the rest of 'em, that way."

Whit faced her. "What is it, then?" he said simply.

Melissa shook her head once or twice, grimly. Then she told him, fully and accurately. "Look here, Whit, since the day he showed up here, he's knowed they was sayin' 'Popish' an' 'Portygee' and 'old Karr was ten times the smith that you be'—an' all like that, ain't he? Steady, it's been. Not a good word for him anywhere. That'll gall any man. And then yesterday come, and for a little while there, he thought he'd got clear of it. And he had, maybe—up till when you quit flounderin' and crep' up and passed him. When you done that, they cursed him. They called him all manner of things—anything come to mind, they flung it at him. They hit him, too; don't you think that they didn't. And you was the cause of it. Right there in front of him—handy to git at—he seen the cause of it. He done no more than was natural!

"And when he come to, he was face down in the stubble and with his jaw all stove-up. That made him funny. That made him something to laugh at. Maybe you and Schoolmaster like somethin' pretty to laugh at. Not the rest of 'em, though. They'd rather laugh at a man who's face down with his jaw broke. And if he's been fool enough to talk big, all the better. This'll last them a long time.

"Joe Felipe knows it. He knows what's ahead of him. And he knows who done it. *You* done it!—not Ensign. Why, if Joe was to live to a hundred, he'd never live that down. He's got that ahead of him. And he knows who put it there: *you* did. Pretty soon he'll be drunk again—soon as that jaw starts to pain him, he will be. And then what? You seen that knife of his under your nose once—and you didn't like it. I don't know as I blame you. Next time, *you won't see it!*" She could, though—all night, she'd been seeing it—just under Whit's shoulder.

"Whit," she begged him, "you *will* keep clear of him, won't you? For my sake. *Please*, Whit! You—I—" She waited for him to say something—for some sign that he did understand. Everything hung there . . .

Whit had been thinking. He said honestly, "I'm sorry if I got him laughed at."

Anger seemed to burst in Melissa. She held her small fists clenched, over her bosom; she was raised up on her toes with rage. She was too angry to try to think of something to call Whit. "Ugh!" she exclaimed. Then she turned away from him, and went blindly up the cart track toward the tavern. She stumbled some because she was crying.

Whit trailed along after her. He hadn't the faintest idea what the trouble might be, but he did know that he'd done it. He'd said the wrong thing, somehow or other—but he didn't know now what he had said. There was Melissa, that was all—about as big as a minute—stumbling up the cart track ahead of him. She was crying. He followed. The day was shattered, of course, but that didn't matter much now. The day was lost in the minute. Melissa was crying. He followed after her, helplessly . . .

Melissa went faster and faster. She couldn't see for the tears now. She didn't know he was following—she was just fleeing in anguish. For her, too, the day had gone. Everything else had gone; everything broken . . .

When she stubbed her toe on a root, she fell down and stayed there. Being alone, there was no need to get to her feet, and lying in the damp grass of the cart track seemed as good a place for crying as any. An elbow crooked under her forehead, Melissa lay sobbing.

Whit came up to her . . . and stood over her. Even if he'd known what to do, he felt certain, he'd have been mistaken about it. So he did what he wanted to—bent down, and lifting her by her firm little shoulders, set her up on her feet—there wasn't much heft to her. It was the first time he'd touched her. It gave him that strange, almost unbearably alive feeling that a man knows in that instant between when he *feels* a noise—say, in a dark, empty place somewhere—and the time when he hears it. But he felt stronger, more certain.

Melissa, before she was properly upright, tried to break away from him. She'd have fallen again if he'd let her. Whit said, "Wait, now. Don't do that." He turned her round, facing him.

"Let me go!" She wouldn't look at him.

"You're all right," he told her. "You ain't hurt any. Stand still, will you?"

Melissa stood, shaken, not looking up at him. She could feel the strength in his hands and arms beyond any possibility that she might break away from him. She began to stop crying.

"That's better," he said. "Spruce root, you fell over. You didn't see it." Melissa nodded.

He let go of her. Then she looked up at him.

Whit had no choice in the matter. He couldn't have kept it back if he'd tried to, and there was in him no question and no fear of the outcome. He knew only her presence. "M'lissa, I love you—" The words came of themselves, and being spoken, remained yet a part of him. Melissa, tearfully, nodded her head.

He knew she was answering. His arms brought her in to him. Up to the instant his lips touched Melissa's, Whit knew where he was.

When they finally came to, they were both surprised to find they were still standing there in the cart track.

Melissa smoothed down her apron. Then she smiled up at him. "Always," she thought, "it will be this way. Always his face here to look up to . . ." She smiled without knowing it. She said in a small voice, "I guess we'd ought to go, hadn't we, up to the tavern?"

As though she'd not spoken, Whit stood there holding her hand. He was looking down at her. There was joy in his face—she saw that, she was sure of it—and she saw, too, almost a sadness. . . . She understood. She was not frightened.

She said, "Now, Whit?"

"Yes," he told her, and gently, in deference, added, "I think so."

"All right."

Together, hand in hand and not speaking, they went down the cart track to the meadow, crossed it, and they came to the place in the woods where the stream ran under the pine trees.

6

The night before, Joe, safely home in his house next to the smithy, had made sober inspection of the state of his jawbone. When he pressed sideways on his chin, he found the pain mighty—so much so that it sickened him. But the jaw, by itself, would lower and raise—in spite of the pain—and it moved all in one piece. Joe concluded that some of the sinews had carried away. They would mend of themselves. His jaw was stove-up, but it had not come abroad. His respect for Ensign was limited. It was wonderful damage for a man to have done with his fist, but it was stupid of Ensign to have risked his hand doing it. A knife was much better. Well, no matter—he had no quarrel with Ensign. The painful time that this jaw would take to heal up was what confronted Joe now. He went to work to prepare for it.

He set three gallon jugs of rum by his bedside, a bucket of water, and a long-handled gourd. That took care of himself. He milked his cow dry and barred her out of the barn, lugged double water for his pig and then fed her, and set out some water in a pan for his hens. Then he came in and closed the door of his house, and he closed all the shutters. The pain in his jaw was getting worse now; Joe knew he was in for it. He drank, filling and refilling the gourd, as much rum through the good side of his mouth as he knew from experience he could hold onto, and then he lay down. There seemed to be no way to lie so that his jaw wouldn't pain him, but the rum took hold after a time and he dozed for a little.

Joe knew the passing of three nights and two days that way, while his jaw swelled so that he couldn't open it. He drank whenever he wakened, but he had to suck it in through his teeth, and the rum spilled all over him. He was drunk and in darkness and in pain all the time.

On the third morning he wakened with a liking for water—and he guessed he'd come through the worst of it. His jaw'd limbered up some—enough so that he could open it a little—and by noon he had eaten. Later on, he went out into the blinding white sunlight and made shift at relieving his suffering cow. He gave the milk to the pig—said the hell with chickens—and went in and lay down again. By the time dusk had come, he was able to think.

He lay on his back, still badly shaken, and tried to think how things stood with him. He thought first of people. He hated Whit Livingston worse than ever, of course, but he wasn't much tempted to go after Whit again. As for Ensign, Joe—his jaw aching—decided to think of the blow as a happening. His thoughts turned to Gowan—the son of an ape! But José Felipe knew that revenge on a priest was something not to be thought of.

Still, he had to get even. He had suffered enough, so that he had something coming.

It was the girl who had started it. Joe thought about her—

After a spell of that kind of thinking, there was no way of getting her but what appeared reasonable. He might even marry her.

The more he thought of it, the more it appealed to him.

José Felipe would make her a fine husband! He was a sailor, and a worker in iron. José Felipe was no thin-blooded farmer. She would see that—or he hoped she would, anyway.

What of her father? Ah, there'd be the trouble! Joe knew his charms wouldn't appeal much to Captain—the dried-up potato!

There was only one thing that interested Captain. That was money.

Up until now, Joe had known he was dreaming. But on a sudden, the thing became real to him. José Felipe muttered, "Deus me valha! . . ." and gazed at his vision.

He had the money.

Nearly two years ago now, on a small British brig—salt from Lisbon to Portsmouth—Joe had shipped in November. That was a mistake to begin with. Nine weeks they were at it . . . sneak along with a fair wind, and heave to when it headed them. Let her start a plank anywhere, and down she'd go like a plummet. Salt's a bad cargo; it got on Joe's nerves. With all of their caution, she was down by the head when they picked up Nantucket, and they had a sweep out to help steer her with Cape Ann not abeam yet. Still, with the help of the tide they made Piscataqua River—with a northeast gale coming on and a thick snow a-riding it.

Paid off and ashore, Joe had started in on his drinking. He'd made some little headway when he fell in with a Spaniard, a mouse-faced little man who was sober and lonely, but who spoke enough Portuguese for Joe to feel drawn to him. Joe was tired of English.

Midway of the evening, José began to grow wary. The other man didn't sing enough, and he appeared to be watching Joe. Another thing was the rat-faced little runt treated just as often as Joe did. That wasn't natural: Joe was a sailor. And when the man paid with a gold piece—tried to keep Joe from seeing it!—José Felipe saw that the man was a pirate. What a pirate was doing in Portsmouth in the middle of winter presented no problem: he was after Joe's wages.

José then demanded that the man tell his business (two or three times the man had said "trader") and the man, in reply, gave a long explanation that made no sense to anyone about duties and prices and a trip to buy bacalao. It wearied Joe mightily. He was ready for women. He turned up his collar and went out of the place—and the other man followed him.

The snow was over their ankles as they stepped from the doorway, and the night was a black one. The nor'easter was on them, and she felt like a beauty. José Felipe stamped his feet in his sea-boots and he cursed the wind happily. He'd cheated her this time! He was safe ashore now and with good liquor in him! . . . he'd forgotten the Spaniard, who was half a step back of him.

40

The rough ruts of the town made for treacherous walking and under the new snow there was ice in some places. José's eyes were half blinded with the snow blowing into them. But he knew where he was going.

Then he stumbled and fell—and the Spaniard on top of him. Joe's brain didn't have to work—he had his knife out before he'd fairly landed, rolled onto his back, and got his left arm round the other man. His right arm was free—and he drove in his knife up beneath the man's shoulder blade, felt a great quiver go through the man—and the man ceased to struggle. José drew his knife out again. He thought, "Now he can't kill me!"

He rolled the man off him, and then he looked him over. He was dead, right enough. Joe put his knife away.

He felt down the man's arm to his hand, to see what kind of knife he had had. He found the hand empty. He felt in the snow for the knife, but he didn't run onto it. He remembered the gold piece, then, and he found the man's money. There was a small leather sack full of it. Joe put that in his reefer.

Then he stood up and thought some. He didn't know much about Portsmouth and had never trusted the English. He thought he'd better get rid of this fellow. He reckoned the tide to have some hours of ebb left, put the man over his shoulder, and came safe to the river. . . .

That done, he made his way to the place that he'd started out for the first time—hiding the gold in the snow at the foot of the gatepost. He retrieved it next morning.

The storm unabated, no vessels were sailing. Still he had to go somewhere, and he took the road down to Exeter, passed through the town, and lay out under a haystack, *frezado,* and the next day kept going. On the third day, the wind shifted southerly, the snow changed to rain, and the wind worked clear round to nor'westerly. By evening the sky'd cleared, and the cold deepened and hardened. He walked all night long just to keep his blood going. He crossed a wide river on ice none too thick for him, and along about daybreak, he came into a village. It seemed to José that he'd gone far enough. He knocked at a tavern.

It had been Captain who'd greeted him.

Joe still had the money—most of it, anyhow—buried under the anvil. The little that wasn't there was what he'd paid for the smithy. Gold didn't move about much in New Hampshire, and Joe had been wary of attracting attention. But gold paid to

Captain would be safe as could be—the old man would bury it deeper than Joe would himself. Nor would Captain say a word, either.

José lay there thinking . . . and in those dusky moments the business looked good to him. He trembled a little. It didn't matter, this way, if Melissa would have him or not: her father would have to see to that part of it. Yes, it was perfect . . . José smiled till it hurt him. Popish, eh? Not after their Mr. Gowan had married him in the church! And dark-skinned? Well, what of it? His wife's skin would be fair enough. . . .

He would be square, then, with the village of Kettleford.

José believed it.

When he could talk, he waited on Captain, got him alone, and laid the business before him—no figure mentioned.

Captain, standing secure behind his goods counter, said when Joe finished, "You?"—and then he laughed a long time, till his wig fell over slantwise across his dampening forehead.

Joe darkened. . . . "Your wig's started," he said to Captain finally—and Captain stopped chuckling, and straightened his wig.

"T' business?" said Joe. "You want t' talk here, do you?"

"Business?" said Captain. "There ain't no business *to* it. You? Why, there ain't a man in the province—nor in Bay Province, neither—that I wouldn't sooner marry that girl to than I would to you, Joe. You know that, don't you? You must be daft, Joe!—Ensign addled your brains. Here—have some brandy. Forget it."

"Sure," Joe agreed. "And after t' brandy, then I show somet'ing to you."

Captain poured for him and had a swallow himself. "What you got t' show me, Joe? You been makin' more nails?"

Joe took a leather pouch out of his shirt front and dropped it onto the counter—keeping his eyes fixed on Captain. He saw Captain twitch at the soft clink of the money.

But Captain drew back. "No, Joe! No!"—his face all twisted up. "You take that stuff out o' here!"

Joe raised the bag, and hefted it thoughtfully. "All of it gold, Captain. You like to see it?" He let the bag fall again. "You want t' look at it? Maybe you want t' feel it?"

"I d' want to look on no part of it!" Captain was breathing hard in his excitement.

Joe loosened the drawstring in the neck of the sack. "You

t'ink maybe I'm Popish?" he said very gently.

"Well, you be, ain't ye?" Captain said shrilly.

"Why?"

"They all say you be."

"Maybe. Who knows? What does it matter?"

"And part black, too," piped Captain. "That ain't so easy."

José Felipe's hand closed on the money and he looked Captain straight in the eye. "I know my father's name, and I knowed my mother. You want t' call José Felipe black? Go right ahead. You won' have to say it only t' once, mi capitao."

"*I* never said it," denied Captain hastily. "I disremember who did say it, Joe."

"A' right. You got any more t' say—like t' 'black' an' t' 'Popish'?"

"No, nary a thing, Joe; nothin'. Not me, Joe!"

"Good."

"I couldn't answer for the village, though," Captain reminded him. "If I was to marry M'lissa to you, Joe—not that I could, or that I'm a-goin' to—it mightn't set good with them—if she didn't want to, what I mean. See, Joe? 'Tain't nothin' against you, I don't mean it that way. Only there's a lot of 'em round here thinks high of M'lissa and wouldn't want to see me go against her when it come right down to marryin'. They're a strongheaded people. Of course I'm her father and I know my rights, but all the same I ain't lookin' for no tar and feathers, nor gittin' rode clean down to Merrimack River atop of a rail 'n' gittin' hove in. That's the way they'd be, Joe, you bein' Popish—or they think you be."

"She your girl, ain' she?"

"Sart'n, she is!"

"Then who can say anyt'ing?"

"All of 'em!" Captain assured him. Then he inquired, "You ain't spoke to M'lissa?"

"No. 'F I had, and she'd a been willin', I wouldn't a come to you. I'd a taken her off—an' t'hell wit' you, Capitao. Tell me: you want me to talk to her?—or *can* you talk to her?"

"Don't go so fast! There ain't naught I've agreed to—'n I ain't a-goin' to. I told you that to start off with."

Joe twitched at the sack, and a strange assortment of coins slid and spread out in a low heap on the counter. "Your Mr. Gowan," Joe muttered gently, "he could baptize me—if t'at what you want. I don' mind."

Captain's eyes had bugged out, and the sweat on his forehead showed very plainly. His tongue was thick in his mouth.

"If you talk to her, Capitao, and make her see the way of it, how I would be a good husband to her—an' I would be!—and we could live righ' alongside of you, righ' here in t'is village, where she can take care of you when you get old—why, what more? You let her do whatever she want to. If you make her see that she does want to marry me—then you can let her. When she does marry me, all of t'is here"—sliding his fingers over the lovely coins—"make a nice present from me to you, Capitao."

Captain said nothing. Joe didn't look up at him, but he heard the man's breathing to be something quickened. Joe stroked the coins . . . "Now t'at piece of money—" with the back of his forefinger he poked it toward Captain—"he is Spanish mill dollar. Very fine money. You don' see any better. All over t' worl' t'ey know Spanish mill dollar. I know; I was sailor. T'ats when I get t'is—one place an' anot'er. Oh, very fine money— ain' a piece in here was made in t'is country. All of it gold—" Joe stirred it and stroked it, confident, waiting.

"Come in here," rasped Captain, "and don't leave that there layin' there, don't for God's sake! There ain't any tellin' who mightn't come in." He led the way to the tiny cubbyhole off the taproom that he liked to think of as his counting room. "T' fox-hole," other men called it. "I bet it stinks same as a fox-hole does, too," they said. Joe followed after him.

7

Whit, after a week or so, went to see Mr. Gowan. He didn't see him the first time because the minister stayed within doors. The next day, Mr. Gowan was out round the barnyard. Whit happened by and Mr. Gowan spoke to him. So Whit stopped, and they visited. Outdoors, Whit had thought, he might find talking easier. And he did find it easier than he had expected. Mr. Gowan talked about rain and Indian corn—how the tassels had dried out this year before the ears were half filled, even—that kind of thing.

"Your hay in?" the minister asked him.

"Better part of it is. She's all cut 'n cocked, anyhow. Got a few jags to haul yet."

"Hay's getting too dry to cut." Mr. Gowan was raking the

barnyard; he kept his place as neat outdoors as his sister did indoors. "Some I cut yesterday, you could trot a horse on all day and he wouldn't sweat any."

"I ain't never rode on a horse," Whit said, "that was meant a-purpose t' ride on."

"No, around here there aren't any. You can't eat a horse—not with any great comfort. That's why it's all oxen. They're a handy thing, though, if you're going a journey. I mean horses."

"Yes, I guess they may be," said Whit. "Still, so is a river. A river'll feed you—if you have any luck—and at the same time it'll carry you—if you want t' go where it goes."

"True. You going north this winter—trapping, Whit, are you?"

"I might, I guess. I'd thought something of it."

"When you going?"

"Fall of the year, sometime. I might go early—I d' know, though—soon as the cider's made—maybe before that."

"You'll be early for fur, won't you?"

"A little mite, yes. Fur ain't worth taking, really, not till after the snow flies. I had in mind that I might look around some."

"Going a tour, are you?"

Whit grinned. "You might call it that."

"Sounds pleasant. Whereabouts, Whit?"

"Well, I ain't never been up into the Grants."

"You won't take much fur in the Grants, will you, Whit? That country is settling. I thought where you went before was more to the eastward. Aren't you a White Hills man?"

"No, sir, I ain't. I been south of there—Pigwacket, Fryeburg, Great Ossipy Pond. I seen t' White Hills. But I never been on 'em. Coruway Mountain's enough White Hills for me, sir."

"Spirits?" Mr. Gowan suggested.

"Well . . ."

"Only Indian spirits."

"Any kind's bad enough."

"I suppose so," said Gowan. "Still, an Indian spirit . . ." He kept on raking.

"You're a holy man," Whit reminded him, "you c'n lay 'em."

"Not I myself, Whit. I'd be only His instrument."

"You'd be a sight handier tool than what I would."

Mr. Gowan said nothing.

"I will say," Whit admitted, "they stay to home, though. They stick pretty close to the tops of the mountains. I been on

45

Coruway—higher than hardwood; I been high enough for the trees to get runty—that's even higher than the bears go in late summer when the lowland berries are by and the acorns ain't come yet—and I never had trouble. They stay up higher yet—up on the rocky part. That's where the thunder is, and the lightning. They like that, spirits do—men that know, tell me."

Mr. Gowan had paused in his raking. "So I've heard," he said carefully.

"They must like t' snow, too—they get plenty of it. Why, I seen it on Coruway—you take in the wintertime, when the wind blows—I seen the snow comin' off Coruway stand out in the west wind just like smoke from a chimbley! I seen that myself. That's a brave thing for a man to see, I think."

Mr. Gowan leaned on his rake handle. "Yes, it is, Whit."

Whit spoke almost wistfully: "A man could see a long ways from the top of a mountain . . ."

"He could, Whit; a long ways." There was silence, both thinking.

" 'F 'twan't a lowery day," Whit added seriously.

Mr. Gowan's face twitched a little. He went back to his raking. "How about spirits on the Green Mountains, Whit?"

"They ain't high enough mountains. And it's like you was sayin': there's a power of people movin' int' the Grants."

"Pioneers," said the minister.

"All right, 'pioneers'!" Whit flared up in defiance, forgetting to whom he was speaking.

"You like them, I take it," Mr. Gowan said quietly.

"Some of 'em, yes."

"I thought you were a trapper."

"What I am is a farmer done some trappin' in winter. I ain't enough of a one to hate all pioneers."

"Most farmers, for that matter, don't speak any too well of them."

"I know they don't."

"Why do you like them, Whit?"

"There's some that I don't, sir. You got to know 'em."

"The men in the towns that the pioneers left, they knew them, didn't they?"

"Maybe. And they know why they left, too."

"Because they liked pioneering?" Mr. Gowan said dryly.

"Why should they like it? What a pioneer does is to start out

46

with nothin' and from there he tries to work up to what the farmer's had all the time."

"Why do you think they leave, then?"

"They got their own reasons. With every man it is different. They are mostly poor people, but that ain't the reason. If bein' poor was enough reason t' go pioneerin', why, all the poor people would have gone before now—or at least them that was able. Bein' poor is the reason that, when they do go, they got t' be pioneers instead of be settlers. No, sir, it takes some other reason besides just bein' poor for a man t' go pioneerin'. And that other reason ain't in pioneerin'—it's back in the town that the pioneer left. You look around and you'll find it."

"Well, then, what is it?"

"Like I said, Mr. Gowan, with every man it is different: family troubles, or maybe they done somethin', or it may be they couldn't get along with their neighbors—all that kind of thing."

"Well . . ."

"But whatever it was that went wrong, the ones that stayed home was against the ones that went off. So if you only listen to the ones that stayed home, what you will hear is that pioneers 're all bad. I know they ain't."

"Still, I never seem to hear the same talk about settlers."

"They got money. They can afford to go to a town that's been started because they can afford to pay for their land. In a town that's been started two or three years ago, things are much easier. They're enough easier so that when a settler leaves home it *can* be because of what he thinks he will find."

"You're not quite equipped to go pioneering," Mr. Gowan reminded him.

"You don't need a great deal. They give you your land and they throw in a cow. You need a few quarts of Indian to plant when you've girdled. You don't need nothin' else that I haven't got."

"Why do you go to the Grants?"

"The land's awful good there—that's what I hear. Interval land with wild hay aplenty—why, there even is places, so I have heard, where you can get a good crop of Indian without touchin' an ax."

"Pioneers," Mr. Gowan said, "can hardly expect to be given that kind of land."

"Well . . ." Whit was loath to admit it.

"Another thing, Whit, you're not the kind of man who'll want to move on once you've made a pitch. You don't want to be a pioneer all your life, do you?"

"No, sir!"

"Suppose you went to the Grants and were just getting started—say, after a couple of years—and the Yorkers won out."

"They won't, sir, they tell me."

"Nobody knows. It'll be settled in England. I'd rather clear land that I knew I could keep."

"If I'd cleared it, I'd keep it—one way or another."

"Not if the King said you'd got to get off."

Whit didn't say anything—but he knew how he'd feel.

"You know the country round Winnipiseogee; you know it till you get up in amongst the White Hills. There is no uncertainty, there, as to who should have granted it. The Proprietors' title is clear to it, and so will be your own. The land may not be as good as some land in the Grants, but at least you could keep it. And where the land is too good, they don't need pioneers."

"I'll think on it, sir."

"I think you'd better. There's yet another thing, Whit. There's a piece of equipment that you haven't got. It may be possible to go pioneering without one, but from what I have heard it is not often done."

"Oh, I got a good gun!"

"You haven't a wife."

Whit's composure deserted him. Mr. Gowan was waiting ...Whit knew that now was the time. "That's what I come about," he managed to say.

"Who is it, Whit?" Mr. Gowan said kindly.

The boy gulped a dry swallow. "M'lissa," he said.

There was quite a pause now . . . until at last Mr. Gowan: "You've done all right, Whit. And I think she has, too."

Whit was touched, deeply. He nodded slightly, and tried to say, "Thank you."

"Come in the barn and sit down," Mr. Gowan proposed. "I broke a tooth out of my loafer rake yesterday, and I got to whittle a new one." He said over his shoulder, "You told anyone else, have you?"

"No, sir, not yet, we ain't."

"How long is it, Whit?"

"Since we agreed, you mean? Let me see now . . . it was the

day after me 'n Joe mowed, I remember. You remember when that was?"

Mr. Gowan said, "Yes." He was looking round for a piece he could whittle from. "Your legs bother you any?"

"Not a mite. I'm beholden to you, I guess. That's what M'lissa says. I didn't see it. I—well, I thank you."

"There," Mr. Gowan remarked, "I guess that'll do it." He'd found him some maple that would answer his purpose—take a long time to whittle, and make a good tooth when he'd finished. "Here—you sit on that." He handed over the milking stool. For himself, he had his own chair. They sat on opposite sides of the doorway, not quite facing each other. Mr. Gowan whetted his knife on a stone from his pocket. Speaking of his rescue of Whit, he said, "I hope you'll not need me the same way a second time."

"I don't think it."

Then a pause.

"What of your father, Whit?"

"I figure I'm square with him."

"I don't think you are. But you're free to go, all the same. How much of a hurry are you in to get married?"

"Well, there ain't any special reason, you might say, that I know of."

"Good. See that there isn't. And you're bound and determined to go pioneering?"

"It looks that way, yes, sir."

"What is your reason?—you say they're all different. You haven't done something?"

Whit grinned. "No, sir, I ain't. But you know how I'm fixed. Our place is out of it, that goes to my half brother, he's younger than I am. Likely he'll have to look out for Pa for a while 'fore he finally comes into it. Still, Pa might go off sudden, then he'd get it for nothin'—though he'd still have Pa's woman on his hands to look out for."

"Who'll look out for your brother?"

"He ain't such a great hand to work, is he? But you take if I was out the way, I think he might do better. I ain't certain he wouldn't. You get him good 'n hungry, 'n he might do some work."

"He might, I suppose . . ." holding up the piece he'd been whittling and squinting along it.

"If I was to fetch home M'lissa t' live at our place, you know how it would be, sir: she'd do all the work. I doubt that my father's woman'd get out of bed in the mornin'."

"This maple's hard whittling," Mr. Gowan observed. "I should have used birch. But, Whit, on the other hand, what about Captain?"

"No," said Whit simply.

"That's good land of Captain's. You could grow more than hay on it. He's got two lots—room enough for a son-in-law. You want me to talk to him?"

"No, sir, I don't. There don't either one of us."

"I can see how you might not want to keep tavern. But you wouldn't have to. Let him keep the tavern, and you do the farming. He might even make over a piece of his land to you— so that you'd own it."

"Captain?"

"Why not?"

"Well, first place, he wouldn't. And I wouldn't take it."

"He owes her a dowry, Whit. She's more than earned it."

"That's true enough."

"If you take her away, he won't give her a pistareen of it."

"He wouldn't anyhow, 'less he was made to. I expect he's the stingiest man in the province—so they say, anyhow; I never see one to beat him."

"It's not your place to judge him."

"How can I help it? There he is, ain't he? I got to think somethin'. When you see a tree, you can't just think 'there's a tree,' can you? You think, 'That's a nice ash tree. Might have a good grain to it.' You judge it, don't you? Or you think, 'That there's a piss-oak; 'tain't no good for nothin'.' Same way with Captain. When I look on Captain, I got to think something. Well, sir, I think it."

"Still, he's her father. Don't forget that."

"He's the one forgot that, sir."

"How do you mean?"

"I mean way he's treated her—in general, that's all."

"Oh. Well, then, let her have her reward, Whit. Let him make over some land to her. Later on, she'll own all of it."

"Only reward that she's after is to get shut of the tavern."

"She'd be a farmer's wife if you were to stay here."

"She'd have him on her hands, though, sooner or later."

"Then it's Captain that troubles her, more than the tavern?"

"Both, I expect."

"She's determined to go, is she?"

"Bound and determined. She'd go tomorrow. I had to talk to her some to let me look out the land first."

"Pioneering's not easy," Mr. Gowan said dutifully. "You have said so yourself."

"I have said so to her, sir."

"And you think she could stand it?"

"I think she could, yes, sir. She's rugged and clever. It's a hard life, I know that. Not many do well at it. I seen some pioneers that had got pretty scrawny—what with bad luck and sickness and one thing and another. Some have done good, though—Frye's men, and round Wolfeboro. They don't go hungry, nor they don't foul up their cabins. Pioneers ain't all dirty. They ain't *got* to be dirty. Why, I slept in more than one lean-to that there wasn't a bug in it. I even heard of a man, come from Falmouth they said he did—I don't claim to have seen this, but the one that told me claimed to—that this man built his lean-to and then built him an office. He let his barn go till later."

Mr. Gowan refrained from any comment whatever.

"Pioneerin', I figure, is about what you make it—barrin' bad luck and sickness, and they can strike anyone. M'lissa can stand it. Better than most, she could, I think."

Mr. Gowan inquired, "When her time comes, who'll tend to her?"

"I'll fetch in a woman. I'll get her a good one, if I have to go fifty mile for her. I'll see to that part of it."

Mr. Gowan gave over his whittling. He thought for a long time. "Well, I've said all I can."

Whit nodded. Then he summoned his courage and he said what he'd come for: "Would you think you could marry us?"

Mr. Gowan was silent. He knew that he couldn't—not legally, anyhow—unless her father approved it, and until they'd been published. "I don't know," he said truthfully.

Whit got up then. It was more of a blow than he'd thought it would be. He bit into his lip and he hitched up his breeches. "I guess maybe the truth is, you ain't got a right to."

"I'm not sure that I have, Whit."

"That's all right, Mr. Gowan." He was having some trouble controlling his voice. "Well, I guess I'll go along now. We figured you mightn't."

"How did you figure it?"

"Same way as you do: her pa and my pa, they'd be both

51

against it. I guess that's all there is to it. You got no call to mix into it."

"I don't know, Whit, I'm wondering . . ."

"We didn't know but we'd ought not to ask you. I'm beholden to you enough as it is. You might get into trouble. We wouldn't want that for you."

"I can look out for that part of it, thank you. Tell me one thing: if I don't marry you—then what?"

Whit looked at him levelly. "We aim to go, sir."

"I see"—and his voice hardened: "That's sin, Whit, you know that—to live with a woman without being married. God punishes sin. He would punish Melissa."

The boy was unshaken.

Gowan got up from his chair; he stood facing Whit, and because of the sill, a little above him. "Bring her to me," he ordered him roughly. "I'll marry you any time."

He turned away, then. "Maybe," he added, "when I can prevent sin, it's my duty to do so. It isn't so often that I get a chance to."

"I'll tell M'lissa," Whit answered, that being the thing that his mind was instantly full of.

"All right, you tell her. She'll be interested, likely." He left Whit alone and went into the barn.

Whit thought things over before he went to Melissa. He'd found he couldn't do very much thinking while she was near him; unless he had his mind all made up beforehand, he was liable to agree to whatever she wanted—and it wouldn't be until later that he'd see what was wrong with it. If he was set on a plan, though, he thought he could hang onto it.

Mr. Gowan's advice, he concluded, was good. Mr. Gowan had said that if he went to the Grants he might find when he got there that they didn't need pioneers. Worse than that was the prospect that, if he should take up land there and get some of it cleared, they might take it away from him. Add these things together and there was only one answer: keep away from the Grants.

All right. Where would he go, then? Well, the country he knew about—at least in a general way—and where he thought it most likely they would need pioneers lay between Saco River and Winnipiseogee—the river on the northeast, the great pond on the southwest. Along the northwestern side was that long row of mountains that began just north of Casumpy—some called it

Squam—and ended with Coruway Mountain. In all of that country, Frye's men, to the north, had the best land that there was. But there was no use trying there unless you had money; they were too far along. In under Coruway Mountain, on the south side of it, there was nobody at all. Twenty miles south and west, at the northern end of Casumpy, he had heard there'd been people for a year and a half. That might be a good place to start looking round.

He decided he'd do that, and he was ready to go to Melissa.

Melissa went out after the cows right after her supper. Whit had got there ahead of her. Melissa ran to him, and after he'd taken her to him and kissed her, Whit told her, "I seen Mr. Gowan this mornin'."

"Oh, Whit, will he marry us?"

Whit nodded. "Ayuh—soon as we're ready."

"We're ready now, ain't we? I am. Tonight, Whit!"

Whit laughed, looking down at her.

"How long you want to wait, Whit? What is there to wait for? I can't bring you nothin'—the way Pa'll feel when we tell him—not so much as a bed sheet."

"I ain't never slep' on one yet. We got to get us a place, though, just to throw down a bearskin."

"I want to go with you."

"Yes, but look you, M'lissa, 'twon't take me hardly a month to go north and look out a place—not if I go alone, it won't, 'cause I won't have to lug much, little corn and some pork, is all. If you was to go, then I got to lug stuff for you, 'n make up a fire and all like that, night and mornin'. You don't want to lay out, same as I do when I'm travelin', you ain't used to it. You let me go alone, this time; I'll make better time that way. Soon as ever I'm back here, we can go north together. We'll get married and go, then. I'll have some place to take you. We'll both know where we're goin'. I couldn't get married and just run off int' th' woods with you, I couldn't be easy if I was to do that. My gorry, M'lissa, they'll talk enough, this way! The least I can do is to know where we're goin'. I got to find me some land—some interval, maybe—and then we c'n go there. It's the right way to do it."

"I want to go with you," she pleaded. "I can travel. Don't leave me! Something might happen. I'm awful afeard, Whit." She laid hold of his forearms.

Whit took her shoulders. "You ain't afeard. Nor I don't think

53

nothin'll happen. If it should, at this end, I guess you can handle it. I don't know anyone better. If it's me you're afeard for—well, I'll keep clear of the mountains, and I won't tackle no bears. And I give you my word I won't lay a hand on a hedgehog." He shook his head as he asked her, " 'Tain't Indians, is it?"

"No, it ain't Indians."

"Portygees?"

"No!"

"Listen to me, now, I'm goin' tell you something: 'twan't more'n two nights ago that I seen clear water. You know what that means. I see a great pool of it—deep, too; it was lovely. I come up on it easy, 'n I could see way down into it. Clear? I never see water more clear than what that was. Then there come a great trout out'n a hole in the bank some'rs—and I want to tell you that feller was handsome! Oh, he was a wonder! He swum proud and lazy, not hardly movin', took a look round, and then he went in again. That was all there was to it; I didn't have nothin' with me. I woke up after that, 'n I felt pretty good over it. There ain't a thing better a man can see in a vision than clear water. You know that, don't you?"

"More partic'ly with trouts in it," Melissa said dryly.

"Well," Whit reminded her, "I had good luck all right that time."

"Better'n you deserved."

"That's true enough."

"Whit—" she was again serious—"how you know Mr. Gowan's sayin' he'd marry us wan't the good fortune the vision meant this time?"

"That was the start of it."

"That might be the end of it. Maybe now it's run out, Whit."

"No, I don't think it. Hadn't ought to, I figure—not with a pool of that size, it hadn't."

In a small voice, she asked him, "When'd you figure t' go, Whit? Soon, did you?"

"Well—tomorrow . . ."

"Tomorrow!"

"Well, sooner I go, sooner I'm back, I guess. It's pretty late now—only three months until snow flies. We got to work fast in that time, I c'n tell you."

"Yes. What would you like for me to do while you're gone, Whit? To get ready, I mean."

"Let's get these here cows o' yourn gathered t'gether, 'n then

54

we can talk on the way up t' the barn with 'em. I'm coming up with you. I got t' trade with your pa f'r some powder 'n hooks t' take with me. I got enough shot, but I'm near clean out o' powder."

Melissa looked up at him. "The cows ain't in no hurry."

Whit went north the next morning.

8

This was Whit's journey: he traveled north along Merrimack River—following the road but not actually in it because of the brush—and passing through Pennacook, he lay the first night twenty-eight miles from home. He kept on the next day, still on the west bank, and along about sundown—at Fowler's, it was, in the town of Boscawen—a man set him across just out of friendliness. He said to Whit, "I c'n tell from your looks I ain't doin' t' ferryman out o' no business." And Whit said, "No, I guess you ain't, prob'ly."

The third day he passed Hucklebury Hill on his right hand, continued north to Great Bay, and still holding north between that and Winnipiseogee, he picked up the shore of Casumpy—the eastern shore, he supposed. All those ponds—Winnipiseogee, Great Bay, and Casumpy—have shores that twist in and out so you can't tell which side you're on; there isn't a place you can see the whole pond from. He went up a tree, though, and found he was correct.

This was a part of the country that he'd never been in before. Last winter, trapping, he'd been more to the eastward and a little bit north. Casumpy—or Squam—was a powerful pond, but still not as big as Winnipiseogee. In the morning, he would work up around it and probably come to the head of the pond about noon. There he'd find the houses of the new town of Sandwich. There were three or four of them, so he had been told—Gilmanton people.

It took him longer next day to get round the pond than he had figured it would, and the day was far gone before he saw the smoke he was looking for. It was some distance off, but it came from a chimney—there was no doubt of that.

For no special reason, he approached the house carefully . . .

and he had formed an idea of the people who lived in it before he stepped from the woods. He liked what he saw: the house was well built, which spoke well for the man, and the dooryard was neat—which said as much for his woman. The clearing was small, but the stumps showed a smooth cut. There was a fine stack of wild hay, and the woodpile was all maple. Stretched on one side of the house, a moosehide was curing that, judged from a distance, looked to be about a week old and to have been well taken care of. He leaned his gun on a tree and coming out into the clearing, he called to the house. It was about ten rods away.

After a minute or two—during which, Whit took it for granted, whoever was inside was looking him over—a woman came out. She was a tall woman, but she stood with her back to the sun and Whit couldn't tell what her face would be like. She had a long wooden spoon in her hand. "Evenin'," she said.

"Evenin', ma'am." He came forward.

"You might's well fetch your gun along, too. You don't look like 'n Injun nor sound like a Frenchman."

Whit grinned and went back for it.

"Nor you don't look to me," she said to herself, "like much more 'n a boy whatever you be."

She stood there by the door and watched him approach—he seemed open and honest—yes, a nice-looking young one. She decided she liked him.

"What's your name?" she inquired. "My man's from home now but he won't be for long. Where you from?"

"Whit Livingston, ma'am. I come up from Kettleford." He could see her face now. She wasn't suspicious and she wasn't uncertain. He felt a lot easier. She looked capable, too. She was a gray-headed woman—no bonnet or cap—and her hair was drawn back and tied so that it lay close to her head. She wasn't smiling exactly, and yet her eyes had a pleasant look.

"Kettleford, eh? You had quite a walk of it. What's your business—a trapper?"

"I done a little last year—over more by the Saco."

"You're early."

"Well, I wan't figurin' t' put out a line right away. All I'm doin' now is kind of lookin' round, you might say."

"Lookin' for what?"

"Well, for land, tell the truth of it."

"Well, I guess you'll prob'ly see some—if you keep your eyes open. Come in and set down. You had any supper?"

"Yes'm, I et."

"Where to?—by yourself?"

"I didn't see any tavern."

"Salt pork and dried corn!" the woman said scornfully. I guess it won't hurt you to eat again, will it?"

"No, ma'am, I guess not."

He set his gun by the door and followed her in.

The house had a clean odor. It was the smell, of course, struck him—as it would have in any house after three days out of doors—and in no house is it pleasant except in a man's own. It takes a few minutes at first to get used to it, and during that time it is much more important than the things that he sees or that anyone says to him. Still, he managed to notice the low bench by the fire, the usual variety of things hung overhead, and in a corner a pallet for two people to sleep on. At the same time, he was searching about—whether he knew it or not—among all the indoor smells, trying to come at that one which in some way redeemed them. He got it finally: it was the hay in the corner, brought in that morning, fresh from its making. It still had the sun in it.

They had a table, hewn out of logs, with wooden bowls and some pewter. They had two chairs: one of them was a rocking chair made by a carpenter. It was an old one. The other was the kind of chair made from a cask.

The woman had gone to the fire and had pulled the crane toward her; she peered into the pot, and then put in her spoon, "How long 'd it take you t' come up from Kettleford?" She was tasting the stew.

"Day before yesterday, I set out, in the mornin'."

She swung back the crane. "I guess that'll do"—and they heard a dog bark, some ways off from the house.

"That'll be Jonas," the woman said promptly, and added, "Not the one barked. That was the dog—he come onto your track." She went to the door, and then out into the yard. Whit stood uncertainly. He had been getting on pretty well with the woman. He didn't know how he would get on with the man. Curiosity pricked him ever so slightly to step over and see what they had in the pot, but he put that aside. Neither did he like staying here in the house . . . and he stepped outside swiftly to where it was open.

The man and the dog were crossing the clearing, the dog on ahead—and the woman was meeting them. She put her hand out

57

to the dog—he was a big, square-headed, black fellow—and the dog thrust up his muzzle, and was glad to be home.

Then the dog left her, and came to look over the stranger . . .

Whit returned the inspection. This was no yapping puppy, but a dog that had dignity. He had the scars on him of a lifetime of work. He looked as though, in his day, he'd have tackled most anything—and as though he wasn't sure that his day was done yet. Whit said to him soberly, "You look to me like a pretty good bear-dog." And the dog sat down and regarded him.

The man had paused for a moment as he met up with the woman, and now they were both approaching the house. "Jonas" she'd called him, so Whit remembered—and he saw that he walked like a woodsman. He was a spare man and tall, and he had a ragged black beard. He was dressed just as Whit was: a soft leather waistcoat, a gray linen shirt, leather breeches, and barefoot. His hair was loose round his shoulders and was beginning to gray. Whit would have guessed him for forty years old, maybe. He carried his gun over his shoulder, politely, and Whit saw that the front sight of it had a gold bead . . .

"Jonas Moore, at your service," the man said, unsmiling.

"Whit Livingston, Kettleford. Your servant," Whit said. He spoke just as coolly as the other man had.

"My woman told me. Come in and set down." And then he undertook to give Whit a welcome—to say that both himself and his wife were really glad that he'd come. He did this by turning to glance at the dog and remarking "I guess the old dog ain't a-goin' t' object."

Whit took it as meant.

Until well into the evening, he and Jonas Moore talked. Moore talked more than Whit did, but the boy did pretty well. Among strangers, for some reason, it was easier for him than it was back in Kettleford. And from time to time Mistress Moore would help out with a question. Much earlier than this—in fact, before supper—they had got past the embarrassment caused by Whit's not drinking rum. It was no longer bothersome. Moore drank rum and water, and Whit had some spruce beer. Whit's only discomfort was that he had nothing to do with his hands. Moore was shaving an ax-handle out of a green piece of white ash, and Whit's fingers itched to get hold of the knife; it was a proper ax-handle knife that had been made for the purpose, and he could see that the blade was perfection itself. And Mrs. Moore had her wheel.

The old dog lay by the fire, outstretched on his side, and deep in good sleep. Now and again his innards would rumble, and sometimes a leg twitch. He looked very comfortable.

"Around here," Jonas Moore said, "there is all kinds of land. You go two-three mile to the northwest now, f'r instance, and you'll come on it wonderful rocky and steep. That's where I got this moose-deer that you see the hide of outside—me'n two others. She got up in there in them rocks and she stove up a leg."

"Foreleg?" said Whit . . . and Moore told the whole story. He concluded: "I d'know as I'd want t' wear any moccasin was made out'n the knee of that leg that got broke. I shouldn't wonder there might be bad luck in it. Was for her, surely."

"You couldn't never be certain," Whit agreed with him; "not unless something happened. Then you would know."

"Yes, you would, I suppose. But now Beede he figures it t' other way round." Beede was one of the other two men who had helped kill the moose, and it was in the dividing up of the beast that the question came up. "He says it was good luck for us that she did get her leg broke, and he'd sooner have the leather from that knee than from her off leg. How would you feel about it?"

"Well, if I was in your room," Whit answered thoughtfully, "I think I'd let him have it, I d'know but I would."

"Why?" Mrs. Moore said.

"I d'know . . ."

"Why?"

"Well, I would say to myself: there is some kind of luck in it, either good luck or bad. You don't know which it is: it could be either way. So the chances are it is bad luck because everyone knows there is more things that is bad luck than what there is good. I think I'd let him have it."

"Well, that's what I done," pronounced Jonas Moore. "Besides, it had a crack in it that he didn't see."

"Dan'l Beede?" Mrs. Moore said. "Don't you believe that he didn't see it!"

"Well, he didn't say nothin'."

"He never does."

It was an unprofitable topic—and his wife had the right of it. Jonas abandoned it. "But what I say about land," he went on to Whit, "—in the township of Sandwich, and Sandwich Addition, there is interval, mountains, wild meadow, and hills. There is rocks of all sizes from boulders to stones, there is clay and there's gravel, and there's woodsmold on sand. There is good loam in places—but I wouldn't say they was plentiful. It ain't so good to grow flax as the land where you come from. But a man can do well with Indian, 'n he c'n grow rye. As for meat, I get plenty. And there are trouts in these brooks—if you can stand to eat trout—that if you wave a worm at them they will follow you home. We ain't never been hungry—that is, not to speak of—not since we come here. You c'n take fur in the winter—of scatterin' kinds—but, the same as everywhere else now, the beaver are gone."

"I never yet took a beaver."

"You never will—if you stay in this province. And you'll never make money takin' anything else. Trappin', round here, is a thing to fill in with. The fur trade has moved about a thousand miles west. If you want to make money trappin', you have got to go after it. There ain't many married men into it now." Jonas Moore paused . . .

But Whit couldn't tell them.

Jonas forbore to glance at his wife. He cleared his throat with some vigor, and spat into the fire. "What you'd better do—if you want my advice, and I d' know why you should—is t' stay here t' my place for two or three days 'n go over the ground. Then, if you liked what you saw, you could go talk to Beede—he's Proprietors' Agent—and you could dicker with him. If you'd like to have me, I could go around with you—I don't mean to Beede, I mean while you look round. We could take the old dog. You can't ever tell—we might come onto something."

"What he means is," Mrs. Moore interposed, "he'd like you to hunt with him for a couple of days."

Whit's emotions were reeling from the impact of kindness. He had to think for a minute to come any words. "You're kind to me, surely," he said to them earnestly. "I would like to stay."

9

It was too dry underfoot for the dog to do his best work, and the leaves were too thick to make for good shooting. At the end of two days all they had brought in was one barren old doe and the skins of two squirrels. But Whit knew as much about Sandwich as Orlando Weed when he'd laid out the town. Neither Moore nor Whit felt that the two days had been wasted.

At supper that night, while they were all of them eating and no one was talking, Whit made up his mind. He had intended not doing this until later when he could be alone by himself—he slept in the barn—but he found it a thing he couldn't put off.

It came down to this: there was land here in Sandwich that was about as good, probably, as he'd be likely to get anywhere. Sandwich wasn't the best land that there was in the province, and he wouldn't get the best land there was in Sandwich. But the way he was fixed, he'd have to take what he could get—in whatever township he should decide on. He couldn't buy land because he had no money. Whatever the Proprietors' Agent was willing to give him, that would be the land—anywhere—that he'd have to take.

Of Daniel Beede, Proprietors' Agent in Sandwich, Moore had said simply, "He's a hard man, but he's honest and fair. He works hard, and he's clever." And Mrs. Moore had agreed.

But the Moores were the main point in favor of Sandwich. Whit couldn't get over the way they had been kind to him. He wanted to stay. Bringing Melissa to a place where the Moores were, wouldn't be the same thing as taking her into a place that was strange. Things in Sandwich had started.

When he thought of Melissa, he was not at all tempted to drag out this business of finding a place. A good many times in the last couple of days he had seen the house he would build—set in this place or that—and in the doorway Melissa to greet him. He had seen her crossing his clearing coming to meet him, and the house behind her. He wasn't minded to comb half of New Hampshire Province seeking the one perfect place for a house. He had marked three or four places in Sandwich that would suit him well enough. If he could get one of them and a cow to go with it, he'd be entitled to figure that he'd done pretty well.

All right, that was that. He had made up his mind.

He remembered his supper, and drew his bowl toward him.

"You ain't eat awful hearty," Mrs. Moore said.

"No, ma'am, I ain't. I have been thinkin'."

Both the Moores waited . . .

"I was wond'rin' if maybe, sometime in the mornin', I wouldn't go up 'n see Daniel Beede."

"Good," Jonas Moore said.

61

And Mrs. Moore added, "I hope he will please you."

"He c'n do that, I guess. I got to please him."

Jonas said unexpectedly, "I got to go up there on an errand tonight. I'll tell him you're comin'."

10

Whit was at Beede's by sunrise next morning—four miles from Moore's, just up over the hill and hard by the edge of a little small pond. Out on the pond, the mist was shifting and breaking.

He wasn't any too early. Beede was out in the yard, and about to set off for a day of surveying. He had his compass slung from his shoulder, and an axman along with him who was carrying the chain folded up neatly in a worn leather sack.

Whit stated his name—and Beede, not even waiting for him to say where he was from or to state the business he'd come on, ordered the axman to go on ahead and make ready some stakes, and told Whit to come into the house. His tone was the same to both men. He was a head shorter than Whit—which made no impression on Beede, and Whit didn't notice it once he had sat down.

Beede took it for granted that Whit had had breakfast—which, as it happened, wasn't the case—but he offered Whit a pint of good cider and drew one for himself.

Whit sat on a bench alongside of the table, and Beede remained standing with his back to the fire. "Jonas Moore," began Beede, "come to see me last night. You been lookin' out land."

"That is correct."

"He pressed me hard for the best part of an hour to get me to make you an offer of land and a cow so's you'd make a pitch here to Sandwich. I had to tell him that I couldn't do it. I would count it a favor if you'd let me tell you why." He pulled at his nose with his thumb and forefinger and thoughtfully took a turn up and down on the hearth.

Whit was entirely ready to listen. He felt no resentment at the way things had gone. He had shut off his feelings when he came into the house. He could deal with them better when he was alone.

"I don't know if you know it," Beede was saying, "but when the Proprietors was granted this township, they had to agree—the same as anywhere else—to get the place settled, one way or another, that is: so many houses and so many men by whatever the time was. And if they didn't do it, the grant was no good. All grants are like that—and some are lived up to, and more of them ain't. Still, nowadays the Proprietors don't like to take too many chances. Governor now ain't so easy as what old Benning was. So they got me to come here, the Sandwich Proprietors—and Gilman, when I did, and Moore come the same time. The year after, the others. Now there is nine. None of us paid anything for our land, and we got something to boot from the Proprietors, too. We shouldn't have come if we hadn't. This wan't the same place then like what it is now. On their side, the Proprietors—well, they had to have us so as to make sure of their grant, and then to get a town started you got to have pioneers.

"But the way it is now, that part of it's finished. Proprietors tell me their grant is safe now and to spare, and you can see for yourself that we've made a good start here.

"So now the Proprietors figure—and I have a letter—that it's time they begun takin' in money instead of payin' it out. I don't know as I blame them, they have paid out a good deal. The grant wasn't give them for nothin' to start with, and since then they've paid us, and they'll have to pay more money yet. They'll have to pay me for this plan that I'm makin'—runnin' the lines on the ranges and lots—and they'll be roads and like that. But anyhow: I am their agent and they have given me orders to quit givin' way land and to sell it instead. You see how it is."

Whit didn't say that he couldn't buy. He had told Moore that he couldn't, and he could see that Moore had told Beede.

"Well, that's 'bout the size of it," Beede concluded. "You didn't ask me to make you an offer, and it may not have been up to me to say why I can't. But Moore certainly asked me to make you an offer—he put it real strong to me. And from what he's told me about you, I wish you could stay."

"I would have liked to." Whit got up to go. "You have spoken fair to me. Moore said that you would. And I thank you for the cider." He moved toward the door.

"Set down," said Beede. "I ain't finished yet."

"I am afraid I have held you too long as it is. That man of yours will have cut a power of stakes."

"I can use 'em. Now, then: where did you figure that you

might try next?—if you don't mind sayin'."

"I didn't know."

"Try Tamworth," said Beede. "You know about how it lays?"

"I would guess about east, and in the main south of Coruway.
As to its lines, sir, I couldn't say."

"You hold still a minute. I got a plan here shows the corners
and courses." He went to a chest at the other end of the room,
drew forth a paper, and spread it out on the table. "Step over
here."

Whit didn't hesitate. A map was a thing he could never resist.

Beede took him a tour of the boundaries of Tamworth; he'd
walked them last winter and hadn't forgotten a thing.

"Now then, you see, Tamworth," he explained when he'd
finished, putting the palm of his hand flat down on the map, "ain't
any further along than what we were two years ago. Do you see
what I mean? They need pioneers, and they need 'em bad.

"Now what I would do," he continued, "if I was in your room,
would be to go over there and quarter the town. Give it a good
going over, and see what they have got. If you like what you see,
you come back here and tell me." He straightened up. "I don't
promise you nothin'—it ain't my affair. But I know two or three
of them Tamworth Proprietors, and I expect their clerk to come
by here sometime pretty soon."

Whit bent over the map, getting it fixed in his mind.

Beede said finally, "If you want to make a copy of that, there's
some gear there to write with."

"I guess I got it all right . . . I don't carry no compass, so I don't
need it too fine . . ." All right, he had it. He stood up and faced
Beede. "I'm beholden to you, sir. I will try to come back."

"Good," said Beede. "And you ain't beholden to me, though
I hope Tamworth will be. We could do with some neighbors. And
I shouldn't wonder but Moore, who don't know nothin' 'bout
leather, might come a mite closer to it when he's judgin' a man."
He showed Whit to the door and out into the yard, where—
without saying a word—Beede simply nodded and left him.

Whit went back to the Moores'—and found that Jonas Moore
had gone fishing. It wasn't quite time yet for the fall run to begin,
when the big square-tails that had lain deep in Casumpy all
summer would begin to move up into the streams, but as Mrs.
Moore said to Whit as they stood out in the yard, "When he takes
it into his head to go fishin', he don't need any reason."

An east wind, beginning, was just stirring the leaves. "Well," said Whit soberly, "it does smell t' me like a good fishin' day."

"All I smell is rain. What did Beede say to you?"

"Moore tell you last night?"

"Yes."

"He done his best—Moore did, I mean. There wan't any reason for him to put himself out for me. Nor for you, too, the way you have done."

"Jonas likes anyone who can smell the same things that he can. You goin' over t' Tamworth?"

"I figured I might. I got to find some place for her. And I d' know really but what I'd ought to get started—if you would tell him good-by for me. Would you?"

"Yes."

"Well, ma'am—good-by. I—I thank you—surely."

"What're you takin' for food? That little bag you got over your shoulder looks t' me kind of flat. Give it here for a minute. You can't go off that way."

"No, ma'am. I'm all right. You 'n him done enough."

"Give me that bag."

Whit handed it over—and as she went into the house, Mrs. Moore muttered, "If I'd had you to raise, I'd have taught you some sense."

Whit put in close to a week in the township of Tamworth. Two days was all it had taken them to look over Sandwich, but Moore had been with him then, and had known what to leave out. Here, he had to look into everything. Behind each ridge there might be a nice little interval—the kind of place that would suit him and that perhaps he could get because so far no one had noticed it.

The rain Mrs. Moore had felt coming lasted only one night, and all through that night he lay dry and warm under the edge of a huge granite boulder. It was a good place in a rain. He stuck some wood underneath the overhang before he left in the morning.

Tamworth, he found, had more good land in it than Sandwich. There were four handsome big intervals, flat as a pond, three of them covered with a mixture of hardwood and soft, and the fourth one all pitch pine. The first three had some wild hay—although no great amount of it—but the pitch pine one didn't. He had no hope of getting a lot in any one of the first three—and he wouldn't have taken a lot in the fourth, because the soil under pitch pine was no use at all. He'd have to have leaf mold.

So he kept on searching. He saw a good many places—just as he had back in Sandwich—that would have done well enough probably, and that he didn't doubt he could get. He supposed they would give him a hundred acres perhaps. But a hundred acres was more than he could see at one time, and whenever he'd come onto something that looked pretty good and then start out to see what the land around it was like, he'd find he was being led on. For example: he happened one morning on a natural meadow that had enough hay in it to feed a half dozen cows. That would be a wonderful thing to have on a place! He started circling to see if there wasn't some land near enough to it that he could clear for a field. He found that there was—but it looked pretty poor—and he went farther and farther away from the meadow. By the time he'd found land that would make a good field, he was too far from the meadow to get them both into one lot. That seemed to be generally the way it would go: he'd find a nice little pond, or a brave stream of water—either one handy to have on a place—twice he came on a clay pit, and he found three or four little meadows just as good as the first one or better perhaps. But he couldn't find all of these things close together and located on land that would be good land to clear.

In the meantime, he had located three of the corners that Beede had shown him on the plan of the town, and keeping in mind how they bore from Coruway Mountain, he could always tell where he was with regard to that plan. That is, he could when he could see Coruway Mountain.

If the clouds weren't too low, it was no trouble to find it. He could go up a tree anywhere, and as soon as he'd get high enough to see out a little, there the mountain would be. There wasn't a minute that he didn't have the mountain in mind. The streams ran every which way, and so did the ridges. There were a good many of them that were too much alike. But Coruway Mountain was a thing you could count on.

There was no other like it that he'd ever seen. The lower part, maybe, was like other mountains. But the gray, granite peak of it, solid and strong and alone in the sky . . . well, that was a thing that you saw and then felt. And once you had felt it, you could see it again just by shutting your eyes—see it more clearly than you could remember a face,—most faces, at any rate.

All day, on the fifth day, there was nothing but rain. He traveled around some, but his heart wasn't in it. He didn't find anything that looked really good to him, and he was wet and uncomfortable and getting hungry, to boot. Not long after noontime he decided he'd go back to his boulder—make up a fire and hole up for a night. Being down in the southwestern part of the township, as he was at the time, it wouldn't have been very much farther to go back to the Moores'. But he didn't like to do that until he'd found what he was looking for—until he'd finished the thing that he'd come here to do.

He worked to his left for a few minutes and picked up a line tree—one Weed had spotted, from the looks of the spot—and then he moved south on the line to a hornets' nest in a hazel bush that Beede had spoken of, and that placed him a half mile north of the corner.

The boulder lay kitty-cornered across the town from him, and eight miles away. He took his bearings most carefully from the line that he stood on, and then faced in the direction that he wanted to go. He stood there without moving for two or three minutes, getting the country well fixed in his mind . . . and then he struck out for it, straight through the woods.

If it had been a serious matter, he wouldn't have tried it; he'd have taken a longer way there, and been sure of his way. But it suited his fancy, just at the moment, to see if he couldn't hit it—right on the nose. That would be pretty good. All through the day, he'd been wandering aimlessly. He was tired of that. He wanted to feel as though he'd done something. He wouldn't need to tell anyone . . .

At the end of four hours, he had to admit that what he had done was to get himself lost in a swamp. He'd been in the swamp for the best part of an hour now, while the boulder sat somewhere on the side of a hill. About the only part of this venture that had turned out as expected was that now he was certain he wouldn't need to tell anyone. And he wasn't sure really that that was just as expected . . .

He thrashed around in there for another hour or more—and when he finally got free of the swamp, he only kept going long enough to find a place to crawl into out of the rain. He had pretty good luck—coming on a big hemlock blowdown, six feet through the butt, and with dead branches beneath it that would do for a fire.

When he'd got a fire to going and had laid up some wood, he stopped the windward side of his shelter, and lay down to eat. It was not a big supper—some corn and dried meat—but it was enough so that his hunger no longer annoyed him.

He was still annoyed, though, about losing that boulder. Not that he needed it—he was comfortable here—but he kept arguing and figuring as to how he could have missed it. He had a strong feeling it wasn't far off from here—a mile was the most he should be out of the way. And yet that whole swamp had been totally new to him; until he was in it, he'd never guessed it was there. Well, he knew it now.

The trouble had been, of course, not having the mountain. If he'd had the mountain to go by, he'd have come across like a shot. Or if he'd had the sun, for that matter. The sun was good one way: you could tell where it was from down on the ground. But it always kept shifting—from summer to winter, from daylight to dark. The mountain stayed put.

He rolled over and thrust some more wood on his fire . . . and lay propped on his elbow, watching it catch . . .

But in the matter of spirits—well, that was a difficult thing. It was a thing that had troubled him always about Coruway Mountain, from the first time that he'd seen it. The spirits were there on the mountain. There was no question of that. Mr. Gowan could doubt it—but he'd noticed that Gowan hadn't wanted to come right out flat and say they weren't there. And what if he had? After all, they were Indian spirits—and the Indians ought to know where their own were.

He poked at the fire, and then lay on his back . . .

Indian spirits, generally speaking, were ready and willing to do a man harm. But they weren't any too clever. There were tricks to outwit them that a hen would have seen through. But the spirits never caught on to them. And another thing was, they stayed up on the mountain. The power they had didn't reach very far. If a man didn't go up there—that is, a white man—there wasn't much they could do to him. That had been shown.

It had been shown in this way: no matter how pesky the spirits had been to the Indians, when it came down to a question of *white* men and Indians, you could count on the spirits to be on the Indians' side. That stood to reason: the Indians were the ones who believed in them most, and you take a spirit that *nobody* believes in, and—well, he isn't anywhere. But in spite of all the help that the spirits had given them, there was scarcely an Indian in this part of the country. They had all been cleaned out. That showed that the power of an Indian spirit wouldn't work on a man except on a mountain. Down here, it had failed.

But the spirits remained—up on top of the mountain. Up there where they lived, in the crannies and caves, they would have pretty good power. A man would be foolish to go up there and try them. It was a bad place up there. A man ought to feel that just to look at it, even—same as he would when he looked at a place that was crawling with snakes.

Yet whenever he looked at Coruway Mountain it made him feel good. It was always that way. And he'd had the feeling a good many times that the mountain was friendly—not in a sociable, talkative way, but in a way bigger than that. He'd even felt himself drawn to it.

That could have been, of course, the spirits trying to get him to come up there so that they could go to work on him. But it didn't feel that way. It didn't feel in the least like—well, like a temptation. For one thing, it was always the same; and while a temptation looks good to you most times, there are times when it doesn't. No, this feeling he got—that the mountain was friendly, of his being drawn to it—looked always the same to him whenever he thought of it. It was quiet, unchanging.

It had puzzled him often; it puzzled him now. And lying there in some comfort—with the light of his fire on the log overhead— he thought of the mountain.

"A mountain like that," he finally proposed, "could have its own spirit. I don't know why it couldn't. And if it did have, why, then this feeling I get needn't have nothin' t' do with them Indian spirits."

He liked the idea . . . and he chose to accept it. And then he thought of various things that would all go to show that this spirit—which belonged to the mountain itself—was a much grander thing than any collection of Indian spirits.

Take the matter of distance. The Indian spirits worked close to home only: they had failed to come down off the mountains when the Indians needed them, and now when he looked at the mountain he couldn't feel them—well, not any to speak of. But the mountain's own spirit could reach out twenty miles. He had felt it do that. He often had felt it when he could not see the mountain—when he was as far off as Kettleford. It takes a powerful spirit to travel that far, and with nothing to bring it—no charms, or like that.

And he thought of proof that the mountain was friendly. Any time, anywhere, a man that could see it could tell where he was. And to get hold of that knowledge, he didn't have to make any medicine, or mess about with the innards of animals, or wait for the moon. All he had to do was climb up a tree and take a look at the mountain—and the mountain would tell him what he wanted to know. If that didn't show that the mountain was friendly—well, then nothing would.

Whit was satisfied of it, and he went to sleep.

Midway of the morning, the rain had let up. He went up a white pine, lopped off a few branches so that he could see out around, and sat up there and waited—pitching bark at a beetle that was climbing the trunk. There was nothing at all to show whether the mountain was in front or behind him. There was nothing to show that the mountain was anywhere. The weather'd come down and had taken it off. Well, there wasn't anything that was stronger than weather. It did what it felt like, and that was all there was to that. There were plenty of signs and omens and so on that would tell what it *would* do, but there wasn't a thing that could *make* it do anything. He had heard of some, yes, but they weren't any good. They might appear to work sometimes—if you happened to try for the weather you were going to get anyhow. Or, if you were willing to wait long enough, you could get what you asked for—because the weather was sure to come round to it sooner or later. But it was safe to say, generally, that a man was wasting his money who paid anything for a charm or a secret that was claimed to work on the weather. The weather was proof against all charms and spirits. There was nothing could touch it; it was on top of everything. He was certain of that.

His thinking broke off—as he felt a strange light all around him. He saw it was down toward the ground—and it was out there in the sky. It was growing now, too, with a kind of slow swiftness—and Whit, his eyes widening, got to his feet and held on to the trunk.

His heart pounded within him. He was scared and he knew it, but he didn't know what . . . The light was brighter and brighter. He could feel in his thighs and the tips of his fingers the oncoming instant. He was all alone now—

And then he saw this: high in the sky—not overhead, but off in the midst of the sky—he saw the mountain come out.

He saw it riding alone in the sky . . . just the gray, granite top with a touch of sun on it—and underneath it was sky, same as everywhere else.

It only lasted one terrible instant—beautiful—clear as a vision can be . . .

—and then it was gone again.

Whit came very slowly down out of the tree.

When he stood on the ground, his knees began shaking. Well, they had a right to! He didn't mind that. "What I seen then," he said half aloud, huskily, "was a sign, and a big one. I don't know what it means. I seen Coruway Mountain on top of the weather . . . and by God, wan't she beautiful! I do know that." And he picked up his gun and his things and set off through the woods slowly and with his head down.

A little above him—he was within five or six rod of it—he passed the gray boulder that he'd sought in the rain. "That's the boulder," he said, "I was lookin' for yesterday," and paid it no further heed. On a long slant to the eastward, he was climbing the ridge on the north side of which he had lain out last night.

This was the thought that kept coming into his head: "Suppose I had been up there—right up on the peak of it—riding along on a mountain on top of the sky—everything else in the world underneath me . . . *What would I have seen?*"

—and then he'd pull away from it, because that wasn't the way that a man ought to think.

But it kept coming back to him . . .

He swung a little more southerly—putting the mountain in back of him—and the hillside rose steeply under his feet.

Spruces and hemlocks were the only trees round him—and none of them big ones: he must be getting up pretty well. Off to his left, he could make out, it was open. Rock ledges, probably—a place to see out. He moved over to look.

As he approached, he had an eye out for rattlesnakes—but there didn't seem to be any, and he supposed without really turning his mind to it that either the place was too easy to get to, or else they hadn't come out yet after the rain.

The sun was free now, and here and there on the ledge there was a thin, wavering steam coming off the damp rocks. From the edge of the woods, he saw that the sky out beyond had cleared clean and blue to the south and southeast. And he stepped into the sunlight—feeling the warmth of it good on his face. Picking his way between the wet junipers, he came up on the ledges—and the country beneath him reached away off for maybe eight or ten miles. He was facing southeast—that was Great Ossipy Pond only a little bit farther north than he'd have said it belonged. On the horizon, there was a white rim of clouds, solid below and with more country behind it, but the top edge was thinning where it met with the blue. Looking down on the country, the white mist

71

in the hollows was as it is in the morning.

He turned round to the mountain—

Whit drew in his breath. All things slipped away from him ... his sight and his mind and his spirit were one ... and he was carried up by the power of the slow, rolling slopes—to the darker green of the pines and the spruces and hemlocks—and on up from there to the great gray of the top—rock in the sunlight—and the blue sky beyond.

When he turned from it, it was to gaze over the valley—a little small interval—that was right down below. He didn't see much at first, and then things came to him gradually, one by one, and he noted them.

There was a flat place of four or five acres, and with a brook running through it, but the soil would be deeper than it would be on a slope. On the far side, the hill that shut in the interval was lower and gentler than it was on this side. And just over beyond it ought to be where the outlet made from the pond lying more to the left. He'd been along that outlet last winter. "Now wait a minute," he said, "—a little ways down below there is a place to cut hay. I remember it well—there's an old broken-down beaver dam, and now that the water is gone, the grass has come in, but the trees ain't had time yet."

He looked again at the interval, lying there in the sun ... near the head of it would be the place for a house—just enough up the rise so it wouldn't be too far to lug water, and yet far enough up so it would be dry in the spring. Logs would be easy to snake down this hillside ...

And as he stood there and thought of it, things came with a rush: a man could probably girdle every tree on that interval in a day—if he worked. In two days, he could. And if he was to fell them off and on through the winter—after he'd got his house— and if he was to get a good burn, he'd have room enough ready by the end of June, probably, to get a fair crop of corn—if the weather was right.

He thought of the interval as it would look cleared and with a crop coming along—a proper log house setting there on the rise, a place for a cow and with a garden beside it, smoke from the chimney ... It looked pretty good. "I don't see no oaks, so the soil ought to be sweet enough, but you can't tell for certain until you have tasted it. You know, I shouldn't wonder but this might be the place ..."

He looked up at the mountain.

And as he jumped down from the ledges and swung down through the trees, he grinned to himself,—because there was no use pretending there was any doubt in the matter: this was the place. "Only thing is, if I can find some clay handy. Nearest I know of is three or four mile. That's a long ways to lug it. But for a chimbley that's right, you have got to have clay."

Late the next afternoon he was on his way back to Beede's. He had tasted the soil and considered it sweet. Until close to dark yesterday and again early this morning, he had followed the streams in search of some clay, and had finally found it at about a mile and a half—which wasn't any too near, and yet it could have been worse.

He was all ready for the Proprietors' Clerk. He'd take a full lot or nothing, and he knew just how he'd bound it: on the northeast by the outlet, opposite that by the foot of the hill, on the south and southeast by the brook—where, after it's come out of the interval, it runs almost due east and then swings to the north—and on the northwest a line to make one hundred acres. That would do him all right. He was on his way back to Beede's—he was on his way back to the Moores'—he was on his way back to Melissa.

When he struck Bearcamp River the rain had raised it enough so that there weren't so many rocks showing as there had been coming in. Still, from what he could see with the sun in his eyes, there were enough to get him across—and he didn't pause very long to lay out a route.

Halfway over or better, a rock turned underneath him, his other foot missed the next one, and he went into the water—holding his gun up over his head. The water was only about up to his waist, but down on the bottom the footing was slippery. He staggered a step or two, trying to stand, and then his right foot slid down. He fell to his left, pushed by the current—and the pain in his leg was a sickening thing. Gun and all, he went under. His right foot was caught.

He got it loose somehow, and scraping and bumping from one rock to another, he dragged himself clear of the river and up onto the bank.

It took him a minute or two to get himself straightened out and then he went to work on his ankle to see what had happened.

He had broken a bone in it, but it wasn't the main one. He

73

could feel the place with his fingers—it was on the outside, and just under the skin. You could feel the two broken ends scrunch against one another . . . yes, she was broken, all right.

His powder was wet.

—and come to think of it, he hadn't any food with him.

He guessed it was up to him somehow to get himself back to Sandwich . . .

Well, the first thing to do was to cut him a crutch. He reached round for his knife . . . it wasn't there.

That seemed like too much.

Where that knife was, was out there in the water. It had come loose while he was floundering round.

He'd have to go get it. Twelve mile into Sandwich, no food, and wet powder—he wasn't going to try that without any knife!

And he went in and got it.

But he had to rest up a bit when he came out.

Then he went crawling around in search of a sapling to cut for a crutch. He found one that would do to start off with, at any rate—and he figured he'd probably see something better before it got dark. It looked overhead as though it was going to be a good night to travel. He'd get to Beede's—well, say around noon. If he kept going, he would. And if he couldn't make Beede's, he might try for Poole's. That would be a little bit nearer, but it was south of his line. They said that old Poole was a great one for talking. Whit didn't know as he'd like that if he was laid up.

If he had enough left by the time he got to Beede's, he might even cut round that, and go on down to the Moores'. It would be downhill all the way once he was past Beede's.

He took a few steps, and the crutch sunk in and stuck. He pulled it out and kept going. He had twelve miles to go . . .

11

Melissa listened and watched for all signs of autumn. The heavy, rich feeling that she'd had of the summer ahead of her, that had gone now. But the fall of the year was a long ways away. It was that she must wait for . . . and all the lingering signs of the summer that in other years she'd hung on to, this year she resented. The swallows dipped and swung foolishly; they had outstayed their welcome. Things that belonged to late summer, like the grasshoppers, or the first of the asters, the halfway mark on the woodpile, and the smell of the earlier apples, these things she noticed, but without any excitement. What she wanted to see was the swamp maples afire! She'd know then he'd be home soon.

For the first time in her life, she liked the talk in the tavern. No man that came in there but what had something to say about the shortness of summer—he'd seen something or other that meant there wasn't much left of it. "I see MacLaughlin down t' the smithy gettin' some irons f'r his breakin'-up plow. I thought that was forehanded, but come to think of it, 'tain't such a great while, once you reap winter rye, afore you go t' plowin'." And another: "I see a mole—must a been two or three days ago—had as glossy a pelt on him as you'd want to see anytime." Talk of the winter, even: "Be an awful winter for snow this winter, now I want to tell you. I ain't see a hornets' nest close to the ground in I don't know how long. That's as sure a sign as I know of. That's an Indian sign."

Let it snow! thought Melissa. She knew where she'd be.

Old David Gillmor came limping in one day. Lord was there at the time, and Ensign offered to treat. David thanked him, and said he guessed he'd take some brandy—if Ensign wanted to go that far; it had been cold in the night, hadn't it?

Ensign said he hadn't noticed it.

"Cold down to my place!" David assured him.

"That might be," said Ensign.

"'*Twas* cold!" averred David. "And what's more you take now my woman—I'd ought not to complain, maybe—but it don't seem to me like nowadays she heats up the bed, not so good as she used to."

"She'd ought to put the pan to it earlier."

"Puts the pan to it early enough. Later on, is when I mean— long towards mornin'."

"Oh," said Ensign, unsmiling.

"You take in the old days a man could keep warm at night. Why, I remember the time when, if a man wanted a bearskin, all he had to do was go git it. Bears was thick around here. You could get a bear anytime."

"Even so, if a man was to get cold at night early as this is, he'd have to wait awhile, wouldn't he?"

"Why would he?" said David.

"'Twouldn't pay him to skin a bear, not this time of year."

"Why wouldn't it?"

"Pelt's too poor, for a while yet."

"No, it ain't!"

"August . . ." Ensign suggested.

"All right, August! Now I'll tell you something. My old father told me: 'Davey,' he said—this when I was a young one—'Davey,' he says, 'it'll pay you to skin a bear any month's got an "r" in it.' "

"Well, it might," Ensign conceded, "maybe last part of August. Still, I wouldn't think so."

"That's all you know about bears. Ain't a young fellow round here now knows about bears like they used to—less it might be Whit Livingston—'n he ain't around here. Where is he now? You know? I ain't seen him lately."

"I ain't seen him either."

"He's went north," said Melissa, "—so someone told me."

"Went north, did he? What'd he want to go north for? Too early to trap yet."

"Went to get him a bear, prob'ly." Lord spoke into his glass.

"How far north was he goin'?" David asked of Melissa.

"I couldn't say as to that."

"Well, I hope he comes back," the old man remarked darkly. "That's an awful mean country."

"Why is it?" asked Lord, just a little bit scornfully. He was tired of David; he didn't know now why he'd treated him.

"I don't feel no call to go there."

"Indians're cleaned out now, you got no cause to worry. Anyhow, one that you cheated, David, would have died of old age by now."

David ignored it. "Look here," he said, "land up there is free, ain't it? Not in the Grants it ain't maybe, but north o' here it is, anyhow. You get something for nothing in this world, there's a reason."

"Land's got to be cleared yet, that's all's the reason. Man ain't goin' t'pay much for land he's got to clear."

"Who cleared the Grants?"

"Pioneers done it. Who'n the hell else would do it?"

"They're worse'n Indians," David said with disgust.

"You talk like a Portsmouth man."

"Not me. I know what I'm talkin' 'bout."

"Then talk about Indians."

"I'll tell you about Indians! There ain't a man now in Kittlef'd . . ."

Melissa left them and went out into the dooryard. The days looked pretty solid between now and his coming. He would come, she was certain. She was not comfortably certain; she was certain because she knew that she must be. The days until then were not now to be counted. If she were to choose one of them, no matter how safely, and then when that day came, it should fail of bringing him . . .

Ensign spoke from behind her: "Put that on my score, will you? That one treat I give him was all I do give him."

Melissa said she would see to it.

"I got to go now. You'd best get back inside there 'fore you're a-treatin' him, too, 'thout knowin' it, hadn't you?"

"Oh, David's all right, I guess."

"Sure he is! Well, good day to you. Where'd Captain go to?"

"Went t' th' smithy t' trade for some nails, he said." She went inside, where she'd have to listen to David.

12

Captain, walking down the road to the smithy, found it a pleasant walk. He was not distracted by nature: he saw no bird, beast, or flower. His mind was on money. He had convinced himself that Joe had a sack of gold buried under every last apple tree within ten rods of the forge and probably two under the anvil. It was in that happy conviction that he greeted Joe largely. "Good morning to you, Joe Philip, my friend, and a very fine morning— though a little warm walking."

Joe never glanced up; he'd seen him coming. He said only, "Capitao," not much raising his voice over the sound of his hammer, and went on beating out nails.

"Nails, eh? Business good, Joe?—not that that matters to a man fixed the way you be."

"Business is no good," said Joe between hammerings. The sound of the hammer was soft on the iron, but rang clear on the anvil. "Nails I make up like I used to make spun yarn—when there's naught else to do."

The nail, cherry-red, lost color rapidly. Joe had it squared and drawn, though, before it had cooled too much. He tossed it into a bucket, where it gave a short, futile hiss—and then he reached for another.

"I come on an errand," Captain Butler informed him. He'd not been asked to sit down yet.

Joe hammered the nail out. "What you come after?"

"I come t' talk business."

The nail hissed in the bucket. "Smith business?"

"No. T'other."

"What about it? She ready?"

"No, she ain't ready! Why should she be ready? You and me ain't agreed, Joe. We ain't agreed to how much yet."

Joe pumped two or three times on the long bellows handle. "I showed you how much t'other day at t' tavern."

Captain, undismayed, smiled. "What! That little sample?"

"You seen it all, Capitao."

Captain seated himself on a worn cross section of white oak Karr had once used for the anvil. "When you get done podgerin' over them nails o' yourn, Joe, then we can talk maybe."

"What's to talk about?"

"Money."

Joe finished another nail, laid down his tongs, and then leaned on the anvil. He still held his hammer. He said, "A' right. You c'n talk."

Captain began. He was a poor man, he said, but content to remain so. He loved his daughter. All he sought was her happiness. Of Joe's money, all he wished for himself was enough to ease slightly the otherwise insupportable pain of a father losing his daughter. He was not asking much. Joe might think that he ought to take more, but he wouldn't.

Joe said, "You can have what I showed you, come the day we get married."

"Now, now, Joe! Don't talk that way!"

"You're t' one's talkin'. What I say ain't talkin'. What I say is trut'."

"Why, God's name, Joe, that's ridic'lous! You don't mean that measly handful! Why, that ain't much more'n enough for to buy a really good black woman!—and if that's all that you offer, I'd say you'd better get one."

"You got one t' sell, Capitao? You in t'at kin' o' business?"

"What th' hell do you mean?"

Joe shrugged his great shoulders.

78

"Now, then, Joe, let's to business. I'm goin' t' be easy. I'll agree with you, Joe—and this is rock-bottom, I didn't come here to trade with you, not in a matter of this sort—I'll agree with you, Joe, my friend, for gold to the equal of ten thousand mill dollars. You can take it or leave it."

Joe never blinked.

"You know damn well you got it, and so do I know it! Why, that's nothin' to you, Joe; I'll wager you've all of that right there under that anvil—say nothin' o' what you got buried out round the place here."

"For ten gallon of brandy, I sell you t'at anvil and all t' gold under it. You wan' t' buy?"

"I don't want no damn anvil! What I want is fair treatment."

"You c'n have what I showed you."

Captain's tone altered. "You know, Joe," he said thoughtfully, "there's one thing I ain't spoke of. I'll be fair 'n open, and I'll take it kindly of you, Joe, not to take no offense. But it might be—I been thinkin'—that I don't want a mite of it. My hands is clean, Joe, 'n what little I've got I've made fair, square, and honest. You tell me this, Joe: where'd that money come from?"

"Oh, it come from all over."

"Well, you know how you got it."

"Oh, yes. I know."

"Then where did you get it?"

"Whit Livingston, he give t'at gold t'me, Capitao, for makin' a scythe blade. Now you know, too."

"You listen to me, Joe: if that ain't clean money . . ."

Joe raised his eyebrows politely and waited.

"If that ain't clean money . . ."

Joe added a smile. "You're in stays, Capitao."

"'Stays'? What do you mean 'stays'?"

"W'en you try a new tack, put 'er 'ard over. You los' your way, ain' you?"

"I d'know what you're talkin' 'bout. Look here, Joe, I'm serious. There—there ain't any blood on it?"

"You see any spots?"

"You know what I mean. And you answer me truly!"

"What good would t'at do? You ain' goin' t' believe."

"Yes or no, Joe!"

"A'right: t'ere is blood on it."

"Oh, God! You don't mean it!"

Joe crossed himself.

79

"Don't do that!" said Captain. "Oh, my God, Joe! But, Joe—Joe, there ain't very much blood . . ."

"A puncheon o' blood t' each piece o' gold, maybe. T'at too much for you, Capitao?"

"A puncheon! Why, a score o' men's blood wouldn't fill up a puncheon! I see—you're jokin'."

"In my country, Capitao, we know where gold come from—back in t' old days. All t' gold in t' worl' has got blood on it, Capitao—one time or another. T' mos' you can do is t' watch out it ain' *your* blood. You look out for t'at now—you ain' got much t' lose. You got more t'ings t' ask me?"

"I tell you what, Joe: I'll say five thousand."

"You can if you want to—say five, ten or twenty."

"All right, then: you name a figure."

"I don' count ver' good. You can have what I showed you."

"You're an awful hard man, Joe."

"I don' t'ink so."

"Well, I know you be!"

Joe didn't answer.

Captain said, "Well, I got no time to waste this way." He got down off his perch. "When you're ready to listen to reason, you come up to the tavern."

"Good day to you, Capitao."

Captain Butler strode out of the doorway. "Oh, er—" He turned back again. "I forgot what I come for. Nails, now—fourpenny. That's what I come about. I could get 'em cross river, o' course, not so dear as what yourn be, and a better nail maybe. Still, if you want the business . . . These here you been drawin', how much would they be? They don't run awful even."

"Same price as before."

"People claim they break over."

"Any nail'll break over if it ain' striken fair—Derry nail or my nail."

"All right. Half a hundredweight. What's to boot? I need pothooks."

"T'ree to boot. For me to boot, rum—same as t' las' time."

"Let's see—pint o' Medford you had the last time."

"Quart—by your measure."

"All right, a quart then. You'll fetch the nails up."

"I send a boy wit' 'em. He can fetch t' rum back t' me."

Captain stood looking out the doorway. "Well, a nice day, like I said before, ain't it? Hot, though, for walkin' . . ."

"I don' know. I ain' walk any."

"All right, Joe"—he swung round to him—"call it three thousand."

Joe raised his hand to the bellows pump and his fire glowed brightly. "I got nails t' make now."

Captain blew up. He cursed Joe pretty liberally.

When Captain had finished, Joe said, "You are a mosquito."

Biting his thin lip, the old man made for the doorway. This was the third time . . . and a third time he turned back again. "Let me look at it once more," he said, almost pleading.

"You seen it already. It don' look any different."

"But I didn't count it."

"You got years comin' t' count it."

The little figure collapsed on the upended oak piece. He was limp now, and hunched over. He was a man beaten. His bowed head nodded slightly. "Yes . . ." he said to himself, ". . . yes, years yet to count it." And without looking up, he put out a small hand to Joe. "All right. It's a bargain."

Joe saw the hand, and reaching high overhead to a cranny, he brought down a bottle. "Here—" he said, "drink on it."

Captain's hand took it. When he'd fumbled the plug out, he drank deeply, not gracefully, and then coughed a little. "Thank you."

Joe plugged the bottle and set it back up where it had come from. With hammer and tongs he went on with his nail-making. Captain just sat there, not even stirring. Joe didn't speak to him, but he was more than aware of him. Because of Captain, Joe couldn't work smoothly: he had to think separately of each thing he was doing. Captain's presence upset him—the little figure in black, there, all drawn in like a spider. It kept crossing Joe's mind, too, how he'd come by the money. Joe never liked thinking of that with another man sitting there. It was too real in his mind—clearer now than it had been the night that it happened. It would come so real before him that it seemed unsafe to have it there: if he could see it so plainly, why should others be blind to it?

Captain stirred on his pedestal. The brandy had worked in him and he felt more himself again. "Joe," he said, "I been studyin', and I'll tell you what you're to do. I'll do the most of it, but I don't want you to spoil it. I know the girl, and I know what she takes to."

Joe wiped his forehead and made shift to listen.

"There ain't been but one man that could ever come near to her. He went away afterward, and there was nowt ever come of it. I seen it all at the time, and I'll give you the benefit. You got to come on her easy, Joe. She ain't like most women. You got to be soft with her. Swearin' and fightin' and singin' and all like that, she's seen enough of. Gentlemen, too, mind you!—she's sent more than one away that might even have married her. I figure what she wants is a kind of a humble man—this one I spoke of, he was properly humble. What I mean is, soft-spoken, and kindly, and helping. 'F you could make out to be that way— 'stead of the way *that* you be—you might get along better. Course, I shall do my part—which, as I say, is the most of it."

"What is t'at? Like I tol' you?"

"You can leave that to me, Joe. Well, I must be going. It's a hot day for walking."

"Here," said Joe, "—finish it."

"Why, that's very handsome! No—just a swallow . . ."

Captain departed, and Joe stood there thinking. He leaned on the anvil first, and then he sat down to think. He thought a long time, and he came round to feel this way: that the kind of man Captain had said she was looking for, well, now that he thought of it, that was the kind of man José Felipe was—though maybe most wouldn't see it, and he hadn't himself till now.

Then he thought of Melissa.

13

Melissa shuddered a little; it was cold and dank in the springhouse. Nor was it warm out of doors even, except in the sun. A week's gray, rainy weather had chilled all the countryside. The wind had changed last night and now the sun shone, but even at noonday, in this second week of September, it had little strength to it for all it was bright. It could not make the grass hot again. Under a white pine, the soft thickness of needles would be wet and chill till next summer, with no proper smell to them; that was lost now. It would come again—far from here—on the other side of the winter. Next year, in the north, there'd be summer for both of them.

It made her work all the heavier, this thinking of next year . . . of Whit's coming before then, of all things in the future.

Because it was only this present that now stood between them. Whit would be along any day . . .

She tried to get on with her churning—but when she laid hold of the dasher, the task seemed too much. She needed something to carry her through it. She knew where she could find it.

Outside, where the pans were set out for their sunning, she stood once again as she'd stood back in the summer, looking down toward the meadow. It was no great disappointment—in that very first instant—that the meadow seemed empty. She'd not really expected that this time he'd be there. There was always a chance though . . . Then, by waiting a moment, she got what she'd come out for: she made herself see him—a clear, distant figure, swinging up through the meadow. She put her hand to her heart, then. But she didn't straighten her apron, or put her hand up to her hair.

Back inside the springhouse, she set herself to her labor . . .

It took a long time this morning. There was weariness in her. Her arms ached and her back, too. She could remember when churning was nothing—she had used to enjoy it. It had seemed fresh and cool in the springhouse—no one to disturb her—and the dasher'd been lighter, too. Now it was heavy.

She kept on with it.

When a faintness came on her, she recollected that she'd eaten little that morning. She was not out of case, really, but— well, Indian pudding that had stood since the night before, cold beef, and cider—she just hadn't felt drawn to them. Later on in the morning, she'd drink some tea, maybe. That was why she was faint now: she hadn't eaten her breakfast. In spite of that, though, she didn't feel hungry. Still, that was nothing to fret about . . . Soon as Whit had got back, everything would be different! She'd be right as a trivet, then.

She kept on with her churning . . . until all she was aware of was the churn right in front of her, with her hands bent to the dasher. She was not crying yet, but she knew in a minute she would be—no one could see her. She spoke Whit's name half aloud—and then knew that was foolish.

After a time, someone spoke to her. Melissa didn't look up at him. She'd got it fixed in her head that, for some reason forgotten, she must keep on with this churning.

"Here—I give you a hand wit' t'at."

She saw a great hand fix itself round the dasher below where she gripped it. The dasher quickened itself—down and up, down and up—and Melissa let go of it. She stepped back and looked at him—

Joe.

Melissa was frightened. She backed to the wall and put a hand out to steady her.

"T' old man said you was out here"—and then he moved his head sideways. "Go out 'n sit down—" he said, "I finish t' is here for you."

She got outside somehow, and she had to sit down then because her knees wouldn't hold her . . .

She gazed at Joe through the doorway. The churn looked to have shrunk some. Joe was bringing the butter!—he'd both hands on the dasher and was making it fly. He was like to pull the lid out of it if he didn't ease up some!—and every stroke of the dasher, his little red hair ribbon would bob up and down. Melissa couldn't help laughing—not because she wanted to laugh, but just because she couldn't help laughing.

Joe must have heard her—and he waved a hand to her.

She stopped laughing suddenly.

But she stayed there too long . . . and Joe, when he'd brought the butter, came out and confronted her. "All done," he said soberly.

Melissa said, "Thank you, Joe"—although she shrank from his nearness.

"T'at ain' nothin'."

"Well—you're stronger than I am." She had to say something.

"You ain' only a woman—and not such a big one. You need a man t' work for you."

"Well—"

"I am a strong man—José Felipe."

Melissa said nothing.

"T' old man," Joe informed her, "he put too much work on you."

Captain squawled from the casement where he'd been listening, "Joe! Look here a minute—"

"What for?" Joe inquired.

"I got a barrel here that I can't break over. Bear a hand, will you?—got too much heft to it—Barbados m'lasses."

Joe went reluctantly, muttering something.

Melissa went to hide in the barn until Joe had gone home again. There was a place up under the eaves, she knew, where no one could find her; she'd treasured it always since she was a little girl. It seemed good to go back to it. Just up overhead, when she'd lie in the hay there, there was a knot in the tie beam that made an old woman's face. There'd been many a time that Melissa had talked to her.

14

At first slowly, then with a chill, indifferent swiftness, October seemed to spread out its days before her—each was empty.

Melissa knew what she was up against. She yielded nothing. She no longer cried out for him, times when no one could hear her, but she'd found this to say to herself and she said it often: "All right, he ain't come today. But he can come tomorrow. And even if he don't come tomorrow, it can't be no worse than today was. One day at a time like this, I'd ought to be able to handle— for a while, I can, anyhow—if I don't think too much ahead." She got along that way. She kept her head up.

She prayed for his coming, but not very often. There was no use keeping after Him. He knew how things stood probably. He would do what He would do.

Things being this way, she didn't pay much heed to Joe's presence.

There came a gray day, though, when she had hard work to keep hold of herself. No matter what she was doing, she could feel the future come closer.

Seeking escape from that feeling, she put on her cloak and stepped out into the dooryard—where she found not the brightness of autumn, but certain and near in the low, heavy sky and the look of things generally, the oncoming of winter. It was cold, too. Over off to one side, she saw Joe at the woodpile. Joe's little red hair ribbon was brighter than any autumn leaves left now. She watched Joe for a moment as she might a bird or a squirrel; he was something in motion that she hoped would hold her attention. It came to her, watching him, that Joe was round there a good deal lately. Most every day, he'd be in for something—and often as not lend a hand in one way or another. Come to think of it, Joe must have lugged all the wood for a week now. It might seem odd, perhaps, that she hadn't noticed it—if she'd had to lug it herself she'd have noticed it soon enough! But she knew it was not odd. She knew where her mind had been—never a letup.

Joe's back was to her. The pile was breast-high to him, mostly all of it maple, and the sticks a handspan in thickness. It was fair enough wood with no popple into it, but it was wonderfully heavy. Melissa never could handle more than two sticks at a time of it.

Joe kept pulling sticks toward him till he had six or eight of them jutting out from the woodpile. He put a long arm out and over them, slid his right arm underneath, and, when he'd gathered them, eased the load to his shoulder, settled them gently, and started into the house with it.

He saw Melissa and said to her, "Mornin'."

"Mornin' to you, Joe. You got quite a load."

Joe grinned like a schoolboy. "I come back and you load me, and I carry some wood."

Melissa smiled pleasantly. "Hold on—I'll get that door for you."

Joe said, "I can get 'er"—and she let him do it.

She went back to the pile then, and waited. This was a pretty thing—her helping the man that she'd once been afraid of. Joe had changed some, of course, but that wasn't the whole of it. She hadn't known, then, what being afraid could amount to. Far as Joe was concerned, she could be as much afraid of Joe as she'd ever been, and it wouldn't bother her any—not alongside of this other fear: that Whit would never come home again.

Joe came out of the tavern, and Melissa smiled at him—half in amusement because Joe was so eager to show off before her.

"You load me up," he commanded her proudly.

One after another, she put eight sticks on his shoulder. He seemed to bear up all right. She put on another. "There," she said, "that ought to do it."

"More," said Joe. "Give me somet'ing to carry."

She put on another stick. "There!"

"Mother of God!" Joe exclaimed cheerfully, "I ain' no more'n in ballast. Put some more on."

"You'll overset 'f I do. You got more on there now 'n you c'n get through the door with."

"I won' overset, I got too much beam t' me." He stood with his feet apart. "If I had a line to secure it, I could carry more yet even."

"You got to set it down when you're in there. Go on, now, be off with you. If you want any more, I guess the pile'll still be here."

Joe stepped off slowly . . . and the sound of his breathing was just like an ox's. It was the biggest turn of wood she'd ever seen a man carry. Melissa stepped round him so as to hold the door open. Her toes gripped the floor while he went through the doorway . . . but he made it all right. She shut the door after him.

"Hold on now, Joe, and I'll take it off of you."

"Get away." Joe moved his left foot back, and then seemed to let himself settle till he was down on his left knee. Then his right shoulder came forward (the one had the wood on it) and he bent his back forward . . . when the weight touched the floor, he was over the worst of it. He set that wood down as nicely as a woman would put down a baby that had gone to sleep in her arms.

"Well, looks 's though you'd done it," Melissa commended him. "Made a terrible clatter, though, if you should a spilled it. That there rock maple's got a wonderful heft to it."

Joe was blowing considerably. "Maple ain' heavy. You ever carry mahogany?"

"No, I don't guess so. I d'know what it is even."

"Kind of a wood," said Joe.

"Give out a good heat, does it?"

"Might. T'ings are made of it."

"Like what do they make of it?"

"Oh . . . all kind o' t'ings. Grows in hot countries—not t' dry ones, t' wet ones. I seen a sloop once come in from t' Islands had some logs of it in her. One went by t' board when t'ey was unloading. She float high in t' water, for such heavy wood. Where's your old man today?"

"Pa's out with the pigs. He enjoys to look at 'em."

"Pretty soon butcher, eh?"

"No, not'll November."

"Pretty soon, all t' same."

"No, it ain't," she said quickly. "Eleven days to November. I know how long to November."

Joe's smile was a knowing one. "You don't like t' butcher?"

"Henry Ferguson does it," she said indifferently.

"I bet you bear a hand. T'ere ain' anyt'ing round here you don' put a hand to. Look here, now: I come and I butcher. I do the whole t'ing for you. You won' get no blood on you, nor you won't have to scrape bristles. All you do, tend t' fire. Tell your old man Joe is comin' t' butcher. Draw for me, will you? A gill o' West India."

Melissa drew for him. "I don't know as Henry Ferguson would take it too kindly, Joe. He don't do any smithwork."

"You don' have t' pay me—not even a forequarter. I do it to help you. Like t' wood, I shall do it."

Melissa, when she'd set out his drink for him, had wandered across to look out the window. She'd forgot Joe for a moment . . . and then it came to her suddenly what Joe had just said to her. Well, she'd got to set him right sometime, and she might as well do it now.

She said, "'Tain't any use, Joe."

She heard Joe set the bowl down.

"What ain'?" he asked her.

"All this helpin' you're doin'." She turned round and faced him. "I'm obliged to you, Joe, but you don't gain nothin' by it."

Joe leaned on the counter and seemed to study the measuring tacks. "I remember," he said, "time was when you laughed at me."

Melissa remembered.

"Now do you laugh at me?"

"No," said Melissa.

"I remember," said Joe, "time was, you was scared of me. You t'ink Joe didn' know it, t'at day in t' springhouse?"

Melissa remembered.

"Now," said Joe, "you ain' scared of me."

"Not a mite," said Melissa.

Joe's eyebrows went up. "And I don' make any headway?"

"No," she said wearily. "No, Joe, I guess not."

Joe's eyebrows came down again lower than they'd been to begin with. "Why don' I?"

There was no way to tell him. "I don't know what you're after, 'n 'tain't my place to say so, s'posin' I did know. But this here's what I do say: when you don't get it, Joe—'tever 'tis that you're after—don't think you been cheated. You could lug all the wood in from now till next summer, and not gain nothin' by it. I got nothin' to give you."

"Not to give me, eh? To some other man, maybe?"

Strangely unmoved, she said, "That's up to me, ain't it?"

Joe was stopped. All he was sure of was that she was not

88

going to be questioned. "Sure," he said handsomely, "t'at's a' right. Pardon. I don' mean to say nothin'."

"Nor I don't," she said dryly.

Joe didn't quite catch it. He still tried to square himself. "I ain' see nobody roun' here—a long time, I ain' seen 'em."

Melissa said almost playfully, "Maybe you scared 'em off, Joe." She felt considerably cheered for some reason or other.

"By God!" exclaimed Joe. "I scare 'em a' right if I see 'em!"

They heard a horse in the inn-yard, and both went to the window.

"Stranger," said Joe.

"The horse ain't," said Melissa. "That's the major's old bay he's got. Must've bated at Suncook." He had come from the north: he *could* have a letter.

"Priest," said Joe, "or a clerk, maybe. Big man, too, ain't he? By God, he's a big one!"

"He's got the clothes on of a minister. You go take the horse, Joe, and tell Pa to come in here."

Joe said, "A' right," and went to do as she told him.

15

The man had to bend his head more than most as he came in through the doorway. He was a big and ponderous creature—dressed all in black but for the dirty linen under his chin—and his face even larger than the rest of him called for. He had a colorless face with the unlighted look that shows on the underside of a cucumber. With his head slightly bowed, he advanced toward Melissa like a one-man processional.

By the light of the fire, she saw that his little eyes searched the room swiftly, though his head didn't move any.

He halted just short of the counter. "The Reverend Josiah Potter," he proclaimed, pronouncing the words in much the way that he walked, "of Durham, in Connecticut. Newly come from the Grants, I proceed now to Portsmouth."

She saw the little eyes go all over her.

"I desire refreshment," Mr. Potter informed her. "And you," he observed, coming as close to her as the counter between them permitted, "are, if I may say so, my dear, most refreshing to a

89

poor missionary who has been long in the wilderness. In the whole of the Grants, I assure you, I have scarce met with a white woman who was not so yellowed by wood smoke that she resembled a heathen more than she did a Christian. You'd be Mistress Butler?" Reverend Potter believed he was smiling.

He laid his huge hat to one side on the counter, and leaned purposefully toward her.

Not greatly troubled that he wanted to kiss her, she drew back to the wall.

Reverend Potter gave no indication of being either hurt or astonished. "Ah, but stay!" he advised her, and held up a fat, dirty forefinger. With his left hand he reached into the bosom of his traveling cloak. "I have something here, child, which I brought especially for you." He kept fumbling for it. "Wait. Wait, now . . . yes, I have it." And then shrewdly not bringing it forth, he added, "But first, haven't you something for me, my dear?"

Melissa could feel no curiosity concerning any small trinket that might come out of that cloak. Standing there with her arms folded, she laughed at the man. And when she had done so, she turned away and walked out of the room.

As he gazed at the door which the girl had pulled to behind her, Mr. Potter's face slowly settled back into sagging solemnity. He was aware, however, that he felt more than a passing annoyance. "What she needs," he confessed, "is a real good blue-beech on her."

It was to Captain—when the latter had set out a bowl of hot flip and promised boiled pork to follow—that Potter yielded up what he had in his pocket.

"I have carried faithfully with me from Pennacook a letter," he said, "intended for your daughter, I think"—and he handed it over.

Captain accepted it. After a careful examination of the outside of the greasy and travel-worn paper, Captain agreed that it was meant for Melissa. Captain then opened it—first glancing at Potter, who appeared wholly uninterested. Even so, Captain explained. "She don't read very good."

Captain himself didn't read very often. Reading, he felt, was in one way like swimming: once a man learnt to swim, he didn't need to go on swimming, day in and day out, just so as not to forget it. Time come he had need to swim, he'd be able to swim all right.

And Captain read all right; he got the meaning.

Dear Miss Butler How are you I am pretty good now my ankil was stuv up som crosing a stream but Is now mended some no Harm done only Delay I have got holt of a good plays some of it intervle and a cow to boot later. I will be to Kittleford soon as I can make out to travil would gess in 3 weeks time I pray you are in good helth same as I be only my ankel It is the right one They give me a full lot 100 acer I will be glad seeing you more than you know or maybe you do some anyhow I hope

Whitfield Livingston of now near to
Sandwich in New Hamp
prov

Slowly and carefully, Captain folded the letter . . . the presence of Potter completely forgotten.

At length, Mr. Potter said the only thing that he could say. "No bad news, I trust?"

Captain came out of it. "Bad? Couldn't be worse, I guess."

"Come now, my good man," said Mr. Potter professionally, "that's not true of anything."

"'Tain't, eh, b' God? Well, b' God, 'tis this time!"

Mr. Potter prepared himself with a long draught from the flip bowl. "I don't mean to intrude, of course, but if there's any way I can help you . . ."

"Look here," said Captain, who thought he saw something. "I tell you what you c'n do . . ."

"Yes?"—the tone lacked enthusiasm.

"Wait, now—let me think." Captain thought quite a ways. Then he said, "Mr. Potter, here's what I wish you'd do: you c'n break this here news to her. I ain't got the heart to. But now you, you're a minister, you'd ought to be an old hand at it. If I was to tell her, I ain't sure she'd believe it."

"What might the news be?" Mr. Potter inquired.

"She's been jilted."

For the better part of an hour—while Captain talked on, and Potter finished a second bowl of flip and his supper—the two men had the room to themselves. Captain found Mr. Potter an intelligent man who always appeared to be listening and who was not too free with his questions. Potter found Captain a magpie.

Until he could make up his mind as to just where to head for,

91

the hard-thinking Captain kept talking round and round in a circle. A good many times he spoke of the trust and confidence he had reposed in Whit Livingston. Why, even the money for the boy to go north with had come out of Captain!

As for the girl, said her father, she'd of course marry with someone—but that would not bring the money back.

Still, he was thankful that the news had come this way instead of straight to Melissa. Because he, her father, could now see to it surely that the news was broke to her easy.

About the fifth time that Captain came round to that, Mr. Potter said coolly, "Is the girl with child by the young man?"

"No!" Captain said instantly. And then, somewhat paler— because this was the first time the thought had occurred to him— he said again, "No, she ain't, Mr. Potter. I asked her that, and she told me—and she tells me the truth, sir."

"You are fortunate."

"Yes, I expect so," the other answered morosely. "He couldn't pay nothin' if she did have a child by him."

There was no comment from Potter.

Finally Captain said wistfully, "I do wish that you'd tell her . . ."

"Why should I tell her?"

"Well, like I said, if I was to tell her, chances are in the first place that she wouldn't believe it."

"You have the letter."

"Sart'n I have! And she ain't goin' t'see it! This here's a cruel letter. 'Tain't *fit* for a woman!—let alone a young girl that's been raised like M'lissy. Why, do you know, Mr. Potter, what this letter says in it?"

"You're the one read it."

"Says he's made him a pitch and he's built him a lean-to and he's got him a woman and she's livin' there with him. He says they both like it, and he aims to hook on to her."

"Pioneering," said Peter.

"That's right, pioneerin'. *I* can't tell the child, sir! I ain't got the heart to. Now, if you'd tell her for me—you know, kind of easy—I'd be most awful grateful. Your bed and your breakfast and all you've et so far wouldn't cost you a penny. Or what the horse'll get, either, or what *he's* had already. I do wish't you'd do it."

"Well, I don't know, Captain. I can't say it appeals to me."

"That's part of a minister's job, ain't it? I always thought so—

92

breakin' bad news to folks—more p'tic'ly women."

"It is often our duty."

"Why ain't it this time?"

"Well . . . it may be. It may be."

"Why, sart'n!" said Captain.

"Very well, then. I'll do it."

"Good! I know'd you would, Mr. Potter, or I wouldn't've asked you. Well, I guess this here letter can go int' the fire." He reached into his pocket.

"I'd best see her alone, I think," Potter said heavily.

Captain turned on him, forgetting the letter. "No!" he said earnestly, "that ain't the way, Mr. Potter!"

"But, my dear Captain Butler!"

"Now here's how to do it. You—"

Potter showed his annoyance.

"Listen here, Mr. Potter, she'd only blow up on you and you wouldn't get nowhere. I know *that* girl, you believe me! Now you listen to me: pretty soon they'll be in here, and—"

"Who will?"

"Why, the ones that come in here. I don't know—half a score of 'em. Three or four, anyhow—men come in of an evening."

"Well?"

"Now, then, look here: you won't any more'n get a chance to declare yourself, afore they'll all want you t' tell 'em how things is t' the Grants. You know how that is."

"Yes, yes, I know. And no sooner I've told them, than they'll say: 'Well, that may be, of course'—and then take great pains to show me that by no possibility could things be as I've told them. That's the traveler's lot. Yes, I well know how that is!"

"Well, like I was saying: you go on and you tell 'em. And whilst you're a-talkin', you make sure she's a-listenin', and then you say, 'Wait, now . . . yes, by God, I remember: I seen a young feller there said he was from Kittlef'd—Livingston, by name I think—if I recollect, 'twas.' That'll open her ears for you! And then you just tell the men like it is in the letter. That's the best way."

"Why is it?"

"Because she can't make no fuss! There'll be other folks round! There ain't anyone knows this about her and this Livingston only me that's her father. She ain't goin' t'want t' tell *them* she's been jilted—not by a long shot! Later on, I c'n talk to her, 'n—well, you know: kind of comfort her."

"Well," agreed Mr. Potter, "all right, if you say so." After all, he supposed, he did owe the girl something for the way that she'd laughed at him. By this means, he could pay her. "There is one thing about it, though, that I find rather troublesome."

"What's that?"

"You have asked me to speak an untruth, Captain Butler."

"You ain't tellin' her only what's right here in the letter. If you want to see it—well, no, I don't know as I'd ought to. After all, it's her letter."

"The point is," said Potter, "that I've never seen the boy."

"Well, I c'n tell you 'bout him so's you'll think that you seen him. He ain't quite so high as you be, though he ain't terrible short of it. And he ain't got the heft that you got by a good half. He's hard and yet withy. He's slow-spoken and soft-spoken, and he steps awful easy. He ain't quite towheaded, though he comes pretty close to it—say about between Indian that's been ground in a plumpin' mill and a dry field of hay stubble when you look across it. He's got blue eyes, I guess, though I ain't never noticed, and his face light-complected—more p'tic'ly so when he's been in the woods awhile, though in winter it's darker. That help you any?"

"I may not have seen him, but I've seen a good many like him. Yes, it might very well be that this boy was among them. Whereabouts is the letter from?"

"He don't say," answered Captain.

"The man who entrusted it to me, said he'd brought it from Wolfeboro. Wolfeboro's far to the east of where I've been."

"That don't signify any. You know how 'tis with letters, they go up 'n down 'n all over. Man undertakes t' carry a letter, 'n then he goes somewheres else, 'n the letter goes with him. I wouldn't doubt for a minute this was wrote from the Grants somewheres. *I* would say, Mr. Potter, that you most likely *had* seen him."

"Yes, possibly—possibly. I hope so—I trust so. Well, in the belief that I *have* seen him, I shall do as you ask, sir. Tell me now of these others."

"There ain't *been* any others! I—"

"No, no, you mistake me." Mr. Potter held up his hand. "I mean the men who'll be in here."

"Oh, them."

"Yes. The townsfolk, so to speak—or I might say your neighbors. Tell me about them. Are they Christians?—men of substance?"

"Well, I guess it's the same way as in most towns round about here: there's some is, and some isn't."

"Who has the most money?"

"No one's got any money. You mean who's the best fixed?"

"Well, put it that way."

"That depends," said Captain. He went to work on the question.

Potter listened attentively.

16

There was no hurry or bustle in the atmosphere of the tavern. Mr. Potter of Durham was doing the talking. In the seat next to the fire—a doubtful honor, most places, where they piled on the firewood in a way to blister the calves—Mr. Potter was comfortable.

Opposite Potter was Lawrence Murphy, the tailor—still spending the money he'd won on Whit Livingston that day at the mowing or he would be in a moment. Just now Mr. Potter was treating him. That was the main reason that Murphy was listening: the man who paid for the drink bought a right to the talking. Murphy was beginning to feel that this Mr. Potter had about had his money's worth and perhaps a bit over.

Old David Gillmor was on the bench beside Murphy. David was nursing a quart of mulled cider which he would himself pay for someday. He'd had to promise his wife that he wouldn't drink even rum tonight because they couldn't afford it. He had hopes, though, of this minister. From time to time, David would say, "Yes, sir, that's right, sir!" or "Ain't that wonderful? Yes, sir!"

Ensign Lord sat with his long legs stretched out to the fire, sipped his drink, and said nothing. He didn't think much of this Mr. Potter.

A little off to one side, and some ways from the fire, José Felipe was sitting alone. No one had said to him, "Pull up, Joe, with the rest of us!"—least of all, David Gillmor. But Joe didn't mind; he was watching Melissa. He called for a pipe, and the girl brought it to him.

"Pull up by the fire, Joe," Melissa said to him. "You're way out in the cold there."

That warmed Joe as no fire could.

William Cauldwell came in, his mind made up at last to buy him a jackknife of a proper kind to split shoe pegs. But finding a traveler there, Cauldwell put off his business, and confirmed Melissa's assumption that he'd take hot rum and water. He sat down on the far end of the same bench as the stranger.

Mr. Potter, reaching a period, said to him, "Good evening. The Reverend Josiah Potter of Durham, Connecticut. From the Grants bound for Portsmouth."

"William Cauldwell, cordwainer. Good evenin' to you, sir. I hope I don't interrupt you."

"Not at all! Not at all, sir," said Mr. Potter—and proved it.

After a while, Thett came in, making twice the noise that he usually did, slamming the door and stamping his feet as though he owned five hundred acres. When they looked round at him, they all saw the reason. Thett had his new coat on. "Looks almighty brave, 'master," Cauldwell said solemnly. "How 'bout some boots to go with it?"

"Sure!" Thett agreed cheerfully. "What'll you take for 'em? Latin or Greek?"

"Well, if you wan't to use 'em no more'n what I would the Latin, they'd last a long time, I guess."

"But if you used the Latin as much as I would the boots, sir, it would not only outlast them but get stronger and stronger."

"Very pretty," said Potter.

Thett turned and bowed to him. "My apologies, sir. I'm afraid I didn't see you."

"All this book-readin', Thett"—Ensign spoke for the first time—"must a pretty near blinded you."

Thett kept a straight face. "Nathaniel Thett, sir," he said to the stranger, "and your most humble servant."

"Josiah Potter."

"*Mister* Potter," said Ensign, "is God's servant, Nathaniel."

Murphy gazed toward the rafters and stroked his chin for a moment.

Captain Butler had missed it, but he saw something was needed, and he asked Thett what his pleasure was.

"Why, I guess the usual." He sat down beside David. Melissa went to the fire to draw out the toddy stick. Thett said to the old man, "What have you got there, David?"

"I did have some cider."

"Have some toddy with me, then." His new coat made him feel that way.

96

"Why, now, that's very kind of you. I don't mind if I do, sir."

Mr. Potter made a rumbling noise, and then said, "As I was saying . . ." It was Mr. Potter's opinion that in another ten years the Grants would be without question the richest part of the province.

"That ain't sayin' much," Cauldwell put in, "the way things are now, it ain't—outside o' Portsmouth. There ain't half o' t' farmers from Bay Province t' Cowas has got proper boots or even two pair o' moggas'ns."

"'Proper' boots!" David said. "Hell, I ain't got any! Nor I d' want any, either. 'Tain't because I'm a poor man, I ain't got any boots, William Cauldwell. T' me, boots is a nuisance."

"There's been times," agreed Cauldwell, "when I've said worse'n that of 'em. How's the Grants t' get rich, Reverend?"

Potter told of the land there. He had seen, felt, and tasted it, and he had seen what would grow on it. It was interval land, and required no clearing. And there was marsh hay for the cutting to take care of the cattle.

"'Tain't all like that, is it?" Cauldwell inquired.

"Well, a good deal of it. And it's now free of Indians."

"Yes, *sir!*" exclaimed David. "We red t' place o' them fellers!"

"Lovewell, Rogers, and Gillmor," Ensign said to the rafters.

The old man turned on him. "What d' you know about it! I've kill't me more Indians 'n what you ever kill't woodchucks! I've kill't two or three white men—'f you call a Frenchman a white man, 'n I d' know why *you* shouldn't."

"I'm sorry, David. I didn't go to offend you."

"Well, that's all right, then, and no offense taken." He took a swallow of toddy.

"When you've finished that," Ensign said, "you c'n look t' me for the next one."

David kept right on swallowing and he sighed when he finished. "You spoke just in time, Ens'n."

They all laughed together, and even Potter smiled faintly. Ensign signaled Melissa.

"What you say of the land, sir," Murphy was speaking, "well, that may *be*, o' course, 'n I ain't never been there. Still, I don't recollect as I ever heard tell of no pioneers had got any too rich at it—not t' the Grants, nor yet t' the east o' them."

"Ah!" said Potter. "Precisely! And they never will, either."

"Why is that, Mr. Potter?" Thett asked him quietly.

97

"Pioneers," Potter answered, "are men without character. They're a low, shiftless lot, sir. I have slept in their cabins, and I speak with authority. They are filthy and verminous out of all reason, and their women are also."

Melissa came round with the toddy for David.

"And that reminds me," said Potter, "I—"

"Does me, too," put in Murphy. "Mr. Potter, you'll do me the honor. M'lissy, you c'n fetch one for the dominie here, 'n as long as you're at it, you might 's well take 'n fill this one up."

"What?" said Potter. "Oh, yes—thank you." The girl took the mug from him. He said to Murphy, "The honor is mine, I assure you. As I was saying—"

"Not too much sugar," Murphy said to Melissa. "I guess I'm more used to it the way Captain does it. Captain holds back when it comes t' the sugar—and the rum, too, for that matter. Though he's got a lib'ral hand when it comes t' the water."

Melissa went on her errand.

"Now, then," said Murphy, "you c'n go ahead, Mr. Potter."

Mr. Potter swallowed, and went ahead. "You are entirely correct, sir, as to the pioneers' poverty. But no pioneer ever gets the best land. That is reserved for those who can pay for it."

"You buy much?" asked Ensign.

"Some," Potter admitted. And he described the land to them. He did it well—he described to them good land, but it was not unbelievable. And he added the price that he'd paid for it.

"You got a bargain!" Captain breathed fervently.

"Yes, I daresay." Mr. Potter settled back in his corner. "Still, I've got to sell some of it when I get to Portsmouth in order to pay for my passage—round the Cape, into the Sound to Lyme, and then up the river. It'll be stormy, too, this time of year. I may decide to go overland."

"Why wait till Portsmouth t' sell?" Ensign inquired.

"I never feel comfortable carrying money."

"Road's safe enough, surely, 'tween here and Portsmouth."

"Yes, that may be, of course."

"Or whyn't you get Captain here t' take 'n give you an order on some Portsmouth merchant—like, say, Langdon, it might be—'n then you wouldn't have to carry no money."

"Sart'n!" said Captain. "I'd be happy to do it!"

Ensign pursued it: "'N let Murphy 'n Cauldwell 'n Thett,

here, if he wants to, all go in on the purchase." Ensign's tone indicated that a problem common to all of them was thus offered solution.

The men looked at Potter . . .

Melissa, coming up with the two toddies, saw that this was not just the moment for her to intrude. She stood there waiting . . .

The Reverend Potter cleared his throat pompously. "Well, now, I—er—"

. . . and then Murphy to Ensign: "Why don't you come in, too, Ensign, along with the rest of us?"

All hands turned to Ensign.

"Twig 'n turf for me, gentlemen. When I buy any land, I want t' be standin' right on it. You men can buy paper. I don't read good enough yet."

There was a moment of silence. Mr. Potter looked up at Melissa. "Ah! Thank you," he said, and took from her his toddy. But the silence continued. Melissa went over to Murphy . . .

"By the by, Captain Butler," said Potter, after a welcome pull at his toddy, "I saw a man up there who claimed he'd come from Kettleford."

Murphy said to her, "Thank you," and Melissa dropped him a curtsy.

"Who was it?" said Captain. "You don't remember his name, do you?"

She was leaving the circle . . .

"Wait, now . . . yes . . . yes, I do . . . he said his name was Whit Livingston."

"No!" Captain said sociably.

Ensign commented, "Well, if Whit's made a pitch, I'll bet he's got him good land. He's seen enough of the other kind to know what that looks like."

Only her father was watching her. She stood there quite motionless.

And Potter remarked, "I trust the same explanation doesn't apply to the choice that he's made of a woman."

After a moment of silence, Ensign said, "What?"

"Yes, indeed!" affirmed Potter, "and as comely a wench as I saw in the Grants, sir."

Captain regretted that his daughter's face was turned from him.

Mr. Potter talked for the company, and the company listened. He kept a weather eye on the girl until he was comfortably certain that she wasn't going to make any fuss. Assured on that point, he cut loose with some detail. It made a welcome diversion.

Melissa heard every word of it. The sound of his name had sent a great upsurge of hope through her . . . and it only came to her slowly what the man's voice was saying. She recognized what the words meant . . . but the horror they builded was a thing gray and apart from her. It was at first beyond her belief that those things which the voice said could be said of Whit Livingston. But she was hearing them spoken—and those other men who'd been sitting there, their identities lost now, they were hearing them also.

She had no thought of the man who had spoken, there was no room in her mind for him; he had no significance.

She saw only Whit as she'd known him. She heard the words spoken of him. But they didn't touch Whit.

It was unclean in here, full of horror, and filthy. She was stifled and sickened. With her hands outstretched before her, she went toward the door. She wanted the air that was outside, and the good darkness round her.

Captain Butler, her father, watched her small figure grope toward escape, and he figured that when she'd put her hand on the latch he'd call out to her, "Hey, girl, where you going?" And in a little torment of triumph, he awaited the instant—

Joe was watching her now.

Joe—so Captain saw—with a sure and purposeful swiftness was, on a sudden, out of his chair and had moved to open the door for her.

Melissa went through it.

Joe's long arm was reached up and he plucked her cape from its peg by the doorway. Then he followed after her, closing the door—

—and Captain, watching the latch descend softly, could hardly contain himself.

Out in the innyard, "M'lissa—" Joe said to her . . . but she returned him no answer.

"Here—put t'is round you"—his voice very different, and he put the cape on her shoulders. "Cold, ain' it?"

She drew the cape round her, but she left the hood down, and she raised her face to the wind now.

"Wind's shifted," Joe offered. "Comin' more out t' nort' now. Be nor'west before daylight, and cold like hell, I can tell you." He looked at the sky again. "Breakin' a'ready. Two hours' time, you won' see a cloud. Be a fine night to run, a' right. Yes, sir, i' 'twill be. You'd have a fine time along tonight!—wit' a course you could lay, you would."

He looked at her again—saw the wind whipping her hair back. "M'lissa," he said to her, his voice urgent but kindly, "t'at old man in t'ere, he don' mean nothin' by it. What t' hell, he talks dirty, but a lot of priests t'ey talk t'at way. T'ey don' know any better. Me, I don' pay no heed to 'em."

He was certain she nodded.

"Forget it," he counseled. "What t' hell; is no matter! They all know you're a good girl an' they know you don' listen w'en a man like t'at feller goes an' takes t' talk dirty—" She made no response "—but I'm glad you come out here." Joe looked all around him. "God, it's nice, ain' it? Come on, we walk up t' road a way an' t'en you forget it." He took hold of her arm, and found she came with him.

It was too much for Joe.

They'd gone only a rod or two, when he stopped and stood facing her. "Deus me valha, M'lisha," he blurted, "I do love you mos' awful, goddammit, M'lisha!" He was shaken and hoarse. "Will you marry, M'lisha? . . . Oh, by God, but I hope so!"

"Joe—" her voice came to him steady and gentle—"Joe, I want you to go home now."

Always, in order to say anything, Joe had had to think of the words first; they never came of themselves. He had to reach out and lay hold on the words before he could use them. José Felipe speaking Portuguese, as a young man, could find the words when he wanted them. But Joe, speaking English, was like a man on a frigate who'd been raised on a sloop. When he'd reach for a rope in the storm and the tumult, the damn thing wouldn't be there. And the more pressing his need for it, the more flustered he'd be.

All words were lost to him. There was not one to take hold of.

And it was borne in upon him—not in an instant, but slowly, while his jaw seemed to droop a little and he lost all his balance— that this little figure before him with her hair blown in the night wind, but she in all other ways motionless—and above and around them both her voice cool and certain—that she was stronger than he was.

Joe did as she told him. "A' right," he said humbly.

"Good night, Joe."

He tried to rebel once . . . but he couldn't quite make it, because long after she'd spoken the sound of her voice lay upon him.

In the dark, very slowly, he went down the road that led to the smithy . . .

Before he'd gone far, he was getting back to himself again. He thought everything over. She hadn't said "No." It was that fact was the biggest, and it was easy to come at; it was right there in front of him. Joe could see it right off, and no two ways about it.

But it was simply a fact and no uplift was in it. It didn't do anything for him.

But under that fact was the feeling that she'd understood him. There was the miracle—as strong and unseen as black ice on a pond at night. José Felipe was now walking where, except for this miracle, he could not have walked. It was exciting and tremulous.

José Felipe—in the night and the rising wind, trudging the road to the smithy—was a little exalted.

She had seen and had answered to—knowing that he'd understand too—she had seen and answered to the best that was in him.

He hadn't quite understood her, but that was no matter.

And because this best that was in him was something that he himself hadn't seen until lately, Joe was impressed by it. He thought it exceedingly doubtful that she could resist it.

He'd go back there tomorrow, and there was a good chance that she'd have him.

It was a chance that seemed to get better every time he came round to it . . .

José Felipe shook his fist at the sky and swore without any difficulty in pure jubilation.

17

Melissa had given to Joe only so much of her consciousness as he'd been able to draw to himself. No sooner he'd gone than that was released. He was now not in her thoughts, being no longer present to demand that he should be.

Standing there in the road, she saw Whit as she'd always seen him . . . and she knew the feel of his cheek to her fingers to be the same as it had been. His face was not changed any. Nothing had touched him. He wore the same garments. The kindness and the look in his eyes were exactly as always. These things she had held to too long in her mind for any talk in a tavern to be able to reach them.

But the talk was there none the less. It existed as talk. And in its existence it was spread out before Whit as a threatening trouble. As a net for a bird, the talk was spread—waiting.

"He could be as the talk said he was." She heard those words in her mind; they came out of the darkness.

"No," she answered, "he couldn't be—no—" her small, solemn face upraised and alone. The wind had brought tears to her eyes. "I have seen him. I know him. I can see him now." And she saw him. It was not strange to Melissa that the sunlight was upon him.

It only lasted a moment.

She turned her back to the wind and pulled up the hood of her cape. Skirting the innyard, she crossed the light from the windows and went down toward the barn. After the company'd gone, if she were about the inn kitchen, she'd either have Potter to deal with, or her father would talk on and on about this news that had happened. She'd be safe from both in the barn. Deep in the hay, it wouldn't be so much colder than what it would be in her chamber—once the heat from the chimney had left it. And if her father should fret himself over what had become of her— well, he'd have to fret himself. This wasn't the time when she could find an answer for everything.

The barn door was braced on the outside by a stout stick of maple that was leaned up against it. By rights, that ought to stay there, because if she left it down they'd know someone was in there. But the other ways to get into the barn all meant crawling and squeezing, or climbing the apple tree, and she was in no mood to bother. She spoke to the cattle, and pushed the brace to one side—heard it fall with a slapping thud into the mud of the barnyard—and stepped in on the barn floor. She was out of the wind now, and she noticed the quiet. When the door was secured, she stood with her back up against it so as to tell where the ladder'd be. There was no light whatsoever; the darkness pressed round her. She could hear the horse breathing loudly, and spoke to him to quiet him—the horse Mr. Potter had come on. The two barn cats came up to her. She went across to the ladder. She was as much at home here as she would have been anywhere; there was no strangeness about it, and no sense of adventure. And by a piece of good luck there were no hens on the ladder.

Up on the scaffold, she made herself comfortable, with a good lot of hay under her and an extra pile for a pillow. She lay on her side then and listened; she was a long way from easy, and not minded to sleep any. She knew what she was here for.

"Up there on the road," she said, "that was a vision, like. A vision is nice when you got nothin' better, but I do wish 't he'd come home again. I thought before that I wished it, but now I feel different. Now he's got to come.

"The way I started in thinkin' was: he may be late comin'. That was some time ago. I couldn't see, then, how I ever would stand it if he should turn out to *be* late. Well, he's late, 'n I've stood it. And for the last month I been sayin: you got figure he may not come at all, y' know. And I thought I did figure it. I know now I didn't. I tried to let on to myself that it might be he wouldn't come, but there wan't any strength to it, because I knowed, then, he would come."

"And I know it yet!" she cried, gripping a handful of hay.

She realized as she said it that she didn't know any such thing, of course.

Somehow or other, it made her feel better. She need not require of herself any longer that she try to pretend to an absolute faith in his coming. It was no use doing that. Such faith was now too far removed from her. It was a relief to her to admit that. It was the talk made her see this—not any belief in the talk, just its presence.

In the stillness and darkness, her cloak drawn close around her, she said, "All right, I'll look at it. He will come if he can. I do know that much. But something may have happened—like a tree, or the river, or his gun, maybe, or something—and he's late enough now so that maybe it has happened. He's late enough now so it's just about even: he'll either come or he won't come."

She was hurrying on with it, because if she paused now for thinking she wouldn't get any further. "What I'll do if he don't come, is to go and tell Mr. Gowan. Whit claims Mr. Gowan's the best man in the village, and there ain't any woman that I know of to go to. They don't come t' the tavern, nor I don't go to church much. I guess he'll be kind to me on Whit's account anyway. And I got to tell somebody.

"If he ain't comin' back, I'll be glad things are this way. It'll give me somethin' to go on. I guess I'm glad anyhow. Seems 's 'ough I'd ought to be. But that's three or four months yet, that's a whole lot of days—'n he c'n show up any one of 'em."

She could not keep it back now. "Oh, God!—God, bring him back here!"

—and she fell to crying.

Her thoughts were all jumbled up. Before very long, the crying stopped slowly. She still knew where she was . . . Pretty soon she was sleeping.

She wakened, and stirred. She had no intention of going way down the ladder, and across up to the inn again, and up the stairs to her chamber. It was too far away. She was warm and comfortable here. She went back to sleep again.

She slept better than Captain, who was devoting most of his night to being afraid he'd hear her come in again. If she'd stay out all night with the Portygee, then Captain's worries were over. He could march straight to Gowan then, and tell *him* what had happened—and it would be Mr. Gowan's duty to force her to marry Joe.

Along about three o'clock, Captain counted it morning.

Just to make sure, he went and looked in her chamber. Finding it empty—he scurried back to his bed. But he was too excited to want to sleep. He lay small in his bed, shivering, and the palms of his hands sweat. It seemed to Captain as though he'd never felt better.

The cockerel wakened Melissa. She opened her eyes and could make out the rafters. She was stiff, now, and cold, but she was no longer sleepy . . . and another day now at hand didn't frighten her any. It pleasured her, too, to know that she'd slept just as late as she would have slept if she'd been in her bed. It seemed like some kind of small victory over the things that beset her . . . and she drew out of the hay, pushed some of it off her, and got to her feet—more hay cascading round her. Hay stuck to her cloak—and she stamped her feet once or twice and blew on her hands, before she took the cloak off and shook it. But she didn't bother to brush it.

As she went down the ladder, she wondered whether or not they'd be up and about at the inn now . . . well, she'd know from the chimney. She doubted Potter'd have stirred himself. Men who wore dirty linen didn't take the road early. But he wouldn't be troublesome. Hot rum and molasses would be all he'd be set on, and after a quart of it, maybe a piece of meat and some porridge. He wouldn't bother her any, not this time in the morning.

She said to the cattle, "I'll take care of you later," and went to the door and unfastened it. Outside it was later than she'd thought it was inside. Even at that, there was no smoke from the chimney. Closing the door, she set the brace up against it.

Then she was free to face into the morning.

It was still as could be, and not a great while before sun-up. She must have slept through some crowing—and just as she thought that, he let go with another crow, back inside the barn there where the night hadn't all gone yet.

But out here it was gone; there was no sign of it anywhere. Look where she would, it was all of it morning—and beyond where she could see, to the north, it was morning. Where Whit was, it was morning.

She would not go up to the inn.

The frost, under cover of darkness, had come into being and been left behind by it, whitening the gray-green of the grasses. The frost was thick on all wooden things. There was thin ice on the puddles. Past the things near at hand, her eyes went away slowly . . . past the red-brown of the oak trees and the dark patches of hemlock and here and there—where it should be—the quiet rising of smoke from the regular fires of morning. Over all these was stillness. They had just been uncovered.

High above all the stillness, the sky was wonderfully busy, with the gray going out of it and the blue spreading everywhere. It was in the sky only that there showed any foreknowledge, any press of excitement, because the sun was at hand now.

Melissa went round the barn and down toward the meadow.

This side of the brook—the place where the spruce root had tripped her—she was not drawn to pause now, as she had done a good many times, and wait for the sharp recollection of that day to come over her. That was not what she wanted. Ahead was the meadow. Soon the sun would come into it.

The brook, as she crossed it, was bustling along as it always did, paying no heed to the night and the morning; rain and drought were what mattered. But the winter would quiet it—the ice would steal over it and snow fall in the darkness.

Ahead was the meadow. Soon the sun would strike into it. Melissa wanted to be there.

She came up the rise, and saw the meadow was empty. She was in time, the sun hadn't come yet. The grass was dun-colored. The whole of the meadow looked flat and even and it was all the same color without any shadows. Round every side of it was the plain wall of trees. That, too, was even . . . almost black at the base of it and gray toward the top; the dark patches of hemlock and the brown of the oak trees didn't stand out from the rest of it. It was simply the edge of the forest, straight up and down, and it came to the edge of the meadow. Both had their places. Neither one, to Melissa, seemed to threaten the other. And the sky overhead was so high over both of them!

She stood at the top of the rise and she watched to the eastward . . . guessing between which two treetops would be the place where the sun would come. Then the sky grew too bright there to see the tree branches.

The true gleam of the sun, in the first instant she saw it, was of the sun itself—and a long ways away from her.

Then across all that distance it came into her eyes . . . and her eyes had to turn from it.

She threw back her hood, and on her face was the morning.

18

Whit was traveling at night for the first time in a long time. It was pretty slow going on account of his ankle, but he was so close to home now he couldn't have stopped if he'd wanted to.

He was keeping clear of the road because of the brush in it. In the woods, it was better. The down trees were the main trouble— that and watching his footing. Uphill it was easy, but downhill it was hard for him. Going downhill to his right he had to feel out each step for fear his ankle would roll under him. It didn't pain him too much, but he couldn't put any trust in it.

Every once in a while—say two or three times in an hour—he'd come to something he knew. He'd go up a steep bank perhaps and when he'd get to the top of it, it would be level ground for a piece with a whole mess of gray birches. He knew where that was. And he went around it. Gray birches at night—little small ones, that is—were worse to get through than juniper bushes. They ranked pretty well up with a high-growing tangle of blackberries and raspberries in a burnt-over clearing, or with a proper spruce swamp full of down trees and bogholes. Or he'd make out a great rock looming up in the darkness. If the rock had a cleft in it, and a yellow birch tree and a maple both growing out of the cleft, then he knew where he stood just as well as in daylight. He knew what was ahead of him, and what lay to both sides of him, and could plan out how to go. That part was easy. It was placing his feet bothered him—because of his ankle—and he was afraid for his eyes, too. But he got along pretty well, and he tried not to hurry.

Along about four o'clock, or a little before that, he lay dowm for a spell when he came to a good place—the dry side of a white pine trunk that lay snug to the ground with some beech leaves under it on top of the pine needles. It would have been a prime place to sleep. Three summers ago, this tree had been standing. He remembered it well. It was five feet in thickness—a good five feet, or more than that—but about halfway to the top it had a kind of crook in it, which was why the masters had left it. He ate a handful of corn and what pork he had with him. From the feel of the bark, the tree had blown down last winter.

The food was good in his belly, and he judged that his ankle didn't feel any worse, maybe, than perhaps it had ought to. He'd been on the thing steady for about twenty-four hours. He was pretty near home now. He was close to Melissa.

He found that he couldn't lie still any longer, and he rolled out from under the log and then, with his hand on it, he pushed himself upright. He tightened his belt and pushed his horn round to his back and also the pouch for his food and some other things. He had a little packet of fur—you couldn't call it a bundle—that he'd taken one time or another; that was slung from his shoulder. He felt for his knife to make sure that was with him, and worked his shoulder a little to settle his blanket. Then he took up his rifle.

"'Tain't a great ways to go now"—and after a long look

overhead, he moved into the darkness. "What I got to do"—his face deadly serious—"is not think of M'lissa until it's come daylight. A man travels at night, he's got about all he c'n swing to when he's got two good feet under him." And he put all his mind to the business before him.

He didn't think of Melissa, but he knew why he was traveling. He knew why he was living.

When it did finally growlight, the last three or four miles were the longest part of the journey. But there was in him no weariness. He was carried along by the blessing of sight, by being able to see things and those things all familiar, each where it should be. There were fields he could use now, and he always skirted the edge of them; there were cowpaths and wood roads. But he stayed away from the houses. He hoped he could work it, some way or other, so that he'd see no other person before seeing Melissa. He knew this was childish, and he didn't figure to tell her, but it took hold on his fancy and he chose his route that way.

He knew perfectly well, of course, that some harm might have come to her, some sickness befallen her, or most anything happened. He had known that every minute since the last time he'd looked on her. There had been no escape from it—as he'd known there could not be. Now in the daylight, it traveled right along with him. Only Melissa herself could take care of that part of it.

He thought he'd go up to the inn through the meadow. That way, he'd come to the barn first, and she might be out round there.

By the brook in the pine trees at the east end of the meadow, he made himself stop and more or less fix himself up some. There wasn't much he could do, but he had a spare pair of moccasins that he'd saved for the purpose—and they were wonderfully handsome! They were deerskin with beads on them. He'd have liked to lay off his leggins—they looked worse now than ever alongside the new moccasins—but he had his ankle bound up and he didn't want her to see that. He did what he could in the way of getting the sticks out of his hair and washing and so on. When he'd finished all this it was just about sunup. He was not quite himself. "The way I feel now," he said, "if I was to see a deer in the meadow, 'twould be a waste of powder to fire. I don't feel awful steady."

He started then for the meadow.

Before coming out into the open, he did just as he always

did—he paused in the last bit of cover to see what was ahead of him.

He saw Melissa.

. . . at the top of the rise at the other end of the meadow, Melissa was standing. He saw her hair in the sunlight . . .

Melissa thought something moved—as he came out of the shadow—but with the sun in her eyes she couldn't make out what it was at first. "Be a cow, more'n likely." She put up her hand so that she could see better—and she made out a man.

In a rush, all at once, she knew what she was looking at—she didn't quite dare to say it—and then she couldn't help saying it: that was Whit coming toward her.

—and Melissa was running, down the rise, through the meadow—

Whit laid down his rifle and held out his arms to her—

He felt so solid!—his arms hard in his shirt sleeves.

. . . so he must have held her a minute or two, before she turned up her face to him, and found him looking down at her.

19

The main question in Whit's mind concerning Melissa she had already answered: she appeared well and happy. This was Melissa. That was all he could think of. He had nothing to ask her that was not already answered. His journey was finished. This was Melissa.

When they got round to talking, when this miracle of reunion—that they'd both of them counted on—was so clearly established that they could talk about it, Whit said to Melissa, "How come you was down t' the meadow so early? You must a knowed I was comin'."

She nodded. "I guess I did—somehow—though I didn't know it. It just seemed t' me like I had t' come down here."

Whit understood—too well to say so. "You had any breakfast?"

"I d' know. Maybe. No, I ain't—come to think of it."

They laughed over this. Sometime or other Whit said to her, "You're all over hay. You must a slep' in the barn, did you?"

"Yes." She'd forgotten about it.

"You done better than I did. I didn't sleep any. What was the matter? Things kind o' rough in the tavern?"

She was suddenly serious.

"What happened, M'lissa?"

"Well—" She told him all about Mr. Potter.

Whit heard her through to the end of it—to where she'd walked out of the tavern. He didn't question her once.

When she'd finished, he stood there thinking it over. The first thing he said was exactly what he was thinking, "I don't understand that." And he went on aloud, "I don't know any Potter. I never heard of him. I ain't been anywhere's near the Grants—it's a hundred miles from where I been t' Connecticut River. You say he's a minister?—with a kind of big face? What in the devil 'd he want to say that for!"

Melissa said nothing.

"He still up t' th' tavern?"

"I guess he may be."

"Well, I hope he is, anyhow." Whit turned to pick up his rifle. "I guess I'll go 'n talk to him."

"No, Whit! Don't! 'Twon't do any good! He can't hurt us now, Whit!"

"No, I don't guess he can. Still, I'd kind a like my turn."

Melissa hoped that somehow between here and the tavern she could dissuade him. They started along . . .

Whit said after a silence, "My letter get through to you?"

"A letter?" Before Melissa there opened the thought of what that would have meant to her.

"Well, I didn't know as 'twould, but I thought I might try it. This feller came through there said he was goin' t' Wolfeboro 'n he'd carry it that far—I guess he did maybe, he seemed t' me like a good, honest feller—but still 'n all Wolfeboro wouldn't no more 'n start it. Well, it's no matter. I didn't want you to fret on account I was late, was all. 'Twas a real pretty letter. I wisht you could a seen it. I put in a power o' work on that letter."

Melissa said something about, well, he was here now.

"What made me late was a fool kind o' business. I'd ought to know'd better."

"What was it, Whit?"

"Well, I'll tell you about it. You might's well know what a lunkhead I be, I s'pose. I was crossin' this stream—I put that in the letter—'n this rock kind o' turned on me that I had my foot on, 'n I started to fall. I know 's well you do what I'd ought to've done, o' course. I done it many a time. But this time I didn't. You see, like it most always is, the sun was in front of me, and I couldn't see nothin' in under the water—it was about up to here, I guess, and a pretty good current. It's an awful nice stream. I bet there's trouts in it that's as big as your arm. You take a month or two earlier, 'f I'd had a grasshopper—or you take along about sundown, 'f I had a mouse, maybe—"

"Trouts," Melissa said sagely. "If Mr. Potter'd said it was trouts, now, why, I might a believed him."

"What?"

"Go right ahead: 'If you'd had a mouse . . .'"

He grinned, and then laughed with her. "Oh, well, what I was sayin', when this rock turned underneath me, what I'd ought to've done was to settle down easy. 'Stead o' that, I stepped sudden—when I couldn't see nothin'—'n my foot took 'n jammed 'tween a couple o' boulders, 'n then I fell over onto it. Well, I got out ont' th' bank, 'thout gett'n' drownded—'n that seemed like a blessing."

"Does to me," said Melissa.

"Well, i' 'twas, I c'n tell you. But then I couldn't step on it. So the next thing, I figured, was to get me a crutch for it—'n then I missed my knife, 'n th' wan't anythin' for it but I had to crawl in again."

"You mean int' th' water?"

"I mean int' the water. I didn't like to—I'd had wettin' enough—but same time in spite o' that, I didn't hanker to go traipsin' round 'thout any knife an' only one leg to walk on. I knew the thing had dropped out while I was wallerin' 'n flounderin' out there in the middle tryin' t' get my foot loose out from 'tween them two boulders. I knew where the place was, all right, so I went out 'n got it. 'N then I cut me a crutch, 'n sometime the next day I come into Sandwich, which was where I wrote you the letter. I stayed there with some people—they're awful nice people—until I could travel. That's why I was late—like I started to tell you."

"Yes." She was thinking about him with his foot caught in the boulders.

"You ain't angry, Melissa—because I was late, I mean?"

"No, I ain't angry—not now that you're back here. I wan't angry before that. I only wanted you back here."

"You been all right? You look pretty rugged."

"Yes, I been all right."

"Joe ain't bothered you any?"

"Joe? No, he ain't bothered me. He ain't the same as he was, though. Joe wants to marry me."

"No!" Whit exclaimed in amazement. "Why, the—"

"Well, I d'know why he shouldn't *want* to."

"*I* know why he shouldn't! Joe nor anyone else hain't got any call t' come anywheres near t' you."

"How does *he* know I'm promised? You said not t' tell anyone."

"Well, you could a kind o' let on to him, couldn't you?"

"I did kind o' let on to him."

"You'd ought to let on to him harder. What did he say to you? When was it, anyhow? Joe! Why—"

"Last night," said Melissa.

"Last night, eh? Wait—Melissa, you wan't up in th' barn with him!" It was not quite accusation, but it was pretty close to it—and yet it didn't cover much more than being up in the barn with him.

"No," she said quietly, "I wan't up in the barn with him."

"Where was it, then?"

"'Twas out in th' innyard."

"Out in th' innyard."

"Mr. Potter'd been talkin', 'n when I'd stood all o' that I could, I c'm out f' some air, 'n Joe come out after me."

"What did he say to you?"

"He asked me to marry him."

"What d'you say to him?"

"Near as I recollect, I said, 'Joe, you go home now'—'n so he went home. 'N I lay in the barn on account o' this Mr. Potter had seemed t' fill up th' tavern with what he'd been sayin'." She was keeping the tears back; Whit didn't see them.

Whit looked down at the ground.

There seemed to be quite a difference between the way Melissa had acted and the way, for a minute or two, he himself had been talking. He didn't want to look up at her.

But when he did so, Melissa was smiling—though she was having indifferent success about keeping the tears back.

Whit said, "I—" but he couldn't get any further.

Melissa came to him.

Within the next minute or two, Melissa had told him how things really stood with her.

Whit was staggered. He knew he ought to have figured that

113

this might be the case. Still, he hadn't. Oh, he'd wondered sometimes, but not any more than that. And now the whole world was changed for him. He felt no elation.

Melissa hadn't expected that he'd throw his hat in the air. But neither, she'd hoped, would he be angry with her—and she could see that he wasn't. But he looked terribly solemn. He looked as solemn as she had when she'd first contemplated it.

"It'll be all right, Whit."

"Yes, I know."

"I—I'm kind o' glad, Whit. Ain't you?—just a little?"

"Oh, I'm glad enough, yes. I got to think what to do, though."

"Give over that for a minute. Now look at me, Whit. Tell me you're glad—I'll know if you are or not, so if you ain't, 'twon't be lyin'. But I want you to say it."

Whit looked at Melissa. He didn't have to say anything. He was glad, and she knew it—and so did he, now he thought of it.

"Well, the first thing, I guess," Whit said to her presently, "is to go 'n get married."

"Yes, I guess we had better."

" 'N then, after that, question is: can you travel?"

"Well, I ain't goin' t' stay here, not if you go away again. And the way I feel now, I could travel most anywhere."

"That's about where you're goin'. When'll your time be?" "May," said Melissa, "you'd ought t' know that much." "Flies'll be bad then, but the weather'll be warmer. You do want to go north, do you?—like we figured we would? I got a place located, 'n I got a lean-to. I didn't put that in th' letter, 'cause it meant too much writin'. But she's there, and a good one. Or if it seems better, you could winter to Sandwich. You do want to go?"

Yes, I do, Whit. I'm ready."

"All right, we'll go, then. I may be wrong, but I think that we'd better. Only risk is, of course, that the river'll freeze. We got t' go by the river—there ain't no other way for it. A canoe 'n some luck'll get us to Sandwich. It might be better for you t' winter in Sandwich. Anyhow, we c'n decide on that after we get there. One way or another, I guess we c'n winter."

"We'll winter."

"Well, then, that's settled. It'll take me the rest of t'day 'n tomorrow t' get things t'gether. I got t' get a canoe—I know the one that I want; belongs t' Peter McDonald over t' Derry—'n I got t' get gear o' one kind 'n other, 'n I got t' get food—though we won't need a gre' deal, but enough t' be safe with. If this

114

weather holds on, I should think we might figure—well, say figure t' leave the day after t'morrow. First thing in th' forenoon, the day after t'morrow. Does that suit you all right?"

"Today would be better."

"Month ago'd been better. It's pretty late in the year now. But I don't see nothin' else *to* do. We got t' get married, 'n soon as we're married we can't tarry t' Kittlef'd."

This was clear to Melissa, and had been all along.

"You know your old man ain't goin' t' take t' this kindly. But I got 'n idea, maybe, that I'd better tell him—get that part of it settled—'fore we see Mr. Gowan. It ain't what you'd call regular for him to go marryin' us without we been published 'n all that kind o' business, so if he's willin' t' do it, least I c'n do is t' meet him halfway when it comes to your father."

"How 'bout your people, Whit?"

"They c'n wait till it's over. Pa wouldn't only complain, 'n then get himself drunk, 'n he c'n do that just as well one time as another. If he was t' come round with a skinful o' rum right while Mr. Gowan was marryin' us, I wouldn't like it. You seen him lately?—since I been away, I mean? He's about the same, ain't he?"

"Yes, he looked to me so."

"Pa don't change a gre' deal. Well—I got t' go up t' th' tavern now, 'n tell your old man that you're about t' get married."

"I want to come with you."

"Well, I d' know now. I was thinkin' that maybe your pa'll want t' speak freely, 'n it might be some better if I was alone with him. Why don't you stay out round th' barn, or go up t' your chamber? Wouldn't that be all right? Then after he's through with me, we c'n go on down 'n see Mr. Gowan, 'n—well, we c'n get married. Why ain't that all right?"

"Yes."

"What's the matter?"

"There ain't nothin' the matter—only—only it's happened so quick, is all. I—I feel awful happy. Really I do, Whit!"

"'Twouldn't seem t' me quick if I'd been in your shoes—settin' round here 'n waitin' since the end o' last August, 'n no word comin' through, 'n then this other business. High time, is what I'd call it."

"Yes. That's true, I suppose. It's because I had all the waitin' that it seems so quick now, I guess."

He first looked—and then gazed at her. "My gorry, Melissa,"

115

he said almost mistily, "you look awful pretty."

"I d'know why I shouldn't. This my weddin' day, ain't it?" She smiled on him bravely.

"Yes, sir, it is"—still gazing at her—" 'n mine, too, for that matter." He kissed her again.

"Well, you go talk t' Pa—and mind you do th' talkin'!—I'll go up to my chamber. I ain't goin' t' be married all over hay, anyhow—e'en though you did cut it."

"I didn't cut much more'n half of it. Joe done his share, I guess."

"Well, it's the half you cut that's stuck to me. Come on, now, we can't stand all day talkin' . . . 'n sooner or later, you got t' eat somethin'."

"I ain't terrible hungry."

"No, I ain't either."

Melissa fell silent. They started up toward the tavern.

—as they came to the bridge, she said, "Whit, d' you remember my mother?"

"Yes, I remember her."

"I—I do, too."

Whit took hold of her hand—and she held on to his firmly.

20

Melissa was going to step into the barn just to see to the feed and the water, and, although Whit said he'd do it for her, she sent him on up to the inn.

He went round to the front door because that was farther—and because it seemed to him somehow to have more dignity to it.

When Whit came in the door, Captain had his back to him, being busily bent before the cask of West India. "Good mornin'," said Captain, "you're welcome, I'm sure—though I can't see who 'tis. Wait'll I get this here drawed—man'll be down in a minute—" there was a thumping upstairs "—that's him getting his boots on. There!" He shut off the spigot, stood up, and turned round—

"Mornin', Captain," Whit said to him.

Captain's hand shook, and lest he should spill any, he set the bowl on the counter. He muttered some exclamation, and then

116

said half aloud, "Where in hell 'd you come from?"

"Sandwich—'n round there."

"When'd you get here?"

"When I come in the door."

"I mean in t' Kittlef'd."

"'Long about sunup. You're the first man that I seen since yesterday forenoon."

Captain breathed easier. The first shock had passed—that of being so suddenly confronted by a man whom he'd injured. Here in front of Captain there stood and awaited him the very great pleasure of informing this boy that Melissa, by God, was the next thing to married to good old Joe Felipe! Captain wetted his lips. "Set down your rifle, my boy. You look like you'd traveled."

"I been travelin', all right."

"Let me get suthin' for you. You ain't growed up to rum, have you, while you been away?"

"No, I ain't, I guess, Captain."

"Cider?"

"No; it's kind of you, Captain, but I can't stay but a minute."

"You got a little packet of fur there. You want me t' look at it?"

"No, that'll wait. Don't amount t' much anyhow."

"No, I can see that. But I'll treat you right on it. It's a little early for fur."

"Not all kinds, it ain't early. But that ain't no matter. We c'n let the fur go till later. What I came about, Captain, is I got somethin' t' tell you."

"You don't say!" exclaimed Captain. "Well, now, that's pretty." He rubbed his hands on his waistcoat. "Maybe we can swap even. I got a little small piece o' news that might interest you, Whit." He smiled after his fashion . . . but not wholly serenely. It seemed to Captain that Whit had grown quite a lot bigger. Captain uncomfortably thought of the letter. Still, when Whit heard the news, that would take care of Whit all right! He'd figure she'd jilted him in spite of the letter.

"What is it?" Whit asked him.

"Tell me yourn," answered Captain, knowing well what it was. "Tell me yourn first, and then I'll tell you mine, Whit."

But Reverend Potter, who now had his boots on and was descending the stairway, forewarned of his coming. He came into the room, looking sleepy and dirty. "Where's that rum?" he demanded.

"Right here 'n ready f'r you, Mr. Potter—all drawed and all ready!" Captain stepped briskly and handed it to him.

Potter shuddered and drank it, wiped his mouth on his linen, and held the mug out to Captain. "Draw me another. That's vile rum, and you know it. But a man's breakfast sets better if he warms up his stomach." He turned to the other man, standing there with the rifle, and said to him sourly, "Trapper, good morning."

"Mornin'," Whit answered.

Mr. Potter sat down. He chose to be irritated by the man's tone of voice, and he looked him all over. "And just who might you be—if I might inquire?"

"You c'n inquire. My name is Whit Livingston."

"Indeed," Potter said carelessly—and then, "What?" He glanced quickly at Captain and was not much astonished to observe that poor Captain was now making faces.

"Livingston here"—Captain did his desperate best—"ain't only just gotten in from a long trip t' th' north o' here. Sandwich, you said, Whit. That's some east o' the Grants, ain't it?"

Whit, in response, nodded his head the least bit, though keeping his gaze fixed on Potter.

"Three months he's been gone," Captain went on, "and no letter come through from him, 'n then he walks in here."

"I see," Mr. Potter said heavily, "quite a surprise for you."

"Yes, 'twas," agreed Captain.

Turning to Whit, Mr. Potter said, puzzled, "But—but you're not the Livingston I know."

"I d' know why I should be; you ain't anyone I know."

Whit's tone and his manner informed Potter and Captain that Whit had been told of what Potter had said of him.

"Captain," said Potter, "you will please introduce me."

"This here's Mr. Potter, Whit," Captain said hopelessly.

"Thank you," said Potter. "And now if you'd kindly bring two of those, Captain, perhaps the young man will join me."

"I won't take any, thank you. Who's this Livingston you know? Let's get that out th' way. I come here to see Captain."

It was Captain who marveled at how Whit had grown up— and perhaps Whit did a little.

But the businesslike Potter—who'd never seen Whit before—wasted no time in marveling. "The Livingston I know," he answered Whit levelly, "does not exist. The fact is, my good man, that I used your name once in an attempt to sell land. If I

118

have done you an injury—as your manner implies—I most sincerely regret it. May I explain to you?"

"Well, you c'n try, if you don't take too long to it."

"Yes, yes, of course. You have business with Captain. So have I, for that matter. Our friend Captain Butler is buying some deeds from me. That is so, isn't it, Captain?"

"It might be," said Captain.

"Very well, then." Mr. Potter now spoke to Whit solely. "I have just come from the Grants where I bought considerable land, a portion of which I now contemplate selling. I sought to sell some last evening to some of your townsmen. I need money, you see, to continue my journey."

"There ain't a better thing you could spend it for."

"I incline to agree with you. Your neighbors, however, were slow to loosen their purses. Earlier on in the evening I had heard your name mentioned. It appeared you had gone north sometime during the summer and had not yet returned. No one had heard from you. It was early for trapping, and someone suggested that perhaps it might be you had gone pioneering. And someone else said—yes, I know who it was: it was the man they call Ensign— said that if you *had* made a pitch, he'd stake his life on it you'd picked good land to do it on."

"Why'd he say that?" Whit interrupted.

"If I recall," Mr. Potter said slowly, "he intimated that you'd had some experience of land that was *not* so good."

"He was correct."

"Yes. That seemed to be the general opinion. So, when the time came and I was trying to sell land to them, I used what I'd heard. It didn't seem serious. In all probability, you had settled somewhere. And no doubt on good land. So why not next to my land? There's good land next to my land. And it was only of that that I sought to convince them. I told them a man named Whit Livingston, from Kettleford, had settled on land that was hard by some lots I owned. It seemed at the time an innocent fiction. And—this may amuse you—I went so far, I confess, as to give you a wife—a most excellent female, let me assure you. You could scarcely do better yourself, Mr. Livingston. Unless you've already done so . . ."

"That the whole o' the story?"

"Why, yes—yes, I think so."

"All right. You're a liar. I guess you c'n go now."

"I fear I've offended you."

"Yes, it looks that way, don't it?"

"You have my apologies, young man, of course. If there are any amends I can make, I assure you, you have only to mention them. I am at fault, and I freely confess it."

"Will you please t' get out o' here?"

"Gladly," said Potter. He rose rather stiffly, and facing Butler, reached into his pocket.

Whit cradled his rifle—

"Captain Butler," said Potter, "here are the deeds that you're going to buy from me. Fifteen pounds apiece comes to forty-five pounds. Bay old tenor, that is. They're very fine deeds. You can sell them for twice that, if you put your mind to it, and I have no doubt that you will."

"But—"

"Captain Butler, you will observe that young Livingston here is not to be trifled with. Please get me the money."

"But forty-five—"

"Livingston at the moment is cradling his rifle. The young man does not wish me to say anything further. Do you, Captain Butler?"

"I'll get it," said Captain, and hurried out of the room. Better forty-five pounds spent on trumpery deeds than a beating from Whit—if Potter should tell him what had become of his letter!

While Captain was gone, neither Potter nor Whit spoke a word to each other.

Captain returned and gave Potter the money. Potter counted the money, and gave Captain the deeds. Mr. Potter said, "Thank you." He took down his cloak, put that on and his hat, and marched to the door. "Well," he said throatily, "I continue my journey."

Captain asked plaintively, "You ain't forgetting your score, are you?"

With his thumb on the latch, Mr. Potter replied, "No, I'm not, Captain Butler. My score here is paid. In fact, I think I've paid everyone. Good day to you, landlord." He opened the door. And over his shoulder: "Trapper, good morning—" and perhaps a little bit hastily, he closed the door after him. They heard him go tramping round down toward the barn to get his horse out.

"Prob'ly steal everything in the barn," Captain said bitterly. "What is he—a land agent dressed out like a preacher?"

Captain said what he was. Then he trailed off into muttering . . . He went over and poured out some brandy and drank it.

Standing behind his own counter, he leaned his back comfortably against one of the casks on the rack, and folded his arms. Now it was *his* turn. "Well, Whit, what is it? Now we got rid o' him, we c'n talk just the two of us. What's on your mind, boy?"

Whit had grounded his rifle. He stood with his long hands wrapped round the barrel, and leaned his weight on it.

"Speak up, my boy!—that is, if you want to talk private. I got a feeling old Joe may come in here most any minute. I been kind of expecting of him."

"Well, I'll tell you now, Captain, what I come to say was." He felt far more excitement because of the words he would say than he did because it was Captain to whom he was saying them. "Melissa and me is going to get married."

Captain said evenly, "Well, now, Whit, you was right. That's quite some piece o' news, ain't it! By God, boy, it is!"

"True, anyhow, Captain."

"Why, o' course, it's true, Whit! You'd ought t' know, hadn't you? Why should I disbelieve it?"

"I d' know as you should, Captain."

"What makes you think that I don't believe it?"

"You ain't sputtered enough."

Captain Butler appeared for a moment about to supply the deficiency. But he recovered himself. "No—the way I feel to you, Whit, is almighty grateful. 'Twas awful kind in you, Whit, t' take all this trouble t' come round here 'n tell me. I d' know as consid'rin' the way you was brought up that 'twould a entered your head t' come in here 'n *ask* me?"

"No, it didn't."

"'Twouldn't."

"Matter o' that, I ain't askin' you now, Captain. Maybe you noticed."

"You think you ain't, maybe. But let me ask you somethin'! Who's goin t' marry you to M'lissa without I give permission? And another thing: just how in the hell did you figure t' keep her? Your old man goin t' give you the mortgage on his place? Or maybe you figured t' hire out mowin'? Wait, though, you're a trapper. Hell, I almost forgot, Whit. I beg your pardon. That there bundle o' rat hides you brought in here with you—where'd you get 'em all, anyhow, under somebody's corncrib? I s'pose you aim t' trade them for enough t' get married." His tone changed to solicitude. "You ain't drunk, are you, boy?—'cause if you ain't drunk, then I do think you're crazy. B'God I could swear to

121

it! I'm sorry for you. When I tell the town this, they'll go'n get Joe t' fit a collar t' you, 'n your old man'll take 'n chain you up out'n the woodshed f' the boys t' make sport of, like that one over t' Goffstown. We ain't had one t' Kittelf'd—not f' some time now."

Captain summed up in disgusted amazement, "You stand there 'n tell me you're a-goin' t' marry M'lissa!" He leaned forward, his hands on the counter, and with a fine show of earnestness—almost as though he spoke confidentially—"I *never* heard *nothin'* in my *life* t'—t' come up to it!"

"You're doin' better. I was afeard back along maybe you didn't believe me. Well, I'll say good day, Captain."

"You'll say 'good day,' hell!" Captain responded. "You'll say more'n 'good day' afore I finished with you! Don't you be in a hurry now! I got somethin' t' say t' you."

"All right, Captain, say it. This your small piece o' news, is it?"

"This is my piece o' news—'n I got the proof of it! That's more'n you offered."

"Why, I'll give you the proof, Captain; I didn't know as you wanted it. You c'n come t' th' weddin'! There, now, how'll that do? 'Twon't cost you a penny, 'n after it's over, I'll stand you a treat—'f you c'n get someone t' drink with you. Maybe I'd ought t' try to m'self, but I guess I won't somehow." Whit wasn't feeling any too steady. He'd had about all of this that he wanted.

Not so Captain, who was pleased to feel his rage mounting. "You're safe enough, boy! You won't have t' drink with nobody! 'N I c'n tell you right now you ain't goin' t' take part in no weddin'. My piece o' news is: you ain't goin' t' marry her! How d' you like it?"

"Why, I d' know, Captain . . . don't seem t' mean much—not'll you put the proof onto it."

"All right: here's the proof then."

"Wait just a minute. The proof'll keep, won't it?"

"What's the matter? You scared of it?"

"No, I don't think so. But tell me this, Cap'n—" he was beginning to slur his words and speak softly the more he grew angry—"this the same piece o' news you spoke of before, is it—when you said we'd swap even?"

"I swapped more'n even! What I'm tellin' you's true!"

"How'd you know, 'fore I told you, that we figured t' marry?"

Fairly caught, Captain was, and he showed it. "Told me

herself." Being checked made him surly.

"That's a lie, ain't it, Cap'n?"

Captain leaned toward him. "Don't you call me a liar!"—his voice thin and piping.

"What'd you do with the letter?"

"What the hell do you care what I done with the letter? You got no call to write to her! I know my rights! You thought you could cheat me! You thought you could take her when I wasn't lookin'!"

"You're lookin' now, ain't you? And now I'm goin' t' take her." He turned his head toward the stairs and called upward "M'lissa!"

Her answer came faintly. "Hold on—I'm a-comin'."

Neither one, for the moment, being in a hurry to speak, they stood there in silence. And they listened together to a sound out of doors . . . the resolute steps of the Reverend's horse as Reverend Potter rode up out of the barnyard, passed under the window, and was crossing the innyard to set out on his journey. And they heard Potter's voice: "Joe, good morning to you."

Captain neglected Joe's answer. But Whit heard it—and it sounded natural enough—maybe a little more cheerful perhaps than Joe usually was. And Whit heard Joe coming up to the doorway . . .

Captain, who had been busily thinking, "How in hell 'd she get up there?" and "How'd Whit know she was up there?" now saw everything clearly. She must have come back with Joe from wherever they'd been all night, and she'd come in the side door and slipped up to her chamber. He hadn't heard her come in on account of Whit's jawing—and as for Whit, more than likely he'd only guessed she was up there because he hadn't seen her around any. It made everything whole; it made everything perfect. Captain, in trembling excitement and gripped by the presage of imminent triumph, awaited Joe's entrance.

Joe flung open the door and to whomever the room might contain shouted lustily, "Mornin'!" José Felipe had put in a good night. He had parted from Melissa as a friend and an equal. That had been in her voice. There was no telling how far he might get today with her . . .

He saw Whit standing there, and in friendly amazement swore at him in Portuguese. "Where d' hell do you come from?" Joe was everyone's friend today.

"Upcountry," Whit answered. "You look pretty good, Joe."

"By God, I feel good! I mow you today, Whit, by God, you wouldn't catch me! Hey? How is that! Eh?"

"I d' know, Joe . . . near as I recollect, it was you a'most catched me, wan't it?"

"Only for Ensign," Joe answered with relish, "I'd a cut t' foot off you! By God, he hit me like—like I don' know how he hit me!" He put his hand to his jaw. "Yes, sir! T'at day we had fun, a' right! Didn' we? Capitao, I want a drink. Hot brandy and water. Where is M'lissa?"

"You're a sly dog!" The Captain smiled slowly. "I'd ought t' ask *you* that." He saw Whit become motionless.

Joe was not even puzzled. "I'm a sly dog? I know what kind o' dog you are!" He told him, and laughed. Captain smiled feebly. "Say," Joe reminded him, "I ask you before, where t' hell is M'lissa?"

"Wait'll I get you th' brandy." Captain moved hastily.

Joe glanced at Whit to enjoy Captain with him. But even Joe could read in Whit's face that Joe was mistaken: there was no joke to enjoy. Joe had never been one to ponder a problem unnecessarily. He reached out for Captain and swung the little man round to him. "T' hell wit' t' brandy! Where is M'lissa?"

Captain's wig was askew. "Upstairs in her chamber! Leave go of me, will you?"

"'Upstairs in her chamber.' You sure of it, are you?"

"Sart'n, I'm sure of it! Leave go of me, will you!"

"Quiet, little old man." Joe straightened his wig for him. "Now get me t' brandy."

Whit wasn't amused. He'd been a long time away. Joe hadn't used to bully Captain.

"Neat," Joe changed his order . . . and taking the brandy, drank it off at a swallow. As he set the glass down, he explained to the Captain. "See? I don' like any jokes about 'where is M'lissa?'"

"Joe," Captain assured him, "you ain't goin' t' hear any. If there's any jokes goin' round about 'where is M'lissa?' they won't be on you, Joe. You'll be the one tellin' 'em. And right here 'n now 's a good time t' begin, Joe. You won't never get nobody more willin' t' listen t' you tellin' 'where was M'lissa' than what Whit is right now, Joe. Whit has just up 'n told me—and you listen to this, Joe—Whit has just up 'n told me that he's goin' t' marry M'lissa. Where was she last night, Joe?"

Joe had turned round to Whit without hearing the question.

124

Joe's arms hung at his sides, or a little before him—and his head was drawn in and lowered.

One look at his face—and Whit shifted his eyes to watching Joe's hands. The instant Joe made a move—for his knife or to close with him—Whit's right hand would go down and he'd strike up with his rifle. He was beginning to wonder what Joe could be waiting for . . .

But what Joe had heard from Captain, his fellow conspirator, had been, in effect, a loud shout of warning. As Joe spun to face Whit, Joe was on the defensive.

But Whit didn't move either . . .

It looked to Joe this way: "I c'n grab hold of the gun before he c'n present it. He's got his knife on him, but he's got to let go of t' gun before he c'n lay hold on it. Captain's t' only one here— 'n I done it before 'n no harm ever come of it!—'n he c'n swear to all hands that Whit come at me first. If I c'n close with him, I can handle him easy. I *want* t' close with him!"

Joe's fingers twitched—

—and Whit's hand began sliding, ever so gently, down the gun barrel. He felt like saying, "C'm on, Joe—" He really felt happy. He wanted Joe to come in to him.

Captain shrilly was dinning "Where was she last night?" over and over. But it had no effect. Captain was out of it. This enraged Captain. He screamed: "She lay out with you last night, by God, and you know it! Tell him, Joe! Tell him!" They heard him that time!

Joe bent his knees—

Then Melissa's voice, "Well, Joe . . . ?" She stood on the staircase, a little above them.

The most Captain could do was to blink at her in anger; Whit, for some reason, felt ashamed of himself; and Joe, seeing Melissa, went numb at the vision and simply gazed open-mouthed at her.

Melissa was dressed for her wedding. She had on a cap of stiff lace, and a very brave apron over a dress that she hadn't dared tell herself—even while she was making it—had been meant for this morning. But so it had been, and now she was wearing it. She had brushed out her stockings, and her shoe buckles shone. When she'd heard Whit call upstairs to her, she'd been all ready to weep for no reason whatever except that her hair wouldn't stay in under her cap. She'd have given most anything for some kind of ornament; her father had sold everything of her mother's.

The halo the sun gave her as she stood on the stairs was a generous thing—but of course she couldn't see it.

What she had seen was Whit—who was lame, hungry, and tired—confronted by Joe and about to fight with him. She could tell from Whit's face there was no use trying to stop him—and a desperate anger took hold of Melissa. It was stupid of Whit! If he fought with Joe now, he'd not only be beaten—but what did Whit think would become of her wedding? . . . and she could hear her shrill little father as he goaded Joe into it. She heard precisely his words.

Whit and her father were both out of her reach. She was scornful of both of them!—a little less so of Joe because he was slow-witted. Still, there was some hope that she could get through to Joe. He might answer her truthfully when he wouldn't her father. She said to him, "Well, Joe . . . ?"

—and she saw Joe turn around and gaze dumbly up at her. She spoke to him quietly. "Why don't you tell him, Joe? Did I, or didn't I, do like he says I did?"—and she moved her head toward her father. It all was as clear as a dream to Melissa.

Joe's eyes, at her gesture, went to Captain—and then back to Melissa. Joe knew where he was, and he knew what she'd asked him. He knew what his answer meant—one way or the other. She'd asked the truth of him. And he meant to give it. But Joe looked too long at her—at the light in her hair—and before the sound of his voice came, José Felipe was wrung by a yearning that he couldn't stand up against. There was Melissa—and all that he knew was to take a step toward her. Out of his thoughts, he may not have answered untruthfully. "Yes, you was wit' me—all night," he said brokenly.

In the awfulness of the moment, she stood perfectly still. But in her eyes there was horror . . .

Whit was the first one to move. He stepped across to Melissa, and said to her gently, "You all ready, M'lissa?"—and he held his hand out to her.

She saw him dimly and put her hand into his. "Yes, I'm all ready."

She came down the two steps, and in response to Whit's leading, around to his right. She passed in front of her father, but she didn't see him. She held onto Whit's hand like a child that is frightened. Whit was walking beside her.

It seemed to Whit a long ways from the stairs to the door . . .

and in the last four or five steps, when he couldn't see Joe, Whit wished in his belly that he never had tried this. Let Joe throw his knife and that'd be all there'd be to it. Joe was good with a knife. The skin on Whit's back, just under his shoulder blades, felt as though it were naked. But he kept his head up and he didn't look round any . . . and when he let go of her hand to open the door for her, he thought maybe they'd made it. Melissa stepped out and down onto the stone.

She had passed from Joe's sight. Joe threw his knife—underhand, like a sailor—and a cry came from Joe as he saw he was high with it. It struck into the lintel, quivered, and drooped.

Whit shut the door, and caught up with Melissa. They crossed the innyard, and had gone a piece down the road in reverent silence, when Melissa looked up at him. "You believed me," she said.

Whit didn't look down at her. His mouth twitched in a smile as he thought of this for the first time: "Well . . ." he said slowly, "th' wan't any hay on him."

Melissa understood perfectly.

Whit's knees had begun to feel wobbly—it had been a long walk from the stairs to the doorway. But that didn't last very long, and after that he felt better.

Halfway to Mr. Gowan's, he thought something of telling Melissa how she looked awful pretty dressed out in that cap and all. He decided to tell her.

From there to the minister's dooryard, Melissa wasn't quite sure whether her feet touched the ground or not.

Back in the tavern, José Felipe was bent over the counter, his head on his arms. Joe was sobbing. At the other end of the counter, Captain was drinking a pint of brandy and water. This was his second. He'd drunk the first one more rapidly, and not so much water. Now and again Captain would look over to Joe—but still he said nothing. This went on for some time.

Joe's knife clattered down from the lintel. Captain started—he saw what it was, though, and he took a deep breath and drank the rest of his brandy. But he couldn't stand it to listen to Joe any longer. "Give over that bawlin', Joe, will you? For God's sake! What you got t' bawl over? You still got the money."

But Joe made no answer. After some minutes, he heaved himself upright, and in a kind of a stagger went out the doorway.

127

"Take the knife with you!" Captain called after him. "Don't leave it there! Joe!" . . . but Joe had gone now. "Joe!" Captain screamed. . . .

He was all alone now.

21

For an hour or more, having finished his breakfast, Mr. Gowan had sat in the kitchen, his great Bible open on the arm of his writing chair. This was Lecture Day—Thursday. He'd been arranging his sermon . . . but all that he'd written—on a page from the almanac—was a dozen citations of chapter and verse; he liked to be accurate. As for the sermon itself, he'd not written a word of it. An idea so unformed that he must needs set it down in order to hold it wasn't fit yet for preaching. In building a sermon he used only ideas that were solid and shapen and that he knew he could handle. That was no more than fair to the people before him. They paid him to preach—not to think in the pulpit.

So far, for tonight, he had arranged his points carefully from firstly to eighthly, and was just about through. Eight were enough. The language was something he never fussed with beforehand. It would either come or it wouldn't once he was preaching; he had good days and poor days.

Now the summation. He shifted his legs, settled himself in his chair, and approached it with confidence. . . .

Here and there round the room—and in and out of it, too—his sister was busy. But she hadn't disturbed him. She was used to his ways, and he was used to her presence. She was not a talkative woman.

Mistress Jennifer Gowan had come to do for her brother not very long after he'd first come to Kettleford. She was older than he was—say, ten years or so, maybe. She was a spinster, spare and unbending, her hair a hard gray, and her face lined and set. People in Kettleford knew this about her: years ago, back in Falmouth, she had been promised to a man who was mate on a snow, trading down east to Sydney—mate and part owner. They'd been properly published and the wedding day fixed, and then he'd gone one more trip—because of the money—and the vessel was lost and never was heard from. Mistress Gowan—she was young then—had persisted in hoping, out of all reason, that somehow or other the man was alive and would someday come back to her. She said things like that *had* happened. And when people talked to her, she wouldn't listen. After a time, they let her alone. In Falmouth they knew that when a man was lost off Cape Breton, he was likely to stay lost. The stories come mostly from parts of the world where the water is warmer.

When she'd first come to Kettleford, various women had tried to be neighborly but she wouldn't let them. For their minister's sake, they had tried hard. But no one could expect them to go on trying forever. Mistress Gowan appeared regularly at Meeting and Lecture and most people spoke to her and she always answered. That was the end of it. People were fair: there wasn't a soul who had ever been in the house who didn't say out and out that the place was neat as a pin, and that from what they could see, she was a pretty good feeder. But try to talk to her!

Her brother stirred in his chair; he had finished his sermon. He leaned his head back and spoke to his sister. "Jenny, that barn cat of yours—Nebuchadnezzar?—the one with the waistcoat: I saw him this morning. I called to him, too, but he wouldn't come to me. How long's he been gone?"

"Must be a week, ain't it? Funny thing, too—all this wet we been having. You s'pose he was out in it?"

"I shouldn't think so. He found a place probably." Some one knocked at the door. "Who can that be, I wonder?"

She was on her way to the door.

He sat there and listened . . . Whit Livingston, that was!—and Melissa was with him. Mr. Gowan's face, for an instant, was troubled and grave. "Bring her to me," he had told Whit last summer, "and I'll marry you any time"—and now Whit had brought her. All right: he'd go through with it!—though the law plainly forbade it. Still, it was he who'd be punished, not Whit and Melissa. Closing his Bible he got up to greet them. If they'd only let him have time he might be able to do something to make the thing legal. . . .

He was glad to see Whit, and relieved he was home again. Whit appeared older.

And as for Melissa!—Mr. Gowan bowed to her, noting the cap, and the apron and stockings, and seeing most clearly Melissa's expression: "This is the hour in which I'm to be married." "Ask her to wait?" he thought to himself. "Ask her to wait three weeks to be published?—after three months of waiting that have brought her this moment? Tell her to bring me a written certificate from the clerk of the town that the match is approved by her father?"

"Well," he said to them both, "I guess there's no question as to what you have come for . . . ?"

Whit grinned in response. "No, I guess there ain't, Mr. Gowan."

Melissa smiled happily.

The minister looked from one to the other. He was proud of them both. "I'm glad you have come," he said.

They had no answer.

"Now, then, first of all: have you had any breakfast?"

Neither one would confess. But from the way the girl looked at Whit, Mr. Gowan was certain that Whit hadn't had any. "Whit," he demanded, "has she had any breakfast?"

"Well, I couldn't say, Mr. Gowan—but not since I seen her."

"And you haven't either. Jenny—" She'd vanished. "Gone to look for her cat. I'll go and speak to her. You two stay right here. Whit, poke up the fire." He went out after his sister.

Whit rocked the back log, and turned over the forelog. "He keeps a nice fire."

"Whit, have I got t' eat breakfast?"

"Looks like it, yes." He stood up with his back to the fire.

"Are you happy?" she asked, standing before him.

"Certain, I'm happy!"—spreading his hands to the heat of the fire. "I d' know as 'twould make me unhappy to eat, though."

"Kiss me!"

"In a minister's house?"—and he kissed her.

"Here they come!" said Melissa.

Mistress Jennifer Gowan, having already spoken to Whit and Melissa, saw no need to do so again. She set to work silently to get ready some breakfast. To Melissa's offer of help, Mistress Gowan replied, "I guess I c'n do it. I know where things be. I'd ought to, 't any rate: I just put 'em away." So Melissa stood by and watched the brisk setting forth of more food than the tavern would put on for four men. This was no shilling breakfast. Some fine-looking butter, and a wide wedge of cheese—not this summer's, last summer's—maple syrup, molasses, and strawberry preserves: these went onto the table. A platter of johnnycake was set on the hob to take the chill out of it. Into the fry-pan, rubbed first with salt pork, she cut some small bricks of cold hasty pudding—and then more salt pork in good liberal slices.

After arranging the pan over the fire, she went out to draw cider.

Whit, too, had been watching . . . and giving halfhearted answers to the questions Mr. Gowan was asking him.

Returned from the woodshed, Mistress Gowan had brought with her a gallon of cider and a couple of eels that had been scheduled for supper.

When Whit saw the eels, his host couldn't help asking, "You like eels, do you, Whit?"

"I d' know as there's anything a man thinks of oftener when he's where there ain't any."

"What! No eels where you've been?"

"I didn't see any." He followed these with his eyes. "You take now t' Sandwich, ten bushel o' wheat'll buy one o' salt. But for a nice mess of eels, I d' know what I'd have given—if I'd 've had it t' give, I mean."

Mistress Gowan took the pan from the fire and emptied the fried hasty pudding and pork onto a plate on the table. She fixed the eels in the pan.

"A good many hold," Whit volunteered, "that a really nice eel is the best thing there is comes out of the river. I d' know but they're right . . ."

"These here," Mistress Gowan could not avoid saying, "ain't so fat as they might be." She set the pan on the fire.

Whit remarked thoughtfully, "If I'd had about half of the oil in them fellers t' put onto my ankle, I might a gotten here sooner."

"I wish't you'd had a kag of it" came from Melissa.

Mistress Jennifer said to her brother, "I guess them'll be ready time he's ready to eat them."

He thanked her, and told Whit to come up to the table. "Melissa, you, too. You can eat with the men today. You won't mind, I guess, will you?"

Melissa said truthfully that she'd rather wait.

Mistress Gowan, listening, approved of this stand . . . and still further approved when, Mr. Gowan insisting, Melissa sat down: the girl knew enough to do what she was told, anyhow.

The minister then asked a blessing . . . the first time in their lives that either Whit or Melissa had ever heard *that* done! They put it down to an excusable quirk—it probably came from his being a minister.

"All right, Whit, begin!" Mr. Gowan invited. And Whit started in. Melissa, after a fashion, made out to eat also.

There was no conversation. The minister had removed to his

chair by the fire, and his sister stood round and watched Whit at his eating. She hadn't seen anyone who really could eat since she'd left the salt water and come inland to Kettleford. On top of the other things, Whit ate both of the eels and drank two-thirds of the cider. By the time he had finished, Mistress Jennifer Gowan was so far won over as to give her permission when Melissa respectfully offered to help her wash up.

Mr. Gowan ignored the fact that Whit now was sleepy; he was bent upon talking. He told Whit to come and sit down on the bench by the fire, and he began putting more questions. They were, for the most part, things having to do with the last three or four hours.

No, Whit admitted, Melissa hadn't expected him. He'd sent her a letter, but it had gone astray somewhere. (He had all he could do to answer the minister accurately, his head was so thickening with his great need of sleep.)

"You know, Whit, last night," Melissa put in, "when that Mr. Potter come in t' th' innyard, the first thing I thought of was: maybe he's got a letter."

Whit's mind revolved slowly. "Well, the way it turned out, he brought word of me, anyhow,—or he claimed that he did."

"'Mr. Potter'?" Mr. Gowan inquired—and he kept on inquiring. Whit wasn't able to pick and choose items. Nor was he able to defend against questions. He worked through the whole story: what Mr. Potter had said in the tavern last evening, and how Mr. Potter had made explanation this morning. Whit didn't know when the story was ended. He went doggedly on through Mr. Potter's selling some deeds to Melissa's old man—and how Captain had paid, even though it hurt Captain to pay money to anyone. Then Mr. Potter had gone.

"Yes. I heard him ride by here. What happened then, Whit?"

"I guess Joe come in, near as I c'n remember." Whit yawned. "There, now, I hadn't ought to be sleepy. Night before last—"

"Let's keep to this morning. 'Joe came in.' Then what?"

From the other side of the room, Melissa came over. She stood watching Whit . . .

Whit was earnestly trying to do what Mr. Gowan required: to recollect what had happened and to tell it all straight.

Mr. Gowan said nothing at all to Melissa. But he knew she was there.

Whit struggled on. He hoped Mr. Gowan would leave him alone as soon as he'd finished. He would go to sleep then.

It was hard work to remember. The outside of his head seemed to press in on his brains . . . but his belly felt good. If he could only let go, he could go to sleep now . . .

They watched his eyes closing.

"'n then Captain said that I couldn't marry her because all of last night she'd been with the Portygee. I d' know why he said it—it seemed awful silly. 'N then there was M'lissa—" His eyes now were closed. They both saw him smile. "—standin' there on the stairway. She looked awful pretty! 'N so I said to her, 'M'lissa, you ready?' 'n she was ready all right—'n so we walked out o' there . . . out o' there . . . 'n Joe never done nothin'—'n—'n walked—in the road . . ." That was the best he could do. He had fallen asleep.

After a moment, the minister looked at Melissa. And she looked at him.

He felt that he wanted to say something to her. But Whit had already put it much better than he could: I d' know why he said it—it seemed awful silly. So Mr. Gowan said nothing. He looked back at Whit.

"He's been travelin' all night," Melissa explained; "all day 'n all night."

"Yes."

Whit was sound asleep now. "Jenny," Mr. Gowan said, over his shoulder, "I'm going up to the tavern. If Ensign should come here to the house looking for me, tell him to wait for me. Tell him to wait here until I get back. Anyone else, you can send them away—you and Ensign between you, I guess you can, anyhow."

"Dinner?" she asked.

"If I'm not here in time, you can give it to Ensign."

Mistress Jennifer sniffed.

Mr. Gowan stood up. "Now, then, Whit, I'll fix you up." He went out of the room and came back with three blankets, spread two on the floor in front of the fire, and then eased Whit off the bench onto them. Whit seemed to half waken and to half understand. The man covered him up with his feet to the fire. "You keep an eye on him, will you, Melissa? I'm going up to talk to your father."

"Yes, sir" . . . but she followed him out into the dooryard. "Mr. Gowan—"

"What is it?"

"You said—that is, Whit said—Ain't you goin' t' marry us?"

"Whit's sound asleep."

"I c'n wake him up, Mr. Gowan—long enough t' get married."

Mr. Gowan looked down at her. "Melissa, I want you to wait until evening."

"But—"

"Till this evening."

"You know what Pa's goin' t' say to you!"

"I think I do, yes. But he can't expect to do all the talking. You be patient, child, will you?"

She looked up at him a moment. "All right"—and she shut her lips tight.

He turned away toward the gate . . . and then came back to Melissa. "I will promise you this: no matter what happens, I'm going to marry you."

Melissa's eyes widened. "Yes . . . That's what Whit told me."

He set off up the road. "Faith," he thought to himself, "is a beautiful thing!—but I wish they'd fixed theirs on a worthier object." He was right up against it. The runaway marriage he'd promised the girl was a poor thing at best. It was one degree better than no marriage at all. That was about all you could say for it—from her standpoint, anyway—though she mightn't see now that that was the case.

As for his share of it—if he were to look at it selfishly—to perform such a marriage was the worst thing he could do. He knew the statute: fine, £50—for marrying a couple who hadn't been published, and who lacked their parents' consent. Moreover, he'd be forever debarred from marrying anyone. In addition to that, Captain could sue him—though there'd not be much left to satisfy judgment once the fine had been paid!

Gloomily Gowan held on for the tavern. . . .

Butler . . . well, yes, he thought he might handle Butler. Because it certainly looked as though Captain Butler—for reasons unknown—had been trying to fix things so that no one but Joe would marry Melissa. A suggestion to Captain that the town wouldn't like that—most people believing Joe was more or less Popish—might have some effect. In fact, the minister thought, the town would like it so little that he was probably justified in hinting to Captain of tar and of feathers. . . . Yes, Captain's consent might well be obtainable.

There was still the town, though. The town would be difficult; there was no getting round it. The town knew the law, too: that a marriage be published three times in advance. That was to give them opportunity to object if they wanted to. In this instance, of course, no one would want to object—Whit and Melissa being both well regarded. But let Reverend Gowan—thus ran his thoughts—ignore the town's *right* to object if it wanted to—and right there'd be the end of his Kettleford ministry!

Why on earth had he promised Melissa "this evening"! There was no use talking that way: he knew well enough.

It was only a little way now to the tavern. All right: Butler first—he rather relished this interview—and with that out of the way, he'd have his mind free to tackle the town.

Mr. Gowan raised up his head and took a deep breath of the morning. He'd been too busy thinking to notice before what a fine morning it was!

22

Early that evening the crowd round the door of the new meeting house was twice what it had been on Lecture Nights recently. The people stood around, visiting. It wasn't much warmer inside the building, and out here they could talk. It was fine overhead and frozen dry underfoot. "Is this here tonight Lecture," David Gillmor's voice quavered, "or is it a bear baitin'? I ain't seen so many in one place t'gether since June Trainin' Day. My soul 'n body, if there ain't t' Captain! That makes it complete. Hi, there, Captain! You treatin'?"

"Evenin', David," said Captain, and took sanctuary inside the church building.

"You say 'treat' t' that man," David remarked, "'n he'll duck into a hole j' like a woodchuck."

"You've shot at him too often."

"Well, I ain't never hit him!"

William Cauldwell asked, "What is it, Lawrence? You know what's the excitement?"

"No more than you do," Murphy responded. "What brought you here, David?"

"Why shouldn't I be here? Can't I come t' Lecture?"

"You ain't in six months."

"All the more reason!" said David triumphantly.

"The truth is, ain't it, David," drawled old Matthew Patten, "someone told you there was goin' t' be votin'?"

"That's what I heard," said two or three others.

"What on?" someone asked.

No one answered immediately.

"What's the difference?" said David. "Where there's votin' there's treatin'—sooner or later. That's why I come. The rest o' you fellers—that ain't here out o' habit, like Schoolmaster here—come out o' spite: so's there wouldn't no one outvote ye. Y' don't care what it's on—no more'n I do."

This was close enough to the truth so that all of them laughed.

"A Presbyterian," another observed, "'d ruther vote 'n eat anytime."

"They ain't so bad as the Congregationals, though."

"Maybe they ain't, but they ain't very far from it."

"Way it is in a Congregational church, even the minister votes. He's got a vote just the same as the rest of 'em."

"How do you know? You ain't never been one."

"No, but my woman was before she changed over."

"She didn't vote, did she?"

"Hell, no, she's a woman."

"I heard this morning," said Cauldwell to Murphy, "that Whit Livingston's back. I heard he'd been t' th' tavern and called that Mr. Potter—right to his face, mind you!—called him a liar. I heard Potter admitted it. You know who told me? Captain himself did."

"Yes, he told me, too."

"'N I said to Captain, Potter had better admit it. I knowed there last night that the man was a liar—soon as he spoke."

"Did you?"

"Sart'n I knowed it! But I didn't say nothin'—maybe you noticed. Give the man enough rope, I says t' myself, 'n he'll hang himself on it."

They had all heard the story of Whit's meeting with Potter. All day long, Captain Butler'd recited it—like a piece that he'd learned—to every man who'd come in there.

"Whit ain't the kind"—it was Murphy's opinion—"t' take 'n live with a woman 'thout he hadn't married her."

There was general agreement.

"Where is Whit?" asked Thett. "Has anyone seen him?"

No one answered. They'd do that to Thett sometimes; it kept him in his place.

Mistress Gowan appeared out of the darkness, marching straight for the door.

"Evenin', Mis' Gowan," Murphy said to her pleasantly.

She cocked her head round like a tall, skinny bird. "Who's that? Lawrence Murphy? Why, good evenin' t' you, sir. Nice evenin', ain't it?"

"Yes, ma'am, it is that," Murphy managed to answer.

—and she kept on her way.

The men gaped. That was more words than Mistress Jennifer Gowan had ever said at one time since she first came to Kettleford!—and before they'd recovered, Mr. Gowan loomed up. . . .

Now, ordinarily, the minister'd stop, speak to this one and that one. . . .

Tonight he stalked through the crowd as though they weren't there.

An odd silence came on them, as of children rebuked. (Thett recognized it.) They moved toward the door. . . .

Inside the church, Mr. Gowan sat in his chair—looking out over them, but, as before, not appearing to see them. They settled themselves. When the bustle and coughing had dwindled to nothing, they heard as they always did the door of the church closed. They waited for the minister to rise and come forward.

Then they heard the door opened again. No one quite wanted to turn clean around to see who it was . . . but they thought the steps sounded like a man and a woman. They came up the aisle. It was Whit and Melissa.

Every wife in the church glanced round at her husband. But most of the husbands declined to confess to the white heat of interest that throbbed in the females. The men thought their own thoughts. They thought that Melissa, putting it mildly, was a fine-looking girl. They were pleased to see for themselves what they'd already heard: that Whit had gotten back safely. The evidence before them that Whit, upon his return, hadn't wasted much time, they found mildly amusing. They wondered how Whit had managed Captain; understood now why Whit had stood up to Potter; and most of them wondered how Whit was going to support her. It was this latter question made them think of Whit's father. And they saw that old Tom was on hand tonight, too. Whit had come a long ways since that time in the tavern. And old Tom had progressed—but in the other direction. Tom looked worse than ever.

The women all wished that Lecture was over. A sudden betrothal awaiting discussion made the hour seem endless.

Straight, stiff, and in black, Mistress Jennifer Gowan was filled with excitement. Melissa was wearing an assortment of items to which, one after another, Mistress Gowan had persuaded her. They were lovely things, too—made for Mistress Jennifer's wedding. Toward midafternoon, she had said to herself, "They were meant for a wedding—and that's what they'll be used for. I ain't goin' back on 'em: I'm doin' right by 'em! It's what they were meant for." Since that moment, whenever she'd realized that the things were no longer up there on the shelf in her closet, she'd felt for some reason, this—well, sort of excitement: she felt like talking to people.

Melissa was radiant. Mr. Gowan had said to her, "One way or another, I'm going to try to arrange it for right after Lecture." It was he who'd suggested she and Whit sit together—he'd like to salvage, he said, as much of custom as possible.

Only Whit was unhappy. Not even his pride in Melissa could make him feel comfortable—here in front of them all.

After Whit and Melissa had seated themselves, Mr. Gowan came forward—and began just as usual. In nothing he said, in no tone of his voice was there any sign whatsoever of anything out of the ordinary.

When he came to the notices, he read out the banns, and he said to the people, "Following Lecture tonight, I want you to remain. There are one or two things that I wish to discuss with you."

Then he preached them the sermon that he had prepared for them—though it suited his purpose to finish with fifthly. By that time they were restless, though not yet resentful.

The service concluded, he gave them no chance to relax into whispering. But with a tangible pause and some change in his manner, he made the transition to secular matters.

"I speak now to the town," he said, "not to the church." And with those words he conceded to them the authority in whatever might follow. There was a visible stir as they settled themselves with judicial air in more comfortable postures. They paid the closest attention.

"Here tonight," he went on, "you have heard me read out the banns for two of your people. Under the law of this province, those banns must be published at three separate Meetings before the law will assume that I have your consent to marry these people. I must have, also, their parents' consent."

"If I break the law—if I marry two of your people without

your consent and the consent of their parents—I become subject to fine, as well as liable to suit. But—mark you this!—the marriage still holds. The law seeks to give you control over me. The law does not give you control over them.

"They may be married by some other minister, provided he have permission of his Majesty's Governor—which, as you know, is not infrequently granted. Indeed, they may achieve the married estate—so far as the law is concerned—without any minister. In New Hampshire Province, any two people living together as though they were married, are just as much married, in the eyes of the law, as though they'd *been* married.

"That, I say, is the law—think what I may of it.

"We come now to apply it. Whitfield and Melissa wish me to marry them. Under the law, I must have your permission. Three weeks, the law gives you, in which to make up your minds."

He spoke not at all humbly. "I ask your approval sooner than that. I believe—and assure you—that in that way alone you may avoid for them unwonted hardship. With your approval, I wish to join together in marriage Whitfield and Melissa before God and this company as now gathered together.

"You have the right to say no. I need not remind you that, where there is right, there is responsibility also. What is your pleasure?"

They appeared very grave.

The minister waited. . . .

Nathaniel Thett, young and earnest, got to his feet. "I should like to ask, Mr. Gowan, about the right to be heard of those who are absent."

Lawrence Murphy, sitting up front, was seen to look round the church. "Them that ain't here," Lawrence said audibly, "is mostly the Portygee."

There was considerable amusement—and Thett chose to sit down again.

David Gillmor got up. "From what you say, Mr. Gowan, looks like t' me that there ain't any use f'r us t' go further until we hear from Captain. If Captain says 'no,' there's 'n end on 't, ain't it?"

Murphy leaned toward his wife so as to whisper, "That old fool 'd kiss a cow's rump f'r a noggin o' brandy."

She reproved him.

Mr. Gowan turned squarely to Captain. "Eliphalet Butler—" and he paused somewhat pointedly until Captain stood up—

"do you give your consent to my performing this marriage between your daughter Melissa and Whitfield Livingston of Kettleford?"

There was dead silence. Everyone in the place, except Whit and Melissa, was looking at Captain.

Captain, however, was looking at minister. . . .

"Or—" Mr. Gowan said.

"I do," answered Captain.

No one thought of Tom Livingston.

William Cauldwell arose; his love of talking was proof against anything. "Sir, and this meeting: Like Mr. Gowan has said, where there's a right, there is responsibility. That means, f'r one thing, that it's up t' us t' be fair an' t' use our best judgment towards Whit and this woman. I think we will. But it looks t' me, too, like our responsibility went further 'n that.

"Now I don't say there is—but I say there *could* be—folks outside o' Kettleford who might have some interest, one way or another, in these two gettin' married. It might even be that such a one as I speak of was at some distance from Kettleford. If we cut down the time between 'publish' and 'marry,' we cut that person out of a chance to object. Oh, yes, we c'n do it; we got the authority. But do we *want* t' do it?" Mr. Cauldwell sat down.

. . . and the story of Whit's having taken a woman somewhere in the north seemed to hang in the atmosphere . . .

They were uncomfortable under it; they didn't like it. But there it was, all the same. And no one wanted to speak.

Mr. Gowan perceived that he was facing defeat. Yet he'd gone as far as he dared in trying to run things. Any move he made now, and they'd turn against him.

Zebulon Porter, disliking Cauldwell, sought a fresh change of subject. Well-intentioned and innocent, Zebulon cheerfully inquired, "I'd like to ask, Mr. Gowan, what is the nature of these here now 'hardships'?—that you said you'd like t' get round for them?"

Whit thought to himself, "I've stood all of this that I've got a mind to."

He rose and faced Porter. "I've made me a pitch just outside o' Sandwich. If you know where that is, you know that t' get there you go up th' river. That means a canoe. If I'm goin' t' take a canoe full o' gear 'n a woman up Merrimack River in th' month o' November, I want t' git started. I *got* t' get started! Goin' upstream, I got t' use th' slack water. That freezes first. Any night

140

now, when there ain't too much wind, she'll begin t' catch over. New ice'll slit a canoe open right at the waterline. If she's loaded down good 'n movin' 't all, it'll lay her wide open. That puts you in th' river with th' gear 'n the woman. As to what Mr. Gowan here means by 'unwanted' hardship, I couldn't tell you. Far as I know, there ain't any other kind. But flounderin' round in Merrimack River with ice 'n gear 'n a woman in a stove-up canoe is more hardship than I want. Does that answer your question?" He was angrier now than he had been when he started.

Porter said, "Yes, it does." Porter was pleased. Whit had pleaded his case better than Porter had thought he could.

Lawrence Murphy said quietly, "Why can't you go overland?"

"Because I ain't got any oxen." And then Whit turned on Cauldwell. "I told Mr. Potter this mornin' up t' th' tavern that he was a liar. I thought that was sufficient. Is it, or ain't it?"

"It is for me, Whit."

"Is it for the rest of ye?"

"Yes," a man growled—and more of them joined him.

Whit, not visibly mollified, sat down again.

Mr. Gowan saw fit to call on Melissa.

She rose when he spoke to her—and she stood very straight.

"According to custom when banns have been read," Mr. Gowan explained by way of easing it for her, "I ask you, Melissa, now to stand forth before this congregation."

Melissa had expected that Whit would be at her side.

"Whitfield Livingston," the minister said to the people, "has already faced you." And to Melissa, "Please turn around."

Melissa turned round. She saw the faces distinctly—there were so many!—but there was no one she knew. She had seen these faces before—but then they'd been people. They were not people now. They were just staring faces . . . without any names to them. She was alone, confronting these faces—she couldn't even feel her legs under her holding her up. Yet she didn't fall . . .

Whit, who was sitting there watching her, did what he had to do: he stood up beside her, and he took hold of her arm. Melissa looked up at him—

"Well, Gavin Gowan—" Mistress Jennifer's voice was high and impatient—"what you waitin' for now?"

Mr. Gowan was startled—

People broke into laughter. Out of the laughter, somebody

called, "Now's the time, Mr. Gowan!" And another man, "Aye! Good for you, Mistress Jenny!"

Over the tumult, Ensign Lord roared, "All in favor, say aye!"

They rocked the church with it.

In a quiet—by contrast more notable—the minister married them. They stood before him and he read from his Bible those parts he had chosen, knowing Whit and Melissa. There was no ritual of question and answer, no admonition. There were only the Old Testament words which he wakened.

Whit and Melissa acknowledged each other as husband and wife.

The minister prayed for them. . . .

". . . Amen," he finished.

"Amen," said the people.

Melissa turned Whit about and they walked down the aisle.

The door opened for them . . . and the night outside welcomed them.

Someone stepped up to Whit. It was Ensign—who had opened the door for them. "Mr. Gowan says, Whit, t' go down t' his place. I guess likely the rest of 'em 'll go up t' th' tavern. He says you c'n do as you like, o' course—but you know what tavern's like after a weddin'."

"M'lissa—?" Whit asked her.

"I d' want t' go back, Whit! I come away from there with you this mornin'."

"Well, I d' know but I feel th' same way." And to Ensign, "Tell Mr. Gowan we take it kind of him, will you? C'm on, M'lissa—"

"My cloak's in the church."

"I'll git it," said Ensign. "You wait down the road a piece, t' other side o' that elm tree."

They slipped away, then . . .

Ensign caught up with them before they'd got to the elm tree. He gave Melissa her cloak.

"G' night, Whit," he said, " 'n good night to you, Mis'ess Livingston."

He hurried back to join up with the others. Ensign knew also what tavern would be after a wedding. And tonight every swallow at Captain's expense! He couldn't escape it! Ensign spoke aloud in the darkness: "I bet that old David has got there a'ready!"

Whit and Melissa walked down the road. The sound of the people faded behind them. They passed two or three houses with light in the windows—dim light, from the fire—and overhead in the darkness, thin-white and unreal, the smoke from the chimneys. These were the houses of the good people of Kettleford. They were warm houses.

Whit struggled to speak. "M'lissa, I'm sorry I ain't got no place t' take you."

"But you will have."

"Yes, I will have."

Then she stopped in the road, and she put her hands up to him. "Whit, I don't care!—not so long as you take me."

Whit couldn't answer. He drew her to him.

Passing Joe's little house, they saw it was dark, no light in the window, no smoke from the chimney. Neither one spoke of it. Melissa pulled her cloak tighter round her.

"You think that tomorrow, Whit, we c'n get started?"

"Tomorrow or next day, I shouldn't wonder. No later than that."

The rest of the way, Whit holding her hand, she went forward in silence.

PART TWO

The River
1769-1770

1

Whit said to Melissa, "Well, now we got started, next thing is t' git there."

They were out on the river, in the long, quiet reach where the river spreads out above the falls at the fishing place. The mist of the morning as it rose from the water was thin now and wispy, and the sun was beginning to narrow the shadow that lay along the east bank. There was almost no wind; what there was was southwesterly. It was yet a little too early for the day to declare itself, but everything pointed to its being a good one.

Underneath all the things that he had on his mind, Whit could feel a great uplift. Melissa was with him. The town was behind them.

He was paddling easy, as a man is apt to do generally at the start of a day or a journey. The blade of his paddle would join with the water, they'd be together a moment, and then be apart again—very much the same way that a man and a woman meet in a figure, go through it together, and cast off at the end of it ... to join again in a moment, carried along and controlled by the music. The firmness of the water, he could feel in his hands, in his arms, and his shoulders. It was gentle and sure; he understood it. He was at one with what he was doing.

This was a birch canoe, high at each end and wide in the waist of it. It was easily ripped but it was easily mended—and he'd brought along enough pitch to pretty nearly build him a new one.

By and large, Whit was hopeful. Now in the morning there appeared a good chance that what lay ahead might work out pretty well for them.

It seemed to Whit, as he thought of it, that he was probably as fortunate a man as you'd be likely to find if you were to set out to look for one. He was going into the woods and Melissa was with him. You couldn't beat that!

He was aware of the happiness in him. Joy he had known, and here and there laughter. This was deeper and gentler. This was a feeling a man could remember and brace against sometime, when he was pressed hard, and know it wouldn't give way with him.

Plenty of men can say "Then, I was happy." Whit was ahead

of them. He knew his happiness at the time when he had it.

Melissa was with him.

That was the main thing. Of course, on the other hand, they were going to run into hardship and certainly danger. But matters of hardship and items of danger his mind kept in their places. They didn't trouble him any beforehand. He knew he was prudent, and he counted that in his favor. He also was thankful that he'd have himself to depend on and no other men around him to worrit him. He liked it that way; it gave him a chance, when something went wrong, to work it out by himself.

He didn't look to Melissa for help on the journey. There wasn't much she could do, really, that he wasn't accustomed to doing himself and that he didn't have an idea he could do better than she could. The job right ahead of him was to get her to Sandwich. He'd manage. There'd be a good many places where he'd have to go easy—where once he'd have poled that this time he must carry—but he didn't mind that. If they'd been coming downstream, though, there were one or two runs he'd have hated to miss.

The sound of the falls was not faint, but forgotten. There were more falls ahead, but they couldn't hear them yet.

He was keeping along at the edge of the sunlight, because he could see that she wanted the sunlight. If he'd been alone, he'd have stayed closer in—more out of the current and where he could see better. But here in the reach there wasn't much current and they had enough to eat with them so that they didn't need to see anything. None the less, all along—because he couldn't help it—he'd been watching both banks for anything stirring. Two musquash and a mink were all he'd seen so far, and he hadn't thought them worth calling to Melissa's attention. A deer would be nice, though—feeding about in a shallow place at the edge of the alders, lifting its feet as dainty as could be, a deer was a thing that belonged to the riverbank—this time in the morning. He'd like Melissa to see one; he thought it would pleasure her.

She was up in the bow and she had her back to him, the hood of her cloak and her small shoulders showing over the top of the baggage he'd fixed there to make a back for her.

The sun coming warmer, Melissa pushed her hood back, raised up her head and shook it a trifle, and it riffled her hair.

It was too much for Whit; it always was when she did that. He couldn't restrain himself: his foundation of happiness seemed so very reliable that he couldn't bear not to add to it some exultation.

147

He grinned and he said to her, "This is pretty good, ain't it?"

"Yes," said Melissa.

The wind—somewhere between them and the falls at the fishing place—had wavered and shifted, and the noise of the falls was much less than it had been. "Wind's shifted," he thought. "Must be more out th' west." He didn't say anything.

Melissa had made up her mind to try to sit motionless. And it wasn't nearly so irksome as she'd thought it would be. But she was beginning to wonder if there wasn't some way she could straighten her legs out. There didn't seem to be any, and she put it off until later. The freedom all round her—and it all belonged to her—was too insistently there for her to think of anything else.

Here the river was wide enough so that they were not walled in by the banks, but were raised up instead so that she could see off into the country. The things that she looked at were farther away than the things that Whit looked for. She looked along the west bank—a bare, tan-colored line—and then went beyond it. The Uncannunucs were plain, but it was not the same mountain. She knew what it was because it couldn't be anything else, but this side of the mountain resembled in no way the face of the mountain that she'd always known. To have the Uncannunucs changed round made it seem all the more a strange and new country in which she was traveling. This indeed was a journey. She was farther now from the tavern than she'd ever been in her life. "How far we come, Whit, would you say, altogether?"

He was slow to answer. "Fourteen mile, I guess, maybe."

She heard his voice as his own but it was not the way he spoke generally. She heard him distinctly—but if she'd been ten feet farther from him she couldn't have heard him at all. And it did seem a short answer. Perhaps, in addition to not being allowed to move about any, she wasn't supposed to speak either. She flushed with resentment, made a wry face, and resolved to keep quiet.

Whit hadn't meant to rebuke her. He'd spoken loud enough for her to hear what he said, and he'd answered her question. It didn't enter his head at the moment that she'd expect any more than that. Chatter, during the daytime when he was out on the river or going along in the woods, wasn't natural to him. It wasn't alone that he was afraid of frightening game—though that was part of it, certainly—but he was at work, he was busy. Everything that he saw he was tucking away; he might need it sometime.

True, he didn't expect to come this way again—not right away, anyhow—but to see and remember was part of his business.

For example: Melissa saw an old blasted pine on the bank of the river. She noticed a brook that made into the river, and alders around it. She enjoyed seeing these things . . . and passed on to the next thing. She could see fifty pines and a dozen of brooks—and not have them take up her mind so that she couldn't talk to her husband. After all, this was her wedding tour. Last night, Whit had been close to her. She couldn't see why, all of a sudden, he wanted to shut her out so completely.

Whit saw the same things—the pine tree, and so on. And if some evening next April a man that he took to were to say to him, "How is it for otter in that part of the country?" Whit would answer him easily, "Well, I come up the river the first week in November, and there was only one place that I see any sign—that is, below Hooksett. There's a little brook there that makes in from the east—lines up with an old blasted pine on the west bank and the top of the mountain. 'Tain't a great ways above Namoskeag Falls. I see a run there, but it looked like an old one. Hadn't been used since the forepart th' summer, I wouldn't say—sticks on it, and so on. I didn't see no other sign of an otter in the whole o' that reach."

Two or three minutes later, Whit began wondering if she thought he'd been short with her. He decided that maybe she might have. "Ten mile from th' tavern, most of them call it, to the falls at th' fishin' place. Where we lay out last night was a short piece above there, 'n we come three mile this mornin'. I ain't a great hand t' cipher, but fourteen is right, ain't it?"

She forgave him. "Fourteen'll do, but I wish it was fifteen. Seems to me ev'ry mile is so much t' th' good."

Whit was distressed. "I was afeard that you mightn't take to it."

"'Take to it'! Whit! I love every minute. I didn't mean the less we got left. I meant the more that we been."

"Oh. Well, we got some ways t' go yet."

"Not too much t' suit me."

"'N 'twon't all be like this."

"Couldn't be any better!"

"It ain't, I c'n tell you. Right along here's th' best part th' river for upstream. You better take comfort while you got th' chance. You settin' easy? You ain't cramped up too much, are you?"

"Not now, I ain't, no. My legs maybe, later."

"Come time t' bate, you c'n get out 'n stretch 'em. You don't want t' stop now, do you?"

"No."

"It's quite a trick t' set still. You never had any practice."

"Not a gre' deal. 'N you know I can't get over it: this time in th' mornin', 'n here I am *settin'*."

He chuckled. "You could knit, I s'pose maybe, 'f you'd be any happier."

"No, I ain't goin' to—'n I couldn't be any happier. I c'n look all around me; I c'n see away off! Everything's new to me, everything's open. The way I feel now don't depend on my legs. I ain't cramped up a mite. Everywhere that I look, it's like I could fly there. You know what I mean?"

"Yes." She was through with the tavern; that was why she felt that way. He had never, himself, felt as though he could fly, but it seemed a reasonable feeling for Melissa to have; it was one that became her.

"I d'know," she said humbly, "bein' shut o' th' tavern, I s'pose, is part of it."

"Be enough, I should think."

"Yes. I c'n remember when it seemed like it would be. I used t' want t' run off. But he'd have sent after me. 'N he'd have made it worse for me when he got me back there. He could do it!"

"Well, he can't send after you this time."

"No, but I wish't he would. You know what I'd say to 'em? I'd tell 'em the truth. 'Who?' I'd say to 'em. 'Who? That old feller's daughter? No, she ain't round here. I'm Whit Livingston's wife.'"

"He won't send after you."

"What good would it do him! That is the truth, Whit. I ain't th' same person."

"Well, you'd ought t' know."

"Certain, I know."

"Whoever you be, I aim t' hang on t' you."

"You ain't got t' hang on t' me! You don't see what I mean. That's who I *am*, Whit. Bein' married t' you is more part o' me now than—well, than an arm or a leg, or that my hair is yellow, or what my face looks like. *Who* I am is what matters. I'm married t' you, that's who I am. Them other things is just things that I brought along with me. They used t' belong t' who I was once.

Now they belong t' who I am now. But they ain't *who* I am. You see what I mean?"

"Maybe. I'm glad you brought 'em along, though. I'm glad you brought your hair. You ain't forgot nothin' that we'd ought t' go back for?—like a hand or a foot or your stummick, or nothin'?"

"There ain't nothin' there that we got t' go back for."

Whit paddled in silence.

"'Nother thing is," she said after a moment, "when you didn't come back—'n one time or another I thought maybe you wouldn't—when I looked ahead, I—I was afeard, Whit—when I looked ahead 'n see next spring a-comin'. Nearer 'n nearer. . ."

"Yes. Well—"

"But I ain't afeard now! I'll be glad when it's May."

"Good."

"You take 'n change a thing round from a thing you're afraid of to a thing you want t' have happen—that you can't hardly wait for—'n it makes quite a difference."

"I should think i' 'twould, yes."

"Settin' here now, I like facin' frontward. I c'n look ahead now. What's near by 'n what's further all looks awful good t' me. Time was, when it didn't—I c'n remember."

"'Tain't a week ago yet."

"Not by days, it ain't, maybe."

"M'lissa, I want t' tell you—'twon't do no good now, but I'd like t' tell you—that if I'd ever have knowed things was goin' t' be with you how they are now as soon as they was, I'd a seen to it that we got married somehow afore I went away. I didn't know it. I'm awful sorry."

"I didn't know either. 'N I ain't a mite sorry. I got 'n idea, while you was away, of what it was worth t' be married t' you."

"Value you set on it may go off somewhat 'fore you get through with it."

"I don't think it."

For perhaps three hundred yards, neither one of them spoke.

Then Whit said, "I didn't tell you. While I was to Jonas's, their agent come by—the agent, I mean, for the Tamworth Proprietors. They own the whole township, the Proprietors do, same as anywhere else—that is to say, a new township that ain't been settled yet. Well, he stopped by at Jonas's while I was laid up, and Dan'l Beede was with him, and Jonas was there, and we agreed on a bargain. I mean the agent and me did. Beede writes a fair hand, and he set her all down. I c'n show you the paper when we get to Sandwich. I left it to Jonas's, hid away safe. He's got a little place under the hearth. You could put a piece of ice in there and then burn down the whole house, and 'twouldn't be melted—or not very much."

"What does it say?—the paper, I mean."

"It don't say only what we did—the agent and me—but it don't sound quite the same, 'n you got to study it out. Still, that is the way with most papers, I guess."

"They're always that way. I've heard 'em read often. What does it say?"

"Well, you see on the day I had looked out the land—the day I hurted my ankle—I had spotted some trees that would do for corners, I thought. I figured the land that they marked would be about one hundred acres. I ain't no surveyor, but I would undertake now that the land that I marked wan't much under a hundred. Someday we will know. And the lines run north and south, same as like in a town. This little flat interval with the brook running through it, that was fairly inside 'em. There was no question on that.

"So I told the agent the corners and how the lines bore, and Beede put it down in the paper. He wrote down the size of it to be 'one hundred acres, more or less,' like they do. But then the agent set up a holler for fear it might be a mile square.

"Well, I says I done enough plowin' t' know what is an acre, and the agent says he didn't doubt that. But he says, 'You take in the woods and an acre looks smaller.' Everyone knows it's the other way round, but I didn't say nothin'. I says, 'I went by paces, I didn't go by my eye.' And he says, 'Well, you don't look to me like a man who would walk in his sleep.' And I says, 'No, sir, not that time.' And he says, 'No, I am sure of it. But still you might have dozed for a spell and not known it, and besides you are kind of long-legged, and we got to put in something or other to limit the size, because if I was to give you more'n half of the town, I would probably get hanged when my people discovered it.' So then Beede spoke up and said he had an idea, and when he'd said what it was, the agent and me agreed to it."

Melissa asked what it was.

"Well, when they come to survey the town into ranges and lots—and Beede most likely'll be the one who will do it—if it should turn out that I've got more than a hundred, then I will give

152

up to them from wherever I choose along the sides of my lot, enough to bring it down to a hundred. If I'm shy of a hundred, they will do the same thing—only they will have the say, then, as to where the addition will be. That seemed to me fair, and so I agreed to it. I can give 'em a piece off the side of the hill."

Melissa inquired, "Did they put all that in the paper?"

"Sart'n they did. Oh, there's a power of writin'! But 'twan't no trouble to Beede to write it at all. Why, he can make a fair letter—like a 'b' or a 't'—in about the same time that I can make a stroke with this paddle"—and after thinking about it for two or three strokes, he said, "any letter you choose."

"What else does it say, Whit?"

"I said I'd clear seven acres inside of three years. I can do that one-handed if Jonas'll help me to burn. It's only felling and burning. He said, 'What about stumps?' and I says, 'Without oxen?' And Beede put in that the stumps could be left."

"What else?"

"I agreed to put up a house, and they agreed to give us a cow."

"A cow!"

"Ayuh. A cow. 'A cow' is what they agreed to. I had almost forgot it, what with everything else, and then Jonas says, 'Hell, ain't you goin' t' make 'em throw in no cow?' and the agent swore some, and Beede laughed at him, and the agent says, 'Where in God's name can I get him a cow?' But Beede wrote down a cow and that was all there was to it. Jonas's rum was gettin' low in the jug, or I doubt that the agent would have agreed to it so easy. Then everyone signed it, and they all had a drink. And then Beede set to it and wrote her all out again—and the agent kep' that one, and they finished the jug. I agreed to pay Beede three shillings for doing the writing, and then him and the agent went home. It was after midnight by that time. It is awful nice writing, clear through to the end."

"Who owns the land now, Whit?"

"What?"

"I mean, do you own it now—or not till after you've cleared it?"

"I own it now," he said. "If I shouldn't clear it or put up the house, why, then they get it back."

"Oh."

"That ain't no more than fair. It's the same way on their side. Governor grants 'em a town, and they say they'll get her settled. If they don't get the town settled, then he can take the town back."

"Suppose they don't settle Tamworth—'n he takes that back from them. What becomes of us then?"

"There don't nothin' become of us. We stay right where we be. They owned her all right, the Proprietors did, when they gave her to us, and so we own it now. All Governor can do is take back the part of the town that ain't been settled yet. When I've cleared seven acres, and built me a house, and lived in it, too, I don't know as I would take kindly to bein' asked to get out. That is the trouble right now over acrost in the Grants. Old Uncle Benning granted the land over there to a whole mess of Proprietors, and they got settlers to settle. Then the Yorkers, their Governor, tried to do the same thing—only he was a little mite late. He knowed he was late, and he knowed there'd be trouble. But there is money, you see, in this granting of land, and so he went right ahead, and right away there was trouble. The Yorkers' settlers come in—they was Yorkers themselves—and they tried to put out the people that was already there. Well, like I say, a man doesn't like that. So they shot at the Yorkers, and the Yorkers shot back, and now there is tarrin' 'n featherin', 'n all that kind of thing. They say it's awful nice land, though. Still, I'd ruther be where I be. Look at that heron, will you? No—along by the shore. He must be after shiners; there ain't any frogs there."

"Ayuh. I see him."

"That's the way it is always, you try to put a man off his land."

"Yes, I suppose it must be."

Melissa was watching the hills in the distance. She saw the dark spire of a pine on the shore—not too far ahead—and how it moved of itself, steadily, smoothly, across the faraway face of the hill in the distance. When the pine tree had done, slipped in and vanished against the same-colored background of a great stand of pine, the hill was still there . . . and more trees had come and were moving across it. If she thought of the trees, then they stood still, and away off in back of them the hill seemed to move forward. But when she thought of it whole, the way it appeared was the trees moving along one after the other . . . and the hill in the distance, quiet, unchanging.

She saw a kingfisher flutter and flash, and two ducks, flying fast, who knew where they were going—and away up in the air, moving ever so slowly, a hawk that belonged there.

Melissa didn't like hawks any better than most people who've had to tend chickens. But here there weren't any chickens. She watched him so long that she had to admire him.

"Flying," she said when she'd watched him long enough so that for a moment it seemed to be true, "looks awful easy."

"'Tis, I guess, for a bird."

She said to him suddenly: "I hear the falls again, Whit."

"That's the ones up ahead."

"Oh."

—and then after a while, "Whit, where d' you figure Joe Felipe went to?"

"I d' know where he did."

"Why d' you s'pose he run off?"

"I couldn't say."

"Two days 'n two nights, nobody seen him. Lawrence Murphy stopped by there 'n dreened his cow for him."

"Well, I ain't goin' t' go look for him. I seen Joe plain enough—there when I had my back to him—so's I don't want t' see him again, even where I c'n see him."

"I was sorry for Joe—in a way, I was—kind of."

"You picked the wrong time for it. I was, once, too—back there in th' summer when you warned me against him. Th' wan't no harm in him then. But this time he was different."

"That was Pa, I think, maybe."

"Maybe 'twas. I d' know as I care much. I ain't goin' t' pine away any if I never see neither one of 'em."

"I don't hate Pa—not this mornin', I don't. Well, no, I won't say that. But with some more mornin's like this one there might come a time when maybe I wouldn't."

"I don't hate him either. If he was t' fall down a well, I s'pose I'd pull him out. But I wouldn't pull awful hearty."

"Who d' you think he c'n get t' do th' work at th' tavern?"

"Prob'ly marry. He ain't goin' t' pay wages."

She didn't answer.

"Y' know, it'd be a terrible thing," Whit proposed dryly, "if he was t' hook on t' somebody, 'n then have it turn out she was able t' handle him. Wouldn't it, now?"

"I guess so." She didn't want to talk of it. "When do we come t' them falls up ahead?"

"The ones you c'n hear? 'Twon't be a great while. After that, there'll be others. There's falls all the way till we come int' th' pond. You know what we're doin'? Same thing as a salmon—in a way, you might say."

"They have a hard time when they come t' the falls."

"So'll we, I guess maybe, but a lot of 'em get there."

Melissa'd talked all she wanted to. But by not talking, she couldn't bring back the silence. The sound of the falls came louder and louder.

2

By late midafternoon, the river had narrowed. When they were close in to one bank or the other, Melissa had to lean her head back to see up to the top where the sunlight still showed on the upper part of the trees. But down in between the walls of the banks it was cold and seemed gloomy. The water was clear, but a dark brown in color, and there were no little waves on it of the kind the wind makes. Instead, it was slick and big bubbles rode by on it. The current was strong. Out in the middle, each rock had a collar round the upstream side of it, and on the downstream side there'd be a kind of hollow and the water trying to tumble back into it. Sometimes, close beside the canoe, she could see down a ways—parts of great boulders and queer, blackened old tree parts. She sat very still, but she didn't sit easy. She couldn't lean back and half close her eyes and just ride along up the river. She wasn't frightened at all, but she had to admit to herself that when they were close in by the bank she liked it better.

Whit was up on his knees and not saying a word. He was working his way up the river, picking and choosing, planning and figuring, taking no chances. He was mainly concerned with getting the most distance upstream that he could in return for his strength. There was almost no danger, because he could see well enough where the current was heavy, and those weren't the places that he wanted anyway. He used the slack water—when he could get it. Now and again, he'd have to cross over at a place that wasn't too good, but he hadn't struck anything yet that he'd have called in any way ticklish even after he'd passed it.

On the whole, he liked the canoe. It handled all right in this kind of water, and so far it was dry. It was light on the carry, as birch canoes go, but it was a delicate thing. It was a better river canoe than it would be on the pond where the wind could get at it, and if he'd been alone he'd have wanted it narrower. But they were doing all right.

As near as he could remember, they had about three-quarters

of a mile from here to the falls—the last part of it, maybe, not so good as this was. What he'd like to do would be to get right up in under the falls—there was a big eddy there that would swing him in easy—and get his carrying over with before it got dark. There was a good place to land there, and a path up the bank that the men used for fishing. He'd lug up a load and Melissa'd go with him, and then she could fix supper while he came back for the rest of it. That way, they'd be ready to make a good start in the morning.

They had come round the inside of a bend on the west bank, and now he'd got to cross over. For some distance ahead it was too fast on this side and there were too many boulders. But along the bank on the far side, it looked pretty good. The river'd built up a beach there, and it would be nice easy going. But he didn't see any place for getting across . . .

There would have been a good place except for an elm tree that had got hung up on a rock out there—sometime this last spring, probably. Well, he'd have to go round it. The downstream side was the only side he could get to, and there wasn't much room between the tree and a place in the water that showed where some rocks were just under the surface. But he guessed he could make it. He didn't see any other way.

When he got out there between the tree and the rocks, he found he didn't have as much room as he'd thought he was going to. He'd figured an elm ought not to have branches sticking out at right angles. But this one had two at least down in under the water—his paddle touched them. They made him feel as though he'd stepped on a snake. But he had to drive forward, branches or no branches: the rocks were too handy for him to ease her through slantwise; there was no room to turn round, and if he'd slackened to stop and try to back out, he'd have been down on the rocks before he could whistle.

He drove her—he had to!

Melissa's small toes curled up in her shoes. She sat leaning forward and her hands gripping the gun'l. She could see the tree and the rocks, and she could feel Whit fighting the current. Along with each stroke, he'd make a sound "uh!" the way a man does when he's chopping.

He paddled wider to swing his bow upstream round the end of the tree . . .

They were through the worst of it . . .

The branches were twigs here, and he could come in close to

them. He got the bow up, and dug in with his paddle. He was heading now almost straight into the current, but because of that "almost" he was easing across it. That was just what he wanted. Half a foot at a time, they were getting on nicely. When he'd got past the tree, they'd be well clear of the rocks, and he could swing to his right again—and in a couple of rods they'd be out of the current.

Melissa misread the state of the struggle. They weren't going forward as fast as they had been . . . they weren't going forward hardly at all. By the twigs of the tree, she measured their progress. A little bit forward—stop—and slip back—then a little more forward . . . oh, they were gaining all right, but so terribly slowly! Whit, by his strength, was lifting them forward. But he was having all he could do with it.

She just had to sit there, part of the weight Whit was trying to lift.

Whit said to himself, "Well, I guess I'm 'bout far enough up now . . ."

Melissa saw close at hand a twig that looked stout enough for her to lay hold on and help pull them along. She reached out her hand for it—

"Stop that!" Whit yelled at her—and he had a time of it to steady the canoe because it had startled her. He couldn't help that, though. If she'd ever got hold of it, there was no telling where they would have been next.

He made up what he'd lost in this little excitement, finished his crossing, and came into a place where the water was easier. Here it was shallow, and he poled with his paddle; they went along famously.

"That danged old elm tree," he said to Melissa, "couldn't picked a worse place. 'Twas narrow in there—seemed so, for a minute. You feel me touch them two branches down in under the water?" He was feeling easy and pleasant, and little proud of himself.

She shook her head.

Whit was arrested. "What's the matter?" he asked.

She was sitting up straight. "Nothin'."

Whit thought back till he came to it. Then he said honestly, "'F you'd a got holt o' that thing 'n been pullin' against it, 'n it had come off in your hand, 'n you'd fell over backward, *then* where'd we a been?"

"I'm sorry."

"I *had* to yell at you."

"Well, you don't have to now."

Whit took his time about answering. "No, that's right, I guess. Well, nothin' happened."

She was still hurt. She had wanted to help.

Whit said, "From here to the falls, we ain't got t' cross over—near as I c'n remember. It's only a little small piece from here till we get to 'em. You can hear 'em good, can't you?"

She certainly could. There was no need to listen. She'd been trying not to.

It wasn't as heavy a sound as the falls at the fishing place that had been with them all night. But it came from above her. The high banks shut them in. Whit, all the time, was going right for the falls; he wouldn't know there was anything fearsome about them.

They came round a wide open bend—the roar opening up—and there was a tossing, white wall. It was some ways ahead. Melissa stared at it. It filled all she could see.

Whit was picking his way from one rock to another, turning and twisting, in and out, thrusting, he was making his way . . .

"How d' you like 'em?" he called to Melissa.

She had shut her eyes for a moment. She nodded her head. When she looked again at the falls she could see what they were. She felt a kind of excitement, as well as just awe.

Out in midstream, the river was jumping about, light-colored, and hurrying. In here by the bank, it was dark and swung slowly.

They were halfway to them, now, from where she'd first seen them. The fascination took hold of her; she forgot everything else . . .

They came closer and closer. She didn't mind it.

She could feel the spray on her face in the terrible noise. The top of the falls was high over her head. Steadily, smoothly, they went in to meet them.

Whit let the canoe drift round with the eddy, saw the place that he wanted, and gently nudged in to it. He took hold of a rock with his paddle, twisting the blade in a crack in the rock. "There now," he muttered. And to Melissa he shouted, "You c'n step out on that little ledge there" . . . but the falls made such a racket he had to holler again to her.

He thought that likely even now in November he could maybe get something out of this eddy that would taste good to her. When he came back for his second load, he might have a try at it.

159

This was the second night that Melissa'd lain out, and she found it not nearly so strange as she had the first night. Whit's presence was between her and all forest dangers— although that didn't mean to her that the dangers weren't there. As for discomforts, Whit took considerable pride in outwitting them for her. Cold was the thing that threatened her most. She confessed it.

Whit was astonished. He said he wished he'd known last night that she minded the cold, he'd have done something about it. He'd fix it tonight, all right.

—and after they'd eaten the trout he'd caught in the eddy, he set to work and spread out the fire over the place that she was to sleep on. He let it burn there awhile, while he picked up around. He picked up everything. When he went so far as to hang up his paddle, Melissa—who felt that this great show of neatness must in some way reflect on her—had to inquire, "What you want t'do that for?"

"So there won't no hedgehogs get at it."

"Hedgehogs? What would a hedgehog do with a paddle?"

"Chew it all up—if he couldn't get nothin' better."

"Oh. Well—wouldn't you hear him?"

"Sooner or later, I prob'ly would."

"Why would a hedgehog chaw on a paddle?"

"Didn't you never get hedgehogs t'your place?"

"I don't remember. Not that et paddles."

"They'll go after anythin's got any salt on it."

"Merrimack River's fresh water, ain't it?"

"Said t'be, yes. But I sweat enough salt water comin' round that old elm tree t'make th' river taste brackish from here down t' Hooksett. This handle's as salty as a piece of beef of your father's—and a little more tender. I don't want t'set round here all day tomorrow tryin' t'carve out a new one. Right here's where they chew 'em, at the base of the handle, 'n a paddle needs all of the wood it's got there. That's where they break when you put too much on 'em—that is, they do if the grain in 'em's right, so that they ain't broken a'ready in some other place. This' a good paddle."

"You got 'nother."

"That's only a spare one. Matthew Patten made this one. He makes a good paddle."

He finished hanging things up. "There, now," he said, coming back to the fire, "I guess that there pan has got your bed about ready"—and he brushed back the fire and ashes from the warmed earth underneath. He felt the earth with the back of his hand. "I guess that's about right. You won't cook, I don't think, but you'd ought not to be cold."

And she wasn't.

"But, Whit, you ain't got nothin' only a blanket!" She had a bearskin and a blanket to boot. "Ain't you goin' t' be cold?"

"No, I don't think it—that is, not t'bother me."

"C'n you sleep when you're cold?"

"Sart'n. Why not? I have often enough. I don't mean *real* cold. But like t'night is all right. My clothes's all dry, 'n I'm out th' wind, 'n I got a blanket. I guess I c'n sleep!"

After a while, Melissa did, too—better than last night.

The next day was lowery, but no rain or snow, and they got along pretty well. With an early start in the morning and no fire at noon, they made more in distance than they had the first day. Whit was hurrying now. He wanted to get above Garven's Falls, south of Pennacook—and maybe Turkey Falls, too, if he could— with still enough time left before it got dark so as to pick out a good place to lay out if a storm came. He pushed right along.

Melissa never had learned to eat salt pork without cooking it, so she didn't get as much dinner that noon as she might have. She said that didn't matter because she wasn't working. Whit agreed with her . . . but when she laughed at him, he saw the joke, finally—near enough, anyhow.

It was around two o'clock when they passed Soucook River, and a mile farther on was the pitch they called Garven's. Whit carried around it without any trouble, and put in again for another mile up to Turkey Falls. And when he'd got above there, he had still an hour of daylight, even though it was cloudy. He thought he'd done well.

He said, "Now, I tell you what we c'n do. I ain't so sure but what it may rain t'night. What d'you think?"

Melissa knew very well it was going to rain. "Well, I d'know—looks's though it might, maybe."

"Or it might snow a little. Now if you want to, we c'n go on

161

a piece fu'ther—'bout a mile 'n a half, I should say it was, prob'ly—'n there Butter's tavern's right close t' th' river. 'F you don't wan't t' lay out in the rain, you might ruther lay there."

"Butter's tavern's t' Pennycook!"

"Yes, we're handy t' Pennycook. Th' road down t'Derry is right up in there." He pointed toward it. "That's th' way we'd have come if I'd had any money."

All her life, she had longed to see Pennacook. That wasn't the way that she felt about Portsmouth. She'd made up for herself a picture of Portsmouth, putting in only the things that she liked: gentlemen, ladies, Joe Felipe's ships, carriages, horses, and Governor John. She didn't much mind if she never saw Portsmouth. She knew it wouldn't come up to the picture, and once she'd seen the real thing she'd have to put it aside whenever she wanted to think of the picture. But Pennacook, now, that was nearer to home. It was bigger than Kettleford, but still enough like it so that she'd tried to imagine it as it really would be. Osgood's tavern was better than Butter's. And McMillan's store—well, she'd often thought of herself walking into McMillan's and buying some buttons and, say, two yards of fustian, and seeing someone buy silk. They kept silk at McMillan's.

If she lay at Butter's, that would be a beginning—that would be part of it. And she'd be a guest, too, and be called Mistress Livingston—and it might come about, if there weren't other guests, that she and Whit would have the same room.

She stood a long time and looked toward the place where the road was—

"All right," said Whit, "I guess that's what you'd better do, then."

"But—but how about you, Whit?"

"I'd like to," he said to her earnestly. "I'd like to put up at Osgood's. I'd like to walk in there and have all of them see you." He stood by the canoe and leaned on his paddle. "And I know it hurts you to know that we can't. Comes down to that, I s'pose we could do it. I got enough money—"

"Come on, Whit! Let's do it!"

"You want to bad, don't you?"

"Well—"

"So do I." He looked down at the ground, and then he looked up at her. "But here's how it is: this money I got is what Mr. Gowan give to me. Half this stuff I been luggin' is stuff that was

162

gave us. And the bulk of the rest of it is stuff that I owe for. I think of that part of it whenever I pick it up. I d'know as I'd want to go 'n lay out the money—proud as I am of you—to show you off in a tavern. That's what it comes down to—my part of it, anyhow. Your part of it's different. I'll spend it for you."

"But—but I—but I can't go alone!"

"I'll go up there with you—to Butter's or Osgood's—see how things are, 'n then I'll come back here. You'd be all right."

She turned away then to hide her face from him.

Whit felt like a fool.

Finally Melissa said, "Can I see Pennycook as we go by on the river?"

"No," he said truthfully. The river swung out around it—like the two curves of a B. The houses of Pennacook were on the straight side of the letter.

Melissa said suddenly, "All right, then, that's that. We goin' t' lay here? I'll make up a fire."

Whit went to work to do the things that were necessary.

It rained in the night, but underneath the canoe Melissa kept dry. She cried a little—not very long—and only when she was certain that Whit was asleep. And she made up her mind that one way or another she was going to see Pennacook. It wouldn't cost any money for her to walk through the town, would it?

Whit said after breakfast, "If you want to, M'lissa, why don't you walk from Butter's up through th' town, while I'm goin' round it? It's 'bout a mile 'n a half to walk through the town— less 'n that, it might be—'n it's a good five or six mile t' go by th' river. You could walk slow as you'd 'mind to. I'd pick you up on the north end th' town—above where there's a brook they call Wattanummun's comes in t' th' river. The rain has let up and it may be goin' t' clear. You could stretch your legs, anyhow."

"Show me how the road runs."

He drew her a map of it. "This here is th' road runs t' Suncook 'n Haverhill, where it crosses th' river, 'n right here is the ferry, 'n right there's Butter's tavern—all the same place. Here's the Derry road here, comes up this way, y'see. They join here t' gether. You c'n go ashore there. Then all you do is walk north. Here's th' Hopkinton road. On th' far side o' that is where McMillan's store is. You go right on by there, past the old garrison, 'n here's th' road runs t' Canterbury—goes past a pond there that's got pick'rel in it. When you come t' th' river, you bide there 'n wait for me."

"All right. I wish't you'd come with me . . ."

"I think I better keep goin'. Come t' half a day, prob'ly, 'f I went along with you. You don't mind goin' alone?—dogs, or what not?"

"No . . ." It suited her thoroughly.

She stepped ashore at the ferry, waved to her husband, and went up the steep, sandy bank of the road from the river.

Butter's tavern, she thought, examining it critically, was about what she'd expected: twice as big as her father's, but somehow not brave; she didn't propose to admire it. A dog came out and barked at her, and she turned up her nose.

She kept on up the road and saw—as Whit said—that the Derry road joined it. There at the junction she stood for a moment and looked down the road in the direction of Kettleford . . . Then she turned very suddenly, and started up the long hill that led into Pennacook.

There weren't many houses. She passed three log houses; they were old and uncared for, half the bark off the logs and the roofs curling badly.

But near the top of the hill, there was a fine-looking house!—two stories, an attic, and big, handsome glass windows. She wondered whose that was—if it were someone she'd heard about.

Going down the other side of the hill—which wasn't as steep as it had been coming up—she came on Osgood's—with a big sign out in front of it, and smoke from three chimneys. Now, that was a tavern! She knew Whit had seen it, but she wished he was with her. She wanted him with her while she was seeing it. And she could understand now that maybe Whit had been right: this was more of a place than she'd really bargained for. When she put up at Osgood's, she was going to ride up on horseback. Still, her curiosity was strong to see what the inside of it looked like . . . new sand every morning, she hadn't a doubt, everything shiny, and probably a crane as big as the tongue of an oxcart! She hadn't so much as a sixpence to go in and buy something. Nor was there a thing she could think of to ask for that she could be certain that they wouldn't have.

She knew now she was going in, some way or other.

—and she mustn't stand here or someone would see her.

She started up to the door without any plan—and then the door opened and a tall man, middle-aged, came out and stood on the doorstep. He glanced up at the sky, and then turned up the collar of his full-skirted green coat. He looked down at Melissa, and was not taken aback to see she was a stranger—as he certainly would have been if this had been Kettleford! He opened the door for her—and she had to go in.

But then the door closed behind her, and she was alone.

This wasn't a room, it was a kind of hallway; the stairs were in front of her, and a closed door on each hand. She stood there a moment, but nobody came . . .

She wished she hadn't come in, but she couldn't go out, because someone might catch her just as she was leaving.

She heard footsteps upstairs, and this helped her somehow to step up and knock at the door on her right.

A man said, "Somebody knockin'"—and another voice answered, "I heard 'em, I heard 'em. Come in, sir! Come in."

Melissa squeezed on the latch, and went in unhappily.

This wasn't the kitchen—she didn't know what it was. Beside a small fire, there was a man at a table, and behind a high counter another man in an apron.

The man in the apron spread his hands on the counter and as a matter of duty wished her good morning.

The man at the table sat there and stared at her, his hat on the back of his head and a quart measure before him. He was having his breakfast. He looked to Melissa as though he might be a horse jockey.

"I came in to ask," Melissa explained to the man at the counter—while the man at the table continued to stare at her, "if you have a letter."

At a sound from the corner away from the fire, she saw in the gloom there a man asleep at a table; his face was turned toward her, but his arm lay across it. The talking hadn't disturbed him, nor was it likely to.

The man in the apron took no notice whatever of her having seen this. "A letter. Well, now, it might be, ma'am. I wouldn't want t' say, really—less'n you'd want t' tell me for who it would be?" He spoke not unpleasantly.

"Mistress Livingston."

"No, ma'am." That was all there was to it; she had asked, and he'd answered.

Melissa said, "Thank you," and turned to go out.

He relented. "From where would it be, ma'am?"—amends in his voice.

"From Kettleford, likely."

"No, there's now't here from Kettleford."

"There's that in the corner," said the man at the table.

If she'd been more at ease, she'd have paid no attention. But she turned and looked first at the man who had spoken—and then from him quickly to the man at the counter, who shook his head kindly:

"There's no letter from Kettleford. What he means is, this here"—indicating the customer asleep in the corner—"is a Kettleford man."

Naturally, Melissa looked to see who it was . . .

She saw who it was . . . as the head was turned heavily and the red hair ribbon showed.

She had her back to the horse jockey then, but the man at the counter could see her face plainly. He said nothing at all. It seemed to him better not to.

Finally the girl simply turned and went out—left the door open—and the man at the counter saw through the window that she went toward the town. After a bit, he said to the horse jockey: "I know who that was—"

"This's fine time to say so."

"Yes, sir. I'm sure of it. Her old man's name is Butler—keeps tavern t' Kettleford. That's who she is. Yes, sir, that's her all right."

"'Livingston,' she said."

"Maybe it is."

"Well, I ain't goin' t' go after her. She's got a man somewhere round in the bushes. She ain't alone."

"'Twouldn't do you no good not if she was alone."

"No?"

"No. She ain't th' kind that you want."

"I d'want any kind. Not this morning, I don't." He drank at some length. "How'd you know she was from Kettleford?"

"She know'd this over here, all right, soon as she looked at him."

"Oh. You know, Charlie, you know what I think? You'd ought t' get rid o' him. Havin' him here puts me off'n my breakfast."

"He's payin'."

"He ain't payin' me nothin'."

"Whyn't you eat in th' kitchen?"

"Stinks o' food too much in there. Rum is f' breakfast—for an honest man, anyhow. Food is for dinner—or better yet supper." He broke out again: "Three days he's been there—right there in that corner! He don't never say nothin', not even at night! I tell you, Charlie, you want t' get rid of him—'fore he blows up on you. That ain't good for a man—settin' there starin', drinkin' brandy the whole time. All of a sudden, he's goin' t' blow up on you. He's a big man. You'll have trouble t' hold him."

"Don't be afeard. I won't ask you t' help me."

"Well, I hope he don't do it while I'm havin' breakfast." Joe stirred in his sleep.

The horse jockey rose. "I'm goin' out t' the stable 'n see t'them nags."

The man at the counter turned his back on him. "Well, don't get too close to 'em; they might one of 'em bite you."

Melissa walked toward the town. That was the way Whit had told her to go—and he'd said that he'd meet her when she came to the river.

She had no interest in seeing the town.

Off to her right, a lane seemed to lead toward the river. It came to her vaguely that she might go that way and perhaps meet Whit sooner—but it seemed too much trouble to try to figure out whether that was really the case or not.

She passed a fine house and, a hundred yards farther, another fine house. She saw what they were—but there was no response in her.

She found she was looking in the door of a smithy as she walked slowly past it. It was a proper big smithy, too, well found and handsome. It was much more of a smithy than Joe's little place.

Why had Joe come here?

That was a tanyard there in the hollow—and this was a steep little hill she was climbing. And that one-story house that set up on the top of it looked like a good house. All this was Pennacook. She always had wanted to see what Pennacook looked like. And these things she was looking at—these things were Pennacook.

But what she was seeing was Joe, drunk and asleep, his head down on the table.

The Hopkinton road came in from the westward. That was where, she remembered, Whit had said it would be, and that on the corner was McMillan's store. Some time ago she had thought she'd go in there—she had wanted to, anyhow—to see some of the things that they had out for sale.

She kept on walking. It seemed a long way. This was a wide road that ran through the middle of Pennacook town. Men had said it was wide. Well, it was.

Then there came a long break with no houses at all. She guessed she'd seen all of Pennacook, maybe.

Why was Joe here?

That must be the garrison around Mr. Walker's. Twice as high as her head, the top of it was. . . . No, maybe not quite that, but still pretty high. Here and there on the top they'd pulled off some of the logs—squared logs, they were—big ones; squared almost to beams. They'd probably used them for building somewhere. But the watchtower, now—it looked like a well house on top of a fence—that was still there. All this had been built at the time of the Indians. That was before she was born. Nobody, now, saw any need for protection. Nobody knew there was aught left to hide from. Pretty soon, now, they'd be pulling this down—using the logs for one thing and another. Then there'd not be a place anywhere—anywhere!—built strong and a-purpose for a body to run to and have safety inside it.

Joe couldn't break through a wall built like that one.

But Joe could get over it . . . and find where she was hiding.

Joe was back there in the tavern—drunk and asleep. Or by now it might be that Joe had waked up.

She began hurrying—

Whit heard her call to him a half mile down the river from where he'd told her to wait for him. She was all wet and muddy clear up to her knees. As he swung in to the bank, he called out to her cheerfully, "What in tarnation you been doin', anyhow?"

Melissa was laughing as she climbed into the canoe—but then that changed to crying.

Whit rested right there. "What happened, M'lissa?"

"Nothin'. I waited so long—'n you didn't come—so I started downstream t' see if I'd meet you. I got kind o' upset, I guess, scramblin' along, 'n fallin' down, 'n like that—What you waitin' for now?"

"I come just as soon as I told you I would."

"I know it! I know it! Go on. Don't wait here!"

"Tell me what happened."

After a moment, Melissa said, "Joe's there."

Whit waited still longer before he spoke than she had. "What did he say to you?"

"He didn't say nothin'. He was drunk and asleep."

"Where was this?"

She told him.

Whit took his time and thought it all over. Finally he picked up his paddle.

"Where you goin'?" she asked.

"I'm goin' t' Sandwich."

"Oh."

"You better take off your stockin's, 'n let 'em dry out."

"They ain't very wet."

"You do as I tell you."

That made her feel better. After a while, she took off her stockings.

4

During that day, they got past Sewall's Falls, ate dinner there, and pushed on upstream past Contoocook River. They lay that night at the mouth of Mill Brook.

It turned cold in the night, and Whit went down to look at the river. In the cold and the darkness, he knelt on a rock where the current was dead and swished his hand gently around in the water—feeling the tiny, loose ice bits not yet caught together. This was the very beginning of freezing. Standing water in pools would be frozen by morning thick enough, likely, to bounce a small pebble. Well, it had come.

He went back up the bank, and put some wood on the fire. Melissa was sleeping. He picked up his blanket, and wrapped it around him; then he squatted down by the fire, with a little stick in his hands, to think what to do.

They'd be all right today. It couldn't freeze fast enough in this part of the river to cause any trouble until maybe tomorrow. All right. By tonight, if everything went well, they'd be to the Forks. (He knew when he said this it would take quite a day to get to the Forks, but he'd say they would, anyway.) When he got to the Forks, he'd have to make up his mind. There'd be three things he could do then—three ways he could go—and he liked only one of them: he wanted to stick to the way that he'd planned. It was surely the best way, except for the ice . . . Well, it turned on the weather—like everything else. First thing to do was to get to the Forks.

He guessed he'd better sleep.

And he lay down and slept.

There was just a skimming of ice by the bank in the morning—and then only in places—and it had stopped freezing. Whit ate a good breakfast of corn meal and pork—he was going to need it; and they were out on the river before daylight was full.

When the sun did come up, the sky in the east was heavy enough so that it made the sun appear small, and a man could look at it long enough to count five and not have it bother him. There was no wind at all. It was a poor sort of day that might mean almost anything.

Whit set his mind on the Forks, folded his hat and put it under his knees, and got down to business.

He pushed it all day without any letup, eating some corn and a swallow of water when opportunity offered.

The day didn't change much, although it began to seem likely that the wind would go into the north and from there to northwesterly. That was the last place he wanted it from.

Eight hours of trying to go a little bit faster put a pain in his shoulders that bit into him badly; he grinned to himself at the thought that he couldn't tell whether the sweat on his forehead came from the pain or from the way he was working.

They made the Forks, though, with a half hour of daylight.

Whit was asleep before it was dark.

Five times in the night, Melissa got up and put wood on the fire. Whit never stirred. She told herself she was glad that he didn't. But he was so deeply asleep that he seemed far away from her. Still, she was more used to the night noises now, and was not tempted to waken him even by accident. A wolf or a painter might have tested her some, or a scream from a rabbit; but little cracklings and rustlings and the stirring of branches, a splash in the river, or the loud squeak of a dry limb as it rubbed on another, she didn't find troublesome.

It was getting cold, though; all the night through she could feel the cold coming, silent and sharp with the winter behind it. She wanted to put her blanket on Whit, but she didn't dare to— he'd only wake up and make her take it back.

She lay there awake and wished for the morning, and thought

170

some of Joe, and looked forward to Sandwich, and thought of her baby and how it would smile at her, lying there in its cradle in the sun of the summer.

She was asleep when Whit, wakened by hunger, stiffened by cold and by sleeping so long, threw off his blanket and bent over the fire, holding his hands to it. He could tell from the fire that Melissa'd put wood on it several times in the night. He hadn't heard her—he hadn't heard anything. He still had some of the feeling that he hadn't been asleep long. But he knew well enough it was close on to morning. And he strode out from the fire to look up at the sky . . .

Every star out—as clear as could be! And the wind easy and confident out of the north.

It was an hour to morning; he went back to the fire.

Melissa looked comfortable; he guessed she was warm enough.

Chewing some corn, he laid out before him the three things he could do: he could take the east branch and try Winnipiseogee, because the pond wouldn't freeze; or he could stick to the west branch—where he'd surely get ice—clear up to Casumpy and round that to Sandwich. Or they could try it on foot.

This last was the safest, and five times the work. Because he'd have to make two or three trips of it, anyway. Winnipiseogee, he didn't like. This canoe wasn't built for one man to handle out on a lake half the size of the ocean, with a good, heavy wind and snow into the bargain. Overset on the river, and a man stood a chance; out there on the lake—well, he wouldn't like it. No, that wasn't the best way.

As for the west branch, from the look of the weather, the slack water'd be frozen. It would be awful mean work. And if he had to stop two or three times to patch the canoe, there was no telling how long it might take.

On foot, from here, it must be thirty mile—between thirty and forty. He could do that in a day; that wasn't anything. The thing was, Melissa—not in a day, but in two or three days? Yes, he thought she could do it. Snow would be hard for her, but they'd take it easy. And when he'd got her to Sandwich, he'd come back here for his things. Yes, he guessed that was the best way. Though it hurt him a little to give up the river; he'd fought it so long, he'd like to have beaten it . . .

He made up some breakfast, and got everything ready, and then wakened Melissa.

After she'd eaten, he said to her soberly, "I want to look at your feet."

Melissa said, "What?"

"I want to look at your feet."

"You ain't touched, are you?" She thrust out her feet in stockings and moccasins. "Didn't seem to me yesterday we had any sun—although you did go bareheaded. All right: look at 'em."

"I want t' see what the soles of 'em look like."

"There they are; look at 'em."

"I mean of your feet."

"Whit, what's the matter? Are you—"

"Matter is, that it's freezin'. It froze in the night." "Well, my feet didn't freeze."

"Tell me: when in the fall did you leave off goin' barefoot?"

"Early. September."

"Then we'll stick to the river." He stood up to get ready.

Almost in earnest, Melissa inquired, "You feel all right, do you?"

"Little mite stiff from yesterday, maybe. That'll work off in an hour or two."

"But—"

"All right, I'll tell you." He came and knelt down by her. He explained where they were, and what they were up against. "I don't like the ice much, nor I don't like a big pond. The woods, I'm all right in. I'd figured that now with the ice on the river, maybe we'd better go through the woods. But I hadn't figured your feet'd be soft."

"I can walk all right, Whit!"

"Them moccasins you got wouldn't last half a day on anything hard. We won't get any crust, perhaps, this time o' year that would cut 'em. But the ground 'll be froze. If we was t' get a light fall o' snow, you'd be worse off than ever—treadin' on sticks that you didn't see, 'n slippin' all over. No, sir. We'll go by the river."

She said again, "I can walk all right, Whit!"

"By the time you got to Sandwich, you'd be leavin' more blood every place that you stepped than a deer does that's done for."

"I don't think so."

"I know you would. Why, we'd have every wolf between Kyar Saga Mount'in 'n Huckl'bry Hill after us."

172

"Think o' the bounty!"

"When I go after wolf bounty, I'll use some other bait. No, sir, we'll go by the river, ice or no ice. If the canoe gets slit open, I guess I can patch it, but it'd take an awful good cordwainer t' make you shoes out of birchbark."

"But s'pose'n it sinks, Whit."

"Then I'll haul you out on the bank. 'Twon't be near such a haul as 'twould be t' lug you th' last half th' way from here into Sandwich." He put his hand on her shoulder. "We'll be all right."

"I ain't helpin' you much."

"You're helpin' me this much: that if you hadn't come, I wouldn't a started—'n I don't mean only this trip: I wouldn't never got nowheres."

"You'd a got somewheres. All right, then: the river."

5

She found the river much smaller, and no longer so threatening. She could, when she tried, begin to see the water as Whit saw it—at any rate, as Whit saw it when he was making his plans. Whit thought of the water as something to use: it took from his back the weight of the load. A man can drag on a sled a much bigger load than he ever could carry; the same way with a horse, and still more so an ox. With the water to rest it on, Whit could move his whole load. But when they came to a carry, he could only take up a third of it—less than a third, if you counted Melissa. When they were afloat, it was the water that carried it; all Whit did was push it.

Where the river'd been bigger, it had been too big to see this. It had been so big there that the river itself had filled all of her seeing: it was a mighty thing, powerful, to be overcome.

But here it was useful. The water from Contoocook, Bow Cook, and Suncook, all of the water from Winnipiseogee, Soucook, Black Water River, Mill Brook, Turkey River, all that was behind them. What was left was less mighty, less something to fear; what was left was some water to float a canoe on.

Melissa enjoyed it that day.

In midafternoon, Whit came in to the bank. There was white water ahead. On big rocks close at hand—on the shady side of each rock—Melissa could see where splashed water was freezing.

173

"This here's what they call the Five Mile Carry Place. I don't know as it's quite that, but it's pretty close to it."

"Five mile?" said Melissa. "You can't do that before dark." She meant take everything over—three trips going over and two coming back.

"I ain't goin' t' try." And he pointed out to her, "Right there's a good place—" for her to step out on.

She was pleased; they'd have two or three hours before it got dark. She could make up a good supper, and they'd fix a fine place to sleep. It was a nice place right here . . . a high, level place at the top of the bank, with dry wood to burn, and fir trees and spruces—she could even see beeches. It was a beautiful place.

Whit got everything up, and he brought the canoe up.

"What I think that I'll do," he said, thinking about it, "is t' take the canoe over, 'n leave th' rest of it here. You c'n stay here 'n see t' th' fire 'n so on, 'n make up some supper—'n I'd ought t' be back before it gets dark."

It was plain to Melissa that it hadn't even occurred to him that she wouldn't like being left alone that way.

"All right." Well—it wasn't for long. She knew she was going to be frightened, but she couldn't tell how much.

Whit swung the canoe up onto his shoulders and settled it there. He had to get it just right—he didn't use any yoke, just the two paddles. "If anything happens that I don't come right back, don't you try to come after me, not until morning. I don't expect that anything will, but I s'pose I could turn this ankle, or something like that. The road's pretty well spotted the whole way across, but you'd get mixed up if you was t' try it at night. I would, for that matter. Well—I'll back pretty soon. You ain't afeard to stay alone, are you?"

"No."

"There ain't nothin' c'n hurt you." He set off into the woods, slowly and carefully, mindful as always that a birch canoe, carried, is in a good deal more danger of getting a hole in it than it is in the water.

Melissa kept busy, but it didn't dispose of her sense of being alone, it didn't do anything to lessen the fact that the distance between Whit and herself, minute by minute, kept getting greater and greater; nor did it provide an escape from the knowledge that when it grew dark he might not come back at all.

The night then began to come toward her.

And before its advance, all she could do was fumble and putter and try to keep busy, try not to look with the eyes of her mind at the darkness approaching, filtering now through the woods to the eastward, closer and closer.

She'd been down to the river for a bucket of water, and now she gathered some wood . . . but her fingers were clumsy as she laid splinters on tow, put on a small pinch of powder, and using Whit's gun got a fire to going.

The fire did help. It gave her something to talk to.

She gathered more wood—taking what there was handy. Fifty feet from the fire was all she could go. She took little pieces, and she even gathered dead twigs. She piled them up carefully close to the fire. They made quite a pile. She admired that pile. She'd have no need now to go away from the fire.

With water and meal and a small lump of grease, she kneaded some cakes, and set them to cook on a stone by the fire. The sun was low now on the other side of the river; it was dropping faster and faster.

She tried to think of some single thing that she feared. Then she could think of some reason, perhaps, for not being afraid of it. A bear, now—or a painter . . . no, they didn't matter. Some wandering Indian that had been overlooked, and who would see his chance now to do some of the things that she'd heard people tell about. . . . But she lost interest in Indians.

It would be night pretty soon.

When it was night, she'd know Whit wasn't coming.

She took up the gun so she could study it while there was yet light enough . . . but she didn't quite want to load it, and she put it aside.

It made her jump so when a pine cone fell near her that she had to admit—when she had hold of herself—that if she was as bad off as that now, there was no telling what the night would do to her.

She got up and went to the edge of the bank and looked up and down the river where it was open and she could see it was empty. But she was too soon aware of the woods at her back. She came again to the fire, and tried to warm her cold hands at it. The cakes were past done, but she didn't move them.

This was the Carry Place. Whit knew it well. Anyone used it who traveled the river, downstream or up—

That brought her to Joe. But she wasn't frightened at thinking of Joe. He'd surely be sober if he'd traveled all day. She could

175

handle Joe, all right. If Whit weren't to come, she'd rather have Joe there to keep the night away from her—than to have the night close in around her while she was alone. Yes, she'd been afraid of Joe yesterday—but now she was afraid of the night. Maybe it was: that she had all this fear in her, and one day it would be one thing that she'd pitch it onto—like Joe, you see, yesterday—and another time something else. When she was little, she'd been afraid of her father; other times, of the men at the tavern. Only a week ago, before Whit had come back, she'd been afraid of the time when her baby would come. Then that had gone—in the instant she'd seen Whit coming up through the meadow. This would go, too—this being afraid of the night. In the very first instant that she knew Whit was back, it would all disappear.

She looked into the woods. Beyond the short reach of the fire, it was black in the woods. She put some more wood on the fire to make it reach farther, to make it push back the darkness farther away from her. But the new wood didn't catch.

Something had happened to him. . . . He was late; that was true now. He was late—it was dark in the woods. Something had happened.

She began thinking of what it could be. She thought of just the same things that she'd thought of for a month back in Kettleford. She remembered them all, they came to her clearly—just the same things.

These were all of them pictures that she'd looked at before. It all seemed so familiar. There was no sharp terror in it . . . .

"This," she thought to herself, "is just like it used to be. It ain't any different. It's just the same thing. I guess I can stand it—I stood it before. . . ." She huddled there by the fire.

Whit called to her out of the woods.

She was all right by the time she'd stood up.

"Brought you a present," he said, "reason I'm late." He held up a rabbit. "Ain't he a nice one?"

"You want him tonight?"

"I don't know—it don't matter. On the way over, I set down for a spell, and while I was settin' there, I see what looked to me like it might be a good place—there was a little tree handy, just about a nice size—'n I says, 'There, now,' I says, 'why don't I do that?' So I rigged me a snare, 'n I thought maybe tomorrow there might be somethin' in it. And then as I come along back, there was this feller in it! He's a good fat one, too, ain't he? You been all right, have you?"

Melissa said yes, that she'd been all right.

"Joe didn't come chasin' you?"

"No," she said cheerfully.

Most of the morning was spent on the carry. Melissa went with him the first trip across, and waited there for him while he made the second trip.

His snare was still set the last time he passed it, and he untied the noose and brought the line along with him. Melissa was cooking the rabbit for dinner.

She told him, when he got there, that she'd been asleep for a while in a place out of the wind where the sun could get at her. Whit said that was fine; he noticed the rabbit was done, though. And Melissa said yes, she hoped he'd never catch her taking a nap at the expense of her cooking.

She didn't tell him that her father had—once.

After they'd eaten, they tackled the river. There was plenty of ice in the pools where the water was slow, and Whit, forced to keep clear of it, found it hard going. They kept at it steady until close on to dark.

When Whit stepped ashore—on a beach made of stones, near the mouth of a stream—he stood up and stretched himself.

Melissa said nothing; what she wanted to say was that he looked so tired that when he stretched his arms she could hear him creak, almost.

Then Whit looked down the river—and a good deal of the weariness went out of his face. He smiled as though something pleased him, and nodded his head. Then he turned his back to Melissa. In respect and affection, he called the river a name. It was between him and the river.

He said to Melissa, "If you ain't seen enough of Merrimack River, you better take a look now."

He shared that look with her.

"What we got tomorrow," he explained with some pride, "is only Squam Brook. That's it over there. Then we put in to Casumpy and go round the shore of it, and then we're t' Sandwich."

"How many days?"

"Depends on the weather."

She looked again at the river. "You done awful well, Whit."

"We done all right, yes. We had pretty good luck."

177

"I hope it holds."

"I hope it does, too. I see signs today both ways. You can't ever tell. Well—that part of it's done with." He turned away from the river—toward the canoe, to take the things out of it. "There's a place to lay out just up above here. 'Tain't an awful good place. But I ain't goin' no further to look out another."

Melissa'd not moved; she still gazed down the river. "No," she said finally, "I guess you can't ever tell."

6

Squam Brook was much smaller than even that narrowing part of Merrimack River on which they'd been for the last day or so. Melissa was freed of any feeling of danger. With that out of the way, all the other conditions lifted her spirits. They seemed to get ahead faster. She said so to Whit.

"I know. But we ain't." He pointed out accurately, "Reason it seems so, is you can't see ahead so far."

Even this didn't spoil it.

If everything went well, this was likely their last day of fighting upstream against the tireless current. She'd felt that current as much as Whit had. But they'd break loose from it tomorrow—they'd be out on the pond then—the current wouldn't be under them, holding them back. That was something to think about!

Moreover, today, she had some variety. Twice in the morning, Whit put her ashore and she made her way slowly along by the bank while Whit hauled the canoe upstream with a line. It was a long loop of line, made fast bow and stern, and under certain conditions he could control the canoe pretty well with it. It was hard scrambling for him, though, in and out of the water. He found it tired his legs. Still, it was faster than it would have been if he'd carried. And one thing it did do, that he was grateful for later: it made him tie all the baggage fast to the canoe and put grease round the plug and the cap of his powder horn.

Late in the morning, and with Melissa in place, he was poling along and just ahead was an island. He could see the far end of it; it was about a hundred yards long. So the right of the island looked to him the best way; the water was deep there—out to the left, it was all shallow riffles. Whit swung in to the run, and had to give up his pole; he couldn't touch bottom.

It was a narrow, dark place, overgrown on the left bank with alder and maple, while the bank on his right rose as high as two houses and with an overhang at the top. The spruces and hemlocks close to the edge showed their roots sticking through where the soil had fallen away from under the overhang. Two rods was as wide as the stream was in some places. The water was black, and moved swiftly and smoothly. But it had no ice in it.

About halfway through, Whit found his way blocked. A big hemlock had fallen from the top of the high bank, its butt with the roots on had slid down and jammed, and the top of the tree was well over onto the island. Upstream of the tree there was a whole mass of dead stuff that had been piling up there for a year and a half. There was no use at all trying to cut a way through it.

"Ain't that a mess," he said to Melissa.

All he could do was turn round and go back—there'd be enough water for him to drag the canoe up the other side of the island.

He let the bow come around . . . and for the first time in a week felt what it was to be carried along by the current. He grinned almost sheepishly, knowing this pleasure was a thing he'd have to pay for going up on the other side of the island; for every foot that he coasted, he'd have to haul the sled up again. But he didn't care, it was pretty near worth it—just to feel it again, and to have her see, for a moment, what downstream was like.

With a touch of the paddle he sidled over a bit toward the high bank where the water was faster. They were winging along.

Then he turned sick as he felt the bow sliding up on a log that was under the water.

He put all he had into a try to back water, his fingers spread on the blade. It didn't do any good. He felt the canoe bottom rip as it caught on a stub. The bow was raised up a foot, the stern swung to the right, the canoe heeled to the left, Melissa grabbed for the high side—and over they went.

Whit made a lunge for her—and missed, as he went into the water. He'd seen her let go the canoe. And when he came up, she was nowhere in sight. He figured that maybe she was caught under the log and he tried for her there. But he didn't see her or feel her. The current sucked him right under the log-and he came up on the downstream side of the log—still holding onto it, but it was a slippery hold. He raised up his head—and twenty feet downstream, he saw Melissa come up. He struck out to reach her. She looked as though she was struggling, and he hollered "All right!"

She was swept in to the bank—and safe from drowning, at least—before he got to her. He stood up in the water at the foot of the bank, but Melissa couldn't stand up. She was coughing and weak, and there was blood on her face where she'd got a cut on her cheek. She didn't appear to know Whit was there.

He looked up the steep bank—and knew he'd got to make it. He took her under his arm and, somehow or other, scrambling and slipping, digging in with his fingers, he got her up to the top, pushed her up over the overhang, and hauled himself up. If he'd been alone, he didn't believe he'd have made it.

He laid her down on her stomach, and let her be sick. She came around. Inside of five minutes, she was able to stand. And then to walk around some. She said she was all right. And Whit told her sure she was. The cut on her cheek didn't amount to a thing—she didn't know yet she had it.

What he had to do was to get a fire to going.

He asked Melissa if she could keep moving if he left her alone to go try for his gun.

She nodded her head.

"You got to," he said. "Don't you sit down. You understand, do you?" Even to look at her made him feel sick himself—her head drooping forward, and her face of no color, and the blood on her cheek. Her hair was matted down over her eyes; she put up her hand slowly to push it aside, and when her hand came away, she saw the blood on it. She looked at it dumbly—

"That ain't nothin'," said Whit, "that ain't goin' to hurt you. Now you keep movin' until I come back. I done this to you, and I'll get you out of it." He hoped he would, anyhow.

He walked to the edge of the bank and looked for the canoe— as well as he could with Melissa still in front of his eyes. First he looked downstream—but he didn't see it; then upstream—there it was: upside down, and stuck under the log, one end of it showing. He ran along the edge of the bank until he was right up above the canoe, and then he stepped off—and slid all the way down on his heels.

His knife had stayed with him. He put that in his mouth, and moved into the water. He felt the cold this time. In two steps he was in up to his hips—and the current pressing him hard against the slippery log. He hung over the log like a man on a yardarm and moved out toward the canoe.

It was the stern that was up out of the water—it probably had air in it that was holding it up.

He wanted the line first. He found that with his feet, got it into his hands, and took a turn round the log with it and made it secure. Then with one arm over the line, he went down underneath, located his powderhorn, cut it loose, and came up with it—his lungs bursting, and dizzy. If it hadn't been for the current, it would have been fairly simple; the cold he could stand for a little while longer. But the current was trying to drag him loose every instant and take him off downstream.

He tied the horn to his belt, and went down after his rifle—couldn't get it the first time, and had to come up again. He wasn't so strong now and his fingers were stiffening. He went down again—and this time got hold of it. He let go of the line and hanging on to the rifle, which was still tied to the canoe, he got his head above water. After a few gulps of air, he cut loose the rifle—and with the gun in one hand and the knife in the other went sailing downstream.

He wallowed ashore about where Melissa had.

For a minute or so, he knelt in the water trying to get his breath back. Then he fumbled his knife back into its place, and slinging his rifle, he tried to crawl up the bank.

But he couldn't make it; his legs wouldn't work.

So he had to go downstream, stumbling along in the water, until he came to a down tree to pull himself up by. It wasn't too easy. But all the same, when he got to the top, he thought he'd begun to feel better—the blood must have started to move in his legs again. He thought to himself that now, if only his powder was dry, he was making some headway.

But when he got back to where he'd left Melissa, he saw she was down. He was able to rouse her a little, but he couldn't get her to stand.

With his hands shaking badly, he went to work for his fire. And when he'd got everything ready—wiping out the lock of his rifle with some dry leaves and so on—he opened the horn.

The powder was dry.

He wasn't so quick at it as he might have been, but he brought a fire. And as soon as he got it to going enough to be safe, he went round like a crazy man, ripping off the dead lower branches of

181

white pines and hemlocks—anything he could find. He'd build up a fire! He'd get it to going!

Then he carried Melissa over beside it.

There was a good heat from the fire, and he figured he still had a chance. All the same, he wasn't certain what cold would do to a woman—who was in the way that Melissa was.

If she'd been a man or a boy, he'd have taken her clothes off and slapped her all over trying to make her turn red. But she seemed so kind of frail, he didn't believe she could stand it.

He took off her stockings and moccasins; and he took off her heavy, wet cloak and hung that up on some sticks to keep the wind off her. He rubbed her legs and then slapped them, and as the fire got hotter, he opened her clothes so she could get some of the heat on her, and he rubbed her back, too. But he didn't dare rub it much, because his hands were so rough he was afraid he'd take the skin off her.

She seemed to perk up a little. Whit tried to encourage her. "You feel any warmer?"

She nodded dimly.

He saw her cheek had stopped bleeding.

"You'll be all right," he said. "You ain't hurt any, are you?"

She shook her head.

"All right, you stay here by the fire. I'll be back in a minute. I got an errand to do."

He'd got to go into the water again, because without any ax he'd never be able to keep ahead of the fire. He took off his leather shirt and the cloth shirt underneath it, wrung out the cloth shirt and hung that up to dry. He laid the leather shirt flat on the ground. While he was doing this, he thought that maybe this time he'd better have a try, anyhow, to bring the whole dang canoe in at once. He thought maybe he could, too.

But when he got out on the log, he wasn't so sure of it. He didn't feel now as though he could handle anything heavy—like trying to get the canoe out from under the log. His arms felt pretty weak. He even was doubtful that he could get underneath, get the ax, and get back again. Maybe the best thing for him was to get back to the bank while he could. He'd go back to Melissa—but what good would that do her?

It was the air inside that canoe was holding it up. Get that air out of there, and the stern would sink down, and the whole thing would slide out from under the log—and fetch up on the line.

Then he'd work it inshore. All right, he'd try it. It seemed simple enough. He guessed he could hold out.

He spraddled the canoe on his belly, and with the point of his knife he jabbed a hole in the bottom. The air came rushing out, and the canoe settled beneath him. He got an arm over the log as the canoe slid underneath it.

The line held. The canoe was slantwise a little, and yawed and tugged, slow and heavy, mostly under the water. He got hold of one end of the line, and was planning to cut that free of the log, and then to bring it inshore along the log and secure it. Then he'd go back and cut loose the other end, and the canoe would swing in to shore. He had it all figured out.

He couldn't get any slack in the line he had hold of—but he cut it anyway. It pulled right out of his hand. All of the strain was put on the remaining line; it stretched—and then parted. Whit was left on the log. And the canoe was off down the river. . . .

He stayed there for a moment, watching it go, feeling a mild sort of wonder. This wasn't what he had planned. But he couldn't think now just what it was that he had planned. The canoe seemed to go slowly. Yes—it went very slowly. It was going away from him. . . .

He came to on a sudden—and began to hitch himself along on the log toward the bank. He'd get it yet—somehow or other.

When he got in to shore, his legs had gone dead. They kept giving way under him. Floundering and flopping, falling down, whimpering, he splashed along in the water at the foot of the bank. A good many times, he went under completely. Whenever he stood up, he'd look out over the river—hoping to see the canoe. He saw it—finally. And it was close in to the shore. But there was no telling how long it would stay there—

When he got there, he found the canoe resting hung up on a rock in the midst of an eddy. The water was just about up to his chest. Tugging and pulling, he got the canoe in to where the water was shallow and the current was easy—and the ice was just forming. His hands were like flippers, but he took five or six turns round a rock with the line, and using his teeth got some kind of knot.

He got his ax, and laid it out on the bank. He got their small iron pot. And he struggled some time with the half a sack they had left of Indian meal—wet to the core, and the deadest weight in the world. Somehow, he dragged it up out of the water—and then he fell on the bank under a sudden downthrust of exhaustion. He raised himself on his elbows, and he brought his knees under him, and he waited it out. Pretty soon, he was able to stand. He ought to right the canoe now—but it was no use to try it. He knew he couldn't do it.

What he must do was get up the bank, take the ax and the pot and some meal along with him. And get back to that fire! He'd be all right if he could get to the fire—he thought he would, anyway. It wasn't the work that he'd done that had taken it out of him; it was only the cold in the water. He wanted the fire. But he couldn't carry the ax and the pot—let alone any meal—and get up the bank.

Yet one more time, he went into the water . . . and he came out with the line from the other end of the canoe. Kneeling, he tied the ax and the pot to it, and the other end of the line he tied to his belt. Then he slit open the meal sack, and fumbled into his pockets as much as he could of wet Indian meal. He put some in his mouth, too.

Then he started to crawl up the bank. . . .

He made it—but he didn't know how. Stupidly, half drunk with exhaustion, and unaware of his triumph in gaining the top of the bank, he sat on the edge with his legs hanging over, and solemnly hauled up the ax and the pot.

The pot was half full of water. Whit thought that was nice: he was going to need water. And with the ax in one hand and the pot in the other, he went a little unsteadily back to the fire.

Melissa lay there beside it.

His head cleared. The fire, he saw, had burned down a good deal. But she'd put on some of the wood that he had left there for her. That was a good sign. She'd been awake enough to do that.

He spoke to her—and she answered, and then, by an effort, she managed to sit up.

It came over Whit that he wasn't near so far gone as she was. That gave him strength.

"Whit," she said plaintively, "you ain't got any shirt on."

"No. It's right here."

"Put it on, Whit. It's awful cold, ain't it?"

"Yes," he said, his head swimming, "it is kind of chilly." Maybe she wasn't quite right in her head; that didn't mean anything. She'd come around soon as she got something hot into her.

He put on his shirt—it was warm in the front and dry in some places—and he put on his leather shirt over it. The leather was stiffening now. When it was frozen, it would keep all the wind out.

Now then: the fire. He put on the rest of the wood. "You better lay down again," he said to Melissa.

"All right," she said pleasantly. And she lay down again.

He set the pot firmly close in to the fire, picked up the ax, and went after some wood.

He found some good wood, and with an hour of chopping and dragging, he had enough wood up close to the fire to get through the night with. It was long pieces, mostly; he could work it up later.

The water was warm in the pot, and he banked red coals around it, and threw in some pine needles to give a taste to it. They were better than nothing.

When the water came hot, he got Melissa to swallow some. Daylight was failing.

The wet meal from his pockets, he put on a stone by the fire.

From then until dark, he cut a good pile of green stuff for her to lie on. And he piled up more stuff to keep the wind off her, because her cloak was now dry enough to wrap it around her.

So they entered the night.

All that night long, Whit never lay down. He kept up the fire, and he tended Melissa. He used every trick that he'd ever heard of to fight the cold from her. In between times he tried to clean up his gun.

The cold that surrounded them was a much harder thing to fight than the current had been. You were out of the current when you came off the river. But the cold lay on all of the country. They couldn't hide from it; he just had to fight it.

Whit thought that maybe a hot stone at her feet might do some good. So he shifted the meal, and used that one. Then he asked himself why—if one was a good thing—more wouldn't be better. Crawling round in the darkness, he located four more, dug them out with his fingers, and put them to heat. All through the night, he kept a row of hot stones along the side of her that was away from the fire.

Every hour or so, he'd try to get her to drink more—and she usually did. Between times, she would sleep.

Late in the evening, her body was warm to his touch, and

185

sometime before midnight, a light sweat came on her. Whit thought that was all right: so long as she sweated, she didn't have fever.

Nor did she seem to have any pains. That eased his mind mightily. That particular danger, he hoped, had passed over her.

Two or three times, he tried the meal on her. But she couldn't take it.

Thus they went through the night.

In the last hour of darkness, she appeared to Whit to sleep easier. He'd have given most anything to sleep some himself, but he didn't dare try it.

She slept right along until well after sunup, and Whit didn't waken her. The way he felt himself may have persuaded him, but it seemed to him sleep might do her more good than swallowing more of that pine-needle water.

When she wakened, she heard Whit stirring round, and spoke to him drowsily—like any morning. Then she cried out in terror.

That frightened Whit more than anything else had. He thought that she'd gone—that she'd never be right again. He knelt down beside her.

It took only a minute. She was all right. She didn't know what had happened. That was all was the trouble. It may have been only a minute—but it was the worst minute he'd ever put in. . . . When he got to his feet, he was pretty well shaken; but he felt like a new man. She was all right. The chances were good now that they would get through.

They stayed there all day. Whit patched the canoe, dried out his gear as well as he could, and ate a prodigious amount of boiled corn meal and pork. Melissa lay there and rested. He told her she had to, and she didn't argue.

He took occasion to go over his gun; he had dried it last night but it was a long ways from clean. So now he went at it, every last little part. He enjoyed doing this when he had plenty of time.

Melissa said, "That gun is longer than most, ain't it, Whit?"

"This here is a rifle. This ain't a smoothbore."

"Oh."

"You know the difference?"

"No, I don't know as I do."

"Some call this a twist-gun. A rifle's correct. Old Captain Karr give me this in his will. He was the best man that I ever knew. You remember him, don't you?"

186

"Some."

"Back when I was a boy—I was eleven years old—he went away in the winter for I guess maybe a month. I felt pretty bad, I know, all through that time because I'd used to go round there when it got too rough at home. Well, my old man heard before I did that Karr had come back, and you know what he done? Well, sir, he took a rope and he tied me up for four days. He'd come around and he'd stand there and laugh, and he'd say, 'Look at him! Eh? By Christ, this is one time when you won't run round to Karr's!' And then he got tired of it because she made him do the chores and he let me loose and I beat it to Karr's.

"Well, Karr he had some work on the anvil and he couldn't stop but he hollers, 'Come in, boy!' And I went right in. I never went in the house, though. And I stood with my backside up close to the forge; it was an awful cold day out, I remember it well. It was just comin' on dusk. Well, he went on hammerin'—he was drawin' a bar—and I commenced to look round because I was glad t' be there. And then I see this rifle high up on the wall . . . and the light from the forge, which is yellow and red, shone up on this stock here and give it a kind of a glow, and when he'd give the bellows a pull and the fire'd rise up, I'd see this here berril lookin' slender 'n long show up in the darkness. I don't know how long I stood there. It made me feel queer.

"Then Karr he come over 'n he reached her down off the wall 'n put her into my hands. It made my knees shake. It was the loveliest thing I'd ever seen in my life—up until then.

"'That is a rifle,' Karr says to me. Oh, I can hear him! 'That's a Lancaster rifle. Laman made her himself. I stood beside him. It took him nine days. I could learn in a year,' he says. 'He wants me t' come back. And I figure to go. I could be happy makin' them things,' he said.

"But he never went back. And do you know why that was? Because nobody cared—not even Ensign. Karr had counted on him. Karr showed him this gun; he showed him what it would do: half the charge of a smoothbore and about half as much lead, and she'll shoot farther 'n straighter 'n any smoothbore in the world. She will strike just as hard 'n she's quicker to load. Why, this rifle here—or any one that's well made—is no more like a smoothbore than a deer's like a cow. You know what Lord said? He said he guessed his musket would serve. That's what they all of them said.

"Down round this Lancaster place they must be hunters, I guess.

"Well, Karr went on mendin' plowshares 'n dung forks and all things like that. And sometimes he'd make a scythe blade—he liked to make them. You know mine that he made. And times when I would show up and he'd not much ahead, he would take this one down off the wall and he'd learn me to shoot. Oh, we had some great times of it! . . . Well, I guess that'll do." He had finished his work, and he began stowing his tools. "And then when he died, there she was in his will." He looked round at Melissa. She had fallen asleep. . . . He was glad that she had, because she needed to sleep.

The next day, they set out again.

Whit shortened the day on Melissa's account—and on his own, too. It seemed to him now that they'd come a long way. He'd be as glad to see Jonas Moore when they got to Sandwich as he'd ever been to see any man. And how he would sleep by Jonas's fire!

Casumpy was easy—with a light wind from the west and smooth water to travel.

Toward sundown, to the north, Whit saw the smoke of the houses of Sandwich. It gave him a catch in his throat. He couldn't speak for a moment.

"That smoke—" said Melissa, "is that where we're goin'?"

"That's it," he answered.

Jonas Moore's house was right down by the pond. Jonas was standing on the little beach, waiting. He was a tall man and bearded, thin and bent shouldered, but a strong-looking man. When the canoe was thirty yards out, Jonas called, "Hello, Whit."

"Hello, Jonas," Whit answered.

No more was said until Whit rested his paddle. Then Jonas remarked, "Well, I see you brung her."

Whit grinned. "Jonas Moore," he said to Melissa.

"Ma'am," Jonas acknowledged this introduction. "You have a good trip, Whit?"

"Well, we got here."

"Have any trouble?"

"No, not to speak of. Overset in Squam Brook, was all."

"No! Kind o' wet, wan't it?"

"No more so than usual."

"Lose anything, did you?"

"Salt."

"Oh." He steadied the bow, and helped Melissa alight. His hand on her arm felt strong and reliable. She liked Jonas Moore.

To Whit, Jonas observed in an unrestrained voice, "She ain't awful big, is she?"

"No," said Whit, "but she's rugged."

"You leave all o' that there, Whit—" the stuff in the canoe— "I'll fetch it up later."

Whit got out and stood up.

"I'm glad to see you," Jonas said earnestly.

"I'm glad to see you."

"Come up to the house. My woman, I guess, has got something ready."

"All right. She been well, has she?"

"Pretty good, Whit."

Whit picked up his gun, and Jonas led the way up the path— then Melissa, then Whit.

Melissa went slowly. Then she turned round to Whit—and Jonas kept going.

She put up her arms to him. Whit kissed her—said nothing.

Then they followed Jonas.

7

If Melissa had come upon Jonas Moore's house at the start of her journey, she might not have thought so much of it. Now the house appeared to her to be handsome and strong. It had a chimney with smoke coming out of it; the walls were stout walls; the roof was fresh bark. Inside the house, supper was cooking. Inside that house there was a woman.

She felt no disappointment at the size of the house; she didn't notice that it seemed to lack windows. It didn't matter to her that the house hadn't a plank in it, a board, or a nail. She scarcely took notice that the door she approached was of skins.

Jonas held the door open—and Melissa went in. But it was so dark inside that once over the sill she turned first of all to see if Whit had come in. He was beside her—and he spoke to the woman who, Melissa saw now, stood by the fire wiping her hands.

Whit said, "Evenin', Mis' Moore."

"Well, Whit, you come back."

Whit stood aside, and to Jonas Moore's wife he said, shyly and proud, "This here is my woman."

"Yes, I thought it might be. Come here, child, let me look at you."

Melissa stood forward into the light of the fire.

Ida Moore took one look at her—and turned upon Jonas. "You two men," she said bitterly, "can go outside and stay there until I call you to supper. It ain't ready yet."

Whit and Jonas went out.

Jonas said reasonably, "I guess we might go down and bring up that stuff o' yourn."

"All right."

They went down the path toward the lake. Jonas observed, "That supper smelled ready."

"Did to me, too."

After a moment, Jonas inquired, "How much salt you lose, Whit?"

"Half a hundredweight, maybe."

Jonas said nothing for eight or ten steps. Finally he offered, "Well, you got here, 't any rate."

"Yes," Whit agreed, "I guess that's 'bout the size of it."

Pity moved Ida Moore when she looked on Melissa. This hollow-eyed, staring, unsmiling child—who from habit held her head up when, from the looks of her, the miracle was that she was able to stand—she was so far beaten down that she didn't even know she was dirty.

So Mistress Moore drove the men out—Whit himself, for that matter, looked as though he'd been dragged through a knothole—and went to work on Melissa.

"Child," she said to her, "you look to me like you had quite a trip. Now you come here and set down and I'm going to see to you. Right here on this bench"—a log split in half and the top of it smoothed. She moved it up to the fire.

"I'm all right," said Melissa.

"Yes, I know: you been sayin' that to him every time that he asked you. Now come and set down." She put her arm round the girl and sat her down on the bench. "I'm twice as old as what you be, and this here is my house. You just take it easy and do as I say. I ain't goin' t' ask you no questions. But I'll tell you this much: I'm goin' t' git them clothes off'n you, 'n git you cleaned up, 'n git some other clothes onto you. When you've some proper food in you, 'n you've had you a sleep, why, then we c'n talk. How was the weddin'? 'Twas satisfactory, wan't it?" While she was talking, she was getting Melissa's clothes off. . . .

Melissa said yes, they had had a nice wedding.

Mistress Moore brought a blanket and wrapped her up in it. She brought hot water and soap. "How far along are you? Three months, it looks like."

"About that, it is. Or a little bit longer."

"Well, don't worry about it. If you'd been goin' t' have trouble, you'd a had it 'fore now. From the looks o' them clothes, you must a been in the river."

"We overset. 'Twasn't his fault."

"No, I guess that's right. Accidents happen. Jonas claims Whit's an awful good man."

"Oh, yes, he is."

Melissa could remember when her mother had bathed her. . . .

"Whit speaks awful highly of your husband, too."

"Jonas' all right. He does like the woods, though."

"Yes—so does Whit."

"There, now," Mistress Moore said, "I guess that'll do you. Now then, you keep that there blanket around you, 'n I'll see what I got that we can put on you. I guess I ain't only twice as old as what you be; I'm twice as big, too. But 'twon't do any hurt; you c'n wrap 'em around you. You ain't goin' t' put nothin' on out'n *that* pile again—" the heap on the floor—"not till I get a chance to wash 'em, you ain 't. Now then—" she was over the other end of the room—"moccasins, stockings, smallclothes, a skirt . . ." She came back to Melissa. "Here—put on these."

Melissa pulled on a stocking—the heel up to her ankle, and folds under her toes. But it felt clean and dry. It felt warm and good to her.

Mistress Moore, at the fire, had now swung out the crane, taken the lid from the middle-sized pot, and was very carefully ladling from the pot into a bowl. . . .

The rest of the clothes, Melissa put on with a good deal of haste and not very much care. What she wanted to do was to get her hands on that bowl.

She did, in due course, and she breathed in its odor, and came almost to crying. She made no effort to think what the broth was made out of. But it wasn't pine needles.

"That started with pa'tridge—" she heard Mistress Moore's

191

voice—"and worked up from there." Mistress Moore was in back of her. "Now if you'll let me, while you're drinkin' that bowlful, I'll give your hair just a lick 'n a promise. You don't mind if I do?"

Melissa had tasted the broth—and her eyelids had closed. She couldn't answer. The taste of the broth went all through her body; she could feel how it loosened the backs of her legs; she could feel in it the promise of sleep. In the long warmth of the fire, she sat there and drank it.

Mistress Moore stood behind her, and fixed up her hair. It was beautiful hair; it was soft in her fingers. But it caught in the cracks of them. Years ago—far away—Jonas Moore's woman had been a girl in Connecticut—Stratford, Connecticut. She could remember!

Melissa had finished her supper when Whit and Jonas were summoned. She sat on a stool at one end of the hearth, her back to the chimney. She smiled up at Whit as he stood looking down at her. "You look different," he said. "What you done to your hair?"

"Nothin'," she answered, pleased with herself. "Mis' Moore done it for me."

"Them are her clothes."

"Yes."

Whit didn't like it.

Ida Moore intervened. "She tried to stop me," she said casually to Whit, "but I c'n tell you, I'm a hard woman to stop. Ain't I, Jonas?"

"'Hard'!" Jonas said fervently.

Melissa looked funny—and Whit suddenly saw it—smiled, and then laughed. Melissa laughed, too.

"Well," Jonas said cheerfully, "I guess we c'n eat, Whit."

Mistress Moore waited until Whit had finished his supper, and then she took him outside the house and laid down the law to him. She told him flatly that on no account whatsoever was he to take that young girl a step farther tomorrow. "I know a lot more what I'm talkin' 'bout than you do," she said. "She's all right now, near I can make out, 'n I don't see no reason why she'd ought to have trouble. But you ain't goin' t' march her no twenty mile in t' your place, nor have her sleep in a lean-to after she gets there. I know you 'n Jonas don't see no harm in it; you'd either one of you—Jonas or you—just as leave sleep in the snow as a bed, I guess. There's times I think maybe that Jonas 'd ruther. He's more'n half animil, anyhow, Jonas—'n I d' know but what you be. You leave her here, d' you understand? You leave her here till I say she c'n go—'n that won't be tomorrow, nor 'twon't be the next day."

"How long d' you figure before she c'n travel?"

"I don't know. But she ain't goin' t' travel a step not inside of a week, anyhow, at the shortest."

"It ain't awful far."

"Maybe it ain't. And I suppose the next thing you'll say is, she won't have to lug nothin'."

"Well, she wouldn't."

"Are you tryin' t' argue?"

"No, I ain't, Mis' Moore—truly."

"*You* c'n go in there t' your place tomorrow. You go ahead. But she's stayin' right here. That's settled now, is it?"

"Seems t' be, yes."

"All right, then, it's settled."

"It's awful kind of you, keepin' her."

"She'll be comp'ny for me. You don't know what that means. All right—I've said my say. You c'n go back in the house now. I'll be in in a minute. When you get in there, you'll most likely find Jonas tellin' the bride how to set up a bear trap, or how to take the guts out of a porcupine 'n not get the quills into you. He's an entertainin' man, Jonas, he's gifted that way. And another thing, now that I think of it, is don't you 'n Jonas think t' set up all night in front of th' fire 'n talk about trappin'. I want her to sleep."

"Yes, ma'am," said Whit.

As he went into the house, he thought to himself, "I never see Jonas guttin' a porcupine. But there ain't only one way that I know of t' do it. . . ."

Sometime in the night, as they all lay asleep—Mistress Moore and Melissa on a thick pallet of cornhusks, Jonas and Whit over across on the other side—and the fire flickering and falling, and everything peaceful . . . Melissa was wakened. She was too deep in sleep to come up out of it suddenly, but on her face she'd felt something cold and wet and alive. Half asleep and half frightened, she put her hand up to it—and screamed and sat up. It was big and alive.

There was noise and confusion and barking and terror. Then Whit was beside her . . . and she clung to him hard.

It seemed a long time before things got straightened out and

193

she knew what had happened. Slowly the terror let go its hold on her. But she was still trembling. . . .

It had been Jonas's dog. The dog, they explained, had come in from somewhere, and finding a stranger, had sniffed at her—naturally. The dog knew Whit and liked him—but she was new to him.

And when Melissa had screamed, Whit and Jonas agreed, she had frightened the dog and set him to barking.

Melissa said yes, she understood now. She was sorry, she said, to have made such a fuss.

Jonas brought the dog up to her. He was a big fellow, black, and part mastiff—the other part hound. They all called him "Major." The dog was uncertain and knew he'd done wrong—and he was still a little afraid of her. Both Whit and Jonas seemed to understand perfectly. "Reach out your hand to him," Whit said to her, "slow."

She did it.

Jonas talked to the dog and persuaded him gradually to sniff at her hand.

"Now," Jonas instructed her, "slide your hand around easy and scratch back of his ear. He wouldn't hurt you! God, he wouldn't hurt nothin'!"

Duly, Melissa scratched back of the ear.

The dog liked it. He pressed his head up against the scratch of her fingers, and he half closed his eyes. When she stopped for a moment, he made it plain that he wanted more of it.

"There, now!" Jonas said to him. "Ain't you ashamed, Major, to been scairt of a woman! And you claim you're a bear dog! Now you go and lie down—go on, now! Lie down." The dog went and lay down.

Jonas apologized for Major's behavior, and Whit said to Melissa, "You're all right now, ain't you?"

She said she was all right—and said again she was sorry she had made such a fuss.

Jonas assured her that that was all right. But Jonas's wife said nothing at all; she was too angry to venture on speech.

They all lay down again, and before very long Melissa could tell that the others had gone back to sleep. The dog lay by the fire,—busily, noisily licking himself. Then he, too, lapsed into sleep, snored for a while, and then he was quiet.

The fire sank farther, and cold came into the house.

Melissa lay wide awake. Tomorrow, she knew, Whit was leaving her here.

But sleep came to her, finally—she was too tired to look ahead any more.

8

Whit got away bright and early next morning.

Leaving Jonas's place, he had in mind no particular path. He didn't need any. He knew where he was, and where he wanted to go. The path didn't matter, the lay of the land being clear in his mind: how the principal mountains bore from each other, the course of the rivers, and where the bigger ponds were. Little ponds, the low ridges, small brooks, and so on were not the things that he traveled by this time of year when the weather was good. The leaves were gone now; a man could tell where he was.

As he stood with his back to Jonas Moore's house, Red Hill on his right hand lay to the south and a little bit east. Israel Mountain, looming up high and easily seen, was almost due north. The line that he wanted was halfway between them. But there was no need to be too nice about it. If he veered to the left, he'd only strike Bearcamp River a little farther upstream than he otherwise would; if he got too far to his right, the steep northwestern slope of the Ossipy Mountains would push him back on his course. These two, the river and the Ossipy Mountains, made a kind of angle into which he was heading from the wide-open end. At the point of it, the river and mountains came so close together that no man in his senses could, without knowing it, squeeze through between them, except at night in a snowstorm—when no man in his senses would be traveling anyway.

He would pass to the north some of Beede's house, this way, and well to the northward of Poole's. Well, that was all right.

He was traveling fast, his ankle not bothering him. But he was carrying a pretty good load all the same. He had his gun and his ax, both held in his right hand, and slung from his shoulders were a half dozen traps—each with a chain—his blanket, his powderhorn, the tools for his gun, and a small sack of corn, with two pounds of pork in case he should need it. He had a spare axhead that weighed close to four pounds, and he had his knife and his bullet pouch hitched to his belt. All in all, what he carried would have weighed forty pounds probably.

Yet he stood on the farther bank of the Bearcamp, ten miles— on a bee line—from Jonas Moore's house, in what looked by the sun to be less than two hours. This was the stream in which he'd hurt his ankle. Today, the water was higher than it had been then. It looked ready for winter . . . and it felt like it, too.

Now he turned north, cutting across the flat interval covered with pitch pine that lay between Bearcamp and another river that joined it farther downstream. A plain covered with pitch pine made the best going there was: it was good underfoot, there was no brush to speak of, and the branches weren't troublesome. If there was enough sun coming through to keep a man straight, he could go just as fast as his legs would let him. He had nothing to worry him.

He was going due north, right on a line for Coruway Mountain—right dead for the peak of it. Now and again where there'd be a tree down, he'd catch a glimpse of the top of the mountain— the dark line of the shoulders, and then up above, the gray, granite peak. Whenever he saw it, it seemed to him higher than he'd thought it was going to.

Whit smiled when he saw it. . . .

When he picked up the stream on the far side of the interval, he crossed it and followed up the east bank for about a mile and a half until he came to a forks, where he took the east branch. He stayed with this for about a mile, it might be, and then worked around the northwesterly shoulder of that hill which he'd stood on the first time he'd been in here.

Here, for the most part, it was heavy, old spruce—high and dark overhead, and with a scattering of boulders, windfalls, and seedlings down on the ground. Then the beeches and maples began to come in, as he came down off the hillside.

His load wasn't heavy. He was pretty near there.

As the land leveled off at the foot of the hill, he moved over a little so as to pass a big maple. This was a line tree, spotted both sides. He put up his hand to it—and stepped onto his land.

Coming around to the front of the lean-to, he saw that no one had been there. He struck his ax in a corner tree, hung up his gun carefully, shucked off his load, and stowed things away. Then he came out and looked up at the mountain. . . .

It hadn't changed any.

Whit stayed there twelve days. He had rain off and on, but nothing out of the way really, for that time of year, and some days it was bright. Mornings, of course, it would be pretty cold. But at night he had a good fire and he slept under shelter. There was only one day that he had a hard time of it because of the weather.

That morning, he stood in front of his lean-to and saw the ground covered with really good tracking snow. The sky was all clouded in and there was a steady wind blowing between west and northwest, but there was no feel in the air of any more snow coming: from the way the snow lay, the wind that had brought it had been from out of the east more, and then had worked round. It was a day that was sent by the Lord for a man to go get a deer—and Whit reached for his knife and felt of the edge. . . .

He didn't believe he'd stop to eat breakfast—he'd had a pretty good supper—he'd just take something with him. It was close now to full daylight and he ought to get started.

He turned and bent down to go into the lean-to—to take down his gun and go over all parts of it—and when he put up his hand to take hold of the gun, he caught sight of his ax.

He wished he hadn't seen that.

As he sat down and began unwrapping his gun, he was already bringing up reasons why it was all right for him to go hunting and leave for a while the work he had come for. He said, "I've eat nothing but trout the last four or five days and it's gettin' so now that my stomach don't take to 'em. If I had some deer's liver, now, I could work better."

When he pulled off the wrapping, he could smell the grease and the metal.

"And the thing of it is," he said aloud now, "a man gets along faster—in the long run, he does, I think—if he suits what he's doing to what's the best time. Now like this morning, with this snow to work on, I might get a deer in no time at all; where if I was to leave it, this snow might be gone and I could hunt a couple of days maybe and not come on a thing."

All the time he was busy with one thing and another, getting ready to go, he kept adding more reasons: he'd done pretty well with the work that he'd come for; he had forty logs cut for building his house, and only twenty to go. He needed a deerskin as well as the meat—and the skin was a thing that would be for Melissa. All winter long there might not come a day as near perfect as this one. It was bad luck—there was no question of it!—when good luck like this happened not to make the most of it. And what he didn't eat of the meat, he could pack out to Jonas's.

When he was all ready, he stood in front of his lean-to, his gun in his hand, deciding with care as to just where to go.

The best way would be to go down to a pond, and work all around the edge of it. Of the two ponds that were handy, he thought he'd try the larger one—the one that brook on his own place went into. He'd have a better chance there, the shore being longer, than he would on the little pond more to the west; also, if more snow should come, he'd have the brook to come back by.

The pond lay a little to the right of the mountain, and he looked up to see if the mountain was out.

Solemn and black, with the gray sky behind it, the mountain looked down at him, and slowly there left him—there slipped away from him—all his assurance that he was about to go hunting.

He knew when he was licked. There was no use going now. There'd be no pleasure in it.

He turned back into the lean-to, stuck his gun in a corner, and yanked his ax from the cornerpost. He didn't want to eat anything. He flung down his powderhorn, and went striding off bitterly to the place where he'd been working last night at dusk. Here he tackled a spruce tree, not even pausing to blow on his hands, and when he'd lopped off enough limbs to let him get at the trunk, he struck into it viciously.

He was throwing his ax, striking as hard as he could. His lips were set in a line, and his eyelids were lowered. With the ax, he bit into the spruce tree as though it was to blame.

He knew what was to blame—or he claimed that he did. It was simple enough. And it had nothing to do with conscience or duty. It was something he'd known for a long time would happen—but he'd forgotten about it, somehow, since last summer. All there was to it was this: now he was married, he couldn't go hunting any time he felt like it. He would never be able to. So long as he lived, he would never be able to do as he pleased—as he'd once thought he would be as soon as he'd left his father.

All right, what of it? It was nothing to cry about. He'd known it would happen. And he hadn't been cheated. He had Melissa.

Yes, he had Melissa—but still, all the same, he hadn't expected that when he couldn't go hunting it would make him feel sick to his stomach—the same as it used to when his father'd prevented him.

He struck harder and harder, with his arms straightened full out at the end of each swing, and pulling back with his shoulders. It was a fool way to chop—but he'd got to do something!

Then it happened.

He stood there and stared down at it. He saw what had happened, and he saw that the happening of it was over with. He hadn't seen it or felt it. But now that it was done, he was beginning to feel it: it made the skin crawl on the backs of his legs.

The head of the ax was deep in the ground, just under his foot. As he stared, he said slowly, "No, I ain't cut any." And then he moved his foot, gingerly, away from the ax. The side of his foot had been touching the ax. That was as close as a man could come, really.

He let go of the ax handle, stood up straight, and turned round. He said "Whew!" with a good deal of feeling, rubbed his nose briefly, and then went and sat down.

Pretty soon he felt better. All choppers get cut—sooner or later they do. But he'd missed it this time. He turned and looked at the ax, stuck there in the ground. "If it ain't got a gap in it too big to grind out, I guess things are all right." He got up to go see, and found the bit was undamaged. "I guess the ground being froze, that was able to stop her, instead of her keeping on going until she come to a rock." He wiped off the bit with the palm of his hand. "Went in far enough, though." It had gone in past the temper.

He set the ax into the tree.

"I guess I'll go up and get somethin' to eat. That was good luck enough so that I can't complain if I don't eat nothin' but trouts till I get back to Jonas's."

"What the good luck was," he said, when he'd sat down to eat, "was that I got a warning—instead of a judgment—for the way I went on, there, about not goin' after a deer."

9

The house Whit had in mind would be six lengths of his ax handle, measured on the inside, and half that in depth. That is to say, as he stood in the doorway facing into the house, it would be short of eight feet across to the wall, and the room would be twice that distance in length.

He couldn't build it much larger than that, because there weren't enough men near by for a raising. Jonas was coming over to help him—once Whit had the logs ready—but to handle the logs for a house any bigger than the one he had planned would have called for oxen to haul them, and for more than two men to raise up the logs and get them in place. As it was, he was going to have to use logs a little slimmer than usual, and so to use more of them. It would take longer, but it wouldn't hurt the house any. It was not how thick the walls were, it was how tight were the joints.

He hadn't said anything yet to Melissa, but he'd set his heart on having a chimney. A chimney would take him as long to build, probably, as all the rest of the house would. But he had a feeling that maybe Melissa might be in a way to be tender to cold; she might take some kind of harm from it that he didn't know about—though he never had heard anyone say that was so. Over and above that, he thought it would please her. He himself would be proud of it, too. It would set them apart from most pioneers. When a man builds a chimney, he at least figures to stay there.

Well, it would not be a house like Beede's to Sandwich, but it would be an awful lot better than some he had seen. He'd have a chimney if it took him a month. He'd have a good one. And he hoped, when he had it, Mr. Gowan would hear of it.

He was getting ahead of himself. The first thing to do was to finish cutting the logs. . . .

Eight days from the day on which he had started, he had them all cut and ready for hauling. Five days, in the first place, was what he had figured on. The difference was great, but the reason for it was natural: trees of the right size and straight had turned out to be scarcer than he had suspected. And yet he knew the woods. "Still," he said to himself, "you go through the woods on some errand or other, and you see a nice little spruce tree—straight as a ramrod, and a good size to handle—and you think, 'Well, now, that there is a nice little tree,' but you ain't got no use for it right at that minute, and so you go on thinking about something else. Maybe a half hour later this will happen again. In the course of a year, it has happened quite often. You add them all up—whenever someone says, 'spruces—what I mean to say, little ones'—but you leave out all them half hours that come in between. You get the answer that if you should need little spruces, the woods would be full of them. But when you cut out to look for them, what you come on to is all them half hours."

Another thing was that he stuck right to spruce. He had various reasons, perhaps none of them good ones. But one of them was: he thought the house would look better all of one kind of wood.

The only places that spruces grew to the size that he wanted—except for scattering, single ones, of which there weren't many—were where an old spruce had fallen around thirty years ago maybe—thirty or forty. There, he'd get a stand of a dozen or two. But of those, three or four would be all he could use. The rest would be crooked, or have too much taper, or there'd be something else wrong with them. He covered fifty acres of ground in looking out trees, before he could find sixty trees of the kind that he wanted.

The cutting and limbing was fairly quick work.

Then he had to haul them. He put in a day, almost, making a sled: two small sticks of maple, the butt ends laid forward, and trimmed on the bottom, did all right for runners. He notched these on top to admit two birch crosspieces, and with his ax and his knife he got a fairly tight joint. He was tempted, of course, to try pegging the joints—heating his ramrod to get the holes with—but he decided against it: it would take him too long, and it wouldn't be worth it. He contented himself with binding the joints with wet rawhide—slotting the runners where the rawhide passed under them—and then setting the sled in front of the fire. The rawhide, as it dried, pulled tight enough to suit anybody. He fixed a pole out in front, and was ready for hauling.

Then it came on to rain, and the snow went away.

Whit went down to the pond, and with a piece of pork rind to skitter, and a twenty-foot pole, he flung out pickerel—clear up into the trees—that came down with a plop and was about the length of his arm. It would make a change from the trout. After setting a trap by the shore for an otter, he came home again.

And the sled brought him luck. He surprised a young porcupine that was about to go after the rawhide—but that hadn't had time yet to do any damage—and before the porcupine knew what was up, Whit had joyfully knocked him in the head with the ax. It was a young one, all right, but with six pound of good meat in him, not counting a liver as big as the palm of your hand. Whit had that liver over the fire before he'd even started to dress out the meat. With fresh meat and pickerel ahead of him—both!—his hand shook with excitement.

He ate all he could hold, and after he'd hung up the sled, he lay down to sleep before it was dark. With so much meat in him, his wet clothes didn't bother him; he slept without waking until it was light.

There was fresh snow on the ground in the morning—though not so much of it as he would have liked. Still, it was better than nothing, and snow was still falling. He ate most of the pickerel, some more of the meat, and felt that things generally were in pretty good shape. Then he went at the hauling.

He started in dragging three logs at a time, but this didn't last long; he was soon down to two. The sled worked pretty well until the handle came loose. His feet slipped in the snow and he fell more or less. The main trick, of course, was to keep the logs moving once he had them started, and he had to step pretty lively some of the time. For really hard pulling, a man isn't built right to pull facing forward. He backed into a tree once, sat down very suddenly, and before he could get clear, the logs came in on top of him. One way and another, he put in quite a day.

A good many times he wished he had Jonas to steady the load for him; it would have made half the work. And all the logs he hauled that day—the whole batch put together—wouldn't have made half a jag for a pair of young oxen.

He lay down to sleep sore and aching all over, his weak ankle lame, and his clothes clammy with sweat. He'd hauled twenty-six logs. But there was this comfort in it: he'd brought in the ones that were farthest away.

When he woke in the morning, every last muscle in him was so lame and stiff that it hurt him to spit. Whenever he looked from one side to the other, it hurt moving his eyes. His throat ached, and his head didn't feel any too steady. He didn't know but what maybe he might have a fever. It didn't help any to know that if last night, before he lay down, he'd not been too lazy to dry out his shirt, he might not have felt this way.

He ate what he could, and went at it again.

His legs limbered up before he'd made many trips, and he thought he was getting the knack of it perhaps. It was a good thing he was, because he didn't feel quite so strong as he had yesterday morning.

"Joe Felipe, now," he said to himself, "would be a good man at this job—with them shoulders of his, and them short, stubby legs. Joe's back in Kettleford, probably, now."

When he heaved the last log off the sled and over onto the pile, he leaned forward on it, resting his weight on the palms of his hands. He guessed that would be about all that he'd tackle today.

He turned round and sat down.

Tomorrow'd be easy; he could work in one place.

From the looks of the sky there was an hour of daylight. He guessed he'd get his gun and go down to the pond.

In the trap was a musquash. He brought that home and ate it. It wasn't too bad, and it wasn't too good. The skin wasn't worth anything, but he scraped it clean anyway. It might come in handy—you never could tell.

He slept dry that night, and from dark till past daylight; he wakened hungry, and he felt pretty good.

When he set to work, it took him less than ten minutes to prove that a man, to hew properly, needs more than an ax. He needs a good solid rig that will hold the log steady—one of those three-legged horses with a peg sticking up in it that fits into a hole through the end of the log. They'll hold a log steady. And he needed a chalk line so as to tell where to hew.

He was more pleased than otherwise that all this was so.

Inside of five minutes he was on his way back to Jonas's—because he couldn't go any further without an auger and chalk.

Whit hailed the house when he got near enough to it—stood there and waited . . . and then hailed it again. . . .

Melissa came out.

She looked to be well, as Whit came walking up to her—but he couldn't say anything to her at all.

Jonas, she told him, was off in the woods somewhere; Mrs. Moore'd gone up to Beede's—she'd only left a few minutes ago: she wouldn't be back for an hour at least.

They went into the house.

10

That night after supper, Jonas having agreed to go with Whit on the morrow to help lay up the house, they sat in front of the fire—all four of them—talking things over. Jonas already had had opportunity to report on his day to Whit,—he'd had all of two hours, and he'd used all of both of them. So that he'd covered not only today, but also most of those happenings of the past week or so that really required an appreciative listener—

things that a woman could not understand. He still had one left, though. He told Whit of it now.

Four days ago Jonas had had a shot at a wolf. His gun had missed fire.

Whit understood. Whit understood perfectly. He shook his head slowly, and spat in the fire.

Jonas was satisfied.

But Jonas's wife saw fit to inquire why the gun had missed fire.

There were a score of possible causes for a gun's missing fire, and half of these were preventable.

Jonas said curtly, "I d'know what it was."

There was a very uncomfortable silence.

Whit tried to help out. "Might a' been anythin'."

That did help a little, but it didn't cure matters.

Melissa asked Whit to tell her more of the house.

Whit did his best. "Well, I guess I told you about all there is to tell. It mightn't seem like much for th' time I been gone maybe, but all it is so far is—well, is a pile o' logs, you might say."

It was Jonas's turn to help Whit out now. He did this by saying, "Whit, you ain't told me if you figure to build in a chimbley?"

"Well, t' tell you the truth," Whit said, not without pride, "I had figured I might."

"A stone or a wood one?"

"Stone, to begin with, four feet or so, anyhow. I'll see how it goes before I decide how to finish."

"Well, you'd ought to have something," Jonas approved. "It'll make all the difference. Yes, sir, a chimbley's a wonderful thing."

Ida Moore, who was knitting, didn't make any comment. Nor did Melissa, to whom it hadn't occurred that they might not have a chimney.

"I seen it," said Jonas, "a good many times. A man and a woman will go through a winter, we'll say in a lean-to. The man locates it right, the same as you or I would, and the roof is a good one, and he don't hear any talk about needing a chimbley. Then the next thing he does is to build him a house. It ain't got any chimbley, but why should it have? The fire's outside, ain't it, same as t'was with the lean-to. And if the man was alone, he would leave it outside.

"But if he's got a woman, you can make up your mind to it that sooner or later she'll want a fire inside. They always do. It begins to come on 'em with the first fall of snow. They're all alike; you can count it. So what does she do? She takes 'n staves a great hole in a watertight roof to let the smoke out!" Jonas paused for a moment.

"Well, that'll work pretty good," he almost conceded, "when there ain't any wind and it's a little small fire—about as much, you might say, as I got in my pipe."

Jonas's wife, with chilly serenity, stuck to her knitting; Melissa was interested but a little uncertain; and Whit, wholly expressionless, blinked at the fire.

"A man," Jonas continued, "can cook on a small fire, and there ain't any man thinks he's got to cook every day." He was still talking to Whit. "But you take in the wintertime, she'll want a fire inside the house *all* the time—wind or no wind. You see, she don't want it only to cook over. No, sir. She's got a notion that with walls all around her, and a fire to boot, she'd ought to be warm. She wants to be warm, you see, even in wintertime. I know that ain't natural, but that's how it is with 'em, and there ain't now't you can say to 'em. They want a big fire.

"So she puts the wood to it," Jonas continued, "and maybe she gets warm. I hope she does, anyhow—she sets enough store by it. But she can't take any comfort in just bein' warm unless she can breathe. A woman has got to have everything perfect. And the way it is now, she's got such a big fire that, in spite of the hole in the roof, the smoke in that house's begun t' thicken up some. It is so thick that the only way she can breathe—or him, for that matter—is to crawl round on their belly. So what does she do? You don't know, and I'll tell you: she goes all round the walls and she knocks out the moss—or the mud, or whatever—that he has put in there to make the place tight.

"She gets rid o' the smoke.

"But the wind that blows out the smoke, will blow the cold in, won't it?—and the snow and the rain. Pretty soon she finds that out, and she mosses it up again—until the smoke gets too much for her. Then she starts in on it over again. She gets tired of that. Why, I knowed of a man once who was given his choice: get a new woman or build in a chimbley." Jonas reached out and poked at the fire. "I would advise you to build in a chimbley," he said.

"I'm glad," said his wife, "that you think it was worth it."

"I think it would be for Whit," Jonas said quickly. He tried to crawl back. "She mightn't give him his choice."

"Oh, yes, she would." His wife held up her knitting to see how it was coming. "Women," she said, "ain't so clever as wolves." She turned round to Whit. "When're you goin' to go after your cow?"

"Not till spring, I guess, now. I ain't got nothin' to feed her."

"What you'd ought to do is get hold of one now, 'n then Jonas could winter her for the milk or the calf, 'n then in the spring you could drive her to your place."

"She wouldn't pay you for her keep in the winter."

"She'd come near enough to it, when you figure the dressin'. I never yet see a garden wan't plowed from a cowyard was fit to grow stuff."

"Well—"

"What you'd ought to think of," put in Jonas, recovered, "is gettin' a dog. A dog's what you'd ought to have."

"A dog would be handy."

"A dog is more handy, I claim, than a cow. Way it is with a cow, she won't begin to take hold unless you feed her first. Don't make any difference which it is that you're after, whether it's dressin' or milk, you got to put the feed in the front end t' get the back end to work. But you take a dog, now, that's a little mite hungry, and he'll hunt all the better. A dog, he ain't got t' be paid in advance. He'll do his work first, and then he'll eat his dinner."

"Still, you can't eat a dog."

"That's only your own dog—and it's more you don't want to. Hell, any Indian—or a Frenchman, for that matter—they'd rather eat dog meat than cornbread or greens."

"You can't argue from Indians. Their stomachs're different. You ever eat any?"

"Dogmeat? I don't know. Sometimes I've et meat that an Indian give me, that I thought would set better if I didn't ask." He got up from his place, explained, "I'm awful dry," and came back with two jugs: rum for himself; the other was cider.

Whit asked him to sing, and Jonas sang them "The Robber."

Melissa said he'd done well with it, and asked for another song.

Jonas had a swallow of rum, thought for a minute—while all of them waited—and then announced quietly, "The Death of Fair Martin."

Whit said he'd never heard it.

"It's a good song," said Melissa.

206

"Yes," agreed Jonas, "she's a good one, all right. Twenty-six verses that song has got in it. If I go to leave out any," he invited Melissa, "you set me right."

"All right."

Jonas said, "I can tell you the story, if you want me to, first, Whit, and then you'll know better about what's goin' on."

"I guess I c'n follow it."

"Sart'n you can. It ain't any different from most of 'em, really. All it is, is this Martin—the one in the name of it—he's a young fellow that they go and hang for something they think he done although he didn't do it. There's a time along in there you think maybe they won't, but they hang him all right. Well, he's danglin' down on the end of the rope and about finished kickin', when this woman shows up that claims he didn't do it and she's got the proof of it. She cuts him down, but he don't last long— not more'n a couple of verses—no, wait now—three, ain't it?" he appealed to Melissa.

"Three," she agreed.

"Yes, that's right: three verses. His neck's all stove-up; I've seen 'em myself. Three verses is right I recollect now; I'd forgotten the middle one. Well, then she laments for quite a long spell with his head in her lap, and then she goes and gets drownded. She does it on purpose. The tune's awful pretty." He bowed his head thoughtfully, collecting himself. Then he said honestly, "I don't claim t' sing it so good as I used to when I had more of my teeth." He looked up at Melissa. "Maybe you'd better sing it?"

Melissa declined.

Jonas put his head down again, and they all gave him silence. Then raising his head, but with unseeing eyes, he announced once again, "The Death of Fair Martin." He put his head back and sang it.

It was a good song; there was no question about it.

They all enjoyed it, and Jonas did, too. He left out a verse but Melissa said nothing, and his voice only failed him two or three times, and then it got better as soon as he'd wetted it.

When he came to the end, he spoke the last half dozen words as a sign that he'd finished—and reached for the jug.

They all of them told him that he had done well.

It was Melissa's turn next. She sang "Billy Boy," and she sang it beautifully. She had a nice voice to sing with: it was gentle and cool, and at the same time it was clever. When she went after a note, she didn't slide her voice up or down—the way Jonas did—until she came to it; she could leave off with one note and light on another no matter how far it was in between.

Whit was proud of her. He always was anyway, but he was shaken with pride when he heard her sing.

Jonas said when she finished, "You're a good singer."

Ida Moore sang—not as well as Melissa, but the best that she could, and they were all glad that she did sing. She chose an old-fashioned song, which—as she said right afterwards—"wan't no more old-fashioned than what 'The Robber' was, anyhow."

No one asked Whit to sing. Jonas sang two more short ones, and then Mrs. Moore said it was time they all went to bed.

"I seen a woman once," Jonas informed them, "close to eighty years old. Ellen Stone, her name was. She might a been more than that—later on she got older—but at the time when I speak of, she wan't far short of that. Well, sir, I seen Ellen Stone—Aunt Ellie, they called her—sing a hundred and fifty-two songs between night and morning, and drink three gallon of cider. Henry Benham was there; he sung eighty-five and got trimmed."

Whit wasn't certain after he got to bed whether he wished they'd asked him to sing, or whether he was glad that they hadn't. He'd feel one way, one minute; and the next minute, the other. Nobody ever *had* asked him to sing. . . .

11

Next morning, Jonas wasn't ready to go. Whit had fully expected that this might be so, but he had hoped somehow to get Jonas ready so that they could leave before noontime. Whit hadn't figured on Ida Moore, though. She knew exactly the things Jonas must do for her before she was willing to let him set out.

So the morning wore on with one thing and another—Jonas attending to this, and fixing up that, grumbling and touchy because Whit could see him being bossed by a woman, and also because every one of these things that Jonas had to do now were things that he should have done some time ago. Finally, toward eleven o'clock, he went off to borrow the auger for Whit and himself to take with them. He said he'd be back before noon.

But he didn't come back. . . .

Whit, by this time, was more put out than Jonas. He had been feeling the pull of his house: he had to get back there and work on it. He could see the walls rising, and the thought of the roof kept coming before him.

Melissa, mistakenly, said she didn't mind. She was only too glad to have Whit stay till tomorrow.

Whit said, well, *he* minded!

Jonas showed up at sundown. They heard him singing a half a mile off . . . and to make everything perfect, he'd forgotten the auger.

Ida Moore wasn't angry—and no more was Melissa. They felt the same as they would have about a change in the weather. If it rained, why—it rained; that was all there was to it. It wasn't anyone's *fault*.

But Whit was so angry that, without saying a word, he set off by the path Jonas had come on.

He was back before dark. He wasn't singing and he had the auger.

Jonas went to bed early, and Mrs. Moore, too.

Whit and Melissa sat up by the fire—in silence, of course, so as to let Mrs. Moore go to sleep. Once that purpose was served, they could talk all they wanted.

Melissa was drowsy—with her head on his bosom. . . .

When Whit chuckled, it wakened her.

She asked what was the matter.

"That was funny, now, wan't it?—him forgetting the auger."

She said yes, she supposed that it was.

Neither contrition nor headache assailed Jonas next morning. It was never his custom to eat a stout breakfast: a quart measure of cider and a slab of cold meat were what he had usually—as his father before him—and he had them this morning. He got his gear all together, and he was ready to start.

There was some little discussion over taking the dog, in which Jonas won out. They took the dog. Jonas brought his own ax, and Whit carried the auger. They had a chalk line and chalk—they had everything that they needed. Whit told Melissa that they'd probably be back inside of a fortnight if nothing prevented. What he had in mind was, they'd be back in a week.

She stood in the dooryard—and waved them into the forest.

Whit traveled ahead, Jonas well in back of him. Jonas heeled the old dog, and they went a smart pace.

Within fairly wide limits, Whit took the same route that he'd taken before. He was trying to find the best going. When he was certain he had it, he was going to spot trees to mark it. Once he got Melissa in there, he would want a road out for her, because it might happen sometime that he couldn't come out with her himself. Or it might happen, too, that he'd want to come out in a hurry, and a road would help then.

Jonas, of course, could find his way round as well as Whit could, or better. Jonas had never been lost; he said so himself. He'd been puzzled sometimes to find the place he was looking for, but he'd never been really what you could call "lost." The closest he'd come to it that he could recall was one time in a snowstorm when he'd got into a swamp. It had taken him two days and a half trying to find his way out. He'd been awful cold, though.

They got to Whit's place a little bit after noon.

Jonas had never seen it before, and he had to take what Whit said about most of it now. It wasn't the best land there was in the province—for example, it didn't compare with Frye's land on the Saco. But it was about as good land—Jonas admitted in praise of it—as Whit would probably get anywhere for the terms he had made. And according to Whit, the lot had as much interval as a man would want to work, anyway. If the rest of it was hilly, why, that wouldn't matter so much as it would have perhaps if Whit had planned to sell off a piece.

Whit didn't tell Jonas about the sign he had seen. He didn't think it was necessary.

Whit's lean-to, however, Jonas praised highly. With a lean-to like that, a man could be comfortable winter or summer—a single man, that is—and not have to worry.

Whit showed him the logs.

"They look all right, Whit. You cut only good ones. Well, tomorrow we'll start on her."

"We could start now. We got three hours' daylight—pretty close to it, anyhow."

"Two hours, more like it. I d'know as 'twould pay us. We could go down to this pond that you speak about, have a look round, and maybe get something for supper, though. You take like in th' mornin', if we had a nice deer, now, hung up right in front here, we could work pretty good. Not so good as I might if there was keg to go with it, but I ain't complainin'. I knowed you was a dry man t' work with before I come in here."

"You hadn't ought to complain, had you?—not after yester-day."

"Come on down t' th' pond."

"This's a fine time o' day t' go deer huntin'!" Whit said. This's a fine time o' day t' start buildin' a house."

Whit saw it was hopeless. They went down to the pond.

But they didn't see any deer. They didn't see anything—except a gray squirrel, low down in a beech tree, and he didn't look to be any bargain in exchange for the powder. Still, as Jonas remarked, "We ain't got t' pay any lead for him."

He sent the old dog round the other side of the tree, and when the squirrel came round to Jonas's side, all spraddled out and hugging the bark, Jonas was able to shoot into the tree trunk. He used a slug big enough to break a deer's foreshoulder—if the range was right, that is—but a very light charge. When he picked up the squirrel, its head wasn't on it. Whit went up the tree and pricked out the lead; it was all in one piece.

They ate the squirrel for supper—what there was of it. While they were eating it, Whit said he wondered if the guts of a gray squirrel made as good bait for a trap, if you rotted 'em right, as a red squirrel's did. Jonas admitted that he didn't know; he'd always used red squirrel. Whit said that *he* had. They talked it all over, but they couldn't settle it. It was a question of smell, so Jonas concluded, ". . . and smell is a thing a man don't know much about. All he can do is try this, that, and the other, and then see what happens."

"Well, we can't try it with this one, because the dog's et 'em."

"We couldn't anyhow; it's too late in the year. You got to bury 'em when it ain't too cold weather. If you don't, they won't rot. I bury my guts about the first of September. I bury a jugful. By the first of October, they're just about prime."

"And they'll keep all winter."

"Yes, sir, they will. They're a wonderful thing."

Whit yawned and stretched himself. He fixed up the fire, and he and Jonas stepped out and took a look at the weather. Then they came back in the lean-to and lay down and slept.

The cold the next morning lay heavy about them. It was more than a threat of the coming of winter. It was the very thud of the footsteps of winter at hand. Near at hand, too—not much farther away than the other side of the mountain. Building a house seemed the natural thing for a man to be doing. It seemed so to both of them. And by the looks of the sky, by the feel of the air, and by the urge that was in them when they heard the wind blowing, they both of them knew that they hadn't much time. To Whit, it gave added excitement to a work that already was exciting enough. He was not only building—he was building a house for Melissa. Add to that now this great nearness of winter . . . winter rolling upon them, coming down off the mountain . . . and Whit and Jonas outwitting it right under its nose—well, it made the whole business as exciting as hunting. He spoke in a voice extra gentle and low; he saw tiny things clearly; he tried to move carefully. He had strength without limit.

Jonas worked fast. He could dovetail as prettily using only his ax as Whit could have done with a maul and a chisel. He was known for it.

Stopping a moment to put the stone to his ax, Jonas said cheerfully, "Time we get this finished, there won't be a bear on the mountain will be any more snug for the winter 'n you'll be."

Whit grunted, "Not many"—he was working the auger.

The soft slapping and hissing of Jonas's stone ran along with the words. "You take it with bears, though," Jonas observed, "I never heard of a he-one and she-one denning up for the winter in the same den together. You ever hear of it?"

"No," said Whit, "I don't think so."

"Neither did I." He went back to his dovetailing. Five minutes later—after nothing but work sounds—there was Jonas's voice again. "Nor I never heard of a bear den with a chimbley."

Whit snorted and grinned.

Whit was doing the hewing. Thrusting and twisting, he'd make a hole with the pod auger in the end of a log, set the log over the pin on the horse, and snap a chalk line to go by, two on each side. Then he'd hew to the line.

Neither man had to wait much on the other.

Whit hadn't figured to lay any floor, so the first tier of logs—after smoothing a place for them—they set right on the ground. They'd not last forever, but they weren't going to have to. If things worked out here as they had other places, there'd be a sawmill near by in two or three years, and then he'd have a house that was built out of boards—boards for the floor and the roof and the walls.

But in the meantime, he'd have a good log house. He'd have it tight, and he'd have a chimney.

They worked all day long. There was no question of going off hunting.

Day after day, in fact, Jonas hung to it. When they had the walls up, and the ridgepole and rafters had all been put in place, Jonas discovered that he'd worked for five days. He said that tomorrow he was going to go hunting.

Whit said, go ahead.

"You don't need two men to work on a roof," Jonas explained, "unless you want someone to dance on the ridgepole, like this was a rising."

"Well, you c'n try it. I'll pick you up if you land on your head."

"No, I'd rather go huntin'."

"You go ahead, Jonas. You don't mind if I stay here 'n work on the roof?"

"You know how to lay it?"

"Pretty good—yes."

That was settled. Jonas—they had finished their supper—said, "Old Henry Cotton—he's dead and gone now—used to dance on the ridgepole when I was a boy. They got awful big barns in that part th' country. He didn't mind. He'd get half full of rum, and up he'd go like a cat, 'n right out on that ridgepole the same as a squirrel. 'N he'd jig up and down, 'n cut all kinds of capers, and they'd holler up at him. 'N then sometimes he'd teeter 'n wave his arms round to look like he was fallin', 'n all th' women 'd squawk. I seen different ones since then, but he was the best."

"I seen two or three."

"They claim if you're born that way, it comes easy to you."

"Well, I know I wan't."

"Nor I wan't. 'N I ain't sure that he was. He never got kill't at it—he died of a sickness—but when they'd holler up at him, he never answered. 'Way I look at it, he didn't hear them. He didn't see them. He didn't see nothin' only that ridgepole right under his feet. That's why he could do it."

"Why did he do it? What was his reason?"

"Why, when he'd come down, they'd make a lot of him. He was just the same that way as anyone else."

"Oh."

"Oh, often as not, I suppose," Jonas went on, so as not to make it too pointed, "the man owned the barn would give him a present."

213

"That would've made a lot better reason than the other one was."

"A better one, maybe, but not near as strong a one. Well, he's dead 'n gone now. He can't jig on no ridgepoles, whatever his reason."

"He ain't never come back?" Whit inquired.

"Not that I ever heard of."

"Sounds to me like the kind would be likely to, maybe."

"Yes, you'd think so, now, wouldn't you?" Jonas agreed. "But I never heard tell of it."

"Time'd be likeliest, I should think," Whit said, "would be after a risin', with a lot of 'em drunk, 'n comin' on dark, you'd think somebody'd see him up there on the ridgepole—jiggin' round like he'd used to—prob'ly better."

"Ayuh, it does seem so. Maybe they figured on that, and put him extry deep when they buried him."

"That don't always work."

"No, it don't."

"Or another time they might see him, would be like after a risin', and a man was goin' home alone maybe, he'd turn round and look—*then* he'd be likely to see him, up there on the ridgepole, if he looked toward the west and there was light in the sky. A little man, was he?"

"I don't remember. I couldn't say. 'N I never heard of nobody goin' home alone from a risin'. Not if they could help it. *I* never did."

Whit said, "Whereabouts did you figure you might hunt tomorrow?"

They talked about that until they went to sleep.

Whit was glad to be working alone the next day. He wasn't tired of Jonas, but he liked being alone.

June was the best time of year to get bark in, but still he did pretty well. He had the roof more than half covered with three rows fixed in place, when he heard Jonas holler. He knew Jonas had meat from the sound of his voice. Whit then remembered that he hadn't eaten since breakfast. He hoped Jonas hadn't. They'd have a feed now.

Jonas had forty pounds of meat over his shoulders. He'd dressed out a deer. It was a good one, he said, but he'd had to work for it: four hours tracking clear up on to the mountain before he'd got a shot that he thought was worth risking, and then two

214

miles more. He'd broken the shoulder, but he hadn't stove it up really as much as he should have, because, so he thought, his wadding hadn't been tight enough; it had sounded that way. The second shot was a good one.

Whit examined the meat. "That's awful nice meat. A doe, wan't it?"

"Yes, and right up in shape. There's a half a hundredweight there."

"Easy," Whit said. "You done well, I c'n tell you."

"Yes, she's a good one. You got a good fire?"

"Fire's all ready."

"But I want to tell you, boy, you got more wolves in this part th' country than there is flies in a stable."

"This deer ain't been run any."

"You wait till winter!"

"You see any, did you?"

"You don't have to see 'em."

"I ain't heard any for four or five nights."

"They're around all the same."

"Well . . ."

Jonas assured him, "I won't say nothin' t' your woman about it, 'n I d' know as you'd better."

"She ain't scairt of a wolf."

"She might be of twenty."

"You don't know there is twenty."

Jonas swore. "Twenty! I bet you right now that if you had enough men to make a drive of it, say two hundred men, and a good man for a captain, and you had any luck, you'd kill a hundred. You'd get anyway fifty. I bet you'd get a hundred."

"When there's two hundred men in this town I'll send for you. You c'n be captain."

"I'll come, if you do. You c'n be the leftenant." Jonas noticed the roof. "You ain't set around much."

"I got some of it done."

"You done better than half of it."

"There's some ways to go yet."

Jonas went to inspect it. It was good work. He called out to Whit, "She looks good to me, Whit. Whyn't you get that meat rigged to cook, 'n then while it's cookin', you come over here 'n we c'n finish this row."

Whit said, "All right."

215

Jonas lasted another day, during which they got the roof finished, and then taking most of the deer meat, and with the dog at his heels, Jonas went home.

Whit took his sled and went down to the brook after stones. They were more plentiful than the spruce trees had been. He put in the day collecting a pile of them—prying them out of the bed and the banks of the brook. What he wanted was flat ones.

He did the same thing the next day. That provided a pile about the size of two haycocks. It looked like enough—so he figured tomorrow he could go after clay.

The following day, he made the cut in the wall. The topmost log in the wall he left as it was to keep the house tied together. Out of the next one below it, he cut a section the length of his ax handle—twenty-six inches; he used a handle longer than most— plus a handsbreadth besides. At that point the chimney, because of its tapering, would pass to the outside of the wall of the house. From here down to the sill, he kept widening the opening, taking out sections that were longer and longer. He had a line to go by. It became easier to work the farther down he progressed, because now he had room for the play of his ax. It would have been easier yet if they'd cut the logs first—to leave room for the chimney— before laying the wall up. But that might have slowed them beyond Jonas's patience. And Whit felt that the chimney was his business anyhow. When it came right down to it, he didn't want any help. From the beginning, he'd had a hankering to do the chimney himself.

When he'd cut out the opening down to the sill, he put a notch in the sill four fingers deep and to the length of two ax handles; that would admit the full width of the hearth.

Another day gone.

Between supper and sleep, he thought of what he was doing. He didn't know much about working with stone and with clay. And now that that was the next thing that he'd got to do, he didn't approach it any too eagerly. There were a good many questions that he should have asked Jonas. It might be better if he were to go out there tomorrow and find out some of the answers before he made the mistakes. There was going to be more to this business—now that he looked at it closely—than just laying the stones up and plugging with clay.

No sooner he'd started choosing stones for the hearth, than he saw he'd already done one stupid thing: he had piled up the stones. If he had just dropped them spread out over the ground, it would have been an awful lot easier to find the ones that he wanted. So he set to it and flung the pile all apart. But it disturbed him to have been such a lunkhead. It made him uneasy about the rest of the work.

He got the hearth laid, flush with the top of the sill, and not without some excitement, started in on the walls.

It didn't take long to discover that he was going to need as much as a bushel of small bits of stones to wedge in under the big ones to make the big ones set steady. He went to gathering little stones until it was dark, getting them out of the bed of the brook. The excitement he'd felt upon starting the walls had now disappeared.

The next day, however, he got along pretty well. He had the walls up two feet and a half, and they were solid and steady. He could stand off and look on what he had done.

He ate his supper slowly and thoughtfully. "In this kind of work," he said to himself, "there are all kinds of things that will come up to block it."

He made up the fire, and then he lay down to sleep. "That high sound of the wind is what it makes in the spruces; the lower down sound is when it blows through a pine tree. When you hear the two of them, both together at once, it sounds pretty good. Like it does now."

He fell asleep then . . . and Melissa was with him.

Cautiously, but with confidence, he went at his work the next morning. "If I make a mistake, I'll have to start over. The top part of this chimbley will rest on the bottom part; you get the bottom part wrong, and your whole chimbley's done for.

"And another thing is: you got to be awful nice when you're workin' with stone. You can't leave any play. Every piece you put in has got to fit snug and solid. You leave any teeter anywhere in it, and the whole thing'll come down on you." Shifting the stones, laying them this way and that way, end for end maybe, or turning them over, he went ahead slowly. It was solid and true.

He had now within him sufficient resolve so that there was no doubt in his mind but what it would stand against anything. And he let it. He let it stand against hunger—not taking the time to go after meat—and he let it stand against weariness: while there was light, he scarcely stopped for a second. When he lay down at night, he could touch the edge of sleep only—and even that would go from him before it was morning. While he was

217

sleeping, he would dream he was working.

He kept it up this way for three or four days, or it may have been five—he wasn't quite certain. All day and all night, he had that chimney in front of his eyes, and he had the feel of the stones on the flat of his fingers. It was getting up pretty high now . . .

Up on the roof, he worked more than ever like a man in a dream. He had the chimney pretty near finished. He hadn't eaten for a day and a half, but that didn't matter. Because an odd thing had happened: he didn't need to eat any more.

He put the last stone in place, and he knew he had finished it . . . and he knew what to do next. He must get down off the roof and onto the ground. He lay down on his belly, and slid down to the edge, hung his legs over, and dropped off to the ground. He landed weakly and heavily, staggered backwards a step or two on the hard, trampled snow among the stones and the rocks he'd left lying about, and his heel catching a rock, he fell over backwards.

His head struck on rock, and he lay there—loose-jointed, unconscious.

Jonas had left home before daylight that morning. He'd told the women that he was going off hunting—he'd be back tomorrow, most likely. His wife had inquired what he was going out after, and Jonas had said, "I d' know, Ida . . . I just thought I'd go huntin' . . ." She didn't have to catch his eye, then. She knew where he was going. Whit was overdue now; it was up to Jonas to look for him.

After Jonas had gone, Melissa said to her, "He's gone to see if anythin's happened to Whit, ain't he?"

"Yes," Mrs. Moore answered.

Jonas had come within a mile of Whit's place when, watching the dog, he knew that Whit—or at any rate someone that the dog knew and liked—must be just up ahead. Major pricked up his ears, stood perfectly still, and then wagging his tail went on to meet them.

Jonas followed and listened—but he didn't hear anyone speak to the dog. As he came round a shoulder, he saw Whit coming toward him—no gun, no nothing, just walking slowly and the dog walking beside him looking up at him.

Jonas slowed down, and then he stood there and waited . . .

Whit came almost up to him before Jonas spoke. "Hello, Whit."

That stopped him.

"How you been, Whit?"

There was no sign in Whit's face that he'd ever seen Jonas.

"Where's M'lissa?" Whit asked, his voice dull with no lift in it.

"She's out to my place"—but Jonas still couldn't tell whether Whit knew him or not.

There were only two things that could make a man act the way Whit was: one was a crack on the head, and the other was being just drunk enough. Whit must have got a crack on the head.

"Where's your gun, Whit?"

Whit didn't answer. He said in the same voice, "I finished t' chimbley."

"Well, that's good," said Jonas.

"Where's M'lissa?"

"She's out t' my place," Jonas repeated. "You c'n tell her about it soon as we get there." Jonas spoke loudly, as he would to a deaf man. But it didn't help any—Whit said again that he'd finished the chimney.

Jonas swore pleasantly. "It damn near finished you, Whit. What happened, anyhow? A rock fell on your head?"—there was no blood at all on him, but he looked awful poorly, and there was the smell and the look of hunger about him.

Whit started to speak—but Jonas forestalled him. "Come on," Jonas ordered, "I'll take you to Melissa."

He had Whit turned around inside fifty yards—Whit not suspecting—and he led him back to Whit's place.

Whit had stopped talking.

Jonas didn't quite want to take him into the house because having that chimney so on his mind, if he was to see it, it might set him off again.

Instead, he guided Whit into the lean-to—told Whit to lie down, and helped him to do so. It was then that he felt the great lump on Whit's head. "We'll lay here for tonight," Jonas said to him—although it was plain Whit didn't know where he was, "and then in the morning, we c'n go on to Melissa."—"And I hope to God," he said to himself, "that I don't have to haul you."

Whit lay there quietly and Jonas kindled a fire. Whit's fire was cold—it didn't look to have had any wood on it, so Jonas judged carefully, since day before yesterday. He set some water to heat and threw in a handful of the corn he had with him and a piece of salt pork. There wasn't a mouthful of food of Whit's anywhere round. Jonas was puzzled. Whit's gun was in shape, and he had powder and lead. Jonas stepped across to the house to have a look round for some sign or other that would tell him what had happened.

As a tracker, Jonas was better than average. The water he'd left on the fire hadn't any more than come to a boil before—out in back of the house—Jonas was bending over a stone that had some of Whit's hairs on it. "Didn't strike it quite fair, his head didn't, you see," Jonas told himself carefully. And he added the thought, "Just as well, I guess, prob'ly."

"Well," he said, squatting down so that he could think better, "here's where he come by that bump on the head, and that put him out of his senses. But that don't account for his bein' so hungry, because this happened this mornin'. Them little snow pieces"—he nodded toward them—"that's set up on edge where he tried to stand up, they're fresh 'n sharp as can be—they ain't had no sun on 'em since they was turned up—" he glanced at the shadow cast by the house—"but they're goin' t' get it in about half an hour. It could have happened at night from the way this snow is, but if he'd come out here at night he'd have had something with him, like a stick or his gun, because he'd heard somethin' stirrin'. He fell down empty-handed, or else what he'd had with him would be layin' here yet. I should think it would, anyhow. No, sir, this happened this morning.

"He didn't lay here long, either: he ain't melted the snow that was under him any.

"Well, if it happened this mornin', why in hell's he so hungry? From the smell of his breath and the looks of his tongue, he ain't et a morsel since day before yesterday. Why was that?"

There was no answer.

"Well, he's hungry, 't any rate, so I guess I better go feed him."

The thin, greasy liquor seemed to be just what Whit wanted. He sucked it in greedily. Jonas didn't let him have much, and then made him lie down again. "You hang on to that, 'n you c'n have some more later. Your stummick's all shriveled up. You got to let it soak for a while and kind of unfurl itself afore you try to fill it. You know that 's well as I do. Don't you?"

Whit lay quiet.

"Sart'n you do," Jonas assured him—and went out and left him.

He found where Whit had been up on the roof. That was also this morning.

Jonas did some more figuring. "If he was up on the roof, he went up there to work. If he was up to workin' on chimbleys, he was up to takin' his gun 'n lookin' for somethin' to eat. Why didn't he do it? His food must have run out as much as four days ago, because after that he eat up what he should have took with him if he'd went off to hunt or if he'd set out for my place. And yet he didn't do neither one of them things. He just stayed right on here. Well, let's see if he did— When did it snow? Four days ago, wan't it?" He walked a small circle round the house and the lean-to. There wasn't a footprint crossing it anywhere—except where Whit had come out today, and Whit and himself had come back again.

Jonas came back to the lean-to, shaking his head. He fed Whit again, and then went back to the chimney. He stood propped up against it, leaning his weight on it through his outstretched right arm, and looking down at the ground. "He's worked on this steady for the last four days anyhow—from the way this snow is trampled—and prob'ly longer. All of that time, he was gettin' more 'n more hungry, but he wouldn't give over workin' and go off 'n try to get nothin'. I don't understand it. Well, he's got a nice chimbley." He turned to inspect it. "Yes, an awful nice chimbley. He done better work, hungry, than most would have, fed. I hope when she sees it she'll have sense enough to tell him she likes it—if she ever does see it. If his head is stove-up . . . But I think it ain't, prob'ly. There ain't any blood in his ears or his eyes; there wan't any blood round his nose, for that matter. No, sir, if she don't tell him to his face that this here chimbley right here is the god-damnedest chimbley she ever see in *her* life—then her head's worse 'n his is—" he turned to the dog— "'n I don't think it is."

Later on in the evening, Whit seemed to sleep evenly, and Jonas decided he would sleep some himself. If Whit were right in his head when he wakened next morning, Whit would want to start going. "Long as he ain't got his senses, he'll do the sensible thing—which is lay quiet and rest." Jonas sat by the fire . . . "He's a rugged young feller—'n I guess all his life he's been more or less hungry for one thing and another. 'Where's M'lissa?' he says t' me. 'Where is M'lissa?' He had to find her! 'I finished t'

221

chimbley. Where is M'lissa?' God, if he wanted her that bad, why didn't he come out 'n see her?—'stead of stayin' round here t' finish t' chimbley. *She* hadn't said to him 'It's chimbley or nothin'." Nor he hadn't promised her. He ain't the kind to say what he will do—not till after he's done it. He makes up his mind, 'n then he goes 'n does it, 'n then he says—at the *most* he says, 'Well, I done it, I guess'—'n then he don't even get drunk. *I* couldn't live that way!

"I say to Ida, 'I promise you, this time, that I'll get a b'ar.' Then if I come home with a mushrat, she ain't disappointed. She knows I done what I could for her: I *tried* for a b'ar.

"What he should have done was to have said all along to her, 'Now, you take it easy. I don't mind tellin' you that when I get round to it, I'm goin t' build you one hell of a chimbley.' Then he could have gone at it in a sensible way. Why, he wouldn't have had to have started it maybe until along in the spring."

Jonas concluded that he would turn in. He put some wood on the fire, and then went and bent over Whit—who was now sleeping heavily. "He smells better to me 'n what he did before— 'n I don't smell any fever." He touched the back of his hand to Whit's forehead. "No, I think he's all right."

And Jonas prepared to lie down himself. He checked himself suddenly—and went over and put his own blanket on Whit. "There now, I almost forgot—that was what I brought the thing for."

Then he lay down a little nearer the fire, and he called the dog to him. "Here, you, Major, lay down. No—right here. You lay down. That's right. Now stay quiet. You'll do me as good as a blanket would maybe—if you c'n only stay quiet."

He sank quickly toward sleep. "Ida'll be awful glad," he thought to himself, "if I c'n bring him out there in good shape tomorrow. I didn't dare promise her—I didn't dare tell her—but she knew all the same what it was I'd come after."

. . . and a half-minute later, "You know, he has got an awful nice chimbley." And Jonas settled in sleep.

The pain in his head was the first thing Whit was aware of. It flowed forward in waves from the back of his head and beat on the inside of his forehead. He knew what had hit him. Falling, and the painless white flash as his head struck the rock, were present and clear to him. He knew now that he'd been knocked out for, he supposed, a second or two.

He opened his eyes against darkness, but expected that to clear in a moment—and then he saw the light of the fire on the back of the lean-to. While he was trying to figure that out, a great coughing roar filled everything near him.

Helpless and terrified, Whit lay perfectly still. His head now was clearing. He recognized facts as fast as he could: he was lying on his side facing the back of the lean-to; it was in the night now, the fire was going; he was under a blanket—and then the great sound that was near him broke and tumbled and fell to a whispering. He suddenly knew it—he'd heard it often enough— it was Jonas's snoring. Whit sniffed to make certain—yes, this was Jonas's blanket.

Then he let go of himself, he couldn't hang on any longer. He trembled and shook, his face shaped itself in a grin of relief, and he was half crying, too.

Jonas started in a new cycle—finished it—and began on another.

Whit began taking stock of things. This pain in his head was a fearful thing surely, but here, somehow, was Jonas, and between the two of them they'd be able to take care of whatever it was that had happened. Jonas's being asleep meant that things couldn't be too bad.

Whit got a hand out from under the blanket and located the bump on the back of his head . . . She was a good one! A half inch lower down and she'd have stove in his head properly.

Well, here was some good luck to balance the bad luck. That made him feel better. It meant that he wasn't marked for a long spell of bad luck. It might even be he was in for some good luck, because whatever it was that was bringing him good luck had been right on the job when he needed it most: it had protected his head from being stove in, and then right on top of that it had brought Jonas in to him. Two things like that didn't happen right in a row without something was causing them. Whit was comforted.

The pain made his eyelids close, and it had started the sweat in his hands. But the rest of him was cold. He discovered now he'd two blankets—one of them his own, the other one Jonas's. Still he was cold.

If he had Jonas's blanket, Jonas didn't have any.

Whit didn't like that. It made it appear that he was a sick man. He wasn't sick—all he had was headache. He *felt* like a sick man—he felt sick enough so that he didn't dare to give in to it.

223

He felt so sick that if he didn't do something to pretend that he wasn't sick, why, this pain in his head would get the best of him. Then where would he be?

He'd got to do something.

He knew what he'd do: he'd take this extra blanket and put it on Jonas. If he could do that, he'd have shown this pain in his head which was the better, himself or the pain. He'd have it beat then, and he'd not have to worry about it, because sooner or later it would go away from him.

He raised his head up, hung on for a moment . . . and then couldn't make it. He settled back, and the pain surged through him fiercely. It was the worst that he'd ever known. It was like having the toothache in the whole of his head. He had a fold of the blanket squeezed tight in his hand.

Pretty soon it let up some.

Whit said to himself, "Well, if that's the worst it can do, I think I can make it."

He gathered himself—and tried again. This time he kept going. He got Jonas's blanket off him to begin with, and he rolled free of his own. Then he got himself up on his elbows and knees, hung there a moment—and had to fall back again. But he'd made a start, and that was big in his mind while he lay there . . . and in a minute or two, he was able to get up again.

Crawling along, dragging the blanket, he got over to Jonas. The dog was awake and thumped his tail pleasantly. But Whit couldn't take any notice. His stomach was turning over and over inside him. He dragged the blanket up over Jonas and started back to his place.

He made it, and lay face down by the fire alongside his own blanket. His breath was coming unevenly in little short jerks and he didn't quite know what was going to happen next to him. But he knew that he'd made it. Whatever happened, he had that underneath him. He'd proved he wasn't sick.

But this headache was worse than he'd ever dreamed of. It went back and forth from his head to his feet, and it worked on him everywhere in between, too. If it didn't get better by morning, he would have trouble walking.

He got his blanket around him, and close to the fire he lay still and waited.

The pain slacked up a good deal, and also he got used to it.

He made no effort to think, and his brain flapped around loosely—it touched on Melissa, and some things back in

Kettleford, and he remembered his chimney—and none of these things seemed of any importance. He was breathing steadier now.

He slipped into sleep . . .

When he wakened next morning he had on both the blankets.

Jonas was tending the fire. He had about four times as much fire as he generally would.

Whit watched him awhile without saying anything, and then when Jonas had his back turned, Whit sat up. His head throbbed pretty hard, but still nothing to speak of compared to last night. He pushed off the blanket and got to his feet. It seemed to him for a moment that he was a long way from the ground, and he wasn't so steady as he might have been. What his stomach might do was anyone's guess. He was on his feet, though. He wasn't sick!

Jonas looked up. "Well!" he said, "'bout time you was up."

Whit grinned—and commented, "That's an awful big fire."

"Roast 'n ox," Jonas said, and turned to the fire. He was so relieved and delighted that he could have shouted. Whit's return of the blanket had not reassured him. Whit could have done that while still out of his head. "Set down 'n take comfort, 'n have somethin' t' eat. You ain't eat no more'n was good for you th' last two-three days, have you?"

"Maybe not—I d'know."

"Well, then, you better begin. Set down, damn it, will you!"

Whit sat down—carefully. He felt kind of squeamish but the food smelled good in spite of that. He guessed he could hold it. "How'd you leave the women?"

"Good," Jonas said, "both of 'em." He had johnnycake ready and some smoked moose meat he'd brought along with him. Fresh meat would have been better. He started Whit on the johnnycake.

The food tasted good to Whit, and it seemed to settle his stomach. He ate almost half of what he would ordinarily, and then he had to quit. He just couldn't seem to hold his head up any longer.

Both he and Jonas had eaten in silence.

"You go and lay down again," Jonas commanded. "You'll get the good of that food pretty soon, and then you'll feel better."

"I feel better now."

"Maybe you do, but it ain't the food done it. You think it is, but it ain't. It takes some little time t' get the good out of food. If you was to vomit that now I could show you: it wouldn't look any different from what it did when you swallered it. I seen that happen. That's how I know."

Whit lay down in the lean-to. It seemed to him wonderfully good to lie down. He would lie here awhile and then they'd get started. "When'd you get here?" he asked.

"Yesterday noontime."

"I guess I was out of my head."

"You seemed like it, yes."

"I fell on a rock."

"That's what I figured."

"Where was I?—layin' there?"

"Yes," Jonas said.

"Good thing you come, I guess."

"Oh, you'd a come to, prob'ly—sooner or later."

"Maybe—but not under two blankets nor close to a fire."

"Did you put that blanket on me?" Jonas inquired. "I hoped the dog done it. I figured if you done it, you must a still a been out of your head. He's an awful good dog." He tossed a piece of meat. The dog caught it with a snap and swallowed it whole.

"I c'n travel," Whit said.

"You could," Jonas answered without turning round, "if we had a stagecoach run from here out to my place. You ain't go'n t' walk, though—not today, I c'n tell you. Tomorrow, you might."

"I feel pretty good."

"Yes," said Jonas, "you look good. Jeems Chris', Whit, be sensible!"

"I c'n make it all right."

"You ain't go'n t' try. You're go'n t' stay right where you be for the rest of today, 'n tomorrow we'll see. You could start, I admit. Hell, anybody c'n start. You might get there, too—if I was to lug you. And what do you figure my woman would say to me for lettin' you start?—or yourn either, for that matter."

"I said I'd be out there some time before this."

"You should a thought o' that a week ago, Whit."

There was a silence—while Jonas thought maybe he shouldn't have said that. He heard a noise and looked round.

Whit was standing in front of the lean-to. "I'm settin' out," he said.

Jonas stood up—and then turned to the fire. He kicked it apart. "All right," he said, "I'm comin' with you."

12

Ida Moore and Melissa had sat up later that evening than there was any occasion for. Mrs. Moore had the little wheel up by the fire, and Melissa, across from her, was knitting a stocking. It was Mrs. Moore's wool, and it would be Mrs. Moore's stocking. Melissa, as guest, was doing the work on it.

The wheel stopped for a moment . . . and the sound of the wind was loud in the chimney.

Ida Moore remarked briskly, "I'm goin' t' bed. My eyes ain't so good as they used t'be, really. I'd ought t' spin in the daytime. But you don't get enough daytime this time of year t' get anything done in. You'd better come t' bed, too. They won't be here tonight."

"No, I guess they won't, now. It's been dark for five hours. Whit can travel at night, but I hope he ain't, in a way. What do you think?—I shouldn't wonder they'd be here tomorrow." She went on with her knitting.

"Maybe," Ida Moore said. She was putting the wheel away. "But I wouldn't figure on Jonas. If he was on his way home and he come on a moose track between Beede's and here, he'd turn off to follow it and not come back for a week. He done that once. Truly. He didn't get the moose, either." There was no truth in this, but that didn't matter.

The girl tried to laugh as well as she could. "I guess Whit's the same way. Oh, I ain't worried at all—not now, I ain't, anyhow. If there'd a been anything wrong when your husband got in there, he'd a come back right away." There was no truth in this either.

"That's right," Ida Moore said.

"Prob'ly what they have done," Melissa continued, "is go off hunting together."

"I shouldn't wonder." She stood over Melissa and looked down at her work. "You turn a nice heel."

"I never done much. One set of hosen'll last a Kettleford woman a good many years. I never had any until I was growed. From mudtime to snowfall I always went barefoot. Other times, moccasins. If I'd gone more to church, I'd have had to have boots. William Cauldwell, the cordwainer, said he'd make me some once, if Pa'd find the leather. Whit can tan leather and

227

fashion a moccasin. But he can't make a boot. Still, I guess I won't need any, not for church, for a while yet."

"No, I guess you won't, prob'ly."

"This here is nice wool."

"That's Gilmanton wool. We ain't got any sheep, yet—or Daniel Beede ain't, rather. I ain't sure that Jonas 'd make much of a shepherd."

"Why is that?" said Melissa.

"Why ain't there sheep here to Sandwich? Not enough pasture, I guess, is the main reason. I couldn't say." She could have if she'd wanted to: wolves were the reason.

"It's nice wool to work with."

"You come on to bed, child."

"Let me finish this heel."

"No, you come on to bed." She laid her rough hand on Melissa's fair head. "They won't come any sooner for your settin' up waitin'. Time you been married as long as I have, you'll have give over waitin'."

Melissa wound up the ball. "I done enough waitin' before I was married so's I'd ought t' be used to it." She laid the stocking aside. "I guess I ain't awful patient."

"You're patient enough," Ida Moore said, and turned to cover the fire. "Trouble with you is, you know that you're patient. What I always do about Jonas when he don't come back is say, 'Drat the old fool!' and go on with my work. He always turns up—he always has so far."

"Yes," Melissa said bravely, "so has Whit, for that matter."

"Then let's us go to bed."

The room had grown darker while she was covering the fire with ashes—but it wasn't quite dark, there was a flame or two left, about enough to make shadows.

"Hark!"—and Melissa held up her hand. . . .

Ida Moore crouched on the hearth—not even moving a finger. She couldn't hear anything. After a while, she relaxed and turned round to Melissa. The girl nodded, still listening . . . and then said in a whisper, "I thought I heard someone holler."

Ida Moore listened some more. Except for the wind, there was no sound at all—not even the water down by the landing. The shadows were large . . . and so was a little pricking noise from the fire.

"An owl, I guess, wan't it?" Mrs. Moore said.

The girl shook her head.

Mrs. Moore stood up then, and strode toward the door. "Must a been some kind of a sump'n," she said very definitely. A fox or a weasel, perhaps, got a rabbit. It was too late for a loon. "They wouldn't get in here this time in the night"—she meant Jonas and Whit.

She stepped out through the door and let the skins fall in back of her. She listened, turning her head . . . no . . . not a sound. Only the wind. Wait—she heard the soft thumping of an animal running.

If it hadn't been for Melissa, she'd have backed into the house. She stood her ground, and heard him come nearer. She was scared, all right, yes. And then she knew what it was. It was the old dog coming home. "Major!" she called. "Where you been, you rascal!" And she called to Melissa, "Here's the dog, anyhow!"

"Yes," said Melissa—she was standing right there behind her.

"My stars, but you give me a start! I thought you was back in the house."

"I come out when you did."

"Well, you stood awful quiet."

"I was listenin'."

The dog came up to them, happy but tired, and as soon as Mrs. Moore'd patted him, he went on into the house.

"Hark—" said Melissa, "I heard him again."

"Yes, I did, too, that time."

"That wasn't Whit's voice."

"No, that was Jonas. He always hollers when he gets near the house. Well, I guess we better go in and perk up the fire. I don't know about Whit, but Jonas'll want something hot." She went into the house. Whit was alive anyhow, or Jonas wouldn't have hollered.

Melissa peered into the darkness that lay on the clearing. She knew just where they would come from, but she couldn't hear any voices. If there were two of them they ought to be talking.

Then close at hand there was Jonas's voice, "Evenin', Mis' Livin'ston."

"I can't see you. Where are you? Whit—are you there?"

"He's here, right enough. Whit: speak to your woman."

Whit said, "Hello—" but it didn't sound like him.

Melissa moved forward into the darkness—and then all of a sudden they all three stood together. She could see better now.

But Whit didn't come toward her—he was holding his head up, but he still didn't speak. Melissa stared at him. "Whit—what's the matter?"

"Whit's kinda tuckered," Jonas explained. "We come quite a ways. He ain't had any rum, if that's what you're thinkin'—nor I ain't, for that matter, I'm sorry to say. Well, you got here, didn't you, boy?" And without waiting an answer, he said to Melissa, "He can tell you about it. I'm goin' in 'n see Ida."

Jonas found his wife busy with bellows and poker before a quickening fire. She heard him come in. "Well, Jonas," she said.

"How you been?—all right?"

"Ayuh, we been all right."

He set down Whit's gun and his own, and the other things he'd been carrying. "I want t' tell you," he announced with some fervor, "a more pigheaded youngster than that fool in th' clearin' I never see in my life."

"Well, you don't need to tell *him* so. He's right outside, ain't he?"

"Tell him!" said Jonas. "All day I been tellin' him!" He came up to the fire. "I been callin' him every last thing I could think of since we set out this mornin' from that camp of his in there. You know how we been travelin'?" And in a much quieter tone, "That rum hot yet, is it?"

" 'Twill be in a minute."

"Ten rod 'n then stop!" He went back to his story. "That's all he was good for—a little more on the level now 'n again maybe—but uphill or down 'bout ten rod was the limit. 'Whit,' I says, 'damn it, lay down 'n rest, will ye?' But he wouldn't do it: he'd hang on to a tree for a little spell maybe, 'n then he'd go on again. He knowed well as I did if he was t' lay himself down, he wouldn't get up again—not till tomorrow."

"He been hurt, has he, Jonas?"

"Yes, he's been hurt! Fell off his roof 'n lit on his head, 'n I guess he'd a stove his head in if he hadn't been lucky. Happened 'fore I got in there. He was out of his head until some time in the night last night. 'N then first thing this mornin' he'd got to travel! All day, we been at it, just like I told you. Why, he wouldn't even stop at Poole's house—we come right handy to it, and I wanted a glass—nor he wouldn't stop in at Beede's. All he would say was 'I guess I'll keep a-goin'.' Do you know what was drivin' him?" Jonas demanded. "He was afeard she'd be worried about him! 'Jeems Christ A'mighty,' I said to him, 'Whit, I had more sense than you got the day I was married."

"You was worried yourself enough to go look for him."

"Well, I found him, all right! How is that now?—hot enough, is it?"

"I shouldn't wonder."

"I guess I'll call 'em in." He stepped toward the door. "He's too tuckered out t' have t' leave 'em alone. You been all right, have you, while I was away?"

"Yes," Mrs. Moore said.

Melissa saw the light suddenly come from the doorway as Jonas drew back the skins.

"We can go in there to live," Whit said, "any time that you're ready."

Jonas called to them.

13

Whit made two trips to carry in meal, and then about noon of a bright day in December, they finally left Jonas's.

Ida Moore was the one to whom the parting came hard. Jonas not only knew the place where they were going, but he also knew that sometime during the winter he'd find himself near there and he'd stay a night or two with them. But Ida Moore knew that it would be eight miles in the snow, counting both ways, to Beede's if she felt that she'd got to have a woman to talk to. Still, she was more cheerful than anyone else, or at any rate she appeared to be, and there was no question whatever but what she was more businesslike.

Jonas smoked more than usual, and he twitted Whit a good deal but without much success.

Whit's spirits were low. When they'd left Kettleford, with the whole trip before him and the odds not any too good on their getting there safely, he'd felt quiet and confident. Now that he'd come as close as this to his goal, he was jumpy and irritable. He refused to believe that something wouldn't go wrong. A half dozen times over he made up the pack of things he was to carry. And he couldn't eat any dinner.

When they were ready to leave, Ida Moore found a chance to say to Melissa, "Any time that you need me, you send him out after me."

"I will, Mis' Moore."

"Well, you see that you do. You be on your way, now. Whit seems kind of impatient."

Jonas came up. "He'll quiet down when he's carried that load a ways. Mis' Livin'ston, you come again, will you? And you'll hear me holler outside your house sometime or other 'fore the winter's gone by."

"I hope so," Melissa said. "You've been awful good to us."

"Maybe Ida has; I ain't. Good luck to you, now." He turned round to Whit, who was shouldering his burden. Jonas helped him to settle it. "There now, that set all right?"

"Yes, sir—feels good. Y' know, Jonas, I—"

"Y' know the way, do you, now? You ain't go'n t' git lost?"

"I guess I c'n find it. I d' know as I'll ever get square with you—all you done for us."

"Well, I d' know as I want you to. Go on, now, git started. Don't stand around talkin'. Anyone'd think you was goin' t' Canady. Hell, it ain't more 'n a step in to your place. I could get in there 'n back between breakfast 'n noontime. Go on, now, 'n good luck to you."

"Well, I guess we had better. M'lissa, you ready?"

"I'm all ready."

"Good-by, Mis' Moore."

"Good-by, Whit." And she couldn't help adding, "Take good care of her, now."

"Try to," he said.

They set off on the path—Whit going first—that crossed Jonas's patch of wild hay and that cut through the middle of his acre of stump corn. The sun had melted to mud the frost in the field except for a patch on the side of each cornhill. They went up a slight rise and into the woods for the four miles of uphill that would bring them to Beede's. Whit stepped out of the path and turned to Melissa. "I guess you better go first. Then we won't go no faster 'n what you've a mind to."

"If I could go as fast as I'd like to, you couldn't keep up." She stepped ahead of him.

"Don't worry—I'll get there."

It wasn't dark in the woods; there was sunlight all round them. Here it was mostly basswood and maple, with scattering hemlocks and occasional spruces. There were oaks, too, their leaves all turned to brown and thinned out overhead. They'd be there when spring came, some of them would. Right in here, for some reason, there were not any pine trees. And the trees were all tall trees. The gray trunk of a basswood, for example, would run up seventy feet before there was a single branch on it. The same was true of the maples. The trees were the shape of long, tapering candles, with away up at the top a tuft of bare branches. A man living in Portsmouth who'd never been back into the forest could come pretty close to the shape of the trees if he took a new candle—say half a cloth yard in length—and held his fist at the top of it. If he had a big enough fist that would just about show him how much was trunk and how much was branches.

Down on the ground, it would be as much as eight or ten paces from the trunk of one tree to the trunk of the next tree nearest to it. Melissa could see a long ways. In a good many directions, she could see just as far as she could have in the open. Other directions, there'd be a big boulder that hid what was behind it, or there might be a row of young saplings getting a start on the moss-covered hump where an old tree had fallen; they were spindly things, generally: they had to hurry their growing, they had to try to get up to the sunlight that came through the hole overhead—that the old tree had left for them—before that hole was closed up.

Whit said, "When we get t' th' top th' hill just this side o' Beede's you can come pretty near seein' where it is that we're goin'."

"Can we? Let's hurry!"

"Take it easy; we'll get there. You can see, too, the whole range of the mountains. There's a little pond down in there—just off the top of the hill—and it opens the woods up so you can see pretty good. Would you like to see it?"

"Sart'n I would!"

"This path don't go by it, but Jonas told me about it, and I went down in t' th' pond once to look at it. It ain't only a step. Nor we ain't hard pressed for time, really—not at the rate you been goin'. You ain't figurin' t' get there tonight, are you? You ain't changed your mind, have you, about layin' at Poole's house?"

"No. I ain't changed my mind any. I still know I could a done the whole trip in one day. But you was bound 'n determined to split it into two days—so that's what we're doin'. I ain't changed my mind!"

"Well, when we get to th' top this hill, you'll have come three mile from Jonas's, and it'll be three more to Poole's place. When you stand on the top, if you still wish in your legs that you had fifteen more miles to travel, then I'll say I was wrong."

When she got to the top of the hill, she was a little bit out of breath and her color was high. But she was undeniably happy—and it did Whit good to look at her.

"You come along pretty spry," he said, "for a woman fixed the way you be."

"I told you I could."

"Yes. Well, here's where we turn off t' go down t' that pond."

"Don't you want to lay off your load?—'n then pick it up again when we come back?"

"No, we ain't comin' this way. We c'n cut acrost from down in here to the pond that's in back of Beede's 'n strike the path again there."

Melissa didn't quite understand it—because he had failed to explain that there were two ponds.

They went down through the trees. And when they had come almost to the shore of the pond, Whit said, "There, about here. If you go right down t' th' edge, the trees on the other side'll come up too high for you. Just look out there, will you?"

She saw the mountains.

From well to her left they ranged low on the sky clear around to her right. She was startled to know that all along they had been there and she hadn't felt them. She felt them now. There seemed to be nothing that separated her from them. The sun was upon them—and between the sun and the mountains there was nothing else, either.

She turned and looked up at Whit—he smiled down at her and nodded—and together they turned and went on with their journey.

Whit shifted his load a little, easing his shoulders. He had never felt better.

He cut around Beede's, having no special reason to stop there at the moment, and about two miles beyond that, as the day turned to dull whiteness—losing the yellow and sparkle that had been in it at noontime and giving way to the soft chill of midafternoon that in an hour or two would turn into dusk—they came to Poole's clearing and his house in the midst of it. He was an older man and could remember the Indians; there was no cover nearer to his house than a good thirty yards in any direction. Here they would lie for the night—and Melissa was glad of it.

Old man Poole lived alone. There was one bed in his house— a good, solid rope bed. In it Melissa lay sleeping.

It was now a half hour since she had retired, but Whit and the older man sat up by the fire. Whit sat on a stool, his chin in his hands; Poole was in his own chair. For a time, they'd been discussing the state of the province. Whit hadn't made a very good showing. About all he could contribute were small items of fact, things he knew of himself mostly, such as prices and crops and the amount of game in the woods, what towns were now settling, and how hard it was for a man to get any powder that he could really depend on. These things, he supposed, might all of them go to make up the state of the province, but he thought of them separately and one at a time—which was the way he encountered them.

Poole liked to lump things together, and then to claim that one cause had brought about all of them. "For the last five or six years," he said, "pioneers has been thicker in the northern part of New Hampshire than fleas on a Frenchman. Why is that, can you tell me? You're a sample yourself. Why are you movin'?"

"Well, I guess the main reason is it didn't seem to work out right for me to try it to Kettleford."

Poole made no further inquiry. "Same way with the rest of 'em," he said approvingly. "It ain't the new land that is bringin' 'em—not into this country. Hell, because land is new ain't so much in its favor. You can grow more in a field than you can in a forest. They most of 'em come because they wanted to leave."

"That might be the way of it; I couldn't say. It was that way with me, surely."

"Whyn't they start comin' in here fifteen years ago?— twenty? I mean all comin' to once, like what it is now."

"On account the Indians?" Whit said uncertainly. He supposed that was it. Twenty years ago, though, the problem of moving hadn't greatly concerned him.

"No!" Poole was emphatic. "Indians, anyhow, didn't stop the ones that was in here. And there was quite a few people lived all through here then—scattering ones, I admit, and not so many round here as there was to the south further. But quite a few, all the same. Some of them *never* had no trouble from Indians. Some of 'em did. But it wan't like the Indians was on their necks the whole time. Why, it'd be two 'n three years at a time when there

235

wouldn't *nobody* would get kill't by an Indian—or even run off to Canady.

"Indians was scarce—the woods wan't so full of them. You had to go a long ways when you set out to look for 'em. Lovewell did, didn't he?—though you wouldn't remember. That was forty years ago, that was. Well, he did, all the same. My father told me; my uncle went with 'em. He never come back. They could afford to go a long ways after Indians. You know what was in it? A hundred pounds for each scalp. That shows they was scarce, don't it? The price wouldn't be that high for anything that was plentiful. You done some trappin', you know that 's well 's I do.

"Why even Rogers and them fellers went with him had to go clean to St. Francis before they come on a nest of 'em. That's a long ways.

"I've knowed this country longer'n you have. The flies and the rattlesnakes, the wolves and the Indians, milk sickness in summer 'n measles in March, all them 're a nuisance. But there ain't any one of 'em enough by itself to keep people from pilin' in here if they wanted to. All them things together didn't keep out the ones that did come. So why claim it was Indians kep' back the ones that's *now* comin'?

"Ten years ago, it was, Rogers cleaned out St. Francis. He done a good job: since then, we ain't had no trouble from Indians. But that was ten years ago, mind you. And it wan't nine years ago that the towns begun settlin'—like I mean they are now. Not a bit of it. It wan't for five years that the towns begun settlin'.

"What were they waitin' for? Th' wan't any Indians holdin' 'em back; the war didn't amount to much after 1760; and there was hard times to boot—there was a hell of a drought there for two years a-runnin', 'n that fire round Rochester—you'd think a good many people would've quit 'n come north. But they didn't come. The towns had been granted—why, Benning had granted, in the year '61, threescore of townships on the west bank th' river—Connecticut River—'n close to twenty on this side. Nobody moved into 'em—not right away. Why didn't they, eh? I c'n tell you, boy: money. They was waitin' for money to get in its work."

"That may be so," Whit conceded politely. In 1760, he'd been just ten years old.

"Money!" said Poole. "That's what's settlin' this country. Why did old Uncle Benning, his Majesty's Governor and a son

236

of a bitch—your wife's asleep, ain't she?—grant the land in the first place? Because he was paid to. Not by the King. The King wanted it granted so's t' get things t' goin'—I d' know, I suppose—and Benning, he granted it: to the ones that would pay him. Th' wan't a batch of Proprietors got an inch of land in this province that didn't pay Benning first. Then he'd turn right around 'n make them give him a share of what they'd just paid him for. He was a beauty!

"Well, then the Proprietors had to pay out some more money—for running out lines 'n layin' out roads, because even a pioneer wants to know where he is at. Them things cost money, and it's the Proprietors' money: a pioneer hasn't got any money."

This was too true for Whit to be interested.

"All right. The town's ready. Now who's go'n t' settle it? People own cows 'n tools, and a place, are well fixed where they be, ain't they? They don't want to move, do they? The ones are willing to move are the ones that ain't got nothin'. They can't move, either: they can't afford to. They c'n get along pretty good in a town where there's people to work for. But if you're goin' t' go pioneerin', you got to have stuff of your own, ain't you? You got to have a cow t' begin with. Where's that cow go'n t' come from? Out th' Proprietors' money. Same way with the land the Proprietors give 'em. All of it comes out th' Proprietors' money.

"Money, I tell you, is what's gettin' this country settled. Every Proprietor is a man who's made money. He's made it in masting or trading or rum, one way or another—some of 'em farming. And now they're puttin' that money into gettin' this country settled. They'll get it back again. They'll get it back and a little bit over. That is one reason they're puttin' it in. Another one is, they don't know what else t' do with it. Bein' a merchant ain't what it used to be—that's what they claim, anyhow. Too many laws."

Whit said, "I guess I d' know a gre' deal about laws."

"My father had money," Poole said, now that he thought of it. "That was when we lived to Exeter. I knowed a good many of the Sandwich Proprietors back when I was a young man and they was most of them boys. I been to Portsmouth many a time. I knowed some of the merchants—not a great many, my father knowed more of 'em. He was in a fair way to be a merchant himself until he lost his money. When my mother died, I went int' th' woods. I've lived alone always ever since then—most of the

237

time, anyhow. That's why I talk so much. I beg your pardon. You look to me sleepy. I should have known better. I shouldn't have talked so much."

"No, I ain't sleepy—not to speak of, 't any rate."

"I seen Benning Wentworth a good many times. He's what I called him. But now you take John, him that's governor now, he ain't the same kind, and don't you forget it. He's Mark Wentworth's boy—even if he is Benning's nephew. Mark Wentworth's the richest man in New Hampshire Province. But he didn't get it the way Benning got his; Mark made it masting. There's a whole lot of difference. Young John is a gentleman, and I don't say that he ain't, but he's got a head on him, and it may be he's honest. He knows the woods, too. I don't mean like a trapper, but at any rate he's been in 'em. Why, a feller come by here last year who'd been loggin'—this's a good story, you won't mind if I tell it?"

"Go ahead, do. I'd like to hear it."

"Well, there was quite a crew of 'em loggin' at this place where he'd been. The wages was good and the rum was found for 'em, and they wan't payin' no heed to broad arrows nor nothin'. They'd take any tree that they had a mind to—and if the King or anyone else didn't like it, he knew what he could do. Loggers are apt to be that way, you know. They bring down a big tree and it makes 'em feel pretty good. They see a thing that size layin' there on the ground, and they get an idea that they can lick anyone. I never see many loggers that you'd got to spit in their face to get 'em to fight ye.

"Well, young John Wentworth he heard tell about what they was up to, and he didn't like it. He didn't like either—or maybe he did—that they'd as good as sent word that any King's officer wanted t' come up there 'd get hove in t' river.

"Young John, he went up there.

"They'd heard he was comin', and they was all ready for him—two- or threescore of 'em, all down on the landin'. They'd figured, you see, that he'd bring a big party—which would be all the more fun because there'd be that many more splashes. If he'd bring enough men, there might even be a fight in it—though most of 'em figured that was too much to hope for.

"Well, young John, he showed up—and he didn't bring but only one man with him—a feller to paddle him. This feller laid the canoe right alongside the landing, and John he clumb out—all alone, mind you. And then he just stood there and looked 'em all over. He was dressed just as fine as he would be t' Portsmouth—a long velvet coat, 'n lace, 'n all that. He would a been somethin' t' throw in the river! But nobody done nothin', and young John he just stood there, quiet and easy, lookin' 'em over.

"Then he started in talkin'. He said who he was, and why he had come there: they'd been takin' down mast trees that didn't belong to 'em. Then he says to 'em, 'I will now read you the law'—and he took a roll, like, of paper out'n his pocket, and he went to work and he *read* 'em the law. He read every last word of it—and then he rolled up the paper and put it back in his pocket.

"'You been breakin' the law,' he says. 'I come up here to tell you that you got to stop it.' Then he waited again. . . .

"Now was the time to throw him int' th' river.

"Nobody moved; nobody said nothin'.

"John turned on his heel, and walked toward his canoe.

"They give him a cheer, then—they couldn't help it."

Whit said, "Did they quit takin' mast trees?"

"I couldn't say as to that. I ain't certain that either side figured that that was point."

"No, I d' know as 'twas."

Poole appeared to have spent his desire for talking. "Well, I guess we better turn in," he said. "You go'n t' lay by your wife? That bed ain't a wide one. Or you go'n t' lay by the fire?"

Whit said he guessed that he'd lie by the fire.

He didn't think long on the things Poole had talked about.

Tomorrow night at this time they'd be in their own house . . .

It was a lowery day—more than threatening, really, it was a part in itself of the storm that was coming—as they set out the next morning. Poole wanted them to wait over. But Whit had said he guessed they'd better keep going; they'd make it all right.

There was no question as to what Melissa wanted to do.

So they'd set out as early as politeness permitted.

The wind in the night had worked its way up from the south to east—and in two or three hours it would be fair and square from the northeast. And there it would stay for as much as a week maybe—this time of year. Looking up through the trees where the branches were bare, Whit could see on the face of the solid gray sky, the wispy, lighter gray clouds moving steady and fast. There'd be no mountains to show Melissa today! He'd be lucky to get her in under a roof before she got wetted—before the cold had got into her, and her clothes heavy to carry.

He didn't like her to hurry, and he made her rest now and then. "We got all day to do it in," he had to remind her. He wished it was true.

"It's goin' t' rain pretty soon," she said.

"Not before nightfall." It had held off longer now than he had expected.

"Or snow," said Melissa.

"I shouldn't think so. It might."

"I hope it does," said Melissa. "I hope we get a great storm! We'll be in our own house." Just at this moment the miles between didn't exist for her. She was in her own house—and the storm running outside was a good thing to hear: it was keeping Whit home with her.

Whit understood. He saw it as brightly as she did. He saw her face bright by the light of the fire.

"We will be when we get there," he answered cheerfully—at least he meant to sound cheerful.

Melissa said nothing.

He supposed she hadn't heard him—overhead it was noisy— the wind in the trees.

But she'd heard him, all right.

Whit was traveling first today, there being no well-worn track for Melissa to follow. Before very long, now, they'd come to the river. Always before he had crossed where there were boulders—and if he didn't lose his balance nor slip, he got across dry. With Melissa along, he'd have to cross where it was sandy. He'd wade it and carry her. That would be the best way.

Melissa trudged along steadily. She had tucked up her skirts so that they didn't hamper her much, and while she wouldn't have wanted to have to make the same trip tomorrow, she felt pretty certain she could do it today. Whit was easy to follow; he wasn't going too fast, and with his broad back in front of her, the approach of the storm overhead didn't seem to her threatening. About all she had to watch out for was not to trip over something. This was the day that all along they'd been trying for! This was the day they'd be in their own house.

Her mind wandered about from one thing to another almost as freely as though she'd been at her wheel. Her thoughts would stay for a little with something remembered—or with something looked forward to, it didn't matter—and then be called back to what she was doing by a kink in the thread or a turn in the path.

It was the sound of the wind took her back to that darkness when, in the roadway that ran past the tavern, she'd felt the wind blowing. In front of her then, poor Joe Felipe had been talking—trying to say something—but she'd sent him home. Joe Felipe. He had the same name whenever she saw him—but you could never count on him to be the same man. She'd been sick in fear of him—Pennacook she remembered. . . . There was evil in Joe—but not all of the time. Oftentimes when she thought of him, she called him "poor Joe." That bright red little hair ribbon—

"Here's the river," Whit said. He was leaning his gun up against a big tree.

There was the river. It looked ugly and cold.

"I'll take this stuff over—half of it, anyhow: I d' want t' get all of it wet in case I should fall in. If you ain't any objections, I'm gon' t' take off my pants."

Melissa watched him step into that ice water and go sloshing steadily forward till he was well past midstream. Then he stopped and considered—peering upstream and down. The deep part was before him. When he'd chosen his way, he stepped carefully into it—the water up to his waist . . . and he got safely across. He didn't call out to her, and when he got back, all he said to her was "Water ain't so cold now as 'twill be in the spring."

"Looks cold enough, though!" she answered with feeling. "If 'twas cold as it looks, it would be solid ice."

Whit had started to pick up the rest of his load. He changed his mind. Straightening up, he said, "I guess maybe I'd better take you over now." Another trip through that water might take some of the limberness out of his legs.

"I ain't in no hurry!" Melissa assured him.

"You'll be all right." He picked her up in his arms as he would have a child. "But when we get out there, don't wiggle 'n squawk."

"When did I ever wiggle or squawk!"

"Never," said Whit, wading into the water. "But most women would."

"'Squawk'! Well, I should hope so!—if you was to come at 'em without any pants on 'n try t' lug 'em into a river at this time of year! You might find one or two who would squawk a little bit, maybe, before you had even stepped into the water."

"Maybe. Hold still, now. I want one arm free to balance." He

241

shifted her over, holding her now in his right arm alone. "This ain't like Squam Brook," he said reassuringly. "If I was to step in a hole, you wouldn't no more 'n get wetted."

"That's a nice thing to know," Melissa admitted.

"Shut your eyes, if you want to."

She kept her eyes open, but when they came to the deep part, she didn't breathe . . . his arm and his shoulder felt solid and hard; whatever limit there was to his strength, she knew was far away from them. Looking down at the water, she felt a scorn for it. She gloated over it—and then on a sudden it came up very close to her. She tightened all over—and shut her eyes tight—

"Easy, now—easy—"

She opened her eyes—and the water had fallen away.

Whit set her down on the bank. "What was the matter? Did you think I was goin' t' drop you down into it?"

"No!" She shook her head happily. "I knew you'd hold me up. I wan't so sure, though, you could keep the water down, too."

"Sandy bottom," said Whit. "It ain't all of one hardness. Some places is softer 'n what you think they will be. I'll go back now 'n bring over the rest of it, and then we'll get along. It ain't awful far now." He stepped into the water with no more hesitation than if it had been, say, the end of July.

She shivered, watching him. It seemed a long time before he got back.

Whit drew on his breeches, and was tying his moccasins. "I'll come over here one these days," he remarked, " 'n lay a good tree acrost—down below here where it's narrow. Then you c'n get over without any trouble."

"I d' know as I'll need it right away," said Melissa. "Well, I d' know as you will."

He loaded up with his things, and they set off into the woods again.

They had not left the river more than ten minutes behind them when Whit heard overhead the first hiss of the snow. The wind had slackened somewhat, and the small flakes were sifting unhurriedly down through the trees.

"Here's your snow," he said to her over his shoulder. "Right on time, ain't it? How far is it now?"

"You tired?"

"No."

"Well, I'll show you." He took note of the tree that was the one he was heading for, and then stopped and knelt down. Brushing smooth with his hand a place on the ground, he drew a little map for her—the brooks and the hills—and explained it all carefully. "Well, that's how it is," he concluded. "You see it now, do you?"

"Yes."

"Well, we got plenty of time—" and rubbing out what he'd done, he said, "You show it to me now."

She couldn't do it.

Whit laughed, and said easily, "I'll show you again."

This time she got it.

"Sometimes," he said, standing up, "if you know what you're doin', it don't seem like so much."

They had started along. "That's true," said Melissa. "And you know you wouldn't have scairt me if you'd a come right out and said that seein' now it was snowin' it wouldn't do no hurt, really, for me to know where I was. Comin' thicker now, ain't it?"

"Bound to," said Whit. "Well, let 'er come. We won't get wet, anyhow, with these little small flakes. This is proper dry winter snow."

It was getting harder to see, and he felt some annoyance because he'd neglected to spot any trees along this part of the route. The shadows had gone, and the land here was flat—and every last pitch pine about as much like another as two peas in a pod. A man could get turned around pretty quickly in here. In hardwoods, when it's snowing, you can tell which way the wind's blowing: through the bare, open branches the snow holds to its slant. But when you're in an interval covered with pitch pine, the wind is all broken up by the thick-growing needles and the snow falls every which way; you can't tell a thing.

Whit was beginning to get just a little uncomfortable. He was lining up trees to keep going straight, but it was a poor enough method and he hadn't much faith in it.

Maybe, he thought, he should have stuck to the river. It would have added six miles—the two sides of the angle they were now cutting off—but at least he'd have been certain of not getting twisted. He didn't really believe that he could get turned around now—but he wasn't sure of himself. And he was getting excited.

If he'd been alone (he knew this was so) he'd have been no more than interested to see how close he would come to hitting the stream at the place that he wanted. If he were to miss it entirely—when he was alone—it would be a good joke on him—and serve him well for his clumsiness.

But there'd be nothing to laugh at if he lost his way this time. She was doing her part—and it was the most she could do—by just keeping going. She was depending on him to lead her straight to their house.

The snow was thicker and thicker—and smaller flakes, too. It seemed to be colder. He was constantly tempted to work to his right—because on that side he could afford to go wrong, if he didn't turn clean around—but he tried as hard as he could not to give in to it too much. He couldn't see ahead very far now—say three or four rods.

Strongest of all was the feeling that just ahead was the stream.

He tried to think calmly how much time had gone by since they'd left Bearcamp River. But he couldn't tell. Still, ahead was the stream—just ahead, surely! It *had* to be, now. They'd be all right in a minute. These woods had a hold of him, but they couldn't hang on to him. He'd be free now in a minute or two—

Melissa called, "Whit! You're goin' too fast for me!"

He stopped in his tracks. But he didn't turn round. "I'm sorry," he said, "I guess I wan't thinkin'. You want to rest, do you?"

"No, it's too cold. Only don't go so fast."

"All right." He spread his feet wide so as to keep his direction and turned round to look at her. "You doin' all right?" She looked to be, surely! The hood of her cloak was all whitened with snow—but her face peering out of it was as happy could be.

"Go ahead!" she laughed at him. "I want to git home!"

Whit nodded—and as he turned to go forward, he saw that the trees were thin on his right. "You stay here a minute—" he said to Melissa . . . and inside of a minute, he stood on the bank of the stream.

Even now—though he saw it right under his nose—he couldn't get rid of the feeling that it didn't belong there. He could not, in his mind, shift the country in back of him to fit this little evidence which he saw with his eyes. None the less, here was the stream. By an effort of will, he forced things to come right.

He went back to Melissa.

"Stream's over here," he said.

She didn't quite understand.

Whit grinned and said sheepishly, "I got off some, I guess. I was makin' too much to my left. But we got hold of her now."

Melissa said, "Well, are we—Did we lose very much?"

Whlt shook his head. "We ain't lost any ground. We're a little farther upstream than what I showed you we would be, but we ain't up as high as the place where we leave it."

"Well, let's keep a-goin'."

"Wait a minute," he said. "We got four mile to go yet. Do you want t' try it?—or d' you want t' bate here? I c'n fix you up pretty good so 's you c'n rest here if you want to. I c'n keep t' wind off you, 'n make up a fire. You c'n have somethin' t' eat. Do you want t' do that?—or do you want t' keep goin'?"

She thought before answering . . . while Whit watched her face carefully.

"I want t' keep goin'."

"All right, then: we will. But you understand that if it gets t' be hard for you—I don't say it ain't now, but what I mean is: too much for you—you're to sing out. You understand, do you?"

"Yes."

"All right." And then half to himself and half to Melissa, "From here on, at any rate, I couldn't get lost if I wanted to. Except rounding the hill, I got a stream all the way."

They stayed along close to the bank till they found a good crossing place, and then Whit carried her over—with his pack, gun, and all—up the bank, and along it. She was easy to carry. Of course, she hadn't much heft to her, but the thing was, she was trustful.

"There," she said, "I c'n walk now."

Whit set her down.

The snow was making up fast—better than two fingers thick in a good many places and it had only been snowing an hour. Melissa found it the worst walking she'd struck the whole trip. She couldn't see very much farther than Whit's back, to begin with, and shut in by the snow, she felt as though she were walking a treadmill. She had no measure of distance except the passing of time. Whit had promised her, though, that if she could keep going long enough, when it was ended she would be at their house.

She trod upon sticks and small stones that were hidden under the snow, and they hurt her feet. She didn't think that Whit knew this because nothing hurt Whit's feet. Even now in the snow, he was content with his moccasins—no hose at all. But except for her feet, she was comfortable enough. She could keep going for quite a while yet—following Whit's back—just plodding along. There'd come little short spells when she'd almost forget where she was—and then she'd step on a stone and be awakened again to the storm all around her and the snow and the cold.

After a time, they were going uphill. They'd left the pitch pines. Under the snow, there were dry leaves that slid about and gave her no purchase. She was leaning way forward, trying to get up the hill, and every so often one foot would slip backwards and she'd fall to her knees. Then she'd get up again, and follow on after Whit. The strength that she'd had was spending fast now. Turning his head, Whit saw her stumble; he helped her up and stood holding her arm. "You hurt?" he demanded.

"No."

"'Tain't awful far now. We're about roundin' th' hill. You want t' go on? We're pretty near there."

She knew she'd got to go on.

Whit stayed beside her, helping her forward.

She could tell when they began going down because she could walk almost upright, or it felt like it, anyhow ... Whit had one arm around her and, though he wasn't actually carrying her, he bore most of her weight. She was making the motions of walking, but if he had let go of her, she'd have slumped in a heap.

She wasn't doing much more than kind of waving her feet at the ground.

Whit would have slung his rifle and carried her outright—it would have been easier for him—but he could see better this way, and there was less danger of falling.

They covered a mile in this fashion. He had to go around everything because she couldn't pick up her feet.

In his mind he was seeing the dry wood on the hearth and the fire he'd laid and left ready to kindle. He could see the pine splinters, the curled bark, and the tinder; everything ready, needing only a spark. He'd even taken the pains to cover the top of the chimney so as to keep it all dry.

They were now in the spruces. Here was a stump—capped over with snow—where he'd taken a log to use in the house. There was another.

She was light on his arm now. A little while back, his arm had been aching. She was light as a feather.

He was searching the swirl of the snow that was in front of his eyes and the grayness beyond it for the shape of his house.

Then he saw it: still and white, there it was. . . .

Coming up to the doorway, he set down his gun, picked up Melissa, and carried her in.

The skin over the doorway fell back into place. It was colder in here than it had been outside—cold and dark, too; that was what he'd expected. "We got here," he said.

Melissa stirred in his arms. "Set me down. I c'n walk."

"You ain't got to. We're here."

She opened her eyes—"Whit, I can't see nothin'!"

"You will in a minute."

"Where are we now?" Her voice didn't sound very big. "Whit— We're in the house!"

"That's right," he said. He set her down by the hearth.

When he'd brushed the snow from his clothes, he reached outside for his gun—and blew the snow from the wrappings he had round the breech. Then he unwrapped it carefully, keeping it dry, and stood it up by the fireplace. He sprinkled in powder around the tinder and pine splinters—and he put a stout pinch in the pan of his gun. Now he was ready . . . Holding the gun low and sideways with the breech close to the fire, he drew back the hammer and cocked it—and he let her go.

He got a good flash in the pan and a flare in the tinder—and the tinder caught from it.

With Melissa beside him, he knelt on his hearth, watching the growth of the fire, the cold and darkness behind him.

The pine splinters had caught and were sputtering nicely. The bark crackled and bubbled, it flamed and it smoked. Up from it all—up into the chimney—there rose a thick, yellow smoke. And the flame spread and increased . . .

A rolling billow of smoke seemed to come down the chimney and out into the room. "Chimbley's cold," muttered Whit. Another came, and another—

He had forgotten to uncover the chimney.

He jumped to his feet and ducked out through the door.

Melissa could hear him on the roof overhead—and some snow spilled down the chimney. Then the chimney took hold and really started to draw.

As Whit came in again, the first thing that he noticed was that she'd thrown back her hood and had loosened her hair.

Melissa slept warm that night; she had the fire on one side of her, and Whit on the other. She hadn't that steady assurance of warmth that had used to come from the chimney by her bedside in Kettleford. But she had enough of warmth, all the same, so that whenever she wakened she was conscious of comfort. She would shift then just a little, knowing things were all right, and have no feeling at all of wanting to hurry the night.

Whit kept up the fire. He didn't sleep very long at a time.

Well on in the night he went to the doorway and found it had stopped snowing. That didn't mean anything. But the next time he looked, there were a few stars in the west and the wind fallen to nothing. There was a brightness to the black of the night instead of the dullness that had been there before. He went back and lay down, thinking about it. He concluded it was probably just a break in the storm—not a change in the weather. Because almost always a northeasterly storm, once it gets started, is good for two or three days. It isn't a thing that springs up like a shower; it takes time for its building, and it lasts a long time. Off and on, it gets worse; and sometimes, for a little, it may seem to let up some. But you can count on it, it will never give over until it's blown itself out. Not till the wind has gone well to the westward can you figure it's done with. It would be snowing again in the morning, all right.

When he wakened the next time he could tell by the fire that he'd been asleep this time for as much as three hours. It was still black in the cabin—except near the fire—but outside, grayness had come—and it wasn't snowing. The whole sky had cleared now—and the wind he felt on his face was coming out of the west. The storm was over and done with: that much was certain. And the sun would come up so you could see it and feel it. They wouldn't have to hold to the cabin today. Melissa wouldn't. She could come out and see where they were. And she would take a good deal more kindly to this place that he'd chosen if it were to have the sun on it when she first looked around. He had not tried to tell her what the mountain would look like.

He tightened his belt, and went in to fix breakfast, letting the skins fall over the doorway but not taking the trouble to fasten them down. Daytime had begun.

Melissa lay sleeping. There was no change at all in the light in the cabin. He tucked the coverings round her and she didn't stir, so he knew she was warm enough. He listened a moment for the sound of her breathing . . . and it came even and gentle. She was comfortable, surely. And she had taken no hurt. He held to

248

the thought of her for a minute or two, and then he broke off without hurry and went to the fire.

It would please him, he knew, if when she wakened there was food hot and ready that he had fixed for her. After a day or two, they would come to share naturally the work and the house. They would divide up the work of their living, the things that fell to each one being just and distinct. But for this first day or so, he'd take enjoyment and pride in providing all things for her: tending the fire, making her food ready for her to eat, and fixing a warm place to sleep for them both.

The house and outside would be all of it strange to her. He had prepared it against her coming to share it. It was she who would quicken it. But he had prepared it.

He was molding some cakes with his hands, patting them plump between his palms—corn meal and grease and water and salt—and as soon as he'd shapen one, setting it close to the heat. They didn't take long to cook. It didn't matter much, anyhow, once they were hot. They had just as much strength in them cold and uncooked. But they tasted good hot.

After she'd eaten, they would go out and look round. The sun would be up . . . and it would all be before her, everything shining and the sky bluer than summer. She would stand in front of the doorway and see the whole thing at once—just as he had from the hilltop. He would tell her, of course, that the soil there in the interval was deep and was good, and point out the direction he would go to get hay. But she would see why he'd chosen it.

Then they'd go round in back—and there'd be the mountain.

He heard her stir in her sleep; she was wakening now. A whole winter night and some part of yesterday, she had lain there by the fire, sleeping and warm. He hoped her strength had come back to her. Because if it hadn't, he didn't know what would bring it.

She was awake now, but her face was turned from him, and he waited to speak to her until she was ready. She was probably trying to figure out where she was. He usually did that himself before he opened his eyes; there was less to confuse him. Now, until he could speak to her, he felt separate from her—but their voices would fix that. He waited, not moving, crouched by the fire, hearing the silence. . . .

"Whit . . . ?"

"Ayuh—right here."

"Mornin'," she said to him.

Whit grinned—she was all right. "Mornin'," he said to her.

He went down to the brook to bring up some more water. There was a fox had been by in the night, but nothing else he could see that had fur or meat on it. When he got back to the cabin, she was standing up by the fire. He set down the water.

She said, "I'd ought t' done that."

"Tomorrow," he told her. "You sleep pretty good?"

"I never slep' better."

"You'd know you been travelin' yesterday, though."

"In my legs, I would, yes."

"But you didn't take any hurt? Not—well, you didn't take any harm?"

"No," she assured him, smiling a little, "not that I know of."

"You'd know if you did, I guess."

"And I would tell you."

"Good." He knelt on the hearth to examine the cakes.

"You didn't seem any too spry when we got here last night."

"I don't remember."

"Well, you wan't, I c'n tell you. You was draggin' your feet some. Still, you kep' a-goin'."

Melissa said nothing.

"I guess these here are done now. What'll you start on, a cake?—or a cake?"

"I don't want to eat now."

He'd been afraid of that. "You better eat somethin'—'n I guess this' 'bout all there is."

"I will in a minute. I want to go out first 'n see where we be. It's dark in here, Whit. I seen the sun, though, when you went out through the doorway. I seen it again when you come in here just now. I want to go out 'n see what I'm goin' t' look at—every time I go to the door from now on for a while."

Whit stood up slowly. "All right," he said.

It was only three steps to the doorway—and he drew back the skins and Melissa stood forth. Whit followed after. They stood together in front of their house.

Melissa's eyes blinked before the glistening glory of the sun on the snow. But she could see what was before her—and she wasn't shut in by it. She could see as far now as she had need to see. She felt hope and some promise . . . and she was unaware of her silence.

Whit said, "If you want to step round in the back, I c'n show you the mountain."

But she stood now in that spot toward which she'd been striving for a good many months. The mountain was extra. She felt no need to go look at it.

Whit told her the things that he'd expected he would.

And she said, "Yes," and nodded. But he knew she wasn't seeing the things that he told of.

What she was seeing was the earth down there in the interval, brown in the springtime as it would be when he'd turned it, and the light green on the trees—and the little bugs in the air . . . and on the other side of the springtime, the summer awaiting them. The mountain was Whit's.

But she would go round and look at it. . . .

She picked her way carefully, choosing to go in Whit's footprints in the deep, fluffy snow. When he stepped aside and stood still, she lifted her eyes to the mountain—and she saw it simply and clearly as it rose gray in the sunlight, gray where the trees were, with patches of white, and then the solid and awful bare rock of the top.

To herself, she said hurriedly, "This is his mountain"—and then its greatness assailed her and in the rush of her feelings she couldn't limit her thoughts. It was far away from her, it was away off in the distance! . . . and yet it came close. It was the bigness it had that could do that to the distance—make the distance to nothing right when she could see it was there. But the moon could do the same thing—and not because of its greatness—when she looked at it too long without looking away.

Whit loved this mountain. And back in the days on the river Whit had gone forward happily toward the roar of the falls . . .

Whit loved this mountain. But she didn't love it.

She looked at it steadfastly as in the sunlight it filled all she could see. . . . The threat of it was real to her. She didn't have to know what the threat was. She faced it squarely a moment—and found it too big for her to feel anger or bitterness.

Then she turned away.

Whit had stood hesitant, waiting to see. And now it came to him that she understood. He thought that was the reason that she didn't say anything. She had stood this first time in the mountain's full presence . . . and she had been lifted to wonder . . . just as he had himself.

She put her hand through his arm, and he was glad of it.

As they came round the house, she felt the strength of his body as he walked at her side. The sun was warm on her face as they stood by the door—and together looked down to where their fields would be green. This was their place. This was enough for her. Let them make it to grow—here in this place now in front of them—she and Whit and the child that would be for them in the spring. That was all that she wanted. That was all that she asked for.

It was good that the door of the house opened south to the sun. True, it was in that direction that Kettleford lay, but that didn't matter: she wasn't troubled so often by Kettleford now. Nor could Kettleford come here, because there was too much of distance that lay in between—oh, yes, too many days, and a great deal of distance. Joe couldn't come here; she didn't mind Joe— he was far away now.

They went into the house where the fire was working . . . and she was a little surprised when she found that she wanted to eat.

14

Melissa was the one who kept count of the days. She had reason to. The days remained fixed and she made her way through them. She added the days into weeks and knew how many she'd done with . . . and she knew how many weeks lay ahead between her and her time.

Whit, on the other hand, watched the winter go by. He told off its progress by the sun creeping north, by the strengthening cold in the night yet the sun warmer at noontime, by the frost in the trees that made the maples like iron to threaten his ax; and he watched the wax of the moon and its waning. The deer hadn't yarded but had begun to be poorly. There was not a bear stirring. And on a night when the wind came from the north and the mountain, the wolves would make as much racket as the whip-poorwills in the summer. These were the nights when the stars were the thickest, and when the noise of the ice on the pond was the loudest. At the full of the moon, the moon looked to be smaller when it got up into the sky than it did in the autumn. But it gave out a great light! Three nights in a row he had seen it so bright that a man could pluck a hair from his head and hold it up in the moonlight and see it. And right in front of the cabin where the snow was tracked down, a step made a sound like the squawk of an axle.

He said to Melissa one night, "What do you figure we're in now?—the third week in the month? I ain't reckoned it lately."

"We lack a day of it. Tomorrow is Sunday."

"Yes, that's about right. From the feel of the air, there's a thaw comin' soon. And after that snow. Been too cold to snow lately."

"There ain't no place without it that I can see from the dooryard."

"Next month it'll snow. That's the time when we get it. February's the snow month—February and March."

She spread her hands to the fire.

"You ain't cold," he asked, "are you?"

"No, I ain't cold. But the fire feels good."

"Yes."

"March is close on to springtime," Melissa suggested.

"Well, it's part of the winter."

"But there'll be signs of spring then, when we get into March."

"Oh, yes, there'll be signs of it—same as you can see signs of the autumn in August. And then all through the autumn you can feel winter come on. But spring, now, is different. There can be signs of spring thick all around you. But it won't make no difference: it'll still be the winter. But when it *is* spring, I can tell you, you'll know it! "

He'd been whittling a spoon, and now he rested his hands, holding his work up to the light of the fire to see how it was coming. "That ain't a bad spoon," he said, "or 'twon't be when she's finished."

Melissa said something—but she didn't know what it was.

There came a morning when it was sunny and warm; there was steam from the roof and the sound of snow melting everywhere—from the drip at the eaves to the rush of the brook. Melissa fastened the skins up away from the doorway; it was warmer outside than it was in the house.

Whit was chopping this morning down below in the interval. When he came up for his dinner an hour or so before noon he was carrying his leather shirt flung over his shoulder and his linen shirt was darkened with sweat from his neck to his belt.

253

She said to her husband, "You'd best take that shirt off and let me rinse it out. The other one's dry for you."

Whit nodded, and did as she told him—drying himself by the fire, and then he put on the dry shirt. "That feels pretty good," he said. "You ain't got to wash that one. I'll just wring it out and hang it up here."

"They last a lot longer," she said, and she took the wet shirt outside to a bucket of snow water that she'd caught from the roof.

Whit was easing his back in front of the fire, and resting his eyes in the gloom of the cabin. He had put in a good morning. In a minute or two he'd be past this first weariness, and ready to eat. He could eat now if he had to, but his mouth was still dry and his stomach still tightened from four hours' working. He drew the stool with his foot from the hearth corner to more in front of the fire, and sat down with his back to the heat, and his head in his hands. He still had in front of his eyes the fresh detail of the cut he'd been making in the last tree that he'd felled. He'd been felling all morning, there being no wind: two pretty fair hemlocks and a white oak tree of some bigness. It was the oak that had taken the time. He had been tempted to girdle it and just let it stay there. But now that he had it down, he was glad that he'd tackled it.

He seemed to feel for some reason as though he were sleepy—as though he'd like to lie down. . . .

Melissa had called him—"Whit! Whit, come out here!"— and he scrambled out through the doorway and stood half-blind in the sunlight without any idea of what could have happened.

"Sh, shsh!" she said. "Hush—"

Whit held his breath. He couldn't imagine what it could have been that she'd heard—but he didn't ask.

"A man hollered. I heard him—"

Whit didn't believe it. It had happened to him when he was alone in the woods. Oftentimes he had never found out what it was. He said nothing and listened. . . .

"Hello!"—they heard it together.

For an instant, Whit stood perfectly still. Then he turned to Melissa. "That's Jonas," he said. But he could see she wasn't yet over the start it had given her. "He said he'd be over"—and Whit raised his head toward the woods and called back.

"I guess I'd better go meet him," he said to Melissa. "He's on about the same track that we come in on"—and he set off at a heavy lope down through the snow.

Melissa was trembling. She didn't know why. Now that she knew it was Jonas she ought to be glad. It was what she had wished for a good many times—and stronger than "wished for." But now that someone was here—or would be in a minute—she was startled and frightened. She wished Whit hadn't left her— and she almost called after him. She watched him go plunging off into the woods. And then very suddenly, as Whit disappeared, joy seemed to spring up in her, and she hurried into the house. They were going to have company! She would hear people talking. There would be talking and laughing, and news from outside. She knew Jonas's voice as it had been in his own house, and it would be the same here in the cabin, and he would look the same, too. What must she do now to get everything ready? What would Whit want for him? What were the things that she and Whit would be proud of? He would want to eat, surely. That was the first thing. Oh, she was happy!

In the pot on the fire she had enough stew ready to feed both the men. But now they had company she couldn't be saving and she added some lumps of fat to it and put in some more salt. There were four dumplings in it—and she knew Whit could eat three— but she had no Indian fine enough to make any more. Still, if she herself did the ladling from the pot into the bowls, they mightn't notice that she didn't take any herself.

Not even the freshness of Jonas's coming could make either man talk when they sat down to eat. They sat on stools on either side of the fire, and Melissa, her back to them, filled the bowls from the pot—she gave Whit's bowl to Jonas and her own bowl to Whit. With a nod to each other, the two men fell to eating. Melissa had moved from the fire; she stood by and watched. She had a spoon for each man, but Jonas didn't use his—nor did he eat with his fingers as a good many men would. He used his own knife as long as there was anything solid to spear with it, and then he raised the bowl to his lips. He wiped his beard and his mustache on the back of his hand and said that that was the best stew that he'd ever eat; he spoke to Whit. "Your woman," he said, "is a pretty good feeder."

Whit was both pleased and proud. He said, "She does pretty good. So does yourn, for that matter, if I recollect."

Melissa asked Jonas if he wouldn't have more.

But Jonas before they had started had looked into the pot; he said he couldn't eat any more if she was to pay him.

Whit, when he'd finished, stretched out on the floor, and Melissa ate her dinner while Jonas reported.

Jonas said there wasn't a great deal to tell, not much had happened in the month—or more it was, now, he guessed—since Whit and Melissa had left. There hadn't been any sickness to speak of. He'd helped Dan'l Beede to butcher a pig. He'd had the toothache himself, but he was over it now: she'd hauled it out for him. It had cost him something for brandy, but he'd had to do it because rum wouldn't take hold on him enough to have a tooth hauled. He asked Melissa if she'd ever hauled any for Whit, and she said no—rather proudly—not any yet.

There was a little pause there, and Jonas said, well, he had nine left himself—he thought that was better than most men. And they agreed that it was.

Whit said, "You ain't heard of nobody comin' in here to settle?"

"Not right away, no, Whit. Of course, there's some talk of it. They say down t' Gilmanton—or so I hear, anyhow—that there's a good many have got it in mind."

"This a good time for oxen 'fore the snow is too deep."

"Yes, you c'n get a team through the woods now in pretty good shape."

"I didn't know but you might heard of someone."

"No," said Jonas, "I hain't. Mark Jewell t' Sandwich, I know he's thinkin' of it. I shouldn't wonder but sometime *he* might. He's a good man."

"The young one, you mean."

"Yes. Him 'n his brother's both of 'em all right. You couldn't ask for anyone better."

"Mark Jewell ain't married," Melissa put in.

"His brother ain't either. Still, they c'n fix that, time they get round to it."

"I'm all right now," Whit explained practically, "felling and limbing, I c'n go all right alone. You take later on, though, when I'm ready to burn, I could use someone to help me—'n then I could help him. It'll be another year, anyhow, 'fore I get a team."

"You take any fur so far?" Jonas inquired.

"No, not to speak of. For the traps I got out, I ain't done too bad. I got a fisher that's an awful nice pelt. I'd like you to see it, it's up there on the rafter. But I don't get the time that I'd like to to trap. Two days a week 's 'bout the most I c'n do."

"You stick to your clearin'," Jonas advised him. "There ain't any fun in it like there is into trappin', and fur is quick money, I admit that. But it's quick *goin'* 'n comin'. Twon't be very long 'fore this country's trapped out—same 's 'tis now on beaver—'n then what have you got? If I'd started at your age to work with an ax instead of a gun, I'd be better off."

"I ain't spared the ax any," Whit defended himself. "Two days out of seven is all I've run my line. Wood takes up another, and one day to hunt in. Two days of clearin', and figure one for bad weather. That's about how it goes—wouldn't you say, M'lissa?"

"Yes—that's about it."

Her voice somehow made Jonas a little uneasy. She didn't seem to have so much spirit as he thought of her having. And yet he was certain that Whit hadn't noticed it. Probably seeing her right along every day, it just hadn't struck Whit.

Jonas turned to her. "And what you been doin'? Settin' here by the fire thinkin' on Kettleford? Not if I know you!"

"She does more work 'n I do," Whit answered for her. "She's chinked the whole cabin so's there ain't one drop of water or a whisper of wind can get through the walls anywhere. She cooks for me better 'n I ever eat in my life, and she scrapes a skin clean enough so a fly wouldn't light on it. Three pair o' moggas'ns—one I ain't wore yet—and an awful nice shirt, I think that's pretty good—with winter, you might say, not more 'n half done yet."

"I don't believe that my woman has done any better," Jonas admitted "—not a gre' deal."

Still Melissa said nothing.

"Anybody been by here?" Jonas inquired.

"No," Whit answered cheerfully, "we ain't seen a soul."

Jonas was mystified. He'd never seen her so quiet. And yet she didn't look poorly—except around her eyes maybe the way women did when they were in the family way. Well, he'd let it go until later. But he knew he couldn't go home and tell Ida about it unless he could tell her the cause of it, too. Ida would then tell him that that wasn't it, and also explain to him just what it was. But if he brought no explanation for her to dispose of, she'd fret from now until April wondering what had gone wrong.

Jonas and Whit had a good afternoon. They went out on the pond and built up a fire, chopped a hole in the ice, and waited for pickerel. Whit went off pretty soon to look at two traps and a snare he had set on the other side of the pond. But he found them all empty. When he came back, Jonas had a great pickerel stretched out on the ice that was as big as the leg of a calf. "Ain't he got a jaw on him!" Jonas said proudly. "The size of a shovel— or pretty near, anyhow."

They got three more in two hours of fishing, though none as big as the first one. While they were fishing they would speak off and on of what a fine feed they would have to their supper.

On the way home, Jonas remarked, "Your woman mind it there not bein' no one to talk to?—no neighbor woman, I mean, you might say?"

"No, I don't think it. She hadn't ought to. I ain't been from home a whole night since we come."

"You're lucky she don't."

"Why? What made you think of it?"

"Nothin'. I only wondered."

"She ain't complained any."

"My woman would. Why, even with that girl to talk to that Beede brought with him—Mary Wells, the one works for him— she wan't content. I says, 'Ida, what ails you? You got one female to talk to.' 'I know it,' she says, 'but we need another to talk about.'"

Whit couldn't see what was funny about it.

Jonas concluded, on the path home the next morning, that he'd been mistaken—that the girl was all right. This was the first chance that he'd had to think on it—Whit had come with him as far as the town line—and as Jonas recollected last evening and how she had sung for them, how she had enjoyed everything that he'd said, how she'd joined him in laughing, and how she'd even urged him to dance a jig for her—which he had done, and not badly, at that—and how she'd been the one who had wanted the three of them to sit through the night and not go to bed, Jonas concluded that she *must* be all right!—*he'd* had a good time, he was certain of that.

He told Ida Moore that he'd found them both well, of the pickerel he'd taken, and that Whit was coming on with his clearing. He said Whit had taken a fisher and the pelt was a prime one. He said that last night they all three had been merry—in spite of his being as dry as he'd ever been in his life!—and that he had danced for them.

His wife said, "I'm sorry I missed it. Listen to me, Jonas: you don't think there's any need that I should go in there to see her?"

"No!" Jonas said heartily. "They're doin' all right."

15

For two or three days after Jonas had been there, Whit was repeatedly troubled by what Jonas had said . . . "Your woman mind it, there bein' no one t' talk to?" . . . and he'd come round to thinking that maybe she might.

He finally decided that he'd ask her about it.

After eating his breakfast in absolute silence because he was trying to think what to say, he stood in the doorway, his ax in his hand, with no excuse left for not going off to his work. Then he spoke without hearing the words in his head. "Jonas asked me if you ever get lonely. I told him I didn't think it. Do you?" he asked.

She didn't answer him instantly, and he turned to look at her. She was kneeling down, busy in front of the fire.

"No," she said strongly.

He shouldered his ax, said, "I didn't think so," and set off for the day's work that lay right ahead. As his mind turned to his chopping, he found he'd forgotten his whetstone, and he started back to the house for it—he knew right where it was . . . and when he came in the door, Melissa was weeping.

She told him two or three times she didn't know what was the matter. And when Whit said that she must know, or she wouldn't be crying—all she could do was to say "Go away!"

Uncertain and troubled, after a minute, he went.

He'd forgotten his whetstone again, and had to work all the morning with a very dull ax.

He supposed that when he went up for his dinner, they would start in again just where they'd left off.

But not a bit of it. She was as sunny and chipper as he'd ever seen her.

Whit was more troubled than he'd been before.

He made up his mind in the night, and next morning he told her he was going to Sandwich. He said he'd be back in the evening, and would she be all right?

Melissa said, surely—for him to stay the night if he wanted.

Whit hadn't dreamed of staying the night. He said no, he'd be back.

He made a pack of his fur, including the fisher, and he was a mile on his way when it began to get light. After that, he went fast. He could travel on snowshoes, and he found the snow good. He was at Beede's in just under three hours. His shirt was wet through, but his wind was still good.

Beede was home, which was lucky, and he and Whit traded. It took them two hours. But Beede was fair, and in spite of things being higher in Sandwich than they would have been down the river in Kettleford, Whit did about as well here as he would have done there. Captain Butler would probably have been a little more liberal when it came to something to boot, but that was more than made up for by Beede's not cheating. And Beede, of course, saved the cost of the rum that he generally had to pour into a trapper. Taking it all in all, both the men—Whit and Beede—were pretty well pleased; they felt they'd done well.

Whit left his stuff there at Beede's and went down to the Moores'.

Jonas was off somewhere—as Whit had figured he might be—but he didn't mind that: he'd come to see Mrs. Moore.

Whit sat down at the table and answered her questions while she got him a dish of boiled cabbage and pork. Yes, Melissa was well. Yes, she liked the house all right. Yes, they'd had a pretty good journey the day they went in. She'd got a little mite tired but she'd taken no harm from it—she was really more rugged than what you might think. No, he wasn't away a great deal of the time.

She set his dinner before him.

"Whit, what about water? Does she have far to lug it?"

"Only up from the brook."

"You got a yoke, have you?"

"Yes. It ain't far."

"Why don't you see if she wouldn't let you lug it?"

"I hadn't thought of it. Yes, I could do that."

"Most women do it and never come to no harm by it. Still, this is her first and—well, I don't know, Whit—she ain't an awful big woman."

"I bring in the wood."

"Oh, I ain't blamin' you! And maybe I'm foolish—still, it wouldn't do her no good to fall down—not with two buckets on her and you off in the woods."

"I'll lug the water. You can depend on it."

He hadn't tasted his dinner. But Mrs. Moore didn't urge him.

She could see that whatever he had on his mind, he was getting ready to say.

"What I can't figure out," Whit confessed suddenly, "is—well, she ain't awful steady, if you know what I mean. Would you know what that comes from? I come here to ask you."

"How do you mean she ain't steady? You mean on her feet?"

"No, I don't mean that way. I mean she ain't steady. Like—" He looked up at her. "Maybe I oughtn't to tell you of this. But I thought you might know of some way I could help her. I tried to ask her, but she don't want to let on."

"All right. What is it?"

"Well—" It was difficult for him, but he went ahead. "When I say she ain't steady, I mean—well, you take like yesterday. I come on her crying, and she sent me away. A little while later I come back up to dinner, and she was as cheerful as—well, she was *more* cheerful than what I generally be."

"I shouldn't wonder," Mrs. Moore said. "What had set her off cryin'?"

"Not a thing I could see. All that had happened was I'd got to wondrin' if she could be lonely, 'n so I had asked, and she had said no. So then I went off to my choppin', and when I come back for my whetstone—well, there she was at it."

"Ayuh. Well—?"

"I didn't like that. But I couldn't do nothin': she sent me away. When I come up for my dinner, like I say, she was merry. She was almost too merry, if you know what I mean. And that was worse than before. I got uneasy."

"You don't mean that you figured someone had put a spell onto her?"

"No, it ain't *like* that. And that wouldn't be likely—she's got too strong a head."

"Well, what *did* you figure?"

"Well, it seemed more to me like she wan't *right* in her head."

Mrs. Moore had restrained herself as long as she could.

"Sart'n she ain't!" she said. "They never are." She stood with her hands on her hips and her feet wide on the hearthstone. "And *sart'n* she's lonely! You'd ought to *know* that!" And she added, half muttering, "You eat your dinner, while I think what to do."

Whit couldn't eat. . . .

Mrs. Moore thought in silence. "I ain't goin' t' go in there," she said when she'd decided. "I ain't goin' in because it's up to you two. You c'n swing it all right, I think—though I'm sorry for her. But you bear in mind now, and don't you forget it: she *ain't* right in her head, and she's lonely, to boot. It would be against nature if it wasn't so. Oh, I don't mean that she's crazy. All I mean is, she's different—from what she's been before, and from what she'll be again. You treat her according. You understand, do you? As for the loneliness, she'll get over that, too—if everything goes well. Her time is in May. The last couple of months, she'd ought to feel better than what she does now. Right now is the worst. I'm comin' in there the first day of May."

Whit had supposed that he would decide that—but that was no matter.

"Now get on with your dinner—you ain't et a bite. I'm goin' t' fix some things for you t' take in to her. You're goin' t' take 'em whether you like it or not."

Whit tackled the dinner. Along toward the end of it, it began to taste good. He was reminded that it was a long time, come to think of it, since he'd had any green stuff. It tasted real good.

Mrs. Moore had the bundle tied up when he'd finished. It looked as awkward to carry as he'd expected it would. He hadn't an idea what she could have put in it, and he regarded it glumly. When it bursted apart and fell into the snow, he'd know what it was anyhow.

Mrs. Moore told him that he had a long journey, and he agreed with her. He hoisted the bundle gingerly up to his shoulder, solemnly thanked her, and bade her good-by.

He was gone out the doorway, when she called after him: "Whit—"

"Ma'am?" he said, turning. . . .

"If once or twice in a week you could think of something to smile at, I don't suppose it would do any harm."

Whit said he would try.

He tied up her bundle more securely at Beede's. Beede stood watching. "That is one trouble," Beede said, "with white women."

The heaviest thing that he'd got from Beede was thirty pounds of ground meal. But that would carry all right—it was in a fifty-pound linen sack, and he put half the meal in each end, and hung the sack round his neck. Outside the door, he bound on his snowshoes. Beede settled the pack for him, and fixed the bundle on top with two cords leading forward that he could hold in his hand. Whit thanked him and said, well, he guessed he was ready.

"It's a good thing," Beede remarked, "that you ain't far to go."

"No, it ain't awful far, and the footing is good."

"You got a hundredweight on you, I should think, easy. How far do you figure it is to your place?"

"Not above fourteen mile."

"Well, good luck to you, anyhow—wait now, hold still. I got an idea."

Whit turned his head carefully. "Well, I hope it don't weigh much."

Beede ignored this. "You ain't got a dog in there, have you?— I mean in to your place."

"No," Whit agreed. "I ain't used a dog lately. I used to have one, though, when I was a boy."

"Listen," said Beede, "I got a bitch puppy. She's weaned and she's rugged, and she'll make a good dog. Her mother's a cat dog, and the dog that stood up to her used to be the best bear dog there was anywhere round. Nor this puppy I speak of wan't the last of the litter. You wait'll you see her—" He disappeared round the house.

Whit stood there helpless. It was an hour past noontime. He had a hundred pounds on him or better than that, and fourteen miles to go yet. Beede would claim that the fool dog would follow—and Whit supposed the dog might, once they were free of the house. Well, that didn't matter: he had nothing left that he could trade for a dog.

He heard Beede coming . . . and in the crook of his arm, Beede had a fat puppy—say, fourteen inches long. The puppy was wriggling and jumping.

"This," said Beede, " 's a present."

"That's kind of you, surely. And I wish I could take her. But I don't think she could travel real good in this snow."

"She don't weigh nothin'.—*Here, you, hold still now!*—You could train her next autumn," Beede went on, "and she'd hunt before spring. She's got all kinds of blood in her. She's got bloodhound and setter and some collie dog, too. It's the collie dog blood that'll give her her brains. They're awful knowin', collie dogs are."

Whit said, "Yes, so they be."

"I would expect that she'd be a still-hunter, but you can't tell of course until you've had her out. If she has got a voice, it ought to be a real nice one. She's got enough hound in her to make sure of that."

"You surely oughtn't to give her away, sir. And the way I'm fixed now I ain't got nothin' to trade."

"You ain't got to trade. And what I give away, I'll more than get back. When you get ready to breed her, you bring her to me. I'll put my dog to her, and take two of the pups. You can have first choice, and then I'll take the next two. You couldn't ask for anything fairer than that."

"But I ain't got no way to carry her! You can see that! The way I'm loaded now—why, even my pockets—the only place I could put her would be in the seat of my breeches."

Beede was holding his finger for the puppy to chew. "A puppy'd be company, I should think, for your woman."

"Give her to me," said Whit. "I'll put her inside of my shirt."

It had been dark for an hour when Whit hailed the house. Along about sunset he'd called Beede some things that he'd never heard any man call another before. But for the last couple of hours, he'd been too tired to think. Three times he had fallen, and the fact that the weight of the meal sack had buried his head in the snow had been the least of his woes. He had strained both his wrists trying to keep from squashing the puppy. It had been quite a trick, too, to get started again. But he still had the puppy inside of his shirt, and he was certain, moreover, that it wasn't dead.

Melissa answered his hail—so he knew she was all right— and then the light from the fire came out through the door.

He plodded on slowly to the door of his house, and neither one of them spoke until he was there. He eased the weight on his back against the wall of the house, and his breathing was hard for him . . .

"You ain't hurt, are you, Whit?"

"No, I'm all right . . . I'm just kind of winded. I fetched a pretty good load."

"You surely did."

He reached in his shirt. "Dan'l Beede, God bless his soul, sent you a present," he said.

But by the time he'd eaten his supper, he had to admit that it all had been worth it. He'd never seen anyone so mightily pleased.

16

For four or five weeks, nothing very much happened. The snow was up to the roof round back of the house, and even in front where the sun got a crack at it, it came pretty well up on the side of the house. The furthest Melissa could go from the cabin was down to the brook in the path Whit had trodden when he was going for water. Whit had made her some snowshoes—not very good ones—but when once she had fallen in deep snow with them on, and he'd pulled her upright, both she and Whit were content to let them hang the rest of the winter on a peg on the wall. "If anything should happen to you," she assured Whit, "I could get out to Poole's on them. I should think that I could." And they tried to believe this. Although Whit said to himself that he guessed that a better plan was to try not to let anything happen to him. He never had seen anyone less gifted on snowshoes; he couldn't quite understand it. Melissa hadn't yet been down to the pond, she didn't know what it looked like.

The dog was the one that had the worst trouble in snow—in new-fallen, light snow, she'd go clean out of sight. She was funny to watch. Whit had suggested that they name her "Jennifer" after Miss Jennifer Gowan. "Because I always liked her. And I wouldn't say that she'd ever had anything called for her, would you?—nor is likely to, now. At least not any humans." So they called the dog "Jen"—and, using it often, Jen became the dog's name, and pretty soon they forgot why they'd called the dog that. They just called her Jen now because that was her name. There was no one to ask them why they called the dog that.

Melissa was less and less lonely, though. Of course, she missed a good many things even when she was busy that she'd always been used to before they came here. She missed having things to work with, for one thing. She had had eight different knives in the kitchen at Kettleford; here she had only one. And she missed being able to choose what she would eat. The only choice she had now, a good part of the time, was whether to eat or not eat: if she ate, she ate meat.

Whit kept them in meat without any trouble, and now and again he'd bring in a mess of fish from the pond. They were short of fat meat, though—Whit hankered for it—and she still hadn't

265

laid by enough fat to make soap. But they got along. And they had no sickness at all. Whit cut himself in the foot with his ax, but it was clean as a whistle, and was well in a week. He used three different charms on it—two that he told her, and one that he had to keep to himself. There was no way of telling, of course, which charm took a hold, but one of them must have, from the way the cut healed.

It was in the first week in March, and the winter unbroken, when going down to the brook after water, he came on the trace of a moose. It had crossed the path without pausing—within a couple of rods of the house—and gone on easy and comfortably into the woods. It was heading northeasterly. The track didn't look to be two hours old.

Whit started to run up to the house after his gun—and then he discovered that he still had the yoke on and the two empty buckets. So he went down to the brook again after the water, but when he got back to the house, he had spilled a good deal.

"He may be right handy," he said to Melissa. "I hope he is. I want to kill him right close to the house, so I won't have to pack him too far. There's a power of meat in him! If he's too far away before I get a shot, I'm goin' t' try drivin' him back toward the house. It may take me some time. I may have to lay out. But I'll be back here tomorrow night, moose or no moose. Now, let me see—have I got everything with me?"

"Just that one little blanket?"

"Yes. Now don't talk to me—"

She held his gun for him while he tied on his snowshoes, and watched him go swinging off into the woods. She knew there was not in his mind any thought whatsoever for what was behind him—only what lay ahead.

She came back into the house. It must have been about seven o'clock in the morning.

Late in the evening, when Whit hadn't come back, she lay down for the night and was determined to sleep.

All through the evening, she'd been listening for him—and thinking how he would look as he came in through the door. Now she was certain that he was far away somewhere. He was farther off, probably, than it was to Poole's. But she couldn't stop listening, as she lay by the fire . . . and she couldn't get the thought of that open doorway out of her head. Anything could come in it. It had only skins over it. Anything could push them aside—and step into the house. It didn't have to be Whit that would come in the door.

After an hour of listening to silence, she suddenly got up and put wood on the fire. Then she took up a waistcoat that she had been working on, and tried to sew on it. But her fingers were cold and she didn't do well.

She went to the door and looked out. There was no moon to be seen—it was a solid, black night—and she had no way of telling how much of it had gone.

She came back to the fire, and built it up bright. The dog was watching her hopefully for something to eat and Melissa pulled off a shred from the nearest piece of meat overhead—and the dog swallowed it whole.

Then she took a deep breath, and went back to bed. There was nothing else to do.

She got through the night all right—and when she saw by the doorway a little light coming through, she went really to sleep.

Two hours later she stood in the doorway—and stepped from the doorway out into the yard. The sun was up now, and everything that she saw was notably looking just the same as it had the last time she had looked at it. Nothing had happened—nothing at all.

There was now no night between her and Whit's coming home.

The day had gone and dusk thickened when she was sure that she heard him—and in a minute or two he came out of the woods. He seemed a strange shape and he came on toward her slowly . . . he was laden with meat.

Melissa stood watching him.

Whit set the meat down. He was happy and tired—and he was covered with blood. His face and his hands, all over his clothing—his shoulders were slippery in a thick slime of blood. His hair was stuck in it.

He said, "I got him"—and she saw the dog busily licking the blood on his feet.

"I guess you did, all right. There ain't none of that your blood?"

"No, not that I know of. All I put in was sweat. You hear the shot, did you?"

"No, I ain't heard nothin', not since you left. And once or twice I have listened. When was it, Whit?"

267

"Just about noon. Right up here by the swamp at the head of the pond. I lay last night on the north side th' mountain—clear way round in back, it must be fifteen miles. That is, as the crow flies, but I covered forty to get there—not a yard under thirty, I'm sart'n of that. Them fellers can travel, now I want to tell you!" He got down on one knee to loosen his snowshoes. "I tried for a shot soon after I left here. But I didn't get it: he was too wise. Look here, I can show you—" Still with one snowshoe on, he commenced to draw a plan in the snow.

"You'd better come in, Whit. Do you want t' leave that meat there?"

"No, you can take it. Look, here's how it was—"

"I'm lookin'."

"Bend down here closer more, so you c'n see. A man don't get a moose every day, does he?"

"No," she agreed with him, "I guess he don't."

Whit sketched it all out for her there in the snow. He used a piece of bark for the moose and a twig for himself, and it was all as clear there before him in that square yard of snow as it had been when it was happening. Sometimes it was clearer, because he knew all the time now just where the moose was.

Twice Melissa asked questions, but that was toward the beginning—from then on she kept quiet except for "Ayuh, I see."

Finally, the bark came very close to the twig . . .

"I didn't think that he'd ever turn round. But he did, and I fired. I tried for his heart. And I thought surely I'd missed it— how he did run! He run to about here"—he shifted the bark. And then as it lay there, he brought up the twig and placed it on top. "I cut his throat," he said. "You should a seen the blood come!"

After a moment, he said, his voice uncertain and strange, "That was all there was to it."

And then he stood up very suddenly without looking at her. "I guess I'd better wash," he said.

17

The morning that Melissa announced that this was now April, Whit said, well, if that was the case, he'd got to make a trip out. He wanted to get his fur out to Beede before too many trappers should have taken the edge off of Beede's desire to trade. There were a score of things—easily—that he wanted to trade for—and two score for Melissa. They had talked them over so often that he had them clearly in mind—and if his fur would bring half of them, he'd be doing well. He figured his pack weighed about sixty pounds, but there was a lot of musquash into it that wouldn't bring very much.

He had fashioned a toboggan to bring his stuff back, and he set out the next morning—carrying the pack on his back and hauling the empty toboggan. There was three foot of snow in the woods most of the way, but it was beginning to go, and on the south side of the ridges, there were a good many bare places. The brooks were big with snow water, but not yet over their banks, and although the maples showed red, there wasn't yet any green. It seemed to be that way with everything: for every sign of spring coming, there was still plenty of winter. The bears should have been out, but he didn't see any sign, and he wondered if Jonas had. He would be glad to see Jonas. He would be glad to see Beede. And he would feel happy when he was on his way home tonight hauling a good load of things.

When he got to Beede's, he found they had sickness. One of their people—a man named Peter Brett—was out in the yard, puttering round in a kind of halfhearted fashion that was neither working nor idleness. He told Whit that Beede himself had had to take to his bed. "The fever's got hold of him, same as it had hold of me. I was took down with it the day before yesterday. I had it bad, but I knowed what to do. You can't tell him nothin'. Drop your pack 'n set down."

"You wouldn't say that he felt up to tradin'?"

"Tradin'? Hell, no! I tell you the fever's got hold of him. He won't do no tradin'—not for maybe a week. I could have him on his feet by noontime tomorrow, if he'd listen to me, though."

Whit said he guessed he'd go down to the Moores'.

"They ain't to home—neither one of 'em ain't."

"No?"

"They went down t' Gilmanton. Somebody died. Some kin of hers, it was. I don't know who. I ain't acquainted round there. Exeter's my home. You get any beaver?"

"No, not to speak of. Have they had the sickness?"

"Who? Jonas Moore? No, he wintered good—both him and her did. Your woman well? I heard she was expectin'."

"Appears to be, yes. Well, I guess I'll go home."

"You might as well. You can't do nothin' here."

269

Whit hung his pack up in Beede's big woodshed. It was safe from hedgehogs and rats, but you couldn't tell about fire. He also stowed the toboggan where it would be out of the way. He was about to leave, then, when Nate Beede came up—he was the oldest one of the boys, he was about seventeen. Nate promptly took charge of things—and Brett shrugged his shoulders and drifted away.

Nate shifted the pack to a slightly different location, and urged Whit to come in and eat dinner—or to have some rum at the least.

But Whit said he'd already eaten, and he guessed he'd better go back.

Nate offered to advance him anything that he needed, but Whit said, no, he'd be back in the course of a week. At young Beede's insistence, he did take a peck of potatoes. He knew Melissa would welcome them. She'd have been disappointed if he'd come home empty-handed, she'd been looking forward to so many things.

Before he got home, it seemed like a long trip. It seemed like a long winter. He was more tired before he reached home than he would have been if he'd been dragging a load.

He went back in a week, and he found Beede better. They ate and then traded. It went pretty well. Whit got close to three-quarters of the things that he'd planned on. Then Beede had some French powder and he got some of that, and he got an oak spade with a good iron strap to it. And he almost got a beetle, but Beede wanted too much. A good many things that Melissa had figured on, Beede didn't have there. But he sent her two needles and a half pound of tea, and Whit bought her a handkerchief to put over her head that was about a yard square and as brave as could be. It had colors worked in it.

He saw the Moores, too, and Mrs. Moore said again that she would be in there the first day of May. And she sent Melissa a cabbage.

By the time he had all his purchases fixed on the toboggan, it came to more of a load than he'd thought it would be. But he didn't take anything off—and once he got the thing going, it slid along pretty well. Where the going was level, it gave him no trouble. But when he tried to slant up a hill, it wouldn't track after him, but would fall away to the side. Coming downhill once, he knelt on the back of it and he got a great ride—whooping and shouting, it made him feel pretty good.

It was well on to midnight by the time he got to the house.

Melissa put on the handkerchief, and boiled them some tea, and they had a feed, and were merry.

. . . and then even though it was late and Whit was dog-tired, she'd got to see every single thing he'd brought back.

Whit showed them all to her, one thing at a time. And then he ate some more, and they went to bed.

Outside it was raining.

—they both heard the thunder.

Whit said: "That ends the winter. 'Twon't be a great while 'fore we'd ought t' get spring"—and then he went to sleep.

But Melissa was wakeful.

18

True to her word, Ida Moore put in her appearance in the late afternoon of the first day of May. She had Jonas with her. According to the reckoning Melissa had kept, this was only the last day of April. But none of them argued it, it was the kind of mistake anybody could make. Melissa was distressed not to have everything ready, and Ida Moore understood that. But neither Jonas nor Whit could see that it made any difference. However, Jonas said tactfully that he'd wondered this morning whether Ida was right—and he'd wondered on the way in. It had looked in the woods as though it could have been May, but even at noontime, he hadn't been sure: it hadn't *felt* like it.

Jonas and Whit were to sleep in the lean-to, there being no other way in which they could all be disposed. This was entirely agreeable to everyone but Melissa, but when she'd talked it over with Whit, she had seen there was no other way. A few minutes after the Moores had arrived, Jonas and Whit wandered out there to talk.

"She looks pretty good, Whit—your woman, I mean."

"I don't know but she does. How long c'n you stay?"

"Well, I know Ida figures to stay till your woman's well again. As for me, the ground out to my place won't be dried out for seed for another two weeks yet. I could stay for a while—if you think you could stand it."

"I guess I could stand it!"

Jonas looked round at him. "Don't you go to worry. She'll be all right."

"Oh, yes, I think so."

"Sart'n she will." Jonas spat cheerfully. "You done any fishin'?"

"Trouts? No, I ain't."

They were standing in front of the lean-to, taking in the late sunshine. There was a chill in the air, but the sunshine was good.

"Say, look at them dogs, will you?" Jonas remarked.

"Jen wants him to play with her. She's a great hand to play."

"What do you call her?"

"Her name is Jen."

They watched for a moment. The big dog—old Major—was annoyed and embarrassed at the way the puppy went on— cavorting and yapping and jumping up at his head. Finally, Major lay down and closed his eyes in disgust. The puppy barked at him sharply . . . and then gave him up, and went bounding off toward the house—and fell on her face as she went in the doorway.

Whit said, "The streams are high yet. But then I don't know— I s'pose we could try it. 'Twouldn't do any harm. We might get some little ones out'n the brook."

"You got any worms?"

"I got some in a place that I keep 'em to sweeten. It makes 'em more rugged, some people claim."

"I got some in my pocket," Jonas confessed.

19

The very next morning while Whit was down getting water, Mrs. Moore came out to the lean-to and shook Jonas awake. "Look here, now, Jonas! You hear what I say?"

Jonas said, "How c'n I help it?"

"Well, I d' know, but you generally do. Listen to me, Jonas: you get him out of here."

Jonas said "What?"—and she said it again.

"Me get who out of here? Whit, do you mean?"

"Yes."

"Oh." Jonas sat up. "All right, I c'n try to. She started in, has she?"

"I shouldn't wonder. She thinks that she has."

"Gorry, you didn't get here no more 'n in time."

"I'm here soon enough. But when things get t' goin', I don't want him around—hearin' her holler, 'n all that kind of business. You take him away."

"Couldn't I help you any?"

"No, I don't think it. But don't go too far away. Leave your gun here, and if I need you, I'll fire it. And don't you tell Whit or he won't stir a step. He'd think he oughtn't to leave her."

"Ain't that up to him?"

"No. I told her just what I was doin'. She wants it this way. It'll be easier for her if she don't have to pretend for him that it ain't hurtin' her much."

"He ain't a fool, Ida."

"You do as I say."

"All right." Jonas sighed deeply. "When can we come back?"

"Not before suppertime."

"'Suppertime'! God! I'll have to tie him up to a tree!" He was standing up now, hitching his breeches up, and adjusting his belt. "S'posin' I do that—'n s'posin' he gets suspicious—'n s'posin' he comes right out 'n asks me what in hell's goin' on! What'll I say to him?"

. . . But Jonas's wife had gone back to the house.

Jonas did as she told him. He got Whit down to the pond to see if the ice had gone out yet, and they found that it had. Jonas discovered that he had some pork rind in his pocket, and they skittered for pickerel along by the shore. The wind was in the right quarter to hear a shot from the house, and when Whit with a yell hoisted a thirty-inch pickerel forty feet in the air and it came flopping down through the branches for Whit to pounce on, Jonas felt that his problem was probably solved.

But when it got to be dinnertime, Whit wanted to go up to the house. He said he'd told Melissa that he would be back.

Jonas assured him that, on the other hand, he'd told *his* woman that they wouldn't be back. "It's worse to come back when you've told 'em you won't, than not to come back when you've said that you will."

Whit wasn't convinced.

"They won't have nothin' t' eat for you," Jonas insisted, "and they won't take kindly to havin' t' fix somethin' all of a sudden. I know my woman don't. Most likely they've et. It'd be close on

273

to noon by the time you got up there. You better stay here."

Whit said he'd take his fish up with him and fix it himself.

"That's all right for you, but I ain't got any fish. You cook it here, 'n I'll help you to eat it."

"We didn't bring any salt."

"I did," said Jonas, "I got some in my pocket. You make up a fire 'n we'll have us a feed."

"I'll leave you the pick'rel."

"Why're you goin'?" said Jonas, standing in ice water up his knees. "Because you got your feet wet? You're a hell of a fisherman! Make up a fire."

"I'll make up a fire 'n then I'm goin' up."

Jonas said nothing.

—but he came out to the fire before it was blazing. He said, "That's a nice fire."

"There's your pick'rel," said Whit, touching the fish with his foot. "You want me to clean it?—'n I'll leave you my gun in case you're sca'rt t' be here without one. I d' know why you didn't bring your'n, but I noticed you didn't. I'm goin' up."

"You're awful pigheaded."

"Maybe I am."

"And on top o' that, you ain't got any manners. Here I come all the way in here t' make you a visit, 'n then you don't want t' eat with me." He squatted down by the fire and picked up the pickerel, whetted his knife on his thigh, and began slitting the belly. "These here are better if you clean 'em dry."

"Ayuh. Well, I'm goin' along. You goin' t' stay down here the whole afternoon?"

"Whit, what is your reason? Just tell me your reason. I won't argue a mite with you—if you got any reason."

"I told you my reason: I said that I'd come."

"*When* did you tell her?"

"'Fore I went down t' get water."

"Well, there you are! There! I said to Ida while you was down t' th' brook that we wouldn't be back until suppertime. And she's told your woman, 'n they don't look for us to come. Now you set down 'n take comfort. I'll have this feller ready in no time at all." He was tugging away at the entrails, but they were slippery and tough.

"You didn't tell me you planned t' stay here the whole day. You said you wanted t' come 'n see if the ice had gone out. Here

274

it is noontime—or pretty close to it—'n I ain't done any work. I got t' go back."

"'Work'!" Jonas exclaimed. "You ain't got t' work *every* day! Set down 'n stop fussin'." He tore loose the guts and tossed them over his shoulder. "You take all the fun out of fishin'."

This was a serious charge and Whit considered it seriously.

Jonas felt Whit was wavering, and sought to give him a push. "What I had in mind," he said, "was after we'd et, to try down below by the mouth of that brook. You can't ever tell what you might get a hold of—by the mouth of a brook where it makes into a pond." He spitted the fish, and put it close to the fire.

"Why wouldn't it be all right if I went up and came back?"

Jonas was caught. "Be kind of late, wouldn't it?"

"Best time to fish is the late afternoon. Well, I'll see you later—" He turned away from the fire.

"No, Whit, don't go! Whit, listen to me! Whit—I got a reason."

Whit turned around. "All right. What is it?"

"Well—just don't ask me. It's an awful good reason. You leave it to me."

Whit came a step closer. "What is it?"

"Well—they're kind of busy up there. Why don't you stay here with me?"

"'Busy'?" said Whit. "What at are they busy?"

"I couldn't say, really. But Ida let on to me that they were goin' t' be busy t'day—both of 'em busy, you understand—and for us to stay clear."

"First I heard of it. Whyn't you tell me before?"

"Well, she didn't want me to, to tell you the truth. I shouldn't wonder but what it might be that they're cookin' up some kind of surprise, you might say."

"What kind of surprise?"

"Well, I d' know exactly what kind. It might be one thing, or it might be the other. But they don't want us round there until they got it done. *Your* woman don't, Whit. That's what Ida told me."

"You ain't makin' game of me?"

"Every last word that I've told you is true."

Whit stared at him hard—and Jonas's eyes fell.

"I don't understand it," Whit said.

"I guess you will by tonight." Jonas was studying the fish and the fire . . . He heard Whit draw in his breath—

"You don't mean t' say that today is the day?"

Jonas's heart sank. "Today is what day?" he said into the fire.

Whit stepped across to him, and Jonas didn't dare to look up. Whit took hold of the older man's shoulder and yanked him up onto his feet. The boy's face was white. "You know what I mean! Is that why you been keepin' me?—when I told her I'd come?"

"She didn't want you, Whit."

"You—" but he stopped short of saying it. And he flung Jonas aside with all the strength that he had—and Jonas went staggering backward through the fish and the fire to land sitting down. But Whit didn't see that.

Jonas sat still . . . he heard the fading thud of Whit's running, and he wasn't sure but that he heard the boy sob.

He looked down at his shoulder where his shirt was all torn and the marks of Whit's fingers were beginning to show—and he stood up without comment.

"Well, I guess I'd better go up there." He picked up the pickerel, and he kicked the fire apart. He took up Whit's gun and started up through the woods. "I could have told Ida that this was just what would happen," he said aloud quietly. "If I'd stood in his room, I'd have busted my head."

He was walking slowly and sorrowfully. "He come pretty close to calling me out of my name. I'm glad he didn't do that, because that is a thing it takes a fight to wash out. There ain't no other way if you want to stay friends."

Twenty yards farther on, he said, "I hope they're all right." He walked a little more rapidly, but not very much. "I guess they prob'ly are," he said.

Jonas saw that Whit, running, had taken a route that was chosen as nicely as he could have picked it himself . . . he was skirting the snow patches and avoiding the steep places, and yet adding as little in distance as he possibly could. Jonas guessed Whit was scared just the proper amount for his brain to work good on something like that. But you try to talk to him, now, try to get him to listen to reason—and you'd be worse off when you finished than when you begun.

Jonas tried not to think of what he himself was about to encounter when he got up to the house. It was bound to be bad, whatever it was. If he should live to a hundred, he'd never be able to make Ida see why he couldn't have held Whit at the pond. That was all she'd asked of him—and he hadn't done it.

He plodded steadily upward, the gun over his shoulder and carrying the pickerel in the other hand by the tail.

When Whit came in sight of the house, he had sickened with running. All the fears for Melissa that he'd known through the winter had been close at his heels as he labored up through the woods. All through the winter he had pushed them back somehow. But now he was running, they came on at his back. He fled without gaining, he carried them with him.

The pain of his breathing, the pain in his legs, were things he didn't notice. He saw the cabin ahead—

He had approached from the back of it, and when he came round to the front—

Melissa stood in the doorway.

She was a ghost. Whit had time to believe that she was a ghost. Then he saw her face change and she spoke to him, "Whit! Whit, what's happened? Where's Jonas?"

She wasn't a ghost.

Whit tried to speak, but he couldn't say anything. He was convinced now that she was all right. Nothing had happened—she looked just the same, anyhow. Nothing had happened—he didn't know why. But she'd tell him later. "Jonas?" he said—and then Ida Moore stood beside her.

Whit got the words out: "Jonas—havin' his dinner—down 'th' pond."

Ida Moore had to first stop and realize that Whit wouldn't have come running if Jonas had drowned. Then, with that out of the way, she was able to guess at the truth. She said nothing at all.

Whit turned his back on them, and started to go round the house. Melissa started to follow him, but Mrs. Moore held her back. She said, "I know what's happened. It ain't anything bad. I'll tell you about it."

. . . Whit got as far as the woods before he was sick.

When Jonas arrived in the clearing, he saw no one about. Old Major appeared from the lean-to where he'd been asleep in the sun, stretched himself richly, and, waggin' his tail, came up to his master. Jonas put his hand round the dog's muzzle and squeezed it to make him stay quiet. Then he let go—knowing that the dog wouldn't bark until he was told that he might.

He went toward the house, not causing a sound—and Major following after him, sniffing the fish.

Outside the door, Jonas halted and listened . . .

He passed through bewilderment, and from that to relief, and finally, listening long enough, he acquired some knowledge of how matters stood.

He considered an impulse to go back to the pond.

That, he concluded, was the best thing to do.

All afternoon Jonas hoped that they'd see it was funny, but when he went back up to supper he found that none of them did.

20

The day Whit had promised—that would bring the spring to them—came to them finally, and it was the fifteenth day of May.

With Whit, as he stood in front of the lean-to at the morning's beginning—knowing this was the day—there was no question at all of any attempt to resist it.

This was the spring. There was in the air a sure, confident softness; there was the feel and the color of spring. There would be now no returning of winter. The trees were dusted with green, a light green but a sure one, and the sunlight was yellow and hazy and warm in his throat. The spring was now in the clearing and it lay on the hills.

Well, they had beaten the winter: they were here for the spring.

He brought up the water and saw to the wood, asked Melissa if she felt all right, and heard her say that she did. He put a piece of johnnycake into his pocket. "I thought I might go a little ways in the woods."

"You ain't comin' back for your dinner?"

"I might or I mightn't. But I shouldn't think so. I'll fix it with Jonas to know where I am."

She poked at the fire . . .

"All right," she said.

Whit turned to her. "I—" but all he knew of it himself was that he wanted to be alone in the woods. He couldn't say that to her.

She said, "You go ahead, Whit."

"Well—I guess, then, I will." He wanted to thank her, but he couldn't come at it,—and he went out the door and was more anxious than ever to be away from the house.

But first he went out to the lean-to and stirred Jonas awake. "I'm goin' int' th' woods," he said.

"All right."

"If you have any need to, you c'n pick up my track at that big old white pine tree by the rock by the brook."

"All right," said Jonas.

Whit reached down his gun and the things to go with it.

He swung off down through the clearing, down toward the brook, and following the brook up a ways, stepped across to the pine tree. From there, he struck off southeasterly. He had an idea now as to where he was going, but he didn't want to be sure of it, really. Here in the woods, the great trees rose around him but it was only their trunks that were near to be seen; on all of the hardwoods, the branches and twigs with the little furry new leaves on them were away high overhead. The leaves weren't big enough yet to put shade on the ground, they only softened the sunlight that filled all of the woods. The birds were come back now, both big ones and small ones. There seemed to him to be a good many birds. He knew the names of three or four kinds of them—but beyond that he'd never had occasion to go. There wasn't a thing you could do with a bird, but he was glad to have them about—they were part of the spring.

All over the ground, where his eyes wandered about, there were various flowers. This was the time for them—they were making the most of their time in the sun before the leaves on the trees should shut the sun off from them. He saw a big patch of pink moccasin flowers.

He was walking barefoot again—and would right along, now. He would not have a thing on his feet until the other side of the summer—yes, and the autumn, as well—not until there was snow on the ground. That was a long time ahead! This was the spring and there was summer ahead—and then after that autumn. . . . There would be no more winter for a good many months.

Melissa had told him this morning that she was all right.

He'd been going uphill a good part of the time, and when he came onto a shoulder, he turned to look back . . . and he was surprised to see how the distance now showed in between. He made out the smoke from his chimney coming up through the trees. He was glad that she'd told him that she was all right.

He went on still farther, working steadily higher—not straight up the ridge, but slanting along up the side. The ridge ran north

279

and south, and then curved round to the west. When he'd come out on the top of it and turn to look down, he'd be facing due south.

The top of the ridge was hemlock and pine—with a deer path along it as plain as a road marked with wheels—and he saw that he'd struck the top of the ridge a little bit sooner than he'd thought that he would. He followed along the deer path, going slowly; there were a few shiny, fresh droppings, and plenty of old dried grayish-green ones that had been under the snow. Even up here, there wasn't a great deal of breeze. Down below, there'd been none. What wind there was, came full from the south—and he could feel the warmness it had in it.

There opened ahead of him a great bare place of rock, full of juniper bushes, and all the sun it could hold. It was the same kind of place—though about half again larger—as the place where, last autumn, he had looked down on his land. But this one faced south—in the other direction.

He stepped out on the rock—and there was a wonderful heat from it rising up all around that made him half close his eyes. He took a deep breath of it in a strange, tightening rapture—seeing but dimly and as a part of that which possessed him the far, rolling country that lay outstretched below.

When this moment had passed, and his sight came more clearly, he was able to think by their names of some of the things that he saw—as Great Ossipy Pond, looking flat and spread-out now, but with a glint of sun on it; that was off to his left—and the trees hid the river that ran out of the pond. Right here down in front of him—but a good ways below—was a bend of the Bearcamp. And over across on the far side of the valley, there under the sky to the south, were the Ossipy Hills.

Southeasterly, though, he could look a long ways—over a gentle jumble of hills of no special distinction, low-lying and pleasant, and needing no names. He never had been in that part of the country. Someday he would go there.

The farther off that he looked, the more hazy it was . . . until it was a very thin place to see through between the sky and the hills—and then you couldn't see through it, they were all the same thing in the haze of the distance—and there was no color there: just a gentle forbidding that a man should see farther . . .

But overhead it was blue!

And near by on the trees there was the new green of the springtime, overlaid on the black of the trunks showing through.

The air between him and the things he was looking at was not empty and clear: it had a fullness into it—of little bugs and of sunshine, and a good many smells. You take in the winter, the air is empty and bright; but on the first day of spring it has pleasant things in it.

He laid down his gun then, and sat down beside it—with the sun on his face, but not quite in his eyes, and with the hard palms of his hands pressing on the warm rock—and all that country before him . . .

And he was grateful to God who had let him be here.

This was the richest day in the year for him. Here at hand was the spring, rolling up from the south—and following after the spring, there'd be coming the summer. He had spent none of it— not a single day of it—it was all of it coming—unbroken— ahead.

Melissa had told him this morning that she was all right.

From the separate trees down below his eyes would lift of themselves, crossing the river, to the smooth rounded masses of the tree-coated hills three or four miles away—and from there to the next hills, and so on and on, the hills less distinct, the green turning to gray, until the hills themselves disappeared and he was gazing into the distance where the haze covered everything . . . and then after a moment, the search of his eyes being baffled, his eyes would fall back to the things near at hand. On the rocks at his feet, the lichens were growing; down in a hollow at the edge of the trees, the low blueberry bushes had come into leaf.

He had dropped an acre of Indian the day before yesterday; he'd be able to see it inside of two weeks. Jonas and he had rolled the logs up for burning; they had sweat at it, too. He owed Jonas Moore much. The logs would be burning the first week in June; the fire might help some in fighting the gnats—though he'd need a smudge in the dooryard. Women and cattle, the flies bothered the most. Another year, maybe, he might own a yoke of young oxen. . . . Surely, in a couple of years there'd be neighbors near by. . . . It wouldn't be a great while before there'd be a sawmill— and just as soon as there was one, he'd have a house built of boards; he could see the shape of it now. . . . Another five or six years would make an awful big difference. Still, no man could tell what the future would bring. . . .

Melissa, this summer, would be like herself again.

281

He had expected that for all of this day the presence of spring would occupy everything. It had done so in the past: he'd been contented to wander all day—to wander and sit, and to lie down in the sun.

But now that he had thought of Melissa, he was no longer contented.

He was feeling just as much pleasure in the spring as he ever had—so he knew it wasn't the spring that was lacking, and that it wasn't himself. But while he was enjoying it, he wasn't content by it. Something was missing . . .

And he knew what it was: he was wishing that somehow or other Melissa could share this.

Standing up, he looked out over the country, and the great beauty of it came to him stronger than ever. And there came with it the certainty—simple and clear—that he was correct about what was the matter. He said then, aloud, "I guess I'll go back."

. . . and he picked up his gun, and with his lunch still in his pocket, he went trudging over the ledge and down through the woods. He still had the spring with him, it was everywhere, all about . . . But the pleasure he had of it was touched a little with sadness. It made the pleasure, for some reason, harder to bear.

He didn't hurry—that wouldn't do any good. He didn't know what he would say to her when he got back to the house. It might be, when he got there, that he wouldn't go into the house. He might just get his ax from where it was in the lean-to, and go to work in the clearing. He didn't know. . . .

As he came into the clearing, Whit saw a strange sight: he saw Jonas Moore with the yoke on and two empty buckets picking his way down the path that led to the brook. Whit wondered what Jonas was being punished for now. And he hurried to join him, enjoying the joke—

"What you doin', Jonas? The house ain't afire?"

"Stand back, boy!" said Jonas. "I got work t' do here." He dipped in a bucket, bent watching it fill, drew it out dripping, and set it down on the bank. "You want t' know what? Your wife's had a baby."

"No!"

Jonas picked up the other bucket to fill. "You knew she was go'n to"—and he commenced filling the bucket. He looked up—and saw Whit was halfway to the house.

Ida Moore heard him coming and remarked for Melissa, "I guess this is him now"—and Melissa scraped into a little pile all the strength she could find and resolved to spend the whole of it on one effort for Whit. She heard him come in the doorway, and she saw his face just above her. Now was the time!—and she smiled and raised her hand to him—but she had nothing to brace against when she tried to speak. She felt the hardness and roughness of Whit's hand close on hers—and she smiled without trying to . . . Then she let her eyes close.

She felt Whit kiss her forehead—and when he let go her hand, she was glad that he had. . . .

She lay there in peace and in easement, neither asleep nor awake, but knowing that she had done her work well. She was not troubled. She was content.

Whit went outside the house—and Mrs. Moore followed him. She stood beside him a moment, waiting to speak. Whit's face was working and his fists were clenched at his sides.

"She done awful good, Whit," the woman said quietly.

Whit nodded.

"And the young one is fine."

Whit said, "That's good."

"You want to see him?"

Whit didn't want to. But when he said, "Ayuh," he knew that he'd got control of himself.

Ida Moore went inside and fetched out the baby. She had it all bundled up in a great welter of linen which she poked aside with her forefinger to show Whit his son.

Whit peered into the bundle.

"He's a good one," he lied.

"He's the best baby," Ida Moore said, "that *I* ever see! Ain't you!" she added, with a peck of her head toward the baby.

Whit hesitated. "You seen a good many?"

"'A good many'!"—and then she looked up at Whit. "This the first one you seen?"

"Yes," said Whit solemnly—and his voice sounded hollow.

For a second or two, Mrs. Moore tried not to do it—but then she laughed at him. She hadn't laughed much in the last couple of hours.

She put her hand on his shoulder. "Whit, you go off and set down. Everything is all right."

And Whit knew that she meant it, and believed it was so. She was telling the truth.

He went off toward the lean-to, his knees feeling weak, and with a beginning joy in his heart . . .

Jonas left the next day—and Whit went along with him as far as the town line as he was bounden to do and as he always had done. They spoke off and on, and didn't see anything. When they were parting, Whit thanked Jonas for coming, and said he'd make up the time to him as soon as he could. And Jonas said that was all right, and not to worry about it. He said, "Well, good-by, Whit," and Whit said, "Good-by, Jonas"—and Jonas called to his dog, and went on his way.

Whit watched him a little—his thin, narrow shoulders, and his gun under his arm . . . and then Jonas had slipped out of sight round a hemlock.

Jonas Moore was his friend.

Whit turned around and headed back to the house.

Mrs. Moore stayed a week and two days beyond that. Whit went out with her to Sandwich. They got a good early start, quitting the house before the sky in the place where the sun would come up had begun to look any different from what it did anywhere else.

He found Mrs. Moore was a good one to travel. She'd have got along faster and easier if she'd have tucked up her skirts, but she said nothing about it, and Whit supposed that at her age she was probably used to them. Anyhow: skirts or no skirts, she kept right a-going, and talked hardly at all, and he had to admire her—although of course he always had.

They stopped by at Beede's for some things Whit was to take back with him, and that he put in his bag, and then on down to the Moores' for some more things that Mrs. Moore was to send.

Jonas wasn't about. But he had planted the garden.

She urged Whit to stay—or at least to sit down and have something to eat. But he said he didn't feel very hungry, and he'd kind of like to get back. So she made up the bundle of things for Melissa, and as she was handing it over to him, she told him he'd got to carry it in some special way. He didn't pay much attention. He was trying to think of some way to thank her for what she'd done for them this past two or three weeks. But he hadn't succeeded when the moment arrived and they stood outside the door. "Mis' Moore," he said earnestly, "I—well, I thank you. I—I guess you know that."

"Yes, Whit. I know that."

"If you hadn't 've been there, things might have been different."

"Oh, I don't know."

"Well, I do!—'n so does M'lissa. We're beholden to you, ma'am. We always will be."

"You needn't feel that way. All it was: it happened that I was a neighbor. Someday she'll be a neighbor to some other woman. Now, you get along, will you? And you carry that bundle the way that I showed you! You get along now—or she'll begin wonderin' if you ain't stopped for some troutin' 'n forgot t' come home."

"I ain't goin' t' stop for no troutin'! I wish you'd say to Jonas I was sorry to miss him."

"I'll tell him."

"I'll be out again soon: I owe him some time. He knows that already. Good-by, Mrs. Moore."

She said, "Good-by, Whit. I'll come again any time that you need me."

And Whit told her thank you, and set out for home.

She went into the house and sat down on a stool in front of the fireplace. Jonas had covered the fire before he went out. She sat there and stared into the gray, empty fireplace. She felt tired and old.

After a time, she got up, and squaring her shoulders, she went about getting supper.

Having fixed up the bundle so that it would carry a little bit better, Whit settled into his stride . . . and went about three times as fast as he had on the way out. He never slackened his pace for the whole eighteen miles except when he was crossing the river. And although the shadows were long when he came to the edge of his clearing, still he'd beaten the sunset by more than an hour. He called to the house—and he heard her answer.

She came out of the doorway holding the baby in the crook of her arm—and looking into the sun, she waved Whit a welcome.

He came up beside her, and put down his bundle.

When they had gone into the house, she said, "You get her home safe, did you?"

"Oh, yes. We had no trouble. She traveled better than I thought that she could."

"Better than I used to?"

"Well, I wouldn't want to say that."

285

"She has been more kind to me, Whit, than I thought anyone could be—save my own mother, and that ain't the same."

"Yes, sir, she has been."

Melissa put down the baby in its place by the hearth, and bent over it. She said over her shoulder, "Still, I don't know that I'll mind havin' ourselves to ourselves."

Whit wasn't sure that they had.

PART THREE

The Woods
1770-1777

1

All through that summer and all through the autumn, and month after month as the winter went on, over the whole township of Tamworth there was no house except theirs. There were no thin wisps of smoke from the flat, wooded intervals; there were no men at all in the Ossipy Hills.

But neither Whit nor Melissa was troubled by this. They had their work to do, right under their hands.

Melissa was so much better off than she had been that first winter—because now her days were made out of something besides silence, and waiting, and scraping the fat off of skins— that she felt no rebellion whatever, and she had a good deal of contentment. To be sure, she looked forward to neighbors, she'd be glad when they came. But she wasn't complaining about things as they were.

Sickness, so far, had kept away from her baby. Both she and Whit knew that in this they were fortunate—although it was true that they'd both done their part: Melissa had prayed, and she had taken the best care of the baby that she knew how to take. And Whit—and Melissa, too, on occasion—had used various charms. Whit knew more about charms than Melissa did any day, and she didn't doubt he'd used some that he hadn't told her about. But over and above all of this, they had needed good luck beyond what any charm would be likely to bring. And so far they had had it. The baby was rugged and plump, and most of the time he was happy—although there had been times when he wasn't, of course.

But as Melissa looked back at the end of a year, she readily realized that the times she had been frightened hadn't lasted for long. There had been colic and cramps, and twice the fever 'd been on him—but these had been only short spells, and they hadn't really been bad. Or at least she could see now that they hadn't been bad. Flytime that first summer—not much more than a month after the baby was born—appeared to her now as the worst time they'd been through.

There was no charm, Whit had admitted, that would work on black flies. And every night when the black flies would quit about sundown, the mosquitoes and gnats would come thicker than ever. For two solid weeks, there had been no escape anywhere—no escape and no rest. She had kept the cabin as full of smoke as she dared to—and when the baby had choked on it, she'd taken him out in the air. She had greased him well, too. But his tiny round face had been swollen and bloody, and a good part of the time he hadn't been able to open his eyes. And then he'd get so tired out crying that he wouldn't be able to eat. It had been a good thing perhaps that during that season she hadn't had but a little bit for him to eat.

Whit himself for some reason wasn't greatly affected by flies.

They had got through it somehow, and by the middle part of July, Whit had claimed that there wasn't a fly left in the woods.

They had decided that the baby's name would be Jonas. That part had been easy—there was nobody else. But it didn't seem to come easy to speak of him by name. And there was really no need for it because with only the three of them, it was seldom in doubt as to just who was meant.

Still, his name was young Jonas—and he liked to lie on his side and chew on the corner of an old linen rag.

Along in September, Melissa had suggested that she didn't know but what they'd ought to get him baptized.

"Where?" Whit had asked.

"Well, I don' know—I s'pose Gilmanton's nearest."

"'Tain't what I would call near. It is halfway to Kettleford. You didn't figure t' take him down there?"

"I will never go back."

"Well, I wouldn't have blamed you. I'd like to show him myself. And if someone's got to baptize him, I suppose I'd as soon have Mr. Gowan to do it as anyone else."

"Why don't you want him baptized?"

"Well, I don't know . . . it's too much like a charm."

"How do you mean?"

"You ever seen 'em?—I mean, have you seen 'em do it?"

"No, I never did. I wished often I could."

"Do you know *why* they do it?"

"I don't know as I do, but I know everyone does it," Melissa had said.

"I seen 'em do it, I seen Mr. Gowan. They sprinkle water. Same thing as a charm. It don't seem to me right, but I never told him so. Charms are for spirits. They ain't for the Lord."

"I never thought on it."

"I know about charms. When I stand before Him it would only

make me feel foolish to recollect I had tried to work any charms upon Him."

"What's it a charm against?"

"Supposed to keep God from sending the baby to hell—that is, in case it should take sick and die."

"Oh!"

"Yes, that is just it. I feel just the same way."

But pretty soon she'd said, "Whit . . ."

"Ayuh?"

"It wouldn't be for ourselves."

"I know. I thought of that, too. I said to myself, You got no right to take chances."

"Then what did you say?"

"Well, then I said this: I said, to put a stop to a thing that's as awful as that is, you would need a much bigger charm than what *I* seen 'em do. And I don't care who was to work it—Mr. Gowan, or who. Hell lasts forever. You think of 'forever' and you'll see what I mean. And Who is it they're tryin' t' work this charm on? Sprinklin' water! Why, you could sprinkle the whole of Lake Winnipiseogee and *still* be ridic'lous ! They wan't at it five minutes. There is an Indian charm that takes three days t' do right—and then don't always work, either—and do you know what it's for? It don't aim at no more than a man getting a deer.

"No, the thing don't look reasonable," Whit had gone on. "You put 'hell' 'n 'forever' 'n 'God' into one side of it' and in the other side is some minister and this five-minute charm, and you can't make the thing balance."

"Maybe there's something more into it than what you know about."

"Maybe."

"Or it could even be, Whit, you ain't figured it right."

"That has happened before."

"And there ain't nothin' t' lose, Whit—not for him, anyhow."

Whit had been silent for quite a while then. "I don't know but there is." And when she had done her part by saying, "How do you mean?" Whit had tried honestly.

"Well," he had said, "what it comes down to is this: I believe He wouldn't do it—send a baby to hell. I have thought and thought on it, and there ain't any one reason why I believe this that can stand by itself. Still, I believe it."

"All right."

"I think I will stick by it. A man ought t' do that much, I think, for his son."

And before she could answer, he had said—his voice very different, "I seen a sign today in that little meadow that they say means a frost in the next seven days. I shouldn't wonder but what maybe we'd get one."

"What was the sign, Whit?"

"Pod o' milkweed."

2

Speaking in general, Whit could be made to admit, with a second winter behind them, that things might have been worse. He knew himself they were getting ahead. They had a cow and a pig, with stout shelter for both of them, and during the winter just past he had felled enough trees so that if Jonas would help him to burn once again, he'd have cleared seven acres—or maybe a little bit more. That would meet the agreement he'd made with the Proprietors, and it would meet it in two years instead of in three. He had done this without oxen, and without any neighbors—except Jonas, of course—and he felt he'd done well.

He had kept his word better than the Proprietors had—no other settlers, and no sign of a road, and the town not surveyed into ranges and lots. True, it had not been in writing that these things would be done, but the agent had surely let on that they would be, and Whit had hoped that they might. But he hadn't so much as caught a glimpse of the agent since that evening at Jonas's nearly two years ago. Even the cow that the Proprietors *had* agreed to in writing, they hadn't lived up to.

Whit hadn't wanted her much the first winter because he'd have been put to it to feed her. He would have liked to have had her by June, though—and from then on through the summer. But although he had paid Beede to write two letters to them—and Beede'd found someone to carry them, too—yet no answer had come from them. Finally Beede had said in October—when the summer was over and the pasture had gone, "The trouble is, Whit, you can't do nothin' to 'em. All right, they ain't kept their word. But still, what can you do? And another thing is—and this

291

may be the trouble—like the agent said, you remember: they ain't got a cow handy to turn over to you."

"I don't suppose you would want to sell them one o' yourn for the purpose?"

"Not at a price they'd be willing to pay. They figure a cow at what a cow's worth where they're living. A cow here in these parts is worth an awful lot more. What's a cow worth t' Kettleford?"

"Depends on the cow."

"Well, say a middling good one."

"I wouldn't know. A middling good one, perhaps, would be seven pound ten."

"That'd be cheap to Kettleford, even. You know the cows that I got. Why, even the brindle—and you know what she is, she is so old and ill-favored I had to blindfold the bull—I wouldn't sell you the brindle for not less than ten pound, Whit."

"I didn't figure to buy one. They agreed to a cow."

"Never mind the agreement. What you want is a cow."

"Sart'n I want a cow. And they owe me a cow."

"I know that well as you do. I wrote it, and witnessed. Well, the brindle's a cow. Would you want to take her? I c'n write again to 'em, and I won't charge you for doin' it. If the Tamworth Proprietors will pay me seven pound in hard money, I will give you the brindle—and my blessing t' boot. They could keep their word that way—and you couldn't say nothin'."

"She took bull in the spring?"

"Ayuh, she did."

"Anything come of it?"

"Not a damn thing."

"Then she must be through."

"She's been as dry for six months as any rock in the pasture."

"Why don't you butcher?"

"I was the one drove her up here from Gilmanton. I never had such a trip in my life. She tried to drown herself twice, and she got loose in a swamp, and she was bogged to her belly three times in one day. What I should've done was to butcher her then, I guess. I could a packed in t' meat, and I'd a been better off. But I wanted to show her I was as stubborn as she was. I showed her! I brung her!—every foot of the way. And at the end of it when she stuck her head in the yard here, I give her a great kick, and I says to her, 'There! Now then, my beauty, who come out on the top?'

292

Ever since then, I have been kind of fond of her. I wouldn't want to eat her; she is more like a pet."

"They agreed to a cow."

"Well, then, let's get down to business. I shouldn't wonder but the Tamworth Proprietors might *pay* seven pound—if I was to write to 'em proper—to be free of this business. If you took the money and put some more money with it, I could sell you a cow that would do you pretty good."

"Which one?"

"The dun one."

"How much would you want?"

"I would sell you the dun one for seven pound more."

"How old is she?"

"Four."

"She milkin' now, is she?"

"Well, she's taperin' off."

"I wouldn't want her until she was with calf. Nor I wouldn't say she was fourteen pounds' worth of cow."

"I ain't gettin' fourteen. I'm gettin' seven from you. And you can pay it in fur, if you want to, next spring."

Whit had finally bought her—giving his claim against the Proprietors, plus two pounds and six shillings to be paid off in fur, three days of labor, and ten pounds of cheese.

Beede had never confessed what he'd got for the claim, and Whit had begun to suspect that maybe Beede'd got nothing. This had made him feel better about the whole thing.

Melissa had said that she would wean the baby most likely as soon as the cow was milking again.

The cow dropped a bull calf on the twenty-ninth day of April, 1771, sometime before morning in a place she'd chosen herself—a little thicket of hemlocks near a stand of beech trees about a quarter of a mile up the brook from the house. Whit found her soon after breakfast—or rather the dog found her for him—and Whit carried the calf back to the house in his arms. He had to tie up the cow while he brought in the calf for fear she'd make trouble.

Whit was pleased with the calf—although he hadn't wanted a bull calf—and he was proud of the cow because she had done well. But the calf delighted Melissa out of all reason. She was as pleased as she'd been when he'd brought her the dog. Whit hadn't been at all sure that he'd want to raise a bull calf, but he doubted now that he'd have any choice. He went back for the cow and he led her home slowly, but she appeared to be able to travel all right.

After supper that evening, he reckoned the date with Melissa, and cut it into one of the logs in the wall of the house with his knife.

It was about three weeks after this that he went out to Beede's—and about the first thing he told Beede was that the dun cow'd had her calf.

When Beede inquired if Whit figured to raise him, Whit said he hadn't made up his mind yet; he didn't know but he would.

Beede said, "I think I would, probably, if I was in your room. I hear you're goin' t' have neighbors. He'll be handy for them. He'll be more handy than mine would."

"Who are they?" said Whit.

"Philbrick and Eastman, and Jackman, and Choate."

Whit didn't know one of them. He wanted to ask Beede if they were good men. But he guessed maybe that that wouldn't do. When he saw Jonas, he could find out from him.

The next afternoon Whit was down weeding corn, and the dog keeping him company, when she began to bristle and growl as she would have for a man. Still, a man was the last thing that Whit ever expected to be stirring round in the woods—and he moved toward the stump where his rifle was resting. He waved the dog down, and she crouched and was quiet . . . they waited a moment . . . then they heard someone hail. Whit answered in kind—and the dog apparently feeling that she was released, sprang to her feet and set up a great barking. Whit said, "Jen, you! Lay down!"—and she gave over her barking. But she didn't lie down.

The man came out of the woods then, and into the clearing, and hesitated a moment because the sunlight was bright.

He was the scrawniest, littlest man!

Whit could see that Melissa had come to the doorway—and he looked forward to later when she'd tell what she'd thought.

The man came on through the clearing toward where Whit was standing; he was carrying his gun as though it were a heavy thing, and he was limping a little as if he had a sore heel. He was thin-cheeked and dirty, and his beard sparse and uneven; his torn leather shirt was without any fringe, and his breeches too big for him. He looked like a man who'd been thrown out of jail because it wasn't worth while to keep him. Whit knew who he was now: he had seen him round Sandwich—but it had never occurred to him to ask what was his name. He was a pioneer, all right, no one could mistake him.

Twenty feet off the man stopped uncertainly, and standing a little lopsided because of his heel, he said to Whit sorrowfully, "Dutiful Jackman." He had a bad fly-bite on the lid of one eye.

Whit almost laughed—but he didn't!—and he said, "Whitfield Livingston."

"I guess I seen you to Sandwich," Jackman agreed.

"I shouldn't wonder. I heard you was comin'. Come up t' th' house. I'll tell my woman t' fix you somethin' t' eat. We ain't got any drink."

Dutiful Jackman nodded his head. "Jonas Moore told me. I thought it might be a joke. He's a great hand for jokin', Jonas Moore is."

"Ayuh," said Whit, "I guess Jonas is."

The dog had sniffed at the man, and then wandered away. Whit didn't blame her: he was pretty strong.

Melissa fed Jackman, but it was between dinner and supper and Whit didn't eat. And she kept a watchful eye on the baby lest Jackman should poke at him.

The little man ate with a woebegone air—which Melissa put down to the absence of rum. Whit thought it was probably because his mouth hurt him—his teeth, in the front, being rotted away.

When Jackman had finished he thanked them both kindly— and then sat perfectly still in front of the fire.

Whit asked him where his land lay.

Jackman confessed that he didn't have any land. He'd had it in mind, he said, to make a pitch somewhere and Beede'd suggested that he look around here.

"You mean right around here?—or the township of Tamworth?"

"Well, Tamworth, he said."

Whit wondered how much the agent would pay Beede for Jackman. He didn't look to him to be worth very much. "Well, Tamworth," he said, "has got plenty of land in it. You come over some of it on your way in."

"I come over a lot of it, it seemed to me like. I got an awful bad stone bruise right now on my heel."

"I noticed you did have. Whereabouts did you figure on?—or hadn't you yet?"

"I thought maybe you'd tell me. I guess you know more about it round here than most anyone does."

"All right, I'll tell you." Whit took out his knife and was about to draw with the back of the point in the smooth dirt on the floor.

"You could see better outside," said Melissa.

But Whit had already begun to see the map in his mind, and he scarcely heard her. He said, "I can see all right here," and he went on with his map. He was trying to draw it as true as he could. He had to do this. For one thing, he owed it to the country itself.

He began explaining to Jackman as he went along. "Here'd be the mountain—she lays about north—and Bearcamp River, I'd say, would come along about here."

The two men were squatting like frogs on the floor, with their knees up to their ears, and very intent. Jackman was nodding his head to everything that Whit said, and occasionally snuffling and wiping his nose on the back of his hand.

"And here's where we be now." Whit drew with his knife a little square for his land—and Melissa looked over his shoulder.

He had finished the map. It was about a yard square. "Now, then," he said, and he got down on his knees. "There is three places, mainly, where there's interval land. The first place is here." And he set the palm of his left hand squarely down on the map. "Maybe you crossed that one on your way in."

"I guess prob'ly I did."

"The second one's here—" and he showed where that lay; it was more to the eastward. "And the other one's here—" and he put his hand on it. He was seeing the land he was talking about. But Melissa, not knowing the land, saw only the map that was there on the floor.

In no case had Whit's hand come anywhere near to that little square he had marked as his own.

Jackman said, "Ayuh, I see how it is"—and he got up stiffly because he was tired.

Whit, still on his knees and bent over the map, was going on talking. "Scatterin' places," he said, "there is other ones smaller. But if I was in your room, I think what I would do would be to go where I have showed you."

"Yes," Jackman answered, "I guess prob'ly I will. Ma'am," he said to Melissa, "I thank you for supper."

"You're welcome," she told him—and Whit looked up from the map. He looked from one to the other as though he'd missed something, and then he said to Jackman, "You ain't goin' now, are you? Don't you want to lay here?"

"That's kind of you, too. But I don't mind t' lay out." He picked up his gun from where it stood by the door.

Whit got to his feet. He was still puzzled. "Well, if you locate, come by here again."

"All right," said Jackman, and went out the door. He glanced toward the cowshed, and then down over the clearing—where the shadows were soft in the late afternoon. "You got a nice place here. Your corn's comin' good."

"Ayuh," said Whit.

"Well, I wish you good night"—and he went down through the clearing, lugging his gun and limping a little on account of his heel. . . .

3

The other three men of whom Beede had spoken—their names were Philbrick, and Eastman, and Choate—came during the summer but didn't stay through the winter. That is, they came to Tamworth; Philbrick was the only one of the three who actually came to Whit's house.

Whit took to Philbrick—and so did Melissa. He was a kindly man, gentle and strong. "David Philbrick," he told them—as Whit stood in the doorway with Melissa behind him, but able to see. And they never forgot the good sound of his voice. He was a man who was heavier than Whit was, taller, and thicker, and with more age on him, too. He was fair-haired and wide-shouldered, and his face was burnt a red brown. He hadn't spent all his time in the woods; he had been working somewhere in the sun.

He stayed all through the evening—and they talked until midnight. It was apparent that Philbrick wasn't a great one for talking, but Whit and Melissa weren't choosey at all—and he was a lot better than Jackman! No one was distressed that the silences lasted until some one of the three had thought of something to say.

Whit went with him next morning to look over the neighborhood. And he found the man traveled slowly and carefully, the same as he talked. Philbrick said he'd already been over a good part of the township, and so they only covered the northeastern part. That took them all day. So far, Whit liked the man. He couldn't quite figure why this sort of man should want to go pioneering, but that was surely none of his business and he didn't ask.

When they got back to the house, Melissa'd fixed a great supper. She'd been at it all day. She had spruced up the baby within an inch of his life, and she'd put the house in such order that Whit didn't dare to speak of it. She'd even cleaned off the cow.

Later on after supper, and the baby asleep, Whit asked her to sing for them. She said nothing at first—for so long that Whit didn't know but in some way he'd made a mistake. She hadn't done any singing for quite a long time, except for the baby. But pretty soon she got going, and she sang very well.

They tried to get Philbrick to sing, but they found he was too shy to. Whit said he didn't sing, either.

Philbrick said the next morning that he'd give Whit a day's work to pay Whit for putting in yesterday showing him round. Whit said this wasn't necessary, but that he'd be glad of some help. Whit had had in mind for some time that when the sow was to farrow, they'd be in need of a place for the pigs that would be safer from bears. He couldn't expect to be there himself every time they came round. The sow was due in September, and this was now August. He hadn't got at it before because of everything else, and now that he had someone to help him, it looked like a good chance.

Philbrick proved to be a comfortable man to work with. He had a good head for planning, and he was a clever man with an ax. Between them that day they laid up a log house with walls two feet in thickness and a roof of logs over it that would give any bear pause. It had a heavy door to it that worked up and down, and they drove stakes all around it so that the pigs couldn't root out. Whit was so pleased with it that he said he wouldn't mind to live in it himself—that is, if he could move in there before the sow did.

They had only one mishap. Philbrick fell down while he was carrying a log, and his knee slipped out of joint. He was in hard pain for some minutes, but he knew what to do—and with Whit there to do it, they got it back in. Then Philbrick got up and went on with the work. He said it happened now and again, and that he was well used to it.

Being another man's weakness, Whit didn't like to talk of it— and he didn't even tell Melissa about it until the next morning when Philbrick had gone.

She said Whit ought to have told her—that she could have bound up his knee. She was put out about it more than Whit would have thought. But Whit said he guessed Philbrick could look out for himself: he had never worked with a man who was as able as he. They'd be lucky, he said, if they got him for a neighbor.

Philbrick had told them that he'd be back before long probably, and true to his word, he was back in two weeks. He had taken up land about a mile to the north of them on some flats that there were near the head of the pond. He said he favored the soil there; it was richer than most. And Whit guessed that he probably had in mind to try flax.

He only stayed a few minutes, and then went on to his land.

Whit went to bed that night feeling more confident about things in general than he had for some time.

Each day they expected that Philbrick would come over to visit; but he didn't, and when a week later he still hadn't come, Whit said he guessed he'd go up there and see how he was doing. It wasn't five minutes after that—Whit was eating his supper— that they heard Philbrick's gun.

Whit considered a moment—the direction and distance— and then he said to Melissa, "Be a deer, I should think. That's a great place for 'em there in that swamp just this side of his place. They lay in there in the daytime, specially when it's so hot, and then come out about now to feed along the edge of the pond. Philbrick, most likely, was on that little sandspit. That's about where the shot come from. He'd have cover to lay in, and he could see either way."

Melissa said yes, that was probably it.

"Well, I guess I won't go up now: He'd only figure I come for a present of meat."

"I don't think he would, Whit."

But Whit wouldn't go.

Things having started to happen, they kept right on happening. Inside of an hour, Jonas Moore had appeared. It was two months, or more than that, since they had seen Jonas, but he wouldn't come in, and he wouldn't sit down; he said he was on his way in to Philbrick's: he'd stopped to ask Whit the way.

Whit told him the way.

"All right," said Jonas. "Well, I'll get along. You two look pretty good. So does he, for that matter—" Melissa was holding the baby and he was jumping up and down in her arms.

"You comin' back here t'night?" she inquired of Jonas.

"I shouldn't wonder."

"Mis' Moore all right, is she?"

"Yes, she's pretty good."

Melissa asked—meaning Philbrick, "He ain't got any trouble . . . ?"

"Well, he has, and he hain't, in a way, you might say. I c'n tell you better, perhaps, when I come back by here. About a mile, you said, Whit?"

"'Bout that, I should think."

Melissa said "What—" but Whit interrupted her. "Let him go," he said curtly.

Jonas didn't want it to look as though Whit had spoken for him. He said, "Well, I guess a half minute won't do any hurt. They all of 'em know this to Sandwich; it ain't any secret. His woman left him, as I guess you know, about a year and a half ago."

"No," Whit said, "I didn't."

"Well, she did, anyhow. Feller from Manchester. She went off with him and took their two young ones right along, too. Philbrick's 'n hers, I mean. Girls, I was told."

"No!" Whit was astonished. "Why did he let her?"

"Who? This Manchester feller?"

"No, Philbrick, I mean. They were his children."

"Oh, there wan't any question of that. I guess she just took 'em."

"He'd ought to gone after them."

"Well, I don't know. I'm only telling you the way that I heard it."

"He'd ought to gone after her and brought her back, too."

"What the hell for?—if she was that kind."

"I would have," said Whit, "if I'd been in his room."

"You'd a had to cut holes in your hat, then, for the rest of her life. Once they get that way, there ain't any stoppin' 'em. A man who'll keep one of that kind is just a plain fool. Way I look at it, anyhow. Still, it don't matter with this one because now she is dead. That's what I come to tell Philbrick. His sister sent word.

She's got the two young ones. I guess she don't want 'em no more 'n what the Manchester feller most prob'ly did. Way I got the message, was that if Philbrick didn't come get 'em, she had in mind to turn 'em out on the town. Still, I don't know what Philbrick c'n do with 'em. Man brought the message to me, come up from Gilmanton. He wan't the one that had had it from her. Well, I got t' go tell him. I guess he'll be interested. I'll stop by to visit some on my way back. That's more 'n you done for me, Whit, the last time you was out. Or *wan't* it the last time?" He grinned at Whit.

And Melissa there in the doorway, who could see over their shoulders, said, "This is him comin' now."

Both men looked up at her—saw her staring past them—and then turned around to see what it was that she saw.

It was Philbrick, all right—carrying a forequarter of deer meat slung from his gun barrel—they could see the shank of it sticking out to one side.

Jonas made some exclamation—but neither one of the other two uttered a sound.

When Philbrick got up to them, he nodded to Jonas, and he said to Whit quietly, "I brought you some meat."

"That was kind of you. I thought that was your gun. Up at the head of the pond?—'bout an hour ago?"

"Ayuh."

Whit took the meat. "You dressed out awful quick. I'll go hang this here up. I'm obliged to you, surely." He went off toward the shed with the meat on his shoulder.

"Good-lookin' meat," Jonas commented.

"You come in from Sandwich?"

"Yes. Matter o' fact, I was comin' t' your place."

"Was you?"

Jonas saw that Melissa had gone into the house. "I brought you a message. Your woman's been sick." He was not looking at Philbrick.

Philbrick said nothing.

"Fever," said Jonas. "It come on her sudden. Still, the way that I heard it, her sister got there."

It seemed a long time to Jonas, but finally Philbrick said, "When?"

"Four days ago."

There was another long silence, but at last Philbrick spoke. He said, "Thank you for bringin' the message."

"'Twan't any trouble. You want t' go back to your place? I could go along with you a ways, if you'd like . . ." but he saw that Philbrick wasn't quite ready for that; Philbrick just now couldn't hear what he was saying.

There was nothing to do but stand there and wait. Jonas knew Whit wouldn't come back until they were finished. There was no sound from the cabin.

Presently Philbrick said, "She was a good woman."

And Jonas said, "Yes."

After a moment, Jonas thought fit to add, "Her sister sent word your two girls is to her place. I guess maybe she figured you would want to come get 'em. Winchester, ain't it?"

He thought Philbrick nodded—but he couldn't be certain.

Then Philbrick turned round to Jonas and made an effort to speak. He failed on the first try, but then he succeeded. "I will be glad to see them," he said. He meant it, all right; it was just the words that were difficult.

"Sart'n," said Jonas. "And they'll welcome you, too."

But Philbrick had done all the talking he could. He picked up his gun and started down through the clearing, not the way that he'd come, but heading toward Sandwich—and from there down to Winchester.

Melissa came to the doorway and said, "Ain't you goin' t' go with him?"

"I don't know as he wants me."

"You go with him," she said.

"Maybe I had better. I'd had in mind though to stay here and visit."

"Well, we'd like t' have you. But I think you'd better go."

"All right," said Jonas—and he set out after Philbrick.

4

Once again they faced winter without any neighbors. Melissa had thought she'd be used to it now. But with the trees wet and black in the month of November and the whole winter to come, she knew that she was afraid. And as the great strength of the winter came closer around them, she began to live only in what she could see—the day right ahead, the work she was doing, and whatever it was that she'd have to do next.

Whit seemed to her to be less given to talking than ever. He would come from a day in the woods, eat his supper in silence, and then sit by the fire, not saying a word, but doing some task that made a regular noise—not very loud but over and over—like taking a gap from his ax with a file. And he'd stand in the doorway before going to bed, letting the cold come into the house, staring out at the night for three or four minutes, utterly silent . . . and then he'd turn back into the room again without saying a word. It made it worse, too, that he didn't know that he did this. If she'd asked him not to, he'd have looked hurt and surprised, and have said he was sorry.

In the tavern in Kettleford, it had been bright in the evening. There had been talking and laughing, and the men often had sung. There had been news there of Portsmouth, and sometimes of Boston. Some of the men had been kindly disposed—like Murphy, for instance, and Ensign Lord, he was pleasant—and old David Gillmor had been funny, in truth. Oh, she could remember the other things, too—the hawking and spitting, the filth on the floor. But those weren't the things that she tried to remember— those weren't the things that came back of themselves.

She seldom thought of Joe Felipe, for example, drunk and asleep in the taproom in Pennacook. But she did think of Joe with the wood on his shoulder, and she thought of Joe on that night in the road with the wind in her face when Joe had been kind to her—and she'd sent him away. And Joe had gone, too.

She would think sometimes of Joe and of Whit, facing each other—when she had come down the stairs and there they were below, both of them shaken and ready to fight. That had been terrible. But it hadn't lasted long, it was very soon over, and it had turned out all right.

She didn't want to go back to Kettleford. She had no thought whatsoever of that. It wasn't so much that she remembered her father—it was more that her father was there all the time—in Kettleford, that is. His presence in Kettleford was a part of her life. She would never go back.

But still she remembered the pleasant things there. She had to have something to think about daytimes when Whit would be off and the baby asleep and the sound of the wind in the trees would rise over the silence and she'd see the gray ashes in the fireplace make little whirls. Those were the times when the pain of her loneliness would come on her hard—and her mind would reach

303

out to take hold of the things that she liked to remember. Some of those things she used a good many times.

They had a spell of cold weather toward the middle of January that Whit said beat anything he'd ever seen. He didn't dare to do any chopping for fear that his ax would break right in two. He wouldn't even tackle a white pine—and he couldn't chop maple: that was so hard that his ax only bounced. Splitting was easy, but he couldn't chop.

He kept telling Melissa of these signs of the cold, and he seemed to take pride in them.

She knew it was cold. She got up in the night once to heat some milk for the baby, and the hem of her skirt in the back, while she knelt at the fire, froze stiff as a board where the baby had wetted it while she was in bed.

She told Whit in the morning, and although she hadn't meant to, she got to laughing about it, and then wanted to cry.

They fought the winter—day after day. They thought in March they were winning. They hadn't lost even so much as one pig.

There was a trapper stopped by and ate dinner about the third week in March. He had just come from Fryeburg and was on his way out to Sandwich. He said that in Fryeburg they had had a bad time of it. About every man had been sick, he said, there.

Two days after that, Whit took a chill, and fever to follow, but not enough fever to put him out of his head. He sweat himself for it, and at the end of three days he was able to stand on his feet. But then Melissa took her turn—and before she was out of it, the baby had sickened. Whit took care of them both. He said he felt all right, although not very steady.

By the time they were better, it was more or less spring.

When Whit got out to Sandwich, he learned that the trapper had only made it to Beede's by the skin of his teeth. He'd left his pack on the trail—Beede'd sent a man out for it—and two miles short of Beede's, he'd left his gun in a tree. They said he'd come into the yard on his hands and his knees. Beede himself had been the one that took care of him—claimed he knew better than anyone else, and wouldn't even let one of his people so much as go near the man. It was highhanded, of course, but that was the way Beede was. And the trapper got better. There was that about trappers: they generally did.

No one in Sandwich had died the whole winter. But they said

that in Fryeburg there had four of them died. Beede was proud of this. Sandwich, he said, had beaten Fryeburg for once. Frye had glass windows in his house in Fryeburg. "But," said Beede, "by God, none of my men are dead!" He was mightily pleased by it.

—and then he remembered he had a letter for Whit. He went and got it—he said he'd had it a month.

On the outside of it, under the dust and the dirt, was written: "Mistress W Livingston in the Township of Tamworth"; it was a little small thing, and the seal chipped and broken. There was no telling how long ago it left Kettleford—Whit didn't doubt for a minute that that was where it was from. He said to Beede, "Owe you anything on it?"

"No, not a thing. Jonas Moore brought it. He told me, I guess, who 'twas left it with him, but I don't remember. If Jonas paid on it, you c'n square it with him."

Whit took off his hat and put the letter inside it. "She c'n read writin' better'n I can," he said, and put the hat on again. All it was, probably, was old Butler was dead.

He had a hard trip going home because he was so weak. When he came in, he set his hat on the table and undid his pack to show her the things that he'd brought.

She was pleased by them, but they didn't seem to take hold of her the way they did sometimes. He was disappointed in that. Still, he supposed she was tired.

He was tired himself. He was so tired that he felt kind of sick. He pushed back from the table and said, "I'm goin' t' bed."

"Don't you want to eat? I have kept it all ready."

"No, I don't think it. I'll eat when I wake up." He took his hat up off the table and the letter fell out. "Oh! There now!" he said. "I guess I forgot."

She'd seen the letter.

He said, "That's for you."

She didn't appear to know what it was. She looked at the letter—and she looked up at Whit.

He wanted to say, "Well, it's a letter. Don't you want to see what it says?" But instead of that he took up the sack of salt off the table to put it away—and from the other end of the room, he asked, "What does it say?"

Melissa reached out her hand for it, and Whit, from where he was standing, saw her break the seal and hold the paper up to the light . . . and while she was reading he came over slowly and stood by the edge of the table again. . . .

When she had finished, she laid down the letter, and turned to the fire. She said, "Pa is gone."

"I didn't know but what that might be it." He took off his wet clothes—he'd been soaking in sweat—put on some dry ones and lay down on the bed.

"Matthew Patten," she said, "is the one wrote the letter. It says he was bringin' in wood and fell down—and that night he was dead."

"Well, that's one way. And he had time to repent." Whit pulled up the bearskin. "Why was he bringin' in wood? I never knew him do that."

"He'd been livin' alone there, so Patten says."

"Not even a housekeeper? That don't sound right. What had become of his money?"

"I couldn't say. Patten says he'd been alone ever since the time that we left. He quit keepin' tavern and let the place go— garden 'n everything. The vendue won't bring enough—I guess they've had it by now—to pay what he owed t' Portsmouth for rum 'n like that."

"What about them that owed him?"

"The letter don't say."

"Well, if he hadn't collected it, I guess nobody could. I mean your old man."

"Ayuh."

Still she sat by the fire.

"Patten is square," Whit said. "When he says a thing's so, you can depend on it that that's just about it."

"M-hm."

"Well—you comin' t' bed, are you?"

"Yes, pretty soon."

She was thinking of Kettleford and its fields in the sun, of the road that ran through it, and the people near by, and of how they'd talk to each other a dozen times in a day. She had seen the good things of the village when she was a girl, but they had never been hers because her father was there. He wasn't there now; he would never be there again. She thought of the houses and the people in them. Even in winter there were always sleds on the road. And in the summer, the great fields in the sun . . . the wide, rolling fields that sloped down to the river, and a score of houses and barns to be seen from the hill. Joe Felipe would be there, probably—poor Joe Felipe!—she smiled when she thought of him. The Kettleford women, she'd never known—but that would be different now her father had gone.

She felt the cold at her shoulders and through all of the room. She thought of her baby, and the great woods all around.

It seemed to be summer in Kettleford. . . .

Whit said, "What's the matter? Do you want to go back?"

"Yes"—and her hands on each side of her clung to the edge of the bench. She was glad she had said it!

Then the silence lasted too long. She would scream in a minute if he didn't speak.

"We could go back," he said. "Yes—we could go back. We could sell what we got done here for enough to get a place there. The land mightn't be much but there'd be some in fields anyhow, 'n there'd be a board house 'n a pretty fair barn. They say in Connecticut there is farms awful cheap. Yes, we could go back. There ain't nothin' to stop us at that end, anyhow."

"Do you think," said Melissa, "we could sell this place for enough to get just that meadow that—well, the one you and me raked?—'n maybe a woodlot? I don't mean any house. We could build just a little house there on the rise. Would you think maybe that we could do that?"

It took him some time, but he said, "I should think maybe we might."

He threw off the bearskin, and sat up on the edge of the bed. "I won't pretend that I wouldn't sooner stay here. You know that, I guess."

Slowly and painfully, he got to his feet. Melissa could hear him, but she didn't turn round.

He said, "I want t' keep on with what I have begun. As long as I can, I want t' work for us both. If I can't do that here, then we'll go somewheres else. If everything that I do here, if everything I put up—like a new barn 'n so on, or clear some more ground—if the things that I plan on mean only to you that you got that much less chance to get out of here—why, then, we better go. If you feel that way about 'em, they ain't much good to me."

"Well, we ain't goin' t'night," she said, "you better get back into bed."

He made no answer at all, and after a moment she heard him get back into bed. She still sat in front of the fire. She supposed she had hurt him. But there were these things now that she had to say: "I hear the wind in them spruces times when you're gone. I wouldn't pay no heed to it—no matter how much it cried—if there was someone else round—some other woman—that I could say to, 'That wind makes a racket,' and she would say, 'Yes.' And times when he's sick and I don't know what to do. Or when you're here even 'n don't say nothin' at all for hours on end, Whit. That's when I want to go back. I don't mind the work; I c'n do that all right. It's nobody to talk to. It's no one to hear talk. I get lonely, I tell you. You don't understand."

Whit said, "No, I don't. Well, then, we'll go back."

"You really mean it?"

"I mean it, yes."

After a moment, she got up and went to the door; she stood in the doorway and lifted her head, feeling the wind as it blew from the south. . . .

Whit heard her go out.

He lay there in misery.

When she came in, she said, "'Twon't be much more'n a month now 'fore you c'n plant. Maybe not down by the brook, but my garden you can."

Once more he sat up on the side of the bed.

Melissa was banking the fire. "If I don't have to stay," she said, "I don't want t' go back."

5

Whit's strength returned as the summer came on, and when he realized one evening that he'd done a day's work and still felt pretty good, then he knew he was well.

His Indian corn was more promising now than it had been last year at this time, and he had a good deal more of it. He'd made a garden and they would soon have some sauce from it. Taking his place as a whole, he was now about even with Jonas. This didn't affect their relationship greatly. It certainly didn't on Jonas's side. And the principal change in Whit's feeling was simply that he felt capable, now, if need should arise, of repaying some of the things that Jonas had done for him. Jonas was still the better man in the woods, and both of them knew it. It would always be so until Jonas got old. Even then he would not lose his knowledge and cunning.

As for the rest of the town: Mark Jewell's son—he was Mark Jewell, Junior—was building a house near the top of a hill in the eastern part of the township, and Eastman and Choate—who had spent the winter in Sandwich—had come onto their land again, and were going ahead. Even Dutiful Jackman, who had wintered somewhere or other, had come back again and was making a pitch. He had put up a lean-to and girdled some trees and scratched in some corn, and said he intended to stay. Whatever else he accomplished—or failed to—he brought the total of men in the township to five. Bradbury Jewell—Mark Jewell's brother—was said to be planning to come the next year, as well as a good many others.

There was no question now but what the town would be settled. If things kept on this way, they might get a mill before very much longer. Not right away, maybe, but in two or three years. Or even a blacksmith.

David Philbrick came back again. He came alone in July, looking cheerful and well, and as though he had wintered in plenty. They found out what it was in a matter of minutes: he had married a wife. He said he'd got a real good one—a great woman to work, and that she was kind to his children, they got along fine. She was a young woman, he said—about sixteen, he should think—but she had a good head on her, and he thought she'd do well. He said he'd bought a cow, too. He had left them all out to Sandwich while he came in to put up a house.

Whit said, "I could go over tomorrow; we could get a start on it."

"How old are your girls?" Melissa inquired.

"One of 'em's six and the other one's four. The oldest one she's a great hand to go berryin'. That's what she tells me."

"I should think it was early for berries," said Whit.

"'Tis a little mite, yes, but they'll be along pretty soon."

"You know, I shouldn't wonder," Whit said to him hopefully, "if you was to hoe in some Indian before the week's out, that you might get to harvest it—if the frost should hold off."

"I brought in some seed."

Whit went over next day. He got there soon after sunrise, but already Philbrick had got in a good share of the corn.

They got the house up in very quick time—no chimney, no windows, and leaving the bark on the logs. By the time the borers had spoiled them, Philbrick maintained, he'd either have made a go of it here and would want a new house, or else he would have failed and be ready to move. Logs with the bark on would last long enough for him to find out whether he was going to really live here, or not.

Whit said surely they would.

As soon as the roof was secure, Philbrick went out to Sandwich to bring in his family. They lay out a night on the way coming in, and when they got to Whit's place late the next afternoon, Philbrick was carrying the younger girl up on his back. His wife was leading the cow, and the cow was pretty well burdened: a good-sized iron pot, a fry-pan, a shovel, a beetle, a spade, a hoe, and a bar, and a small keg of rum, and what looked to be a bundle of clothing were all tied on the cow. The six-year-old girl was back of the cow with a stick, but whacking had ceased to get any results. Beginning with Philbrick and including the cow, they appeared to have had about all the travel they wanted.

Melissa took note that Philbrick's woman was healthy and that she was probably not yet with child. She was a big, strapping girl—she would probably scale half again what Melissa would. And she looked a sober girl, too: one could see that a widower— even a man with two children—might look as good to her as a younger man would. Melissa approved of her. She would make a good wife for Philbrick and a good neighbor-woman: she would never run off as Philbrick's other one had, and she didn't look like the kind to make sheep's eyes at Whit.

Melissa had fixed a great supper beforehand. She had three kinds of meat—two hot and one cold—and a great pile of bread, and she had cheese and some butter.

Later on, when they'd gone, Whit said to Melissa, "I remember the first night you 'n me come in here. You remember?—a wind blowin' 'n cold 'n a power o' snow. And I put a light to the fire never stoppin' t' think that the chimbley was covered. You remember that, too?"

"Yes," she said, "I remember."

6

Throughout that autumn of 1772 and the two winters that followed, Whit hunted alone. Philbrick wasn't a hunter. His brother Jonathan—who came later on—had the name of being a hunter. But David was more of a man to do work. David could shoot well enough, and he knew the country, but a deer could outguess him more often than not, and Whit told Melissa that he thought that foxes *tried* to get Philbrick to hunt them. Whit got in the way of doing the hunting for both families, and Philbrick was careful to repay him in work.

The dog Jen was now of an age to be really some use. She was three. Another two years and she'd be in her prime. She had proved a still-hunter, just as Beede had said. That is, she didn't use her voice any when she was working a track. When Whit heard her bark, he knew she had her game.

This was the fourth winter since they had come. It was the best winter Whit had had yet. Because of hunting for Philbrick as well as himself, he spent nearly twice as much time in the woods as he had before, and yet it paid him to do it.

He got more work done that winter than in any winter so far. Philbrick never came over unless Whit was there. They built a log barn that would hold a half dozen head, and they put a floor in the cabin made of logs split and hewn.

What Whit wanted the most was oxen and boards. If he had oxen, he could get rid of his stumps, he could clear better, and also he could plow. And if he had boards, he could build a new house.

Melissa, meantime, was expecting again. She figured on probably the third week in October—and it turned out she was right. Mary Philbrick came over and showed herself to be as knowing and able as they'd had every reason to expect her to be. It did't take so long this time, and Melissa was up and about sooner than she had been before.

Hez Hackett, the hunter, stopped by in November. He admired the baby. "He-one, ain't it?" he said to Whit. "That's what I heard. Now you got two of 'em. You're doin' all right!"

He was a single man older than Whit—a plump little man, but very good on a track and an excellent shot. Whit still did the hunting for himself and for Philbrick, but Hackett killed most of the meat for the rest of the town. Eight families, he hunted for.

Melissa smiled on him pleasantly. She cared nothing whatever for Hackett's opinion, but she'd be willing he'd carry a good report of the child.

"You look pretty spry," Hackett answered her smile. "How long ago was it?"

"Three weeks," said Whit. "Seventeenth day of October, 1774."

"Three weeks!" exclaimed Hackett. "My, ain't he come on!" He poked at the baby, and then turned to Whit. "A boy's a great thing when a man's runnin' traps, ain't he?"

"I expect so," said Whit. "My two are still young."

Hackett cast a glance round. "Where's the other one hid himself?"

"Prob'ly out in th' shed."

"Shy, is he?"

"Maybe."

"Most of 'em is. But what I mean about trappin': the way things are now, a ten-year-old boy c'n go int' th' woods, 'n you ain't got to fear for him."

He explained to Melissa. "My old man always fretted for fear I'd get took. I never did, though." And then he remarked to them generally, "It was the money that worried him most. They never done nothin' to children at all—that is, the ones that could travel. Sometimes they kep' 'em, 'n sometimes they sold 'em. 'Twas only men growed that they burned 'n like that." And he added to Whit, "John Stark come from down your way. He c'n tell you 'bout Indians."

Whit said, "Londonderry, he come from. I'm a Kettleford man. He left there two years before I was born anyhow. That was the year they had him five weeks to St. Francis. I heard all about it a good many times."

"I suppose so," said Hackett. "Well, I'd ought to get on. I only meant to stop by here 'n see how you was doin'. Now I c'n tell people that you're doin' good."

"You better stay 'n eat supper."

"Well, that's awful kind of you." He glanced at Melissa and saw she approved; he liked Whit and her both, and the food would be good; there wouldn't be any rum—but a man couldn't have everything, and Whit understood hunting. Hackett said that he'd stay.

"Your dogs with you?" Whit asked.

"They're outside with yourn. They get along good. She run a deer with 'em one day there last week. A doe, but they lost her."

"I wondered," said Whit. "She come home tuckered out." He sat down with Hackett at one end of the fireplace, leaving the rest of it free for Melissa to work.

The men settled to talking. Hackett told Whit of each place where he'd recently seen any sign of a panther or wolves, and Whit did the same in return. Whit said he thought that the panther were lessening. (He knew very well that the wolves had increased.) They talked together of the state of game generally.

And just as they did every time that Whit saw him, they talked of Whit's rifle and of what it would do. Hackett wasn't quite ready to say that he wanted one, but he was pretty close to it. Whit's was the third rifle that Hackett had come across inside of two years—and all owned by good men. There was a Baker's River man owned one, in the township of Romney, fifty miles west. And Frye himself did—but of course he was a rich man and could afford to own anything. There were some men in Tamworth owned no gun at all.

Whit saw that young Jonas had put a foot in the doorway. Another five minutes, and he'd be inside.

Not till Melissa had finished getting ready the supper did Hackett start in on the news of the town.

He knew where there was sickness and what they should do for it—and sometimes they were doing it, and sometimes they were not. He knew how the work at each place was progressing, and how they were fixed now that winter was near: how much corn, and so on, and the state of their cattle, if any, and what kind of shape their houses were in.

"I see Jonathan Philbrick—that brother of David's—two-three times in the woods. He ain't started a house. Five weeks he has been here, 'n he's still layin' out. He ain't much like his brother."

"I ain't seen him but twice."

"First time I seen him I thought he was a bear, 'count of his color and shagginess. Then when I see the size of him, he looked more like a moose."

"What did you think he was when you hear him talk?"

"You know, he ain't a liar," said Hackett. "Them things that he brags of, I b'lieve he has done—at least a part of 'em."

"You b'lieve them bear stories?"

"No. But if you c'n believe a bear story, it ain't any good."

"Fourteen in one season!" Whit said with disgust.

"He'll tackle a bear, though. He ain't afraid. B'God, if he had enough rum in him he'd tackle fourteen."

"I shouldn't wonder. The way he looked t' me he was wild enough to."

Hackett refused to give in. "He's a kindhearted man."

"Drunk or sober, you mean?"

"He's kindhearted sober, but he's more generous drunk. You heard him sing, have you?"

"No."

"Bellers a lot, but they're pretty good songs. Some of 'em are funny. He'll even sing in the woods."

"Sing in the woods?—when he's goin' along? Sounds like a Frenchman. And you claim he ain't wild!" Whit took up again what they'd been saying before. "You'd say that, in general, people 'd be all right until spring."

"I would think so," said Hackett. "But they're liable t' be hungry between spring and a crop."

Melissa stood leaning against the chimney and listening. It was some time since she'd seen a man talk while he ate. She would remember each word that he said, though. Each bit and each item she would think about later, tomorrow and next day, probably a good many times. She did like to hear what other people were doing.

Hackett told them of Sandwich and a few things about Gilmanton. He mentioned Boston, and Whit said he'd never been there. "Bigger 'n Portsmouth," Hackett advised him, "but they ain't so highborn to Boston, I mean the rich people ain't."

Whit said he didn't know. He'd never been to Portsmouth, for that matter, either.

"No, nor I ain't," Hackett confessed. "But I seen Governor John times when he was to Wolfeboro. They don't come no higherborn 'n what he is, I guess."

"They say he's a good man."

"That's what I always thought. I guess you ain't heard about him and them carpenters . . . ?"

"No, I don't know as I have."

"Well, the story I heard was: this Britainer general they got down to Boston—Gage his name is—he wanted some men to put up a place for his soldiers to sleep in. He couldn't get nobody in Boston to do it because they don't like havin' the soldiers around. So he sent word up to Governor John to send him some carpenters."

"Whyn't the soldiers do it themselves?"

"Well, I don't know. I guess they wan't up to it. Anyhow, Governor knowed he couldn't get any carpenters to go down to Boston for that kind of work. So he hired 'em on without tellin' 'em nothin'. All they was told was 'twas carpenterwork. They didn't find out till they got clear to Boston. And *then* wan't they mad! I want to tell you! Why, right down here t' Rochester—you know where that is—they made Governor's Agent—he was the

314

one done the hirin'—get down on his knees and apologize to the town."

"The agent, not Governor."

"No, hell, no. Not him! Governor wouldn't get down on his knees for the devil."

"I didn't think he would either," said Whit. "Still, he'd ought not to 've tricked 'em."

"No, sir, you're right. That's what they thought."

"Man tricks his equals, is one thing; or in a trade is all right. But not them that are under him. He hadn't ought to do that."

"Specially when they're so many," Hez Hackett agreed. "Why, you take in Boston, where they can all get together, they're up to something 'bout half of the time. Same way to Exeter—same way to Rochester. Same way to Connecticut, I should expect."

"I shouldn't wonder. I never been there. Connecticut people, they say, has gone into the Grants."

"Oh, God A'mighty, I should say that they had. They're thick over there."

"How many provinces is there? Do you know?" Whit inquired.

"I would say a good many."

"As many as ten?"

"I shouldn't wonder. Close to it, I guess. Say, now that I think of it, you wouldn't like to trade for the knowledge of where there's a bee tree? I lined 'em to it back along in the summer, 'n I marked the tree. But I been so busy I ain't been back to it since. I could tell you about it so's you could walk right up to it blindfolded. I wouldn't say it was a step over four mile. Whatever honey you get, you c'n pay me in meal for it."

"To balance?" said Whit.

"Well, I had hoped t' do better than that."

"Then you couldn't have figured to trade for it with me. How thick is the tree?"

"She ain't awful thick. You could get her down in an hour."

"She must a shrunk since I seen her, then."

Hackett said nothing.

"A whackin' old hemlock stump forty feet high?—a gray boulder beside it 'bout the size of this house?—twenty rod from the bank of the big brook to the north of here?—just before it goes in t' that steep-sided place?"

315

Hackett said ruefully, "Twenty rod from *which* bank?"

"The near bank, goin' up. And your bees is late-comers. I pitched a rock int' th' top of that stump a year ago in late August and never stirred up a bee. If they made ten pounds of honey in the time they been in there, I would say they'd done well. If you want to take down that hemlock and bring me the honey, I'll trade you meal for it when I see what it's like."

"You talk like Beede."

"I been here five years."

Hackett laughed and stood up. He said he'd got to go. He turned to Melissa and said, "Ma'am, I want to thank you. That was an awful good feed. And you got as handsome a baby as I ever see. I c'n tell all the rest of 'em. You got a name for it yet?"

"No," said Melissa.

Whit said to Hackett, "It's been dark for an hour. You better lay here."

—and after some slight discussion, Hackett stayed overnight. He slept out in the hay.

Whit said the next morning when Hackett had gone, "I like him all right. But ain't he a terrible feller to talk!"

7

It was the following April that David Philbrick was killed. A white pine fell on him. There had been three of them working—that is, two besides Philbrick. They were Elkanah Danforth, who wasn't more than sixteen, and Stephen Mason, an older man. Danforth and Mason were felling the tree—not such a big one, three feet at the butt—and Philbrick, near by, was lopping the limbs off another one that was already down. He wanted the limbs off so they could roll the trunk up to burn.

Mason and Danforth—both of them—called out to him two or three times that she was about ready to come—but he must have thought he was clear, because, though he answered, he kept right on working. They thought themselves he was clear but still a little too close. They finally quit chopping: that would make him come out.

Philbrick heard them quit chopping, and he called out, "All right, just let me free this one—"

Then a gust of wind came and they heard her crackling deep in their cut, and they yelled, "David, she's comin'!"

He looked up—and he saw the top of her beginning to move, and he started out. They said he didn't look scared, and that he hung on to his ax. He came wading out through that whole mess of branches, and they thought that most probably he'd make it all right. But then he fell down. He went down sideways and rolled onto his back, and they saw him throw up both arms to try to cover his face. Danforth screamed like a woman—

And the green tree settled over him.

They got to him in no time, but they couldn't do any good. A limb of the tree had gone right clear through his chest and as much as ten inches into the ground. He was dead when they saw him. It was a limb maybe five inches through.

They got him out and they tried to make him look better before they went for his wife.

Elkanah Danforth came out and told Whit of it. Elkanah looked pretty badly, and Whit said, "You stay right here and keep an eye on these young ones. I'll go in with my woman. I shan't be gone long. If you're hungry, eat something. I ain't got any rum."

Whit thought on the way, "It was prob'ly that knee of his give way underneath him. That was why he fell down." But when he saw David, he didn't try to find out.

Mary Philbrick was quiet, and so was the younger girl, who was with her. The older girl wasn't there. As soon as they'd told her, she'd gone off by herself.

Whit and Mason decided that they'd better wait till tomorrow to bury him—and that they'd better send word out to Sandwich in the meantime, as well. Mason said he would see to it.

Whit went home for the night finally, and Melissa stayed there. The reason Whit was so late leaving was because he thought he ought to have a look round for the older girl before he went home. He found her in no time. She was out in the barn.

He could just make her out—she was in a far and dark corner, huddled over and crying, but not making a sound. He put his hand on her shoulder, and said, "I'm goin t' set down over here for a while" —and he went and sat down. After a time, she'd stopped crying. Whit got up and went over to her. He didn't know what to do, and he didn't know what to say. Once again, he laid his hand on her shoulder. "I'm goin' in 'n tell your ma that you're out

here. You ain't got t' go in right away, but I would pretty soon."
She nodded her head. And Whit went away. He didn't feel that
he'd helped any.

Daniel Beede himself came over from Sandwich, and two or
three with him—Jonas Moore being one. They brought in some
boards, knowing there'd be none in Tamworth.

Late that afternoon, David Philbrick was buried—at the foot
of a gray, granite boulder about a quarter of a mile from his house.
Beede read from the Bible. They all were agreed that he was the
one who should do it, although he favored the Quakers and they
thought Philbrick had not. David, his wife thought, had been
more of a Baptist. But she thanked Beede for reading, and he read
quite a lot.

Afterwards, Beede went back as far as Mark Jewell's;
Melissa stayed for one more night to help Mary Philbrick; and
Jonas was planning to lie at Whit's for the night.

Jonathan Philbrick hadn't showed up. No one knew where he
was—somewhere off in the woods.

Whit was glad it was Jonas if it had to be anyone, but Whit
didn't feel much like talking. He didn't want to think, either.

On their way home, Jonas talked along easily. He said Ida had
told him to bring Philbrick's woman and both the two young ones
out to his house to stay. He had spoken to Mary Philbrick about
it this noontime, but he wasn't certain that she'd understood. He
would go over again and see her in the morning. She could stay
on in Sandwich until they'd had the vendue—there wasn't much
to sell really except the place and the cow—and then, he
supposed, she'd go back to her people. "Although she could get
married as easy as not, if she didn't go back there. Jonathan
Philbrick would be the natural one—although she'd have to tame
him before she could marry him. Still, women are scarce in this
part th' country. You know how old Dan'l got Dolly Scribner t'
come 'n live there with his family? Told her he'd give her the pick
of his sons. She took the oldest one."

Jonas had told him of this once before, but Whit didn't say
anything, and Jonas went on. He tried a new topic. "They been
havin' some fightin', I hear, down t' Boston."

"Have they?"

"That's what I hear, and a good many killed."

Whit said, "Them two young ones of his, I am sorry for them."

"I guess so is most everyone. Still, she looked to me like a kindhearted woman."

"Oh, she is kindhearted, far as that goes."

"Goes quite a ways—if you got some sense to put with it."

"Yes, I suppose so," said Whit. He made an effort: "Who was fightin' to Boston?"

"Soldiers on one side—'n them that live round there. Bay Colony men. Soldiers marched out t' git aholt some powder the militia 'd got stored in—hold on now, they told me th' name th' town. I guess I forgot it."

"They git it?"

"The soldiers? No, sir, they did not. Not so much as a grain. They got more lead than powder. This place that I speak of where the powder was stored—wait now, it's got kind of a queer-sounding name. You know the names of any towns around Boston?"

"No."

"I wished I could remember it. I c'n remember faces real good."

Whit said nothing at all.

"Twenty mile, or close to it," Jonas said resolutely, "this town is from Boston that I can't think of its name. The whole way back to Boston, the fellers lived round there shot at them. They was at it all day. I don't know how many there was of 'em—soldiers, I mean—but there must a been a good many started if any got back. Either that, or to Bay Colony there can't many shoot."

They had come along the path now till they were almost in sight of Whit's house. Whit—as he always did here—was wondering how his children had fared. There was a young girl there who'd come over to tend them, but she didn't know much. He wanted to see them . . .

This loosened the grip that his thoughts had had on him. He spoke now of David. He said, "I think he was the most gentle man I ever see."

Jonathan Philbrick finally put in his appearance—not at Whit's, at his brother's. He had a deer on his back—so Mary maintained—bigger than most men could carry. He gave her half of it and then went away.

8

They came to a morning that was the middle of May—and there was still no word from Jonas. This was the day Whit was going to Sandwich to fetch in the oxen he had agreed with Daniel Beede to buy. He told Melissa that he'd go down and see Jonas and find out how things stood.

Melissa said, "You'd better go down to Jonas's before you stop at Beede's. Once you get your hands on them oxen, you won't want to leave."

"You wait till you see 'em. I tell you they're pretty."

"Are they, Whit? Really?"

"Oh, my gorry, yes! And yet as I said before, you take now with oxen—" he was all ready to go; he'd even said good-by to the children— "with oxen, it ain't how they look, it's more how they're broke in. I never see oxen work as pretty as these two. They swing right together; they step alike, too. You gee 'em or haw 'em, 'n they turn like one beast. When they go up int' th' yoke, she don't seesaw a handsbreadth! And I want t' tell you that them fellers can pull."

"You ain't got to sell 'em t' me, Whit."

"I just want you t' know. You'll see 'em tonight, I guess."

"Well, I hope that I will. Don't forget to go down to Jonas's."

Whit said he wouldn't forget. He told the dog to stay home, and set off through his clearing and into the woods. He was not taking his gun.

Spring was ten days ahead of time. There was no snow at all anywhere in the woods, and where the sun could get at it—like back there in the clearing—the cold and the wetness had gone out of the ground. The trees hadn't begun to leaf out, so he could see as well as in winter. And the flies hadn't come yet. It was a fine time of year. But Bearcamp River was cold!—it was so cold that it made his legs ache as though he'd been knocked on the knee with a billet of wood.

He kept clear of Beede's, knowing Melissa was right— probably more so than she thought—by going around the north side of the pond, and went on down to Jonas's. Jonas was there— he was making a garden. And Mrs. Moore was there, too. If she hadn't been there, Jonas wouldn't have been at the garden, because there was a haze in the air and an east wind coming up, and Jonas should have been fishing.

Jonas said to Whit, yes, that he'd been to Fryeburg. But that he hadn't found anyone there that he thought would be likely to suit. He was going to keep it in mind, though, and have another look round—if he ever got through with this garden. He asked if Jonathan Philbrick had shown up as yet. And Whit told of the deer.

"I wished she'd come and stay here," Ida Moore said with such earnestness that both men were uncomfortable. She saw that they were and went on, "There's twenty men, anyhow, in Sandwich ain't married, and that ain't as wild as what he is. If she was to stay here with us she could see the whole lot. They come by this mornin', one at a time, t' get Jonas t' fish with 'em. Didn't they, Jonas?"

"Yes," Jonas said sadly. "But they won't come again."

Whit only stayed a few minutes, and then went back up to Beede's. He wanted his oxen; he wanted to know they were his.

Beede had noticed that Whit didn't have his gun with him, and as Whit was leaving the yard at the head of the near ox, his goad carried forward and his face very solemn, Beede said to him, "Now you look like a farmer."

Crossing the river was the only place that had worried him, and when both of the oxen had humped themselves safely up the far bank and had settled again to their walking, Whit's mind was at peace. The near one was named Beauty, and the off one was named Neb. By Beede's chain Beauty had girt six feet and a half, and Neb wasn't less than that by much more than an inch. Beauty was piebald and his eyes didn't quite match, but as Beede had said, " 'Tain't often you'll see both his eyes the same time." Neb was almost all black with a white blaze on his face. Whit had told Melissa that if she was real set on it, she could change the names of them. He liked the names that they had on them now.

Having the oxen would give him a new feeling about a whole lot of the work on the place. He could command the strength now that he needed to tackle most anything. There were a good many things that for years he had had to pass by, knowing they were too much for him. Near the east end of his field, there was a fair-sized granite boulder. It was too small to leave there and have it look right, but it had been too big to get rid of in the time that was worth. That boulder had mocked him. But now he had the victory: he had the strength.

He could fence his field round with stumps. He could free it of rocks. He could plow it deep now—and he'd get a great crop. When wintertime came he could haul wood and logs. When other men wanted the work of his pair, he would lend them out to them—and later on he'd be paid. But no man would drive them excepting himself—although it wouldn't be long now before he'd be teaching the boy . . .

This was the spring. Everything was beginning.

Beede had told him how over west in the Grants, Ethan Allen had captured the great fort on the lake—Fort Ticonderoga. Allen, said Beede, was a great one to swagger and swear. He'd taken the fort by surprise, and then with the danger all past and nobody hurt, Allen had spread his legs wide and stuck his thumbs in his belt and roared out to the general who was in charge of the fort, "Now, then, you God damn old rat, you come on out of there!" It had made Allen comic—or so Beede had thought.

Whit had said he supposed it was more or less the same kind of business that Jonas Moore had told of: some fighting down around Boston?

And Beede'd said, yes—it was all the same thing.

Beede would have been more than willing to talk a lot more on it, but Whit hadn't wanted to—any more than he wanted to think of it now. It was a puzzling business. He didn't at all understand it—and although that rather attracted him, still he wanted more to think of his work.

He wished David Philbrick were coming over tomorrow to enjoy the oxen with him. David and he had talked often of oxen. And as much as a hundred times—easily!—he'd said to David, or David to him, "If we had a pair of oxen here now—"

David himself had been a man of great strength—except for that knee of his. That could mean, of course, that there was some flaw in the goodness of strength, and that he, Whit, ought to watch out for it. But it was bad luck had killed David. Bad luck could beat anything. David had known that. Everyone did.

Whit watched the steady, slow beat of their walking. They were coming across the pine plain now where the going was smooth . . . their heads nodding and swaying . . . and little small wrinkles would come and go on their shoulders.

322

Whit walked beside them, not often urging them or guiding them. It was flat here and no trouble to get through the trees.

9

During the first month that Whit had the oxen, five families moved into the town. It seemed, in a way, as though the oxen had brought them.

Three of the men had bought land near to each other in the interval the other side of the hill a mile to the south of Whit's place. It was Dutiful Jackman who told Whit about them; he'd just come by there. They had been there three days, so Jackman told Whit, and he didn't appear to approve of them. He ate in silence what Melissa set out for him, and she guessed that the new people hadn't asked him to eat. But when he had finished neither Melissa nor Whit could quite bring themselves to the point of suggesting he stay. Jackman thanked them as sadly as he always did . . . and took the path toward the Philbricks'.

Whit, watching him go, said to Melissa, "You don't suppose that he figures to *speak* to her?"

"No!" She was scrubbing with sand the plate that Jackman had used.

"Well, now, I d' know. They say any man c'n get married."

"But they don't say to who."

"He looked to me a little cleaner than usual. I shouldn't wonder but that might be it. I never thought nothin' would make Dutiful wash! When was he here last?"

"Four months ago."

"He has washed in the meantime."

"Not more than once."

"Well, maybe not."

"He smells worse'n ever." She took her broom from the corner and began to sweep round the hearth.

It was well on in the evening. The sun had gone down. Over in the corner at one end of the cabin, both of the children were soundly asleep. Dutiful Jackman's diffident tones hadn't disturbed them. Nor had they wakened when Jen had barked at him.

Whit sat down in the doorway. "I hope he does speak to her. I really do."

"Why?"

"Because she'd have to laugh. She couldn't help herself—nobody could."

"She wouldn't laugh," said Melissa.

"She'd not take it serious!" Whit said, turning his head to look at her.

"No, I don't mean that." She'd finished sweeping the hearth and, putting her broom back, took up the flat wooden shovel to cover the fire.

Whit waited. The mosquitoes weren't bad tonight compared to what they had been . . .

"Married to Philbrick," Melissa explained, "she felt pretty safe, didn't she?"

"Why, I d' know; maybe."

"Well, she did, anyhow, because anyone would. Then to come down from that—and as sudden as she did—to the place where *Jackman* could speak to her—no, I don't think that she'd laugh."

Whit sat in silence a moment. Then he said, "I wish she'd perk up. They had some bad luck—her and David did both. But it ain't as though there was somethin' for her t' be ashamed of."

"Give her time," said Melissa. "It ain't but two months."

"Oftentimes they are married a lot sooner than that. But she don't show no *signs* of it."

"You don't begrudge her the meat, do you?"

"No, not a mite. But she can't stay there this winter without any man. And I got t' make the house bigger if she comes over here."

"She ain't asked t' come yet."

"She ain't *got* t' ask! She ain't any family: what else can she do? She ain't got t' say *nothin'*! You 'n I 'n her know that if I got t' look out for her 'twould be handier here. There'd be only one fire, and it ain't an awful lot harder t' cook for seven than four. And then if she was right here, why, she could help you out, too. Them things are so true they don't have t' be said. But it also is true we'd sooner be by ourselves."

"Nor that ain't got t' be said t' her either, I guess."

"No, I guess not. But what can she do? There's them two little girls."

"How about Jonas Moore?"

"They don't seem so anxious as what they did before."

324

"That ain't like Ida Moore. She ain't one t' go back on an offer t' help."

"Yes, I know that. Well . . . it ain't winter yet."

"No," said Melissa. She was getting ready their bed.

There was dusk in the clearing, and away off in the woods a whippoorwill sounded. Whit said, "I ain't heard an owl for as much as three or four days. I wonder where they have gone to?"

Melissa said she didn't know.

"You reckoned the day lately?"

"No, not the day. But I know it's the fourth week in June."

"I thought it was, prob'ly. It looks like it round."

Melissa was thinking that the bed needed new cornhusks.

Whit's voice was gentle and quiet. "Takes a long time to get dark, don't it?—this time in the year."

"Yes."

10

He went over the next night to see the new people who'd located over the hill. Melissa wanted to go but she had to stay home with the children. Whit said he'd be back again before very long.

He was back in two hours. She questioned him eagerly.

"Look all right to me," he said, coming up toward the door. "Children asleep?"

"They're quiet, at least. What are the women like?"

"Well, I couldn't say. There's quite a mess of 'em, though. Must be as many as four or five, I should think. They didn't talk any."

"Did—did they have on bonnets?"

"I didn't notice, t' tell you the truth. There are six men that are grown between the three families; they got a brave pair of oxen; and there's quite a good many boys."

"Ain't they got any girls?"

"Oh, yes. And I want t' tell you that they made a good start! They got one house about roofed, and a garden all dug, and they even got some hay up in stacks from off that little meadow that there is over there. I guess you never seen it. I didn't ask what they paid for the land. I guess a good deal, though. Them oxen were right up in shape."

"Where did they come from?"

"They hauled in their goods with 'em."

"The people, I mean."

"Rochester people." He hung up his hat. "They come up the Salmon Falls River to East Pond and lay there the first night, and they lay the next night at the south end of Great Ossipy. Then they come in from there. They could do it, all right."

"Rochester," she said. "That's where they had the great fire."

"Ayuh. Twenty mile, more or less, up from Portsmouth it is. They had news about Portsmouth. Been a high old time there."

"Always is, ain't they? I used to hear."

"You never heard nothin' like this one before. I ain't sure really that I got it straight now."

"What happened?"

"Well, the way they told me—" He went over to peer down at the children, and seeing young Jonas still about a quarter awake, he caressed the boy's head and saw him wriggle in comfort and settle nearer to sleep. Whit watched him a moment, and then without saying a word went outside and sat down on the bench with his back to the wall, his chin on his chest, and his legs stretched out in front of him. Up overhead was his long witch-hazel pole, resting on pegs where the roof would protect it.

Melissa sat down in the doorway, the light from the west coming over her shoulder. "Most Portsmouth stories," she said, "you'd ought t' be sure they're asleep."

"Oh, it ain't so bad as that, really—at least not in a way."

"What is it?"

"Well, as near as I could make out: some feller I don't know his name that Governor had put into General Court—that is, he wan't sent by no town same as the rest of 'em be—well, they didn't like that, so they took and voted him out. So he went round to a tavern,—I guess they all of 'em did. And he begun to talk loud and to say what he thought. So I guess some of 'em went for him. Well, he ducked 'n got out, and he made for Governor's house, 'n he went in there 'n hid.

"That made 'em mad. If he'd stood up to 'em in the first place, they might a backed down. Or if he'd kep' a runnin', they'd a quit 'n come back for more drink. But when he hid behind Governor, that made 'em mad. I shouldn't wonder but what it did Governor, too. He ain't that kind—or at least he didn't used t' be, once. Anyhow, they hauled a great cannon up in front th' house, 'n they said if this feller didn't come out, that they'd touch her off. So then he come out. I don't know whether Governor sent him or not. Still it may be that he's softened up some. I don't like to think it."

"What did they do with the one that come out?" asked Melissa.

"I don't know. Governor, he took his people and went off to some fort. And he'd no sooner gone than they broke into his house, and stove it all up, and took about everything they could lug off. Ain't that a fine business?" He spat on the ground.

"Portsmouth people?" she said.

"I don't know who else."

"But—well, I always had an idea they was rich people t' Portsmouth."

"Yes, a good many's rich. But th' town ain't all Wentworths. They got sailors and whores and speechmakers, too." He added morosely, "They been fightin' t' Boston again. I guess worse 'n before. A proper battle, this was—same as 'twould be in a war."

"Who between?" asked Melissa.

"Britainer soldiers 'n m'litia, they say."

"M'litia? Like—like the same as t' Kettleford?"

"Bay Colony men, I guess, mostly they was. They ain't the same as nobody."

"Who won?"

"Soldiers, I guess. They was on top at the finish. But th' wan't so many of 'em as th' was t' begin. M'litia done well. They kill't more 'n you'd think for."

"Right in Boston?" she said.

"Handy to it, I guess. 'Twas up on a hill. Wait now—Breed's Hill."

She was troubled and puzzled. She shook her head. . . .

Finally Whit said, "You know there's one of them fellers that I really took to. I got to thinkin' about it comin' over th' hill. He ain't married or nothin'. He might be just the one."

"For Mary Philbrick, you mean?"

"Ayuh."

"How is he featured?"

"'Bout th' same as the rest. He ain't much to look at. But he can dovetail as good as what Jonas Moore can. I see where he done it."

"What's his name?"

"I forget now. He only said once."

"What 'd th' rest of 'em call him?"

"Well, 'him,' like, or 'you,' 'n nod their head or look at him. You know how it is. He didn't talk much. I guess except for his name, he didn't speak only once. But you c'n tell to look at him he's a great one to work."

"How old did he look?"

"Why, I couldn't say, really . . . 'bout th' same as most men."

"But you do know he can dovetail."

"Yes, sir, he can!"

"I'll tell Mary tomorrow," Melissa said grimly. "I don't see as there's anything more she could ask. Still, he don't own a rifle, does he?—just to make it complete?"

"No," said Whit blandly.

"What did he say?—the one time that he spoke."

"He asked me," said Whit, "if I liked to ketch trouts."

The name Whit had missed turned out to be Onesiphorus.

They saw him off and on during the summer—maybe three or four times. He spoke his name "Phorus"; it was his brother told Whit what the whole of it was. Whit took him fishing after they'd been there a month. They got a sackful. On their way home, they stopped by at Mary Philbrick's to leave some of them there.

She gave them spruce beer or syrup whichever they chose, and she was glad of the trout. But Whit didn't think that she really laid herself out to make an impression on Phorus as much as she might. Although, he admitted, she was cheerful enough.

"How're they off for meat?" Melissa inquired.

"He'd been there again, I guess. They got enough."

"That makes the third time he's been there in a month."

"Does it?"

"Maybe he ain't quite so wild as you think."

"Oh, he's wild enough, surely. She ain't goin' t' tame him!"

11

Whit was pounding dried corn on a fair day in September when he saw that someone was standing in the door of the shed: it was Mark Jewell, Jr. He had no gun with him, so he couldn't have happened by hunting; he seemed easy and natural, so he wasn't bringing bad news; Whit couldn't imagine what his errand could be.

Mark Jewell, Jr. lived on the hill over in the western part of the town near the border of Sandwich. He was a sober, slow man, very careful and accurate. In that, he resembled his father, who was next to Beede in Sandwich. Young Mark was so careful that, although he'd had his place now for three or four years, he hadn't yet brought a wife to it. Everyone knew that he planned to marry Ruth Vittum as soon as he thought he was ready. She, in the meantime, appeared willing to wait—or it may have been she knew no one could hurry Mark Jewell.

Whit was sure *he* wasn't going to . . .

"A dry day," Mark said finally, "is the best to pound Indian."

"Cracks better, yes. But it takes a long time any day. We'd ought t' have a mill handier. With a mill and a smith, we'd be right up in shape in this town."

"Moulton promised a smith when I took up my land."

"I'd expect one a lot sooner if he hadn't promised."

"You 'n Beede, I guess, feel the same way about him."

Whit leaned on his pestle. "Dan'l Beede," he said, "is a proper surveyor. He run out Sandwich in 1769. Now Jonathan Moulton comes along six years later and claims Beede was wrong and wants part of the land. There ain't no man on earth can get so upset 's a surveyor when you try t' tell him he has made a mistake—specially if the surveyor is Beede and you're Jonathan Moulton."

"I guess maybe you're right," Jewell agreed. "Tell you the business I come on: I been countin' the town."

"You been what?"

"Countin' how many people there is in the town. They're at it everywheres—all of the towns."

Whit didn't quite like it. "They never done it before."

"Well, they're hard at it now, anyhow. Sandwich is finished. 'Tain't the Proprietors doin' it. It's Gen'ral Court."

"Oh. Well, you didn't need to come way over here to find out there was four of us—that is, if you count the two young ones. Not that I ain't glad to see you, of course."

"They count," said Jewell. He had a book with him and he wrote it down. "Two ain't so many, though."

"How many you got?"

"Another question," said Jewell: "do you own a gun?"

"I own a rifle."

"The kind of berril don't matter—not so long as she'll fire."

There was an uncomfortable pause. "She'll fire," said Whit.

Jewell hadn't looked up. "In Sandwich," he said, "in the whole of the town, there is two hundred and forty-three people. Joshua Prestcott and my father signed it. There is forty-six men who can vote, and more 'n half of them have got guns."

"Not in Tamworth," Whit told him. "They ain't half of 'em guns,—and half of the guns that they have got wouldn't shoot a hole in a snowbank. Some of them that own guns are too poor to buy powder, and them that have powder don't know how to shoot. Sandwich has two hundred and forty-three people. Well, I expect Tamworth's a hundred and fifty. And out of that hundred and fifty, there is only one man that a sensible deer would try to run away from. That is Hez Hackett."

"Dutiful Jackman—they say he can shoot."

"I never been out with him. What do they want to ask about guns for?—I mean, whoever it is that's payin' you t' go round."

Jewell said honestly that he didn't know.

"They figure the Indians are comin' back, do they?"

"I hadn't heard of it."

"Neither have I. You wouldn't think, would you, that they was goin' t' put a tax on 'em?"

"I shouldn't think it," said Jewell. And then he suggested, "If there was a war goin' on, I suppose they'd want to know."

"There ain't any war in New Hampshire. They ain't been fightin' to Boston since away back in June."

Mark Jewell, Jr. said he must go. He was trying to put his book in his pocket—it didn't fit very well. "Elkanah Danforth," he said, "has joined up with the army. He went off the day before yesterday. He is the only one out of the town."

"Elkanah has gone? There, now, I didn't know that." Whit came to the front of the shed.

"I guess bein' a soldier ought t' suit him pretty good." Jewell tried turning the book upside down. "They tell me he was drunk a month steady before he went away. Claimed the only way he could get it out of his head, seein' David Philbrick get killed, was to get full of rum." He fussed with the book, and finally got it all tucked away . . .

"How old is Elkanah?"

"Sixteen, I should think. Well, I got to go now. Stop by to my place when you're handy to it sometime."

Whit smiled—but not brightly. And Jewell went on his way.

Mary was married to Jonathan Philbrick—tamed or

330

untamed—sometime in that fall. There was nothing sudden about it. He had got in her grain for her, and in fact all through the late summer he'd been around the place there a good part of the time.

Whit was relieved, of course, that she'd married someone—although he didn't like it that she'd married Jonathan after his telling Melissa that he was certain she'd not.

He said to Melissa, "You know, I'm glad he hooked on to her: it's up to him now. He c'n pull his load, 'n I c'n pull mine. I would have helped her; I owed it to David. But I won't pretend that when I'm luggin' in wood, it ain't lighter to carry if it's meant t' keep you warm—you and the children—than what it would be if it was for somebody else. That may be selfish. I hope that it ain't."

"No . . ." said Melissa.

"You don't sound awful sart'n. Well, maybe it is. But it's natural, too. I don't think I could change it. M'lissa, you couldn't expect that to work for another man's family would feel the same to a man as to work for his own?"

"No, I know that. Are they Jonathan's family?"

"Well, they are now. At least they're all that he's got."

"But they're not his own. And they ain't rightly hern, either—only through David, and now he is gone. Them two little girls, I feel sorry for them."

"He'll look out for them."

"I don't doubt he will—well as he can."

Whit said, "She's been their stepmother. She still is that."

"Yes," Melissa admitted. But without pausing long, "It's the older one, Whit. I feel sorry for her."

Whit said nothing at all. He simply got up and went out of the house.

12

That was the month that the British burned Falmouth—seventy miles to the east from Whit's place.

Falmouth didn't all burn, but it burned pretty well. They were British from Boston who had sailed up the coast. Going and coming, they went right by Portsmouth. A good many Portsmouth people thought that they might be next—seeing Governor John wasn't there any more because they had succeeded in driving him out. They loaded their things into carts and went back into the country—away from the seacoast, where they would be safe. But they didn't go any seventy miles. They were just being careful—they weren't out of their wits. None of them went up to Tamworth.

Between Tamworth and Falmouth there was nothing but woods. There were no rivers to follow; they ran more to the south. No one in Tamworth had ever seen Falmouth. "Mr Gowan," Melissa said, "didn't he come from there?"

"Yes, now that I think of it, I guess maybe he did. Still that must a been quite a long time ago."

Whit couldn't help thinking of that young one of David's. He couldn't help seeing her as she'd been that day in the barn— huddled over and shaken from time to time with her sobs. And then slowly grown quiet . . .

He knew that all summer she had been much by herself. She was the one who did most of the berrying, and who went looking for herbs. Any task, Mary had said to Melissa, that would take her away from the house, the girl would try to get for her share.

Whit came on her one day by the side of a brook. She hadn't heard him because of the noise of the water. Her face, so he thought, looked a good deal more cheerful than it had any time since her father had died.

Whit called out to her—

—and she didn't turn around, she froze perfectly still, the same as a rabbit will do.

Whit spoke again. When she knew who he was, she looked up and was easier.

They talked of the brook for a while—where it rose, and so on—and finally Whit, knowing now that he must for the sake of his conscience, said, "How do you 'n your uncle get on?"

"All right," she said. The way that she said it made it perfectly plain. He knew, and she knew, that that was just about it.

"That's good," he said. "And while I think of it, any time you get a feeling you'd like t' go somewheres for a visit, you're to come over t' my place. All you got t' do is show up, 'n I'll go talk t' your ma. You understand, do you?"

"Oh, yes," she said. "Thank you."

"You ain't got t' say nothin' t' nobody. All you got t' do is t' come. I guess you know the path."

332

"Oh, yes." She nodded. And looking up at him, "You think Mistress would like it?"

"Sart'n!" he answered. "No question at all!"

The girl nodded gravely.

"That's between you and me, then."

"Like a secret."

"Well, yes, in a way."

"I know about secrets. I used to have 'em with Pa. He never told nobody. Neither did I."

"No, I guess you didn't," said Whit. "You know, you favor your pa."

"Do I?"

"Oh, yes."

She said to Whit suddenly, "Do you think he'll ever come back?"

"Well—how do you mean?"

"I mean in the night. Come and talk to me—sit on the side of the bed. I wish he would."

"I have heard of it happenin'," he said, "but I don't think you'd ought to count on it. My mother never come back, though I hoped that she would. I used to dream of her—I still do oftentimes. But she never come back in just the way that you mean."

"Were you bigger than me when she—when she died?"

"No, about the same size. P'raps a little more heft, but not any more old."

"How did she come back?"

"Only that I remember her. It ain't the same that you mean. But when you get older, it will seem the natural thing."

"I never saw him to tell him good-by." But still her terror had gone, and her bitterness, too. Whit looked down at her face—a thin little face, and her hair bleached by the sun. Her eyes were light blue as her father's had been.

"You will see him again."

"Oh, yes, I expect so. Prob'ly will when I die. Well, I guess I better go home now. I been gone a long while. Good-by." She scrambled up onto her feet and went running off through the woods on a line for the house.

Whit stood there and listened—until he knew that the sound of her feet in the leaves was no longer heard.

Then he went slowly home through the October woods.

Melissa thought he was more cheerful that evening than he had been for some time.

333

13

Whit said to the Moores one day in December when he'd gone over to Sandwich to bring home a grindstone, "I wish't you'd come 'n visit. I have built on t' th' house. There wouldn't even Jonas 'n me have to lay out in th' barn."

"At the end, or the back you built?" Jonas inquired.

"Back."

"You got th' good of the chimbley, then. Still cold, ain't it, though?"

"Some."

"Jonas, I want t' go!"

"Well—" he said, "I d' know."

"You ain't got t' lay out in th' back, even," Whit said to Jonas; "you c'n lay any place that you like—within reason, that is. We'll let the two youngsters lay out in th' back. They c'n snug up to the chimbley 'n be warm 'n sleep—while you set up in front th' fire 'n sing 'n tell lies —'n I have to listen. When do you want to come?"

"February," said Jonas. And Ida Moore added, "You c'n look for us the first good day that we get!"

It was the third week in the month before there came a day when Whit and Melissa agreed that this was probably it. There was good snow for traveling and a fair day overhead . . . and the sun hadn't set when Jonas and Ida Moore kicked off their snowshoes in front of Whit's door.

Old Jen made quite a fuss over Jonas—they didn't know why Major'd not come—and Whit's welcome, though quieter, was just as sincere. Melissa, who'd not seen Ida Moore in a good many months, could say nothing.

Young Jonas stayed clear of it. He stood in the doorway, with his small brother behind him, and as long as no one moved toward them, they were content to stand there and watch.

Whhit called to the youngsters, "Jonas, Gowan, come out here—" and they disappeared into the shadows like small trout from a pool.

Whit was put out, and he was disappointed as well; he was

proud of both boys, and he wanted to show them both off.
"Generally," he said—and he spoke half to himself, "when I call,
they come runnin',—that is, if they ain't busy with nothin' else
at the time."

"Shy, I guess, ain't they?" Jonas Moore said offhand. He
couldn't see that it mattered. He'd never seen a child yet that
didn't hang in the doorway and disappear when you spoke to it.

"Maybe," Whit said.

Jonas took a few steps to his left and looked out in the back.
"Who done the dovetailin'? Looks pretty good."

"'Phorus Mason," said Whit.

"He done all right,—for a Rochester man."

The women moved in through the door, and Whit followed
them in. But the two boys had retreated and were nowhere to be
seen.

Jonas came in and took off his load and then he and Whit went
out to the barn.

Melissa commenced fixing supper, and Ida Moore rested—
she had come eighteen miles—and two small, silent figures
showed in the door of the new room at the back. Ida pretended
that she didn't see them, but the boys knew that she saw them,
and their mother knew, too.

Ida Moore and Melissa kept on with their talking. The two
little boys, grinning and silent, and their eyes very bright, came
farther and farther into the light of the room. Young Jonas was
dressed just the same as his father, in breeches and shirt, and his
hair was long enough now to be clubbed in the back. He'd be six
in the spring. He was featured like Whit, but still he didn't look
like him—perhaps because the boy at the moment was just ready
to laugh. Ida Moore hoped that he'd hang on to that. But there
was that in his face that made it unlikely. He looked as though he
would always take things kind of hard—as though he'd feel
them, at any rate. That was like Whit. Well, he could pick out a
worse person to be like than Whit. . . .

Gowan was the one that she wanted to get her hands on. He
was stubby and square and he had the soft hair of his mother, and
he was bursting with excitement, and there were large crumbs of
johnnycake stuck on his face. . . .

Old Jen had been watching them and thumped her tail on the
floor.

"We miss Major like anything," Ida Moore said.

And young Jonas laughed loudly, and so Gowan did, too.

Whit hadn't one barn, but several: a row of log buildings, joined each to the next, but none of them bigger than three men could put up. The roofs were no higher than he had thought needful, and were made of bark slabs held in place by long poles and rocks. There were no windows for the cold to come in. The barns were unfloored and dark and they were hard to clean out. But they sheltered his cattle—and they'd been built with few neighbors and without any boards.

Jonas began with the oxen. He saw that they'd put on weight—and he said that they had. And Whit said that they'd ought to—peas 'n oats every day. There was a cut on Neb's knee that Whit asked Jonas to look at. The knee was a little mite swollen. But the cut had come from a rock hidden under the snow, and after going over the leg carefully from shoulder to hoof, Jonas said that he thought the swelling probably came from the bruise. "He favor it, does he?"

"No more 'n you'd think."

"He will," Jonas said, "even after it's well. That cut ain't goin' t' give trouble, or it would have by now."

Jonas noted that Beauty was almost blind in one eye. He said nothing about that, and neither did Whit.

All the rest of the cattle Jonas saw just as carefully. He examined the hay and the grains and the Indian corn. He didn't miss anything. . . .

But when they had finished, they came back to the oxen.

Jonas sat down on the sill in the doorway, picked up a chip and began scraping his moccasin. Whit rested his elbows across Beauty's back. He and Jonas were comfortable here. They would go into the house when Melissa called to them. . . .

"Your p'tatis," said Jonas, "don't run awful big."

"And few to the hill. And yet I worked on 'em. I don't know what it was. Yourn do any better?"

"Some. Not a gre' deal. Her garden done well."

"Good."

Whit scratched Beauty's ear, but the ox pulled away.

"You take twenty years ago," Jonas said very casually, "and you wouldn't have dared to have all of this here. Wouldn't the Indians have loved t' get into this! They'd shoot both the oxen, and set fire t' th' house, 'n prob'ly run off your woman 'n youngsters to sell—although the littlest one, prob'ly, bein' short-legged t' travel, they'd whack his head on a rock and throw him to one side—and prob'ly you'd a been fool enough t' try t' stand

336

up to 'em, and so you'd be face down in the ashes without any top to your head. Wouldn't that have been pretty! But a man startin' in now, he c'n afford t' do like you're doin'. What I mean t' say is: take 'n build up a place." Under his eyebrows, he glanced over at Whit—and then down at what he was doing. "You know that you're safe."

Whit didn't even look at him. "You c'n have fire," he said, "without Indians. You c'n have fire with wind and with sparks. You don't need Indians t' take off your children. The croup and the fever can do that just as good. It wan't any Indians that killed David Philbrick; I don't s'pose 'twas an Indian that went off with his wife—his first one, that's dead, I mean."

"Feller named Duffy," Jonas supplied.

Whit hadn't heard him. "I ain't a fool," he said. "I ain't been showin' you things that I own. I been tryin' t' show you what I'm tryin' t' do—part you can see, anyhow."

Jonas spat very carefully. "I c'n see pretty good."

"You said that I thought that t' winnow ten bushel of rye was the same thing as knowin' who'd be here t' eat it."

"Well, maybe I did, then. But I take it back."

"What's the news out t' Sandwich?"

"Hell, there ain't any. Mark Jewell got married."

"To a woman too good for him."

"You're a great one to talk!"

"I asked you for news."

"All right, then: they got some new kind of State Government—what the hell ever that is, 'n I don't know as I care. Oh, sure, there is news. Arnold and them fellers tried for Quebec is come home again now. That is, them that are comin'; I guess quite a few will have to stay there. That one didn't turn out so good."

"'Twan't the fault of the rifles."

"Oh, no, I know that! Well, now, let me see . . . in the counting to Sandwich—the signing, I mean—thirty-eight favored fightin' to eight that said no. 'Test Act,' they call it. It don't mean a thing. Take the Weeds: they are Quakers so they can't say that they'd fight. But I never see a Weed that would thank you to spit in his eye. As for the thirty-eight others, they all of 'em signed. Why shouldn't they sign it? It don't mean anything. A thing like that ain't a promise. In order to promise, you got to have someone to promise to—not just a paper. I signed it myself."

"Yes, so did I."

"But if I don't want t' fight, there can't nobody make me. I don't care what I signed. If I do want t' fight, they got t' fight me t' stop me."

"Most of the rest of 'em feel the same way?"

"I couldn't say. Biggest part of 'em, prob'ly, don't give a damn." He turned to spit out the doorway. "You been huntin' much lately? Jen don't look t' me as if you'd pushed her too hard."

"I don't know as I have."

Jonas was frowning as he gazed toward the woods. "Who in the hell is that comin'? I got the sun in my eye."

Whit came over beside him . . . but he couldn't tell, either.

Jonas commented, "Don't walk very spry."

Whit shook his head in agreement. "He ain't carryin' nothin', so he can't have come far. Still, from the shape of him, he don't live around here. Sun's right square in back of him so I can't see his face."

"That's what I said."

Whit stepped over Jonas and out into the barnyard so that the man would see where he was. Then he stood there and waited. . . .

Whit didn't know who it was until he'd come in through the gate—leaving the bar down. It was Elkanah Danforth.

Jonas stayed in his place in the doorway—the boy was looking for Whit, he wasn't looking for him.

Whit went forward to meet him. "I didn't know you'd come back from the army."

Elkanah was skin and bones mostly. He was dirty and pale, and his face was all broken out. He had enough clothing—he even had spatterdashes—but he didn't look warm.

Whit said, "Elkanah, come in t' th' house."

"I come over t' see if you had any work."

"Come in t' th' barn."

But Elkanah stood still. There was no life in his face.

"Well, right now, Elkanah, there ain't a great deal. Chores 'n wood's about all. I ain't buildin' nothin'. What did you have in mind?"

The boy shrugged his shoulders. "You ain't got nothin', then . . . ?"

"No, Elkanah, I hain't."

Elkanah nodded.

"But come in 'n set down, won't ye? There ain't nobody here only Jonas 'n me."

"No, I'm goin' back." He turned and went out through the

barnyard and down the hill toward the woods.

Whit crossed the yard slowly and put the bar up again. Then he went back into the barn. There didn't seem to be much to say.

Melissa called to them, and they went toward the house.

It was blue-gray and cold as they went toward the house. The sun had set now and the sharp shadows had gone.

Whit saw that young Jonas stood in the doorway awaiting them. He said to the boy, "Where you been all this time?"

Young Jonas grinned. "Nowheres," he said. Then he announced, "She can whistle."

"Who can?"

"The woman."

"You know Mrs. Moore."

Young Jonas nodded. "Pa, you come 'n listen."

"All right."

Jonas Moore asked, "I c'n come, too?"

"Sure," the boy answered and ran into the house.

14

Although the snow would stay in the woods for another two weeks probably, it was gone from the fields before April was out. Whit was uneasy and restless; he wanted to plow. The shortness of summer was in his thoughts all the time. The frost never held off in August because they'd had a late spring. He hitched up the oxen before the ground had dried out enough— when the buds on the red oaks were still fuzzy and furled—but the mud stuck to the plowshare and he couldn't free it. This was on the high ground up back of the house. Down in what he still called the clearing, down in front of the house, with the little brook running through it—the first place that he'd cleared— there were great patches of water.

So he had to wait.

He didn't take to it kindly. He was short with the children; he was moody all day, and at night he couldn't lie quiet. Melissa wished that he'd go on an errand that would take him two or three days. She asked him one morning why he didn't go trouting; she thought that might help.

He said, "Brooks 're too high,"—and didn't speak again until noon.

He was so tight-strung and nervous that Melissa thought to herself that if he were to stub his toe good and hard maybe, or bang his shin on the fire bench when he had his arms full of wood—well, it might be a good thing. It might clear the air, maybe. But she knew this wouldn't happen: he wasn't the kind to bang his shin on the bench. . . .

Whit watched the snow patches dwindle high up on the mountain; he saw the water gone off from down on the low field; the sound of the brook wasn't so loud as it had been . . . and the winter they'd passed began to fade and grow dim. At the same time the next winter began to lose some of its threatening. The space in between them was here and at hand.

The soil was now ready. He could start in to plow.

Neb and Beauty had grown in the two years that he'd had them. They had weight on them now in addition to strength. And they knew how to use it.

It was hard plowing here on the high field. He had hauled out the stumps, but there were still some roots left, and under the surface, new rocks had worked up. But now that he was at it, he felt pretty good. This was the field from which to get a view of the mountain. It was with him all day. And he rejoiced in his oxen, and his oxen knew him. Beauty was used to being blind in one eye; it didn't bother him any. They were all three of them working to just the same purpose; they went well together, and they knew that they did. Whit could feel the same easy and uplifting comfort in working with them that two or three years ago he had known in working with David. He liked to plow—but it made his arms ache.

He was using a new white-oak yoke that he'd fashioned that winter, and it seemed to set well.

Stopping to rest at the end of a furrow, after making the turn, he leaned on the plow . . . and he counted the smoke from six neighbors' houses—and wondered how many had started to plow.

All day he was plowing, until evening had come. And then in the dusk, he stumbled about at the chores.

Melissa wanted to laugh at him because he was so changed and so cheerful—and yet he didn't seem to realize how he'd been before. The only thing that he said that had to do with his feelings was when, the chores finished, he came into the house. He said, "I feel as though now I'd got a holt on the season. I got her hooked, anyhow. I hope she don't get away."

She tried to get him to eat something, but he was too tired. He just lay down and slept, not stirring all night. He seemed to her like a boy.

It was that way for three weeks while he was plowing and harrowing, broadcasting, brush-harrowing, and dropping his Indian corn. The leaves of the red oaks had unrolled and were green now, and the warm smell of the spring was on all of the land.

He didn't come in to his breakfast one morning, and she went out to look for him. He was nowhere about—and the chores were only half done-and when she came into the house and looked in the place where he kept his fishhooks and saw it was empty, she knew everything was all right.

He was back by midmorning with a sack half-full of trouts, and carrying one on a twig that looked as big as his arm . . . and it was as big as his forearm and about half of his hand.

He ate enough breakfast for two men.

She took his dinner out to him—because he'd said he wanted to stay with the oxen or something like that—and she charged the two children not to go away from the house.

15

Whit kept too busy through the fore part of the summer to kill his own meat, even. But they suffered no lack. Jonathan Philbrick brought a quarter occasionally—for which he was paid. But it was Beauty and Neb brought in most of the meat—as well as other things, too: such as labor in mowing time, a nice piece of leather, linen cloth and some findings, and cider, as well. They were a pair had a great reputation. A man would pay more for a day of Whit's oxen than he would for any other pair in the town. He could afford to because he'd get more work. There were enough people wanted them to fill six days a week. Whit had to plan out his time, though, and he couldn't spare a great deal of it from off his own place no matter how much they'd pay. He had ten acres cleared, and although his hay didn't need tending, two acres of Indian and one of potatoes were enough to look out for without very much else. Add two acres of rye, a half acre each of oats and of wheat, the garden to work, four cows night and morning, the pigs and her hens, and the water to haul—and it wasn't so easy to find time to go off.

There were quite a few men who, the second week in July when they heard that the Congress had voted for Independence and so on—Liberty and Freedom, and all that kind of thing—appeared to think it important. Over in Sandwich there was a good deal of treating—they even treated Dutiful Jackman, who for once ran into luck: he just happened to be there.

Whit heard the news of how the Congress had voted when Hez Hackett brought it.

Hackett himself wasn't certain—that is, in his own mind—whether it was quite as much of a thing as they'd made out to Sandwich. Still, he didn't hold on to it, he didn't wait till they'd eaten, he sprung it right off—as they stood there in the field where he'd come on Whit hilling young Indian corn. And Hackett added the comment, "Maybe we'll get somewhere now." He'd heard another man say that.

Whit leaned on his hoe. It was late afternoon. He'd been hilling since dinnertime. It was muggy and hot, and they needed the rain from a thunderstorm that was making up now in the southwestern sky—but he didn't believe that they'd get it, it would probably go round. And if it did come, it would come hard and sudden, flatten the corn, and perhaps wash out the hills. So he leaned on his hoe, and the little pain between his shoulders and the tireless flies didn't make him feel too polite. He wiped some of the sweat off the back of his neck and his forehead, made a pass at the flies, and said to Hez Hackett, "Why?"

Hackett had known Whit for several years. He took no offense at the tone—although he felt that it put on him the need to defend what he'd said. "Why? Well, the way that I see it: now we're onto a track. We know what we're after. Up to now, we been wanderin' round in the woods—some of 'em hopin' t' jump a deer, you might say, maybe, some of figurin' a couple rabbits would do. But now we know what we're after—'n we c'n hang on till we get it. That is, we c'n hang on till we get it, or don't."

"Independence, you mean."

"Independence," said Hackett.

"All right, Independence. You think this Indian corn's goin' t' come on any better whether it's New Hampshire Province or New Hampshire State? Independence from what?"

"Well, from England. The King."

"I wouldn't know him from Adam if he was to come over that wall—only for the way they would have him rigged up. England ain't never bothered me that I know of."

"She might not have you, but I guess she has some."

"That may be so. But I couldn't cut mast trees, it was too far to haul 'em. I never used any stamps—I never even saw one. This trouble they had about tea down t' Portsmouth—and Boston, I guess—I ain't goin t' shoot nor be shot at for a noggin of tea. They talk about taxes. I never paid any taxes to any King's officer, they never come after me. Nor I ain't a slave, either—not so far as I know."

"No," Hackett agreed, "I don't know that you be."

"And where's your Independence if you got t' tie up with Yorkers, Virginians, and Connecticut people, and—and, well, whoever the rest of 'em be?"

Hackett said he didn't know.

But Whit wouldn't stop. "Britainer soldiers are bad, that I grant you. I don't want 'em around no more 'n anyone does. But they ain't none around here, are they? I ain't see any sign. In Boston there is, but that's nothin' to me. There are plenty of rattlesnakes up on the mountain, but I don't feel no call to go tackle 'em, not until they come round. When they do, then I will. I don't care nothin' about no Independence—not so long as they leave me alone t' work my place as I please. Let 'em get drunk to Sandwich, and to Gilmanton, too. They can have Independence. I got work to do here." And he added, "And rum don't set on my stomach so well as it might."

Hackett said, "Yes, I can see how you feel. You about done here now, are you? We could go up to the house. I got a deer's liver here I thought your woman might like."

"Yes, I'm about done. I'll just hang up this hoe."

"Your Indian's good, Whit. It is higher than most."

Whit had stepped over to hang his hoe in a tree. "We'd ought to have rain," he said.

"We will, in a minute."

"I think that's goin' round. They generally go down th' Bearcamp to Great Ossipy Pond."

The lightning was hot and the thunder close by. Hackett said, "We're goin' t' get it, all right."

Whit said, "Maybe the edge of it," and they started up toward the house.

Melissa came to the doorway when they were a little ways off.

343

She had on her blue apron, and she had moccasins on—in spite of its being full summer. They were beaded deerskin. Her hair was twisted up tight.

Hackett and Whit were both looking at her. Hackett said, "Whit, she holds her age good." And he looked forward to supper.

"I guess maybe she does. She don't hold back on the work, though. And we ain't had any sickness. We been lucky in that."

"And you ain't got but two young ones." He enjoyed coming here. The inside of their house always smelled clean and felt clean. He was as much at ease in their house as he was in the woods. He could hear the rain coming now, but he said nothing to Whit—and the first drops started falling. . . .

A dozen yards off, they could see she was smiling, but she hadn't spoken—and wouldn't—until they were up to the door.

A hard thrust of lightning, and the splitting and jolting, rolling crash of the thunder filled the whole place. Still, neither man hurried.

Melissa stood to one side as they came into the house. She said, "You two had walked any slower tryin' t' show off to each other, you'd have looked awful temptin' t' that lightnin', I think." And then she greeted Hackett and asked how he was.

Hackett said he was well. "I see a cow once that had got hit by the lightnin'. By God, she was stiffer than as if she'd been froze."

Whit had turned in the doorway and was watching the treetops. The wind had them tossing, but the storm hadn't struck yet. He still thought that the worst of it might go around.

16

Taking things altogether, Whit made a good harvest. It was better than last year, he was certain of that, although he couldn't reckon it to any one figure—as so many bushels, or dollars, or pounds. It was this thing, and that thing, some better than others—while his late Indian corn, for example, hadn't done well at all. It had had too much rain in the middle time of its growing and had run all to leaves, the ears not filling out. But the stalks and the leaves would feed his cows in the wintertime, and he could not call the planting an absolute loss. The big yellow squashes that Melissa should have had in her garden were missing; they'd done more or less the same thing—they'd put out big blossoms but they didn't head up. But his early Indian corn—that he had been hilling the day Hez Hackett came the second week in July—had come up after the thunderstorm and gone on to bear a good yield.

His potatoes were wonderful—the best he'd ever had. He enjoyed every minute of digging them—on raw, windy days with November close by. The frost had blackened the plants and they drooped and looked poorly; it didn't seem as though they could bear anything that would be really worth while. And then he'd turn over a forkful of earth with a little thin frozen crust on it—and there'd be potatoes as big as his fist!—not to mention the small ones that would fatten the pigs. Another fine thing there was about a potato: it was finished and ready when he took it out of the ground. Grain cut and shocked wasn't more than half done yet; it had to be thrashed and winnowed and cleaned, and it had to be ground into meal before a woman could cook it. Indian corn had to be husked and then pounded. But pick up a potato and knock the dirt off—and there she was ready to throw into the pot.

Of his cattle, as well, he had had a good increase, both among his neat cattle and also his swine. He would dress out enough pork later on in the winter so that they could eat wild meat or not as Melissa might choose. There wouldn't be many in the town could say that.

Whit took as much comfort as he could from these matters. He knew he had done well, and he was proud that he had. But there was too much ahead, there were too many things lacking, for him to sit down and gloat on the present as compared with the past.

What held him up now was that he was ahead of the rest of the town. He had got there the first, and so he was further along. He felt the need of things that most other men didn't need, things he was ready for that the rest of them weren't. He was tired of living in a little log house, he wanted a board house—and Melissa did, too, although she never fretted at all. But boards meant a mill. Everyone else, of course, would have been glad to have a mill handy—but they weren't quite ready to go after one yet. They felt the same way that Whit had in his first three or four years: they had so much to do that was right under their hands that they

345

couldn't pay much attention to anything else. Their log houses would serve till they had their land cleared; it would be time enough then for them to think about boards.

It was the same way with grain. You take a man who grew only stump corn to feed himself and his wife—and perhaps a few children—he could pound it at home, or she could anyhow. He didn't need any mill. But Whit had got beyond that. He wanted a gristmill where he could get his corn ground. He wanted a miller who would trade for his grain—that is, over and above what he needed himself.

But the town wasn't ready to get together and put up a mill, the Proprietors didn't, and so no miller came. Nor was one likely to come of himself until he could count on more than one customer to make his mill go. Until it would pay, there wouldn't be any mill. Still, it couldn't be long—Onesiphorous and the rest of the Masons would stand in need of a mill pretty soon. Bradbury Jewell did now,—but he lived nearer to Sandwich.

Roads were another thing. A man who stayed on his own place and ate all he could grow, could get along while he did that without any roads. But Whit had stuff now that he wanted to haul. Roads would have helped him, and bridges, of course. But he couldn't build bridges alone by himself, and he couldn't cut roads just himself and his ax. But not until the day came when enough felt the same need would they get together and do anything.

Still, there were signs of its coming, and it wasn't far off. Men at least argued over the proper site for a mill—everyone wanting it nearest his place—and while talk wouldn't build a mill, still it had to come first. They talked of bridges and roads more than they did of the war. The war was petering out. General George Washington appeared to get trimmed every time they caught up with him. He'd had to clear out of New York along in September, and from then on he lost battles every time one was fought. He was retreating across the state of New Jersey—but a good part of his army was on its way home. They had enlisted to fight in a war; the war had been lost—and so they went home. If they stayed with the army only two things were certain, and they were hunger and cold—although there was a good chance of sickness, a good chance to get captured, a good chance to get wounded, and a fair chance to get killed. And all to no purpose because the war had been lost. Anyone could see that except General George Washington—who by the end of October still had his white horse and about three thousand men. Nobody knew why the three thousand had stayed; the horse was well fed and couldn't get loose to go home.

But whatever their reasons, these men hung on. And then one night in December, they crossed over a river and jumped on some Hessians who were drunk and asleep. General Washington's army might not have been able to do very well when the other side was awake. But they did all right this time: they killed all the Hessians they could lay their hands on.

This was on Christmas Day. It kept the war going.

Soon after this, on the third day of January, General George Washington offered his men ten dollars extra if they wouldn't go home. Enough of them took it so that, if they were to stay on through the winter, he'd have a crew to start up with again in the spring.

With Whit and Melissa, the winter went well. The snow wasn't deep—but enough to haul on—and Whit got in his cordwood; and he cleaned most of his rye, and hunted a little, but didn't get very much. Four times in that winter when the weather was bright, they went to a neighbor's. Twice, at the Mason's, they stayed most of the night. But when they went to the Philbricks', they left the children at home so as to have an excuse to come back before Whit should say anything. Jonathan Philbrick rubbed Whit the wrong way. If it hadn't been that Whit had known David and been friendly with him, he and Jonathan Philbrick perhaps might have got on. But Jonathan Philbrick was loud in his talk, and all he talked of was things he claimed to have done. And although Melissa pointed out to Whit—once, anyhow—that Whit was the one who had most wanted Mary to marry again—and to marry Jonathan Philbrick—it didn't do any good.

When they went to the Masons', though, they had a great time. There were a half dozen Masons who all lived near together, and they would put all the children in one house to sleep, and then in another the grown people would visit and talk, and drink cider or rum, and pretty soon sing. Onesiphorus, though he didn't seem like that kind, was a great one to dance, and they'd get him to jig. They had a floor in their house, and Onesiphorus would put on boots with heels on them, and with the rest of them singing and clapping, he'd go to it good. If they'd had someone to play, he could have done better, he said.

When they'd get back home, they wouldn't have more than

time to lie down before Melissa'd have to fix breakfast and Whit tackle his chores. It was surprising, though: all the next day he would feel pretty good.

17

On the first day of February, a man coming through told them that Jonas Moore out in Sandwich was in a bad way. He'd got the prongs of a fish spear run clear through his hand, and his arm had swelled up, and a fever come on.

They heard this at noontime—and it was snowing hard then.

Whit was in Jonas's dooryard with two hours light left.

He stepped off his snowshoes and hung them up on the house, beat the snow off his clothes, and turned to go in the door. But Ida Moore'd heard him, and she had come out.

Whit knew from her face that the man's story was true.

She said, "You didn't need to come, Whit. Melissa all right?"

"Oh, yes, we're all rugged. How're you comin' on?"

"Well, Whit, I don't know."

"That's what I was afraid."

"You want to come in and look at him? He won't know that you're here."

Jonas was lying on his bed on the floor; he had his face turned to the fire. The man whose turn it was watching was sitting at one end of the hearth, but Whit didn't know him, and gave him only a glance. Jonas's lips were drawn back, and his eyes sunken and dull. He lay perfectly still, but his breathing was short—although not so fast as it might have been. They'd cut off his shirt at the shoulder and bound a poultice of flaxseed the whole length of his arm, and his hand was tied up in bacon fat.

Whit stood and looked down at him—and then he knelt down. But Jonas's eyes never moved. Whit could see by the veins at the side of Jonas's neck that his heart was going along at a terrible rate. He was bad, right enough—there was no question of that. But he didn't look wasted. And Ida Moore'd managed somehow to keep him wonderfully clean.

Whit, for some reason, didn't feel upset at all. He stood up and went to the other end of the room where Mrs. Moore waited. Together they went outside and stood in the lee of the house. "When was it?" Whit asked.

She told him the story. A week ago yesterday, Henry Chadburn and Jonas had been a mile down the shore spearing fish in the night. The way the accident happened: Jonas was watching on his hands and knees by the hole, and Henry Chadburn was touching up one of the points of the spear with a file. Jonas saw one, and keeping his eye on it, he said to Chadburn, "Give me that spear—" Chadburn stepped toward him, tripped over a piece of wood for the fire, and trying to save himself thrust down with the spear—and jammed it down squarely through Jonas's hand.

Chadburn claimed Jonas hadn't even cried out.

. . . and it had been Jonas himself who, one at a time, had filed the prongs off the fish spear so that they could be drawn on through his hand. They had to do this on account of the barbs.

Ida Moore said the hand hadn't looked very bad after she'd washed it up—only the four little holes in the back and the front—and he could work all his fingers. Still, they'd put the bacon fat to it right then and there so as to be on the safe side, and Jonas had got full of rum and had slept pretty good.

The little holes in his hand had closed up right away—but then his hand had started to swell and it had gone clear up his arm. Then the fever had come. He was quiet right now, but night before last it had taken two men to hold him. "The people," she said, "have been awful kind. There's been somebody watchin' day and night ever since."

Whit nodded. "I don't suppose you ever watched any for them, did you, before?"

"Well—"

"He can't eat nothin', now, can he?"

"No, but he'll drink. Since the fever's been on him he's dry all the time no matter how much he drinks. I steep pine spills in water and let him drink that."

"Best thing," Whit agreed.

"Dan'l Beede has offered to send and bring up a doctor. But you know well as I do what he'd want to do. That hand isn't bad; it ain't rotten at all."

"Didn't look to me like it. And you say it wan't stove-up any?"

"Not a mite. No."

"That's a sign, then. You couldn't fit them four prongs through his hand without stavin' up somethin' no matter how hard you tried. That hand is meant to be saved. I wouldn't let a doctor go near it. Anyone bled him?"

"Beede did, yes. Didn't seem to do any good."

"In his leg, I guess, didn't he?"

"Ayuh."

"Whatever's got hold of him is up in his arm." He was silent and thoughtful. . . .

Ida Moore said, "You know anything else?"

Whit went right ahead. "There's one thing you could try. It ain't quite the full moon yet, but it will be pretty soon. You know them little blisters on a fir balsam tree? When the moon's got its bigness, them blisters swell up. You take the juice out of one, and give him five drops of that. It's awful rugged, they claim."

"He can't wait for no moon."

"Well, then give him ten—his stomach is strong. I ain't quite certain how much of their power'll be into 'em now, but I should think prob'ly enough. If it don't seem to take hold, we c'n try it again when the moon's right up in shape. I know where there's a tree. Do you want to try that?"

"You mean he's to drink it?"

"Yes, that'd be best. You'll have to add somethin' to it. Them little drops by themselves wouldn't get past his tongue. I would say water. If you give him rum, it'll heat his blood all the more."

"Where is the tree?"

"Well, I d' know but I'd wait till the moon has come up. That won't be more than an hour or two. It ought to work through the snow even though we can't see it."

"Well, all right. You know best. But, Whit, in the meantime, if there's anything you want to try . . ."

"Yes, ma'am, there is. Will you leave me alone with him?"

"Go ahead in to him. Tell that feller that's in there to come out here to me, John Dillon, his name is." She turned away.

But before Whit had taken a step, she turned back again. "And—and—"

Whit nodded.

"Go ahead in," she said. "I'll wait out here."

As Dillon went out the door, Whit knelt again beside Jonas. He passed his hand in front of Jonas's eyes—saw that they didn't move—and then took out his knife. He cut off a strand of Jonas's hair, and held that in his lips. Then he lifted Jonas's hand—the one that was hurt. The ends of the fingers were free, but they were swollen and hard.

350

Jonas stirred . . . and was quiet.

Whit got a small shred or splinter off of each fingernail. The nails were brittle and dry, and hard to get at. The thumbnail was hopeless, and he let it go. He figured this was all right: if it had been anyone else, he'd have taken a piece of the nail from only one finger.

He laid Jonas's hand down very gently again—looked in his face for a moment—and then turned to the fire.

Whit's heart was beating as fast as Jonas's was.

He drew some hot, burning coals out onto the hearth . . . and his hand shook as he sprinkled the gray hairs on the pile and added the fingernails. The hairs puffed into flame and shriveled up tight, and then twisted and writhed, and the pieces of fingernail smoked and curled up.

Whit spoke in silence the words that he knew. . . .

. . . and his whole body was shaken. He heard Jonas stir—and Whit's lips moved faster. Sweat ran on his face—and he heard Jonas cry out.

Then Whit sat back on his haunches, and his arms drooped at his sides.

As soon as he could, he got to his feet. He looked down at Jonas, who was quiet again.

Then he went to the door—and the cold wind on his face made him feel stronger. He went round the house and as Mrs. Moore turned to him, he said, "I'm goin' t' go git the fir balsam. I guess the moon's up enough."

Ida Moore went inside, and when she bent down to Jonas she thought he seemed a little mite easier than he had before. When she turned round to the fire, she saw the coals on the hearth. She looked back at Jonas—and then again at the coals . . . and then she took her broom and brushed the hearth smooth.

She took a deep breath and stood up very straight. She felt more hopeful than she had before.

Jonas came through all right.

He wasn't really himself again until late in the spring—at least he had his two hands. Ida Moore never told him of the coals on the hearth, and Jonas's fever dreams were something he didn't talk much about.

Jonas went trouting with Henry Chadburn in May. Chadburn knew why he did it, and was grateful to him.

18

Whit was having his dinner on a hot morning in June. He was glad it was dinnertime. The hearth was empty and cool; they'd moved the fire outside. A man can get pretty tired of the smell of warm earth on a muggy June day with the flies round his head. It was quiet here, too. Jonas and Gowan were out by the cowyard where they'd get some good from the smudge.

Melissa came in with a big dish of boiled greens. "Mason's boy, Henry—he's the middle one, ain't he?—is comin' up through the corn. He ain't hurryin' any, so I guess it ain't much—either that or the weather." She set the dish on the table.

"Them look pretty good," he said, and took up his knife. "Prob'ly want me t' come over 'n help 'em roll up to burn. They let lay some big trees there till it was too late for the snow."

"You goin'?"

"I don't want to tomorrow, but I might the next day. I thought this mornin' that Beauty's off shoulder might be a little mite lame."

"You want me to tell him?"

"No." He had his mouth full. "This a nice mess o' greens, you know it?" he said.

The boy stood in the doorway. He was about ten or eleven years old. Whit said, "Come in."

But young Henry Mason had his mind on his own words. He hooked his toes over the doorsill, and recited, "Pa said to tell you Town Meetin' Day's set. A week from today. Richard Holcomb's, he said."

"Thank him for me. You get your dinner yet?"

Henry nodded his head.

"You could eat some syrup and johnnycake, though, if you tried."

They could see his quick grin—and he said politely, "I might."

Melissa gave him a piece, which—syrup and all—he took in his hand—and he disappeared from the door. Melissa'd intended that he take the plate in his hands, and she was wondering—mildly—why she hadn't seen to it he did . . . and then she turned round and saw Whit. He was staring off into space, sitting perfectly motionless. It was on the end of her tongue to ask him what was the matter—but then she held herself from it.

He got up, on a sudden, and went and stood on the edge of the hearth with his back to the fireplace, and she saw him, from habit, spread his hands to the warmth as though the fire'd been there.

"I want the bridge," he said, "where it'll be the best place for me. I think that Fred Mason would be a good selectman."

—Melissa was wiping the syrup drops up from the floor.

"But they can vote to build their dang bridge halfway up Claybank Brook, where Hez Hackett and deers 'd be the only ones cross—and I'll work with 'em on it! They could vote Dutiful Jackman, or worse'n him, even, to be selectman—and I shouldn't wonder they will. All right, then, let 'em. Let him be selectman."

He swung round to Melissa. "You know who votes at Town Meetin'?"

"Why, all of you do."

"That's right—that have places"—and he said it so fiercely that she didn't know what to think. And with his voice rising, "Not Jonathan Moulton. Not Leftenant Webster. Not any Proprietors. This is them that *live* here. This here is for us. This here is Town Meetin'!"—and then his voice fell away—"like they used to have it to Kettleford, only I couldn't go."

He stepped across the small room, and leaned in the doorway, looking out across his hot field as it lay ready to work. Over on the other side of the hill, in the Masons' big interval, they were right at it most likely; they were great men to work. More off to the right would be the line to the Jewells', and still more to the right, and four miles away, the Birch Interval men were probably bending their backs in amongst their stump corn. Face any direction, there would be men at work—or it might be they hadn't finished their dinners quite yet.

"Seven years," he said to her—"come this autumn, it is."

"Ayuh, seven years."

"I never voted at nothin' before." . . . And then he hitched up his belt. "Well, I got to get back to work. You want me to call them two young ones?"

"You ain't eat your own dinner, yet."

"There, now, I ain't! Well, I'll call 'em up anyway." And he did, with a long-drawn-out "Yo-o-o . . ." that could have been heard at Jonathan Philbrick's if the wind had been right.

They would vote at high noon. It lacked a half hour of that
. . . and Whit moved about past one group and another in the
shade of the big sugar maple in Richard Holcomb's dooryard. He
gathered that Bradbury Jewell would be first selectman. There
were more people living in Jewell's part of the town than there
were in any other one part. Well—Jewell would probably be
better than some. He was square, so they said, and he would not
be afraid to stand up to Jonathan Moulton or anyone else. And he
had started already to build a brick house.

There didn't seem to be a great deal of argument among the
men waiting about. There were not many drunk, and there hadn't
been any fights. The women were all round the other side of the
house, but children were plentiful wherever he looked. There
were almost no dogs. Some of the talk was of the meeting to
come. But not all of it was. There was also some scattering talk
of the war. "Burgoyne," a man said, "what he figures to do, is t'
keep comin' south the whole way t' New York. Down the lake
first, and then down Hudson River."

"How does he figure to get past Fort Ti?" That was it.

"Well, I couldn't say."

"And no more can he," the second man said. "By God, when
you tell me how he's goin' t' get around Ti, then I'll set up 'n take
notice of Gen'ral Burgoyne."

This seemed to suit everyone.

But then somebody said, "How about Indians?"

Nobody wanted to tackle this one. So they looked at the man
who'd disposed of Burgoyne, and he had to say, "Oh, was you
speakin' t' me?"

The other man shrugged his shoulders. "You or anyone else.
I said, 'How about Indians?'"

"You mean that they claim he has got on his side?"

"He says so himself, don't he? Thousands, he claims."

"It don't cost very much to claim you got Indians."

"It don't cost a damn thing. But it'll cost a good many the tops
off their heads if he turns out to be right, won't it?"

"Well, I never did fancy to live in the Grants." They all
laughed at this—but not very hard.

Someone said, "Eli, that old boar o' yourn poorly yet?" Eli's
pride in his pig was a long-standing joke. "Poorly!" said Eli. "He

ain't no good 't all. You want t' buy him? I'll sell him cheap."

Whit moved along. He'd made up his mind he was going to vote for Fred Mason. He was a neighbor of Fred's. He didn't see Jewell five times in a year.

Bradbury Jewell sat on a hemlock stump, one leg over the other, and chewing a twig. He didn't appear to begreatly concerned. Except for a pair of new bright yellow breeches— deerskin, they looked to be, with a touch of saffron for dye—he wasn't dressed out any more than was anyone else. True, he had on moccasins, which some didn't have, but his gray linen shirt could have been any man's. He spoke to Whit pleasantly when Whit came in range, asked him how his oxen were doing, and in fact called them by name. He said he'd seen Jonas Moore back thereone day last week, and that Jonas had said he was feeling all right.

But Jewell didn't say or do anything to try to get Whit to vote for him, and Whit took it that Jewell knew he was already in.

Jewell turned to another man, and Whit walked away. He himself had whittled the buttons for the front of his pants; the buttons on Bradbury's breeches were brass.

He saw Fred Mason standing in the rim of a circle of five or six men. Fred appeared to be listening while the others talked past his face. Fred never said much when there were many around. Still, he had a good head on him, everybody knew that. Get him alone, and that was the time he would talk. Cutting wood, it might be, two men working together, and when they'd sit down for a spell, then he'd open up. Whit had worked with him; they got along well. Mason could read, and sometimes in winter he would read in a book in the evening just to pleasure himself—not spelling it out, but going right ahead, fast. Whit hadn't seen him, but he didn't doubt that he could. Mason was taller than most, and easy and strong—in some ways a little as David Philbrick had been. But with more quickness than David, at least in his face.

But Jewell had the most neighbors, there was no getting round that—and every man wanted the bridge to be handy for him. If it had been only a question of just the two men, Whit wasn't sure but what Mason might win. He'd have a chance, anyhow. He was related to a good many here.

Then Whit got an idea; if Bradbury Jewell was certain to win, the bridge was gone anyhow. All right, let it go. Let Mason say

355

to them now that *he* favored putting the bridge wherever the bulk of them wanted it put. Then let them vote for a selectman . . . and see who would win.

He made up his mind to go and suggest this to Fred. And he found himself walking over to do it—when he was stopped in his tracks by the full noise of a drum.

Everybody looked round—

Charlie Griffin was doing it; he'd been a soldier back in the time of the war—that was some time ago now, that was twenty years back. Charlie's face was set hard . . . he could handle a drum! The sound came in waves . . . and then stopped.

Richard Holcomb stepped forward. He called out to Fred Mason and told him to come up. Fred, looking unhappy, did as he was told—and Holcomb said for him to stand over there a little off to one side. Bradbury Jewell still sat on his stump. Then Holcomb told all of them that he would read out the names of those who were to vote, and when a man heard his name called he was to come up and stand with either Jewell or Mason.

Then he began. "Anthony Cogswell,"—as loud as he could. Nobody moved . . . and they began looking round. "Anthony Cogswell . . . ?"—and a dozen men commented, "I see him round here a minute ago."

One said, "The hell with him," and some, "Call off the next," and there were suggestions as to where Anthony was.

Finally Holcomb took a look at the roll, and bawled, "Israel Meacham"—just as Cogswell appeared hurrying out of the barn. They all shouted at Cogswell—who made no defense—and after some little bewilderment, he went over to Jewell. There was no doubt from Cogswell's expression as to just what he was thinking: he was wishing he could take a dull knife and cut the two ears off every man in the crowd.

Israel Meacham also voted for Jewell.

Things got very quiet. Three men to one were going over to Jewell. There was no cheering, no voices were loud—just the low murmur of whisper and nod.

The women had come round the end of the house and were watching in silence.

Bradbury Jewell with his thumbs in his waistband, his feet wide apart, and his head tilted back, appeared to be gazing over the heads of the men . . . and now and again he'd look down at the ground at his feet. He gave no greeting to the men who came and stood by him, and his face didn't change any—he had it set. But Whit could see his eyes moving: Bradbury Jewell was taking count of the men who were voting against him. He'd never have to ask anyone who they had been.

Whit looked round for Melissa two or three times. He didn't see her, but he was sure she was there.

There weren't many left now—eight or ten, maybe . . . now only six.

If Whit's name wasn't called—if Holcomb had skipped it—Holcomb would say to him afterward, "B' God, Whit, I missed you. I don't know how I come to do that. But I guess it don't make any difference." And Whit would have to say, "No."

"Whit Livingston," Holcomb called out.

Whit took it for granted they were all looking at him. He knew Melissa was anyhow . . . and he held his head up. Each step was separate. He looked straight ahead. On either side, he couldn't see anyone. . . .

He was proud of himself, and he was proud to be voting.

Then Fred Mason, in front of him, said, "H'lo, Whit," and Whit answered, "—Fred." Onesiphorus moved over a step. "We got plenty of room," he said. "We ain't crowded at all." And Whit grinned a little and turned round to face out. He felt lightheaded and free. Bradbury Jewell, his thumbs in his waistband, was looking off somewhere. . . . And then Whit saw Melissa, and he saw her smile.

Holcomb called out the names of the ones there were left. They all went to Jewell. Whit was glad that they did.

When the last man had voted, there was a stir, and a rising of voices in talk—but nobody cheered. Holcomb shouted to all of them, "Now we'll eat dinner."

A hand was on Whit's shoulder a second, and Fred Mason said, "Thank you," and then turned away.

Whit started across to where he'd seen Melissa. He felt thoroughly happy . . . but not quite like himself. And then he saw her making her way through the moving crowd toward him. She had her sunbonnet back, and she was smiling a little bit because she enjoyed having all the people about. She had the two boys with her, one on each side. When she caught sight of Whit, her face lighted up—and Whit felt pretty certain that she was not going to ask him why he didn't feel worse that Fred Mason had lost.

They ate the lunch that they'd brought—and there was laughing and shouting and some visiting round, and wrestling began to break out, first among the young children, but then working up through the boys and young men. Anthony Cogswell started a fight with a man, but they got them apart and took Anthony's knife. Awhile after that, they tried to have some more meeting, but a good many were drunk now, and the meeting didn't get very far. And with milkingtime coming on, people began to go home.

Whit and Melissa walked home through the woods. The two boys were on ahead sometimes, and sometimes behind. It was three miles to walk home. They talked for a time of the people they'd seen, but before long their talk lessened. There were months of evenings ahead.

Walking, the flies didn't bother them much.

There was no need to talk of how Whit had felt. He would remember it always. . . .

The longer they walked, and as they approached their own place, Whit found that the day—the men and the meeting, the noise and the talk—dropped further and further behind him till his mind turned ahead to how the things that he'd left to look out for themselves might have fared through the day. He guessed they were probably all right—they left them at night in the winter, they ought to be all right by day in the month of July. He'd left a smudge in the cowyard, was all; the cook-fire, he'd covered. There wouldn't be any bears come around, and the kind of man who would steal would sooner go to Town Meeting in hopes of free rum. You take back in the old days, though, it must have been hard—back in the Indian times—a man wouldn't leave his place then with nobody to watch—or he would probably feel worse when he was on his way home if he had left his wife and his children at home . . . his house burnt to the ground, his cattle killed or run off, that would be bad enough. But if he'd left his family, too—

Well, there was no use thinking that way. Those days were gone. Threescore of families now in the town.

He could hear the two youngsters back a ways on the path—

In a few minutes more, they came to the edge of the woods . . . and there up on the rise, up across the low corn, his house and the buildings in the late afternoon sun looked peaceful and quiet.

The smudge was still going, but it wasn't putting up a great deal of smoke. Old Jen had heard them: he saw her come round the house—

He hadn't known it, but he had stopped and stood still—and Melissa came up beside him.

He said, "I like to look at it."

PART FOUR

The Mountain
1777

1

Whit was on his way down to the edge of the pond to try for a pickerel. There were reasons why he had to do this. July was the month for them, and he hadn't been yet—and the first week in July had already gone by. It was a lowery day without very much wind, and Melissa, that morning, had killed a mouse with her broom. When Whit had asked her at noontime if she'd like a pickerel to eat, she had said that she would. So now he was on his way down. He had the mouse in his pocket.

He found his pole near the pond where he'd left it the last time, and he sat down on a spruce log to rig up his bait. The mosquitoes were thick and it was a delicate task, but with some waxed linen thread he finally got the mouse tied to the shank of the hook—and it looked pretty good. He made his line fast through the eye of the hook, and then he fastened a hemlock cone onto the line about a handsbreadth in front of the nose of the mouse.

He took this down to the water just as it was—without any pole—to see how it would float. . . . It seemed perfect at first. The mouse stayed right side up because of the weight of the hook, and as he drew it along on top of the water, it appeared to be swimming to catch up with the cone. It was a beautiful rig. Whit grinned with delight. But then the mouse sank. Its fur had got wetted through.

Whit lifted it out and considered . . . and the mosquitoes grew thicker and tried to hurry his thoughts.

He knew what he wanted: he wanted some air in that mouse—and he had no liking at all for putting that mouse's head in his mouth. If he'd had an oat straw right handy, that would have been just the thing.

With the point of his knife, he pricked loose the thread that was round the neck of the mouse, and then he hung the whole business safely over a twig, and went in search of a small, hollow stem of some kind. This took a lot longer than he'd have supposed, but he got one at last . . . and it was no trick at all to blow up the mouse. It really looked better than it had before. And it floated most handsomely—although it canted a trifle, but not enough to do any hurt.

Four foot of line was what he used to skitter with generally, but he thought this time he'd use six.

With the mouse dangling and bobbing from the end of his pole, he waded into the water—his eye fixed on an open space in the lily pads well out from shore. He had about twenty feet to his pole. When he saw that he'd gone far enough, he got his feet firmly set—the depth of the water was now about up to his chest—and he lowered the mouse to the surface with the greatest of care and started to tow it out across the open space in the pads. There was a little small wave at each side of the mouse . . . and then Bang! the light green of a pickerel curved up out of the water, his great jaws were wide open, and he hit that mouse a blow that carried the end of the pole a yard under water—and held it there, too, with a steady pull mostly, and occasional jerks.

Whit set his hook, and then began to back up. The footing was soft and uneven, and as he was stepping over a log on the bottom that he'd missed going out, the fish came up out of water and seemed to stand right up on his tail, shaking his head—and Whit, dipping the pole to him, nearly sat down.

Well, it went on for some time, the pickerel off and on making a dive for the bottom and the grass and the weeds, and then again his fin showing moving slowly along, and Whit trying to keep the pole at an angle to the line of the pull and at the same time backing up trying to get in to the shore. But the time finally came when, with his heart in his mouth, Whit hoisted him up out of the water and swung him up onto the bank, dropped the pole—and went for him on his hands and knees like a boy. He got him!—and, oh, he was a beauty! He must have been easy a yard or more long.

The mouse was stove-up too much to be any more use—and Whit tossed him into the bushes for the first fox come along. The hook was all right.

Whit didn't know that he wanted to fish any more. He put his pole up, and with the line and the thread and the hook in his pocket, he picked up his fish, and started up through the woods home.

It had been pretty near perfect.

—he would joke Melissa about it, and claim she hadn't believed that he'd do so well, but that he'd known himself that he would. Why, any time she wanted a pickerel, all he had to do was to say so, and he'd go get her one.

It worked out that way, too, when he got up to the house.

But before he could set off to clean it, she said to him, "Whit, there was a man come by here while you was down t' the pond. For Fryeburg, he was."

"What was his name?"

"Collins, it sounded like. He said you didn't know him."

"Well, he was correct."

"He said he was just on his way. He said to tell you they had taken Fort Ti."

Whit laid down the pickerel. "Tell me the rest."

"Well— They give it up, he said, without any fight. He said the Britainers—General Burgoyne and them—had them covered, he said, and they went off in the night."

"Had them 'covered'! Fort Ti?"

"That's what he said."

"You can't have a fort covered. That's what a fort's for! Who is this Collins? What's he look like? You mean to say they just up and *surrendered*? What'd they do that for? How long ago was he here?"

"Half the time you been gone, maybe. 'Bout that, I should think."

"Was he travelin' fast?"

"He wouldn't stop to eat nothin'."

"He seem like a sober—a sensible man?"

"Ayuh."

"They just give it up! They run off in the night!"

"That's what he claimed."

"Well, I don't understand." He started walking about, turning this way and that, and then he caught sight of his fish—and he looked at it as though he were saying "How'd that ever get here?"

Melissa said, "Do you want me to clean that?"

"No, I'll do it," he said. "I'll go do it now." He picked up the fish.

"Whit, where is Fort Ti? I never knew, rightly. I heard you speak of it, but I never knew."

"Hundred and fifty mile west, I should think."

"Will they come over here?"

"Will who come over here?"

"Britainers."

"No"—and trailing the fish with its tail in the dirt, he went down across the dooryard and round back of the shed.

Whit wasn't concerned about Britainer soldiers, they would move slowly. And they weren't headed this way. Indians, though . . .

364

He had a bad time of it cleaning that fish. He wanted to think, but this was not a good chance. The insides of a pickerel don't come out as slick as do those of a trout, and there is a smell to them that mosquitoes like. Whit needed both hands to the business, and care not to get cut. And he was hungry, to boot. With mosquitoes pricking his face and on the backs of his hands, it was hard to get anything straight in his head.

He had better luck with it when supper was done. There was enough smoke in the house to keep down the mosquitoes and midges, and the black flies and his children had both gone to bed.

Whit said to her finally, "They must a sold the fort out. The head one, I guess, prob'ly—name of St. Clair. How else could it be? Can you see any way?"

Melissa said, no, she supposed that must be it. "Whit, how do you figure they won't come over here?"

"Nothin' t' bring 'em. They head for big towns—like the same as New York. Even for Boston or Portsmouth, they would go some south of here. And another thing is, they got too much to lug. They got women and cannon and—oh, all kinds of truck. Where they are now, they can haul that in boats. If they was to come here from Ti, it'd be mostly all through the woods."

"Well, all the same . . ."

"All the same, nothin'. They won't come over here. You can take my word for it."

"I heard they got Indians."

"Who told you that?"

"Two or three women. Town Meetin' Day."

Whit took the short route. "Yes, I heard the same thing," he said. "No one knows if it's true. I ain't sure that it is."

"You ain't sure it ain't, either."

"No, I'll admit that."

"Two hundred mile," she said, "ain't much to an Indian. They used t' come down from Canady further 'n that."

"Yes, they can travel. They ain't loaded down—a knife, and a gun, and them little hatchets they got. But why should they *come* here? Ain't there enough cattle to steal in the Grants? For ten years I been hearin' how rich the Grants be. That's what brings Indians. They ain't in it to fight."

She said "Maybe" reluctantly . . . and went to the doorway to the other room where the boys were. She listened a moment, and came back and sat down. "They're asleep," she assured him.

"I ain't holdin' back nothin'."

"All right," she answered, "then neither am I. 'They ain't in it to fight,' you say. All right, then, they ain't. What they're in it for is the same as before. I know the stories. I heard 'em too often. I wan't hard of hearin' when I was a girl. I know about burnin' and stealin' and all. And I know the rest of it—the part that ain't talked of when women 're there."

"You heard it wrong. They ain't hot after women, Indians ain't."

"I mean the torture. I know what they do. I heard them tell of it when I was real small. There was some of the words then, maybe I didn't know what they meant. But I ain't forgot any, nor I never will. When I think of them comin', my bowels turn sick. It's the same way with most people. You know that it is."

Whit examined a scratch on the inside of his wrist. "You don't even know," he said, "if Gen'ral Burgoyne has got so much as one Indian joined up on his side. Do you, now?"

"No."

"And neither do I. Then why do you talk that way?"

"Because that's how I feel. I get kind of tired of not lettin' on—now and again, I do. Don't you ever . . . sometimes?"

"Everyone does. The way you feel about Indians is the way a good many do. Women do, anyhow. And a good many men. In the Grants, more so."

"I am sorry for them."

"In the Grants, you mean; yes. I am too, in a way. But I ain't so certain there'll be Indian trouble. I have thought about this—" and as she opened her mouth, he said, "Let me say my say." And she let him.

"This Gen'ral Burgoyne can't be quite a fool. Because if he was a fool, he wouldn't have got so far: Montreal to past Ti—he has done pretty good. And he ain't got t' be awful clever t' figure out why. Who's tried t' stop him? The army, is all. He can handle the army. He done it at Ti. All right. If he keeps this business between armies, you see, he c'n keep right on a-goin' till he gets clear t' New York. There's Tories enough t' sell him food on the way. And as for the bulk of the people—well, they ain't done nothin' yet, and if he knows what is good for him—and I figure he may—Gen'ral Burgoyne'll let sleepin' dogs lie."

"Maybe," Melissa said.

"Because what happens next when he turns Indians loose? You know there ain't any Indian goin' t' hold back just because a man is a Tory. No, sir. The first house they come to they'll carry

366

on just the same whether a man is a Tory or Sam Adams's son,—
or if he ain't the one nor the other, same as most around here. All
right. You let 'em fire one haystack, let 'em rip off their first
scalp—and every man in the Grants'll be down on Gen'ral
Burgoyne. He won't get time t' turn round in his tracks. I'd be
tempted myself—I d' know but I would."

"What?"

"I d' know but I would be."

"You mean that you'd go?"

"I don't know but I might. It's the same as you said yourself:
there hadn't anyone ought t' do that—turn Indians loose."

Melissa tried to go back—but she knew it was too late. "Still,
I shouldn't wonder but you'd figured it right," she said. "He
won't turn 'em loose. And supposin' he should, they won't come
over here. I ain't afeard at all. I wan't t' begin with. It was only
the way some of them women talked."

"Yes. I understand." He got up from his place. "Well, I got t'
go do my chores, I guess."

"Yes. It's pretty near dark. I hadn't noticed."

Whit stood where he was. "Now don't you fret. I ain't goin'
t' morrow. I may not go at all. Nor I wouldn't go off and leave you
unless I thought 'twas all right."

"I know you wouldn't."

"We don't know nothin' yet. We'll have t' just wait and see."
He went out to his chores.

. . . and Melissa sat there and waited—hearing his step in the
barn, hearing his voice as he spoke to his beasts—she sat there
and waited for him to come back.

2

Late the next afternoon, Whit walked across the hill to the
Masons'. He wanted to talk over these things with some
man.

When he was still a quarter-mile maybe short of the place, he
could hear the sound of a man who was notching to hew . . .
probably down by their barn. He tried to guess from the sound as
to which one it was. Two blows to a notch and never an extra one,
that would be Phorus; sometimes an extra one, that would be
Fred; no rhyme or reason, would be one of the young fellows.

Whit listened carefully . . . and judged this to be Fred.

When he came out of the woods he saw that he'd been correct. Fred was squaring some white oak with an ax and an adz. It was a nice piece of wood.

Fred, Whit soon discovered, wasn't nearly so certain as Whit was that St. Clair had sold out. The way Fred had the story was that the Britainer soldiers had hauled up some cannon to the top of a hill that was right near by the fort and that was higher than it was. The hill was so steep that nobody had figured you could get cannon up there. But they'd done it somehow—block and fall, might have been—and when St. Clair had seen they could shoot right down in on top of him—well, there'd been no need to pay him to pack up and get out. That was the story that Phorus, so Fred said, had brought back from Sandwich an hour ago.

"What become of the men that was inside the fort?"

Well, the way Phorus had it, they'd got clear of the fort—it wasn't yet light—when some dumbhead or other set afire some building. That woke up the Britainers, and the men had to scatter.

"If there's a Britainer round who's awake, then they all got to run!"

Fred said he guessed there was probably more than one Britainer.

"Yes, I shouldn't wonder. I wasn't there."

Anyhow, Fred said, General St. Clair had put in a good part of the day trying to collect them together again, and he'd done pretty well. Toward evening, he'd left Colonel Seth Warner's regiment, Colonel Francis' men, and Colonel Hale's crowd as a kind of rear guard on the Hubbardton road.

"General St. Clair, though, he kep' a-goin.'"

"Ayuh," said Mason.

"Ayuh," said Whit.

"Well, then, the next mornin', so Phorus says, these fellers was cookin' their breakfasts when the Britainers jumped 'em and they had a fight. Colonel Hale, so they claim, took his men 'n run off. Colonel Francis got kill't, 'n three-four hundred men lost, 'n Colonel Seth Warner, who was the main one in charge, he hung to it, I guess, 'bout as long as it seemed t' be any use, 'n then him 'n the rest of 'em beat it int' th' woods."

"Who'd Phorus get this from?"

"Dan'l Beede, he said."

"Then that's the way Beede heard it. You think it's correct?"

"I don' know why not."

368

"*Cookin'* their breakfasts'!" Whit said it slowly and bitterly—"'and the Britainers jumped 'em'! I don't wonder they did." He walked around for a minute, and then he came back. "What about Indians?" he demanded of Fred.

Fred seemed to take it more calmly. "They're with him, all right. I guess there ain't any question. But they wan't in this fightin' on the Hubbardton road. They was still busy robbin' the fort."

"That won't last 'em forever."

"I d' know as 'twill."

"You figure Burgoyne'll keep on headin' south?"

"Sart'n to. Yes, Whit. Hudson River, he's for. They say there's a road from the south end of Lake George. You know how it lays, do you?"

"Yes, I been showed."

"A good many don't know. If you was to ask me, I'd say that he'd make it, too—and then maybe from there clear way down to New York."

"I don't know what's to prevent." Whit was looking about him for something to chew.

"No, it's hard to say, now. Fort Edward is next. That's on the river. General Schuyler is there. He might do somethin'."

"Do the same as St. Clair, if he's a gen'ral, I guess."

"Maybe he'll have to," Fred Mason said. "This Burgoyne knows his business; looks to me so."

"So far, he's done good," Whit said over his shoulder. "It's the Indian part of it sticks in my craw. I don't like that."

"No more does anyone. What can you do?"

Whit had picked up a chip and was slicing a splinter off. He turned around slowly. "Well, I don't know. I will admit it don't seem like there's much . . ."

Fred Mason assured him, "There ain't a thing, Whit. All you c'n do is set tight. They won't come over here. And then again, if they should come—well, you'd want t' be here."

"Oh, I ain't sayin' I plan t' join up. What'd be the use? St. Clair and this Hale—Still, all the same: if Burgoyne turns loose Indians . . ."

After some time, it was Mason who spoke. "You used to trap, didn't you?"

"Some,—more or less." Whit wasn't thinking about it. "That's what your trouble is."

"What do you mean?"

369

"That's why you're uneasy. You think of these things bein' nearer-to than do most. A hundred mile to a trapper ain't more'n a couple of days. Why, there's men in this town ain't been a hundred mile their whole lives—that is to say, in a line, I mean. You're a farmer now, boy. You want to stay home. You leave the Grants to look out for themselves. They ain't your lookout. Your family is. I know how you feel. But you take my advice. Anyhow, you couldn't go now: you ain't got your hay in."

"Ayuh, I know."

"Well, then," said Fred as though the whole matter were settled. He stood up and picked up his ax. "How's your woman been?"

"She's been pretty good."

"Ayuh. That's good. Well, now, you hold still a minute till I get this side done"—he prepared to cut a new notch—"'n we'll go up t' th' house 'n set down for a spell. I ain't seen you t' talk with since before Town Meetin' Day."

"I got t' go back. I ain't had supper yet."

"You eat kind o' late. Must be near six o'clock."

"Her and them have had theirs."

"Yes. Gives you a chance to eat quiet, I s'pose."

"Your people all right?"

Fred said that they were, and Whit said good night.

On his way home, he couldn't see that he'd gained a thing. He felt more uneasy than he had before.

3

If Phorus Mason could come back with that much news from Sandwich, Whit was more than half tempted to go try it himself. Still, he didn't feel that he ought to take the time for the trip just for the sake of news only. His scythe blade had been ground until there wasn't much left of it; it would be time to mow before long: he would go out and trade for a blade, although he never would get one that would come up to his first one—the one Karr had made for him. That was ten years ago.

He waited four or five days, and then he went over to Sandwich—and he came home in the evening without any blade.

Melissa was certain before he'd said a word that this wasn't simply because he hadn't found one to suit, nor because he was having one made: he brought nothing else with him, he hadn't traded at all. She asked about Ida and Jonas, and Whit said they were well.

"Well, it's begun," he said finally. "They killed a woman. Indians did. Beede told me."

She watched his face for a moment—and then she said, "Where?"

"Somewheres around Ti." He turned to hang up his things. "South of it, some, I guess—Gen'ral Burgoyne—wherever his camp is. They was his Indians. She was comin' in t' th' camp t' see some Britainer officer she was goin' t' get married to."

"Oh, Whit!"

Whit thought he knew what Melissa was feeling because, when he'd first heard it, he had felt the same way. Melissa was thinking about the young woman. He had got past that. "Maybe Burgoyne has found out that when you stir up hornets you can't fix it with them as to who they're to bite."

Melissa said yes. But she made no effort to think what he meant.

He sat down on the bench in front of the fireplace. He had his back to Melissa. "I don't know why it should be any worse," he said, "that she was about to get married, but it does kind of seem so."

And again she said only "Yes."

. . . Whit left it.

He turned to the rest of his news. "Committee of Safety," he said, "for the Grants has sent word to New Hampshire asking for help. Gen'ral Court has gone home, but our Committee of Safety is callin' 'em back again so's they can decide. I don't know what they can do, though."

Melissa hadn't made any effort to follow him. She said, "What was her name, Whit?"

"Whose name? Oh—McCrea. You ever know any?"

"'McCrea' . . ." She shook her head. "No."

Whit tried again. "Grants fellers claim that if we don't send help to 'em, they may go under—'n then New Hampshire'll be next. Makes a good argument."

She said, "Why ain't it true?"

Whit was relieved. "I don't know but it would be, if it was only us and the Grants. But you got to figure that Bay Colony's into it, 'n the Yorkers as well. The Grants will have asked both of them to send help—'n I shouldn't wonder but Connecticut, too."

"Why ain't that all the better?"

"Because the more that is into it, the less chance there is that what will be done will be the right thing for us."

"How do you mean?"

"I mean that whatever place sees Burgoyne headed toward them, what they want to do is to have him headed off."

"Surely."

"Toward who?"

"Oh. Well, yes, I c'n see that."

"Why should we help," he went on, "to head him off from New York—when all it would do would be to turn him toward here? Or you think any Yorker's goin' t' try awful hard to head him off from Bay Colony? I c'n tell you they ain't!"

"Why would it be any different if it was just us and the Grants?"

"Because the Grants is between us and Gen'ral Burgoyne. He is travelin' south, down along their far side. Neither us nor the Grants wants t' have him turn east. No, we could work together all right, if it was only us and the Grants."

"Then you think we won't send any?"

"I don't know. You can't tell. But if we do send any, we want to know who is in charge. Gen'ral Schuyler—a Yorker? The men wouldn't go! Nor they wouldn't want to go, either, t' be sold out by St. Clair. You c'n be sure of this much: if we send any men—'n I ain't sayin' we won't—it'll be a New Hampshire man who'll have the say over them: he'll say when they'll fight, and he will say where."

"Who do you think it'll be?"

Whit shook his head. "Gen'ral Court ain't met yet. You can't tell about them. But I know who it ought t' be—and so does everyone else. So do you, for that matter. He'd be the best one. He'd be the best one they could possibly get—even if he was born over on the east bank."

"East bank . . . You mean Stark?"

"I mean Colonel John Stark. He ain't a gen'ral, 't any rate, 'n that's all t' th' good. He'll be all the more for New Hampshire, the way that come about. You remember last year there—I told you about it—when the Congress was makin' new generals 'n Stark got left out . . . ?"

"You never told me."

"Well, then, maybe not. Anyhow, that's how it was. So he quit 'n come home. He figured they'd told him they didn't want him around. He is through with the Congress. He knows well enough now he'll never get nothin' from them. He ain't got to listen to a word that they say. He can be all for New Hampshire; he can be for New Hampshire only. I want t' tell you that's worth a good deal. He is honest and square—or I always heard he was, anyhow. He knows about Indians, and he's a hard man to scare. If they was to put him in charge, then you'd see 'em join up! I don't know but I'd—well—I think he'd be a good man."

Melissa couldn't see that it made any difference that he hadn't said it right out. She was heavy with fear . . . and she hated John Stark.

4

The days counted slowly to a full seven days—and no news came. Then it came all at once. Hez Hackett showed up—appearing as usual in time for Melissa to add to the pot the little present he'd brought. He said he was partial to rabbit and he hoped that they were. And while they were waiting for the rabbit to boil, Hackett sat in the doorway and told them the news.

General Schuyler had quitted Fort Edward without any fighting at all, but at least he had burned it—which was better than Ti. It made it look more as though he hadn't sold out, because if they'd paid for the fort they'd have wanted it whole.

Whit made no comment—and Hackett went on.

At Thetford and Lyme on Connecticut River—that would be less than halfway from here over to Ti—the women and children had moved out of the houses and come over this side because they were afraid of attack.

Whit moved his head slightly as a sign that he'd heard.

Melissa came from the fire. It was only two or three steps. She had a spoon in her hand, and it dripped onto the floor.

"You heard what happened to Exeter?" Hackett asked Whit.

"We ain't heard nothin'."

"Stark," Hackett said.

Melissa watched Whit. He turned his head slowly and spat out the door. Then he gave a hitch to his breeches, and said, "He's a good man."

"None better, I guess."

"What you doin' tomorrow? You want t' help get in hay?"

"Yourn ready to cut? It don't look it to me."

"I'm goin' t' cut some t'morrow—if the weather is right."

Melissa said, "I c'n help you. I done it before."

Whit said to Hackett, "You should have spoke sooner. Now you have lost out. When her and me hay together, we don't need any help."

They didn't try to pretend that Whit hadn't made up his mind. All through the day's haying, as it had been all through the night, Melissa lived ringed about by a cruel circle of thoughts: he would be gone to the fighting, they would be trying to kill him, there was no way of knowing whether he would come back. There would be no escape from this circle until it was over: until he had come back, or until she should get word.

Somewhere out beyond this, she did the things of the haying; she made the load, and she could hear her own voice speaking the words that had to do with the work—of how the grass had more of its fullness than she would have thought, it was about ready to cut, and it was a good day to make. She spoke of the oxen, and of the chances of rain. These things she could speak of because she didn't feel them. The other things she could not speak of.

Toward the end of the day—though it still lacked of evening, and there was more hay to haul—she put her fork in the rick and walked over to Whit where he was steadily raking the made hay into cocks.

He looked up at her coming—

She stood there before him, her hands at her sides, and their life together was shown in her face. They would speak now of his going—and then not again.

"Why must you go, Whit? I want to know. If I could feel the way you do, it—might not be so bad."

He had no feeling of wanting to tell her; he had no sureness that she'd understand. He wanted to gather her to him, and with his face bent to her head, try in some way to keep her from being afraid.

But they had shared things too long.

"I'd sooner go meet 'em than to wait for 'em here. I expect we can beat 'em. I expect to come back. It seems t' me kind of— well, if it's for you, in a way, I might 's well go 'n help out instead of just let someone else. I ought t' be as good at it as Elkanah Danforth."

"Do you want to go, Whit?"

"Sometimes I do, yes."

374

"Why?"

"Well, I ain't never been a great one for fightin', I know, but—but I don't like the idea of them comin' around."

"You could look out for us better if you stayed to home."

"You'll be all right. You c'n go over to Masons', you 'n the boys, 'n come back here daytimes t' milk 'n t' feed I shan't be gone such a great while—at least, I don't expect."

"You're set on it?"

"Yes."

It was all over, then.

"When do you want to go, Whit?"

"Three or four days—soon 's I get in some more of this hay."

"The rest of 'em ain't even started to mow."

"Then I c'n get men t' help me. I didn't want no'ne t'day."

She came and put her head down on his chest, and he put his arms round her, and she cried for a while—scarcely making a sound. Whit couldn't see that he'd done very well—he hadn't made her feel any better about his going away.

And though Melissa, for her part, knew she ought not to be crying, she had no wish at the moment to try not to cry . . .

But they couldn't stand here forever, and when, in due time, that was plain to both of them, and when it seemed to Whit that because she had quieted, she must be feeling better, he said to her, "Now, then, you come 'n set down. We hauled enough hay for one day; we c'n let the rest go for now."

So they went and sat down by the edge of the field at a place where the moss had come between two white ash trees. There were not many mosquitoes; it was the last day of July.

They were aware of the stillness that lay on the field and the woods . . . they saw the sun settle swiftly behind the mountains . . . and they felt the oncoming coolness that ran ahead of the night . . .

The first star was showing as they went back up to the house.

Neither one of the boys seemed to have missed them at all. Jonas asked where they'd been, and they said they'd been haying. Jonas was making a house out of twigs on the floor, and Gowan was watching him and wanting to help.

Whit was pretty sure in that moment that he'd made a mistake. But he had made up his mind; he had said he would go.

Three days later, he went.

. . . Melissa walked with him down through the clearing and a little ways on the path as it went into the woods. Then she said,

"Well, I guess I'll go back now," and Whit said, "All right," and laid his rifle aside. She stepped into his arms—and he knew as she kissed him that she trusted him perfectly that in going away he was doing what he thought was right . . . and then the hard pain of leaving her took away any thoughts.

After a moment, she pushed herself from him—and she said, "Now, then, get along—you got a long ways to go." She was smiling—or trying to. "There is your rifle," she said, "there by the tree. Have a good journey—and don't forget t' come back."

Whit picked up his gun—but then he stood there in the path because he could not turn away from her.

She had more courage than he had: she turned away . . . and he stood and watched her go from him, farther and farther, until at a bend in the path (far enough now, she hoped, so that he could not see her face clearly) she turned and waved to him—and turned again toward the house.

Whit answered her wave . . . then he swung about slowly, and set out on his way.

Inside of an hour, he was traveling smoothly and hard.

He stopped by at Beede's to get some French powder, and Beede said two men had already gone. Stark, so the word was, had gone to Number Four, or was going there. That would be the likeliest place, Beede thought.

Whit said he guessed he'd try there, then—and to add the twelve ounces of powder onto his score. Beede said, "To hell with it. What else are you shy?"

"Nothin' else I c'n think of."

"You goin' by Jonas Moore's?"

"I shouldn't wonder. I thought prob'ly I might. What d' you want me t' carry him? I hope it's a message; I'm travelin' light."

"I don' know as it's anything. She was up here last night. Wanted me to talk to him. She thinks he's got it into his head that he wants t' go, too. He ain't said nothin', but she thinks that he has. She claims he ain't in shape for it."

"What do you think?"

"I know well that he ain't. He's come on pretty good from what he was there in the winter. He c'n fish, 'n work round, 'n all that kind o' thing. But he'd oughtn't t' travel—why, God, he'd kill himself."

"You want me t' talk to him?"

"Well, that might be the best. Still, he's like an old dog, you know. He see you settin' off t' go gunnin', 'n he'd feel pretty bad that he couldn't go 'long. If he was a dog, you'd have t' tie him up good."

"Try to follow, you mean?"

"He *couldn't*, Whit, no. He ain't got the legs for it. He can't go it all day. Look, I can show you. Noontime, it is now, or pretty close anyway. Where will you lay tonight?"

"Baker's River, perhaps."

"Forty mile from your place. And the same thing tomorrow. Well, it ain't more'n a week ago, Jonas was up here—four mile at the most from his doorstep to mine—and he was tuckered out when he got here. He ain't in good shape."

"Don't sound like it, no. Well, I'll go along. I thank you for the powder. I'll try t' put it to use."

"Well, if you get any Indians, I'll trade for the pelts. Good-by and good luck—and you do as you're mind to about stoppin' there. I just thought I'd let you know."

"Ayuh," said Whit.

And he went down to Jonas's.

But he didn't stay long. He didn't stay to eat, even. Jonas laughed at him for going off to the war. Jonas said all Whit was after was the ten-dollar bonus that Stark had said he'd pay in hard money to anyone who'd join up.

Whit said he hadn't heard of it.

"The hell you ain't heard! Why don't you take Dan'l Beede along? He's a great one for money. He's worse 'n you be." And so on and so forth. It wasn't like Jonas: he talked too loud and too fast. Whit tried to joke back at him, but he didn't do well.

"And your woman," said Jonas. "A fine way t' treat her! Leave her do all the work while you go traipsin' off! You expect t' find her there, do you, when you come home again? You're takin' a risk, Whit. Maybe you'd ought t' go back."

Whit said, "I guess she'll be there. You been off yourself, ain't you?—now 'n again? If a woman 'd wait for a husband like you, I d' know but my chances ought t' be pretty good."

Ida Moore asked him, "Whit, she there alone?"

"No, only daytimes. She'll lay to Masons', I guess, mostly, nights. That is—well, you know, if more stories come in."

Whit said he must go now.

They didn't press him to stay because they could see he

wanted to go. Ida Moore said, "I was goin' t' say you might stay longer here on your way back, but I guess that on your way back you prob'ly won't want t' stop."

Whit said he'd stop, all right.

Jonas stood up. "Come on," he said, "I'll go with you a piece. I wouldn't want t' give any offense."

For a quarter mile, maybe, they talked about hay—though it wasn't their custom to talk in the woods, and neither man, really, had much to say about hay. Jonas cursed and swore more than Whit had ever noticed him to.

Then at the top of a ridge, Jonas stopped and said quietly, "I'll go back, now."

"All right, then, Jonas. And I take it kindly that you come this far. There wan't any need."

Jonas paid no attention. He was looking just past Whit's head. "Reason you're goin' alone, my legs ain't any good. I would be a drag on you. I couldn't keep up. It's because I was sick and because I am old."

The truth of what he was saying was in Jonas's face. Whit couldn't say anything—not one single word.

Jonas spoke evenly. "If you don't come back, we'll keep an eye on your woman—I guess you know that—Ida 'n me will, as long as we live. Well—I got t' go back now"—and before Whit could speak, Jonas had turned and was off down the hill.

Whit watched him going. Downhill looked to be hard for him . . .

Then Whit swung about and headed into the west.

5

This was the first time he had taken this road. Once he was free of the settlement, the cart tracks became dim, but he could still make them out with no trouble at all, and he had the spots on the trees, and the path was trodden some, too. It was pretty fair going—not as good as a pine plain, but still not rocky nor steep, and generally speaking the footing as good. There was nothing to check him from going as fast as he liked.

For the better part of an hour, the path held to the west; then it swung to the south round the base of a hill and kept south for a time until he stood at a forks. The way to the left would take him still farther south along the shore of the pond until he picked up Squam Brook. Follow that down, and he'd come to Merrimack River not very far south of where he wanted to go. That was the way he and Melissa had come. If he were to go that way now he'd pass right by the place where they'd overset that time. He grinned as he thought of it, and he wiped the sweat from his eyes. It had been as cold that night as was hot in here now! He'd like to go by there—and to tell Melissa he'd seen it. He'd like to see if the bank there really was a hundred feet high. But it would be a longer way round, and he didn't suppose he ought to spare the time to it. He wiped his forehead once more—and took the path to the right . . . and it went straight uphill for a good, solid mile . . . until it began to pull at his wind and to bother the backs of his legs. But he hung to it all right—until the rise of it slackened, and then it leveled off for a moment and began dropping down.

He was running well now, and as his head cleared after the climbing, he was pleased with himself: he might not be as good as he was eight or ten years ago, but he could still run the woods. He'd undertake to stay with most farmers close to thirty years old.

It would be downhill now, on an average, until he came to the river. If he'd had a load on his back, downhill wouldn't have helped him, but as it was he didn't suppose he had twenty-five pounds—that would be counting everything: spare clothing and food, gun, powder, and lead, his knife and his belt, and the things for his gun, as well as what he was wearing—light leather pants and old hunting shirt. In his food satchel, besides corn and salt pork, he had a pair of good-looking moccasins, his best linen shirt and all that was left of a hat. The hat was an afterthought; he'd brought it along on the chance that he might be tricked somehow into having to fight with the sun in his eyes. The linen shirt he would need if it should turn cold or wet, and it would be a handy thing, too, if he should chance to get hurt. The hair ribbon and moccasins were in case he had to dress himself out.

The other things that he carried all had to do with his gun. The last thing before leaving, he'd taken them out of the bag and counted them over just as he always did . . . frizzen pick, file, spare flints, and so on . . . they came to fourteen in all.

He'd thought some of bringing a water bottle along, but he never had carried one, and so he'd decided not to this time.

All of these things were slung over his shoulders—that is, his bag and his bullet pouch and the two powderhorns. Only his knife was hitched onto his belt. He had a thong round his waist to keep these things more secure, and the way he could tell whether his running was smooth was by whether his bag would bounce and flap at his side. It did a little—but not very much.

He was enjoying it now; he felt pretty good. Going as fast as he was, he didn't get much chance to think about where he was going or why he was here. He had to keep his mind on the path. Not very often would there come a stretch where for a dozen steps in a row he could put his loot down without picking the place.

The times when he stopped were when he could see out around: he had to keep the country in mind as well as marking the path.

It was past midafternoon when, because it was flat, he could tell he was approaching the river . . . and he came out on the bank with the sun three hours high.

The river was wide here, sandy bottomed, and brown. Over across was where Baker's River came in. The ford from here over was marked out with stakes. The river was down. It didn't look like a hard river to cross. Peeling his shirt off and stepping out of his breeches, he wrapped them both round the gun and bound them tight with his belt. Then he stepped into the water— which was as warm as Coruway pond.

Halfway across, it came to him that if there were any Indians had come this far east, they would never get a better shot at a man than he was giving them now. What they'd probably do, though, would be to wait till he came out on the bank, so that, when he fell, his gun and his other things wouldn't get wet. This possibility began to seem real to him. And though most any river will turn out to be deeper than it looks from the bank, this fool river had places where it didn't come up to his knees . . . and his skin was so white! Well, if he was shot now, he deserved it—there was no question of that.

When he recollected that both his gun and his knife were tied up so he couldn't get at them—then he was suddenly scared. He was scared enough so that he wanted to run. But the water was too deep to run in and the bottom was soft. He couldn't have run a single step if he'd tried. And then he did try—just to see if he could—and he almost fell down, and terror came on him as it does in a dream.

. . . when he was free of the water, he stumbled a few steps up the beach and crawled in under the bank amongst the roots and the spiderwebs and lay there and listened—and the mosquitoes came . . . but there was no other sound.

Ten minutes later, he was again on the path. But it was a good hour or more before he began to feel like himself.

And he must now carry with him these things: first, that he was liable to find any minute that he'd done something foolish it was too late to mend; and second, that fear was close to him— more so than he'd thought.

At his regular suppertime, he stopped and sat down, and he opened his satchel—but his stomach didn't feel hungry, and he got up and went on.

By sundown he was tired, and he turned aside from the path to look for some place to sleep.

He found a good place about a half a mile from the path where there was an old hemlock blowdown, as dry as a bone, with the top of it tight up against the face of a rock. Not even a bird could get in under there without making a noise. And it was a place where no one would come anyway.

He took off his shirt and put his linen shirt on underneath it, ate his supper in comfort, and then crawled in and lay down. He was tired and safe, and he didn't want to think about anything . . . . Sleep came over him quickly and stayed with him all night; it was a good sleep, but not as deep as it might have been in his house—and from time to time he'd wake up enough to know where he was. . . . He took an extra hour of sleep after it began to grow gray in the morning.

The stiffness and lameness he had when he stood up would work off as soon as he got going again.

The first part of the morning he would follow up Baker's RIver through Rumney township and Wentworth, it might be fifteen miles. Then he'd cross a height of land somewhere, and go down to the Connecticut River through Orford—and there he would get his first look at the Grants.

In the first couple of hours, he passed a half dozen houses, but from then on they were scarce—it was hilly and rough. It was along in here somewhere that John Stark had been taken—thirty years ago, that was, when there were no people at all. And it was still better country to hunt in than it was for anything else . . . and that was about all you could say for it for a good twenty miles. Then he came to a farm and beyond was the river: he had finished his westing. Now he would turn south.

For two hours he passed one farm after another. This was no

wilderness; this was all taken up. And on the west bank of the river—when he could catch a glimpse of it—it looked to be even more settled than it was on this side. It was beautiful land, there was no question about it—a strip on each side of the river that was of uncertain width but that in a good many places was as flat as the ice on a pond. It was flatter than Fryeburg—or as flat, anyhow. And the soil must be the best. They had natural meadows with rich-looking hay, and they had Indian corn that was as high as a man. If the whole of the Grants, he thought, was like that little part over there, there must be no country to equal it anywhere in the world.

A few minutes later, he met a man riding a horse—he hadn't seen that since he didn't know when.

Overtaking a farmer, and feeling ready to talk, Whit gave him greeting and told him his name.

"'Livingston,' eh? That might be a Scots name." He was an older man, square-built and blue-eyed, and his short beard almost white. "My name is Hamilton. I live down the road. You say you're of Tamworth? I know where it is. Where are you for?"

"Number Four. Colonel Stark."

"I've a boy is with Warner. You'll stop with us for tea." Whit said he didn't mind.

. . . but when he saw the house—with a fence round the dooryard, and painted pure white—and with glass in the windows—he was glad of the moccasins he had in his bag, and he asked leave to wash at the well before going in.

Hamilton brought him a basin and a dish of soft soap, a piece of coarse linen, and left him alone. When Whit was done washing, he put his linen shirt on, his moccasins, and his hair ribbon. He felt a long way from home. Then he picked up his rifle and went toward the house. It seemed a good deal of fuss for a saucer of tea. He didn't care much for tea, and he was hungry besides.

Hamilton's wife—a tall and gaunt woman—put him in mind of Mistress Jennifer Gowan. And then he saw the table . . .

He hadn't eaten since sunup, and he must have come fifty miles. They had more things on that table than he could have named.

He stayed the night there, and he slept in a bed. He couldn't help thinking, as he climbed into the bed, that so far he was doing pretty well in this war.

He was on the road early next morning—but so full of breakfast that a moderate walk was the best he could do. This was the township of Lyme. He approved of it. It was to this place, two weeks ago he had heard, that some people had crossed who were afraid of attack. Well, they had showed their good sense, fears or no fears—and he smiled to himself and his belly felt good. Number Four, they had told him, was sixty miles south. He had in mind to keep going until he got there.

The names of the towns he crossed during the day were Hanover, Lebanon, Plainfield, and Cornish, the township of Claremont . . . and at seven o'clock he had made Number Four.

But there were no soldiers gathered in front of the tavern; there was no sign of Colonel John Stark.

Tired and hungry, he went into the tavern. He called for his supper—after telling his name—and then he sat down and ate it alone, asking no questions, not talking with anyone. He gathered from listening that Stark had gone to Manchester; he didn't know even where Manchester was.

When he rang down the money to pay for his supper, the landlord came over and asked if he wanted a bed. Whit didn't like his looks much: he was a fat little man who kept rubbing his hands. Whit said, "No, I don't think it. Where does Manchester lie?"

"Over the river and west twenty-five miles. You ain't goin' t'night, are you?"

"Not all the way."

"You come quite a ways?"

"Orford, this morning."

"God, you done well. Fifty mile, ain't it?"

"I didn't count 'em. Might be, I guess."

"You'd be a hunter, I take it."

"I'll be a soldier tomorrow, if I can catch up with Stark."

"I knowed you wan't a militiaman."

"You seen more of them than you have hunters, I guess."

"By Jesus, yes. God, this place has been thick with 'em—all headin' west. They been comin' through here from clear east of the Merrimack—Chester, and Nottingham, all of them towns. Exeter, even."

"I shouldn't wonder."

"Oh, he won't lack for men. From the river towns, too: Goffstown, 'n Kettleford, 'n Hooksett, 'n them. When John Stark gives a holler, I want t' tell you, they come."

"Kettleford?"

"Kettleford, yes—a dozen or more of 'em. They crossed over here—I guess 'twas three days ago."

"Who was in charge of 'em?"

"The captain, you mean?"

"Ayuh."

"I don't remember. No . . . I couldn't say. Friend of yours, is he?"

Whit rubbed the back of his forefinger under his nose. "I couldn't say." And he got up to go.

"You can have a bed reasonable," the other man urged, "cleanest you ever saw, and a candle is free. You can't do no better anywhere in the town."

"How do I get over the river?"

"You ain't goin' on!"

"Well, a little ways, maybe."

"I'll send a boy down with you to see you across. And I'll say for you, mister, you got more legs than brains."

Whit looked down at him briefly. "I suppose there ain't nobody ever told you the same?"

The boy rowed him across, and Whit gave him three coppers. And he slept well in a haycock about a mile from the town.

6

It was an easy trip the next day: twenty-five miles to Manchester, with Bromley halfway . . . and the camp in Manchester no trouble to find—not with three hundred fires and twelve hundred men. He was able to smell it for the last mile and a half. And there were carts coming and going, and men on the road. There was a high excitement about it, the closer he got—and this was not only because he was nearing the end of his trip. It was also because of the signs that there were of a big business afoot in which he was to share.

. . . but nobody paid any attention to him.

When he came in sight of the camp, the very size of it made him want to hang back. Twelve hundred men in one place was more than he'd ever seen in his life. . . .

But he went down in amongst them and wandered about—

and felt more alone than he ever had in the woods. To see that many faces—and none that he knew—it was a strange thing. He didn't know what he'd expected, but he knew this wasn't it. And he found he was looking for the Kettleford men. . . .

Often he'd think of a man a little ways off, "There, that looks like someone that I used to know." But when he'd see the man's face, then he'd know he was wrong.

So he went through the camp. He had forgotten John Stark. He wanted to come on somebody he knew.

Many looked up at him—and a few of them spoke.

Most of the men in the camp were just lying about—some of them talking, and not many were drunk. Here and there at a fire, there'd be a man cooking meat. And he saw a good many men sleeping. Most of the guns that he saw were smoothbores. The men were all ages: there were quite a few boys—and there were some men who were older than Jonas Moore was—but they had probably come from near by.

He didn't see many hunting shirts; the men were in waistcoats and shirt sleeves as they would have been for work. Not a uniform anywhere—although he did see an officer wearing his sash.

Those men who were moving about were either bringing in wood, were bent on some errand, or were just looking round— two or three at a time, they were strolling about, looking this way and that, taking everything in. They were strangers, as Whit was.

A boy came up to Whit and asked if he knew where the Epping men were. Whit said, no, he couldn't say. Whit would have said something more, but the boy turned away . . . and as Whit started on again, he saw Ensign Lord coming straight toward him. Lord looked up and saw Whit—and for an instant was puzzled, and then broke into a smile, and said, "Where'd you come from?"

"Same place as you did—some time ago."

Ensign said, "Whit, you look good."

"I been all right." It seemed to Whit that Lord's face hadn't changed a great deal. He enjoyed looking on it. "How have things been?"

"Pretty good, Whit. I'm single and healthy, though I ain't very rich. You?"

"We been all right. There's four of us now."

"Well, I'll be damned."

"How's Mr. Gowan?"

"He's in good health. Whit, how long you been here?"

"I just got in."

"You with a comp'ny?"

"No, I come alone."

"You want t' join a good comp'ny?"

"Well, I don' know, Ensign. I figured I just stay around till the fightin' was over, and then I'd go home. I still got the best part of my hay to get in."

"So has everyone else. They all feel the same way. But you got to join up with someone to get your ten dollars. Come along with me, will you? We're just over here."

Whit didn't budge. "Who is captain?" he asked.

"Oh, we got a good captain. We got the best one around. We got about the best captain that we ever had—if I do say so."

Whit let his pleasure show in his face.

"Better'n Butler?"

"We-ell—I would say yes."

"Whereabouts is your pitch?"

Lord led the way. "There is one or two there you'll remember," he said, "though we have got some that wan't long out of dresses time you went away. You say you got two young ones—?"

"Two is all, yes. Boys, they are—both of 'em."

"Well, you're ahead of me, anyhow."

They wound their way between the cook-fires and among the men whom Whit no longer noticed—and although Lord told him as they walked along that Colonel Stark was not here yet but was still expected today, it didn't sound important to Whit.

Whit was wondering what men he would see in a minute or two that he used to know. He was wondering what they would think of him . . . whether they'd see that he had come on, or whether it would be the same way it had been before. It began to seem more and more as though it would be the way it had been before. These men would know nothing of his oxen and fields. They would see only himself.

And almost aloud he said, "Well, that's all right."

. . . and then they came to a little group clustered tight round a fire, six or eight men standing close to each other, watching, their heads bent, something going on in their midst. They had their backs to Lord and to Whit.

Lord said to them clearly, "I got a recruit" —and they twisted their heads round and then stood apart. . . .

In an old leather apron—a pair of tongs in one hand—Joe

Felipe stood there, staring at Whit. He stood in back of a little small forge.

Joe Felipe's eyes got bigger and bigger. He muttered something, and he crossed himself.

Whit watched him, and waited.

The fright that had been in Joe's face began to disappear from it, and Joe—from behind his big mustache—appeared to be trying to smile.

Whit met him halfway with it—or at least he thought he did.

And Joe whispered in Portygee, and then said, "I t'ought you was a ghost!"

He looked funny to Whit. "No, Joe, you missed." But Joe didn't get it. And Whit said, "You're still smithin', I see."

Joe nodded—but Whit wasn't sure whether Joe had understood him or not.

"He surprised you, eh, Joe?"—that was Lord speaking.

Joe turned his head. "Aye, captain," he said.

And Whit saw the little red hair ribbon. He saw it was faded now almost to pink.

7

Whit was sitting with his back and his head leaned up against the rough trunk of a big red oak tree. He was feeling hopeless and sick. In a few minutes now the fighting would start. His stomach and bowels were troubled and sore, he ached in his joints, and his head seemed to sway. John Stark and Indians, Melissa at home, Britainers, Hessians, the cool of his house, and the weight of his rifle as it lay in his lap, these were the things that went through his head. There were other men round him; they were all waiting, too. Whit guessed it must be now about halfway from noon until darkness—but they'd have the fighting, all right, there was plenty of time. There were four or five hours before darkness would come.

They would have had the fighting yesterday—but then it had rained. Today it was bright. It had been hot all the morning. It was hotter still, now. Even here in the shade, the air that he breathed was thin and uncomforting. It would not rain today.

It was over a week now since he'd come into the camp at Manchester. He hadn't joined up finally—but no one seemed to care. He had marched with the rest of them from Manchester to Bennington, and then a few miles westward to this place. He was one of them now. Stark was around here—oh, yes, he was here, all right! And the Britainers, Indians, Hessians, and Brunswickers, their cannon and muskets—and their long bayonets—they were all waiting, they were all ready—they were on top of a steep hill over across a small stream. Burgoyne wasn't with them. Colonel Baum—Bum—was their head man in charge. They had a good place. They were on top of a hill. Whit and these other men round here—as soon as Stark gave the word—would go down and cross over the stream and try to get up the hill, and when they got to the top of it, then there'd be the fighting.

Whit knew what Stark was waiting for now—and it couldn't take much longer. Stark had sent other men to go the long way around and come up from in back, on the far side of that hill. When they were there, they would start firing. It was only that sound that Stark was waiting for now. Whit would hear it himself—it would strike hard on his ears—and he would get up and go with the rest.

For a long time this morning, Whit and a hundred other men had marched round and round a small knoll in the sun. As they went round the far side of it, they were shot at—but mostly with cannon, and nobody got hit.

No one except Stark had any faith in the trick. And Stark said himself that he didn't know as it would fool anybody but Bum. Still, he did order Joe Felipe out of the line. He said, "Even old Bum would recognize your shape if he was to see you twice in ten minutes. I guess you better stay out."

Whit had felt worse and worse all the time they were marching. At first, he'd thought it might be the sun and he'd put on his hat. He thought now that most likely he had eaten bad meat.

Lord came up and spoke to him. "Whit, you look kind of peaked. Don't you feel right?"

Whit opened his eyes, and the light struck against them. He said, "I feel all right."

"Well, by God, you don't look it, boy! You think you can fight?"

"I shouldn't wonder. I figured to try. I might get kind of lonely if I was to set around here."

Lord said, "If you got a sickness, you better stay here." He was distressed . . . he kept looking at Whit.

Then there was suddenly with them the far sound of the

muskets—uneven, many—from behind the high hill.

Lord looked annoyed—as though they'd picked a poor time for it.

Whit put a hand back on the tree trunk to try to get up—and then took Lord's hand and was pulled up onto his feet.

"How about it?" Lord asked.

Whit said, "All right."

Lord turned away to shout to the men.

Whit simply stood there—but anyhow, he was standing; he could do that much. . . .

Stark spoke to the men.

They gave a great shout and began moving off—cursing and happy,—or it seemed so to Whit.

Whit followed them—running and stumbling . . . but not far behind.

. . . he had fixed his eyes on Joe's hair ribbon and was following that.

It seemed to Whit strange that he could keep going at all. There was nothing holding him up, no strength in his legs, and he couldn't see anything—except that little pink hair ribbon, swimming and bobbing in front of his eyes. That held him up, somehow. If he were to lose hold on that he would fall on his face.

He was aware for a moment that he was wading a stream.

Sometime after that, his weakness won over him: he was down on all fours, he was retching and sick.

He heard the roar of a volley just up ahead of him.

Someone crawled back to him and said, "You been hit?" Whit shook his head and said, "No," but he didn't see who it was.

When he began to feel better, he raised his head—and had a look round. Forty feet up the hill from him, he could see some of the men. They were lying down, kneeling, or standing in back of some tree. All of them were loading.

Whit watched them curiously. . . .

Then on top of the hill, he saw one of the cannon go off—much nearer, much louder than it had been this morning. This was the battle.

Up there on the hill, coming out of the smoke—but not coming toward him, going off to one side—he saw an Indian. He was a perfect Indian, too—half naked and painted, trotting along, carrying his gun at one side. In his other hand, he had a cowbell. There was another Indian following him. The first Indian was ringing the cowbell as he trotted along. A third one followed

389

them—and another—another . . . there came a whole line of them. They were all hollering mournfully—Whit could hear them as plain! . . . and then the last one disappeared round the side of the hill. There had been a hundred or more of them—anyway that.

It was a strange thing to have seen. But that was just what he saw.

Whit sat back on his heels, and then got up onto his feet. He felt a lot better! . . . and he clambered up the steep hill to join the men just in front.

The first man he came to was a man lying down. He turned his head and looked up at Whit—and said, "For Chris' sakes, get down!"

Whit knelt beside him—and watched the man cuddle his cheek to his gun, aim . . . and then fire—peer ahead for an instant—and he turned round to Whit. "I got him!" he said, "—right 'tween the two eyes!"

"Pretty good shooting."

"You're God damn right it's good shooting!" Then he looked closer at Whit. "What's the matter with you? Ain't you goin' t' get in this?"

"I s'pose I might 's well." He lay down on his belly and brought his gun round. He was all loaded—he had been since noon. But he wasn't primed. He put his powder flask up to his teeth, pulled out the stopper, and poured some in the pan.

"What is that—a twist-gun?" the other man asked.

"Uh huh."

"Thought it might be, from the length of the berril."

Whit had her all primed now. He settled himself and drew back the hammer. He was searching the smoke up on top of the hill. He wished he could see better; his head wasn't real clear. He said, "What I come after was Indians. You see any now?"

"I guess they went home. That's the trouble with volleys. We fired one volley, 'n them Indians beat it while we was all busy loadin' 'n nobody could shoot. So now it's 'fire-at-will' like it should a been t' begin with. Well, we hadn't ought to run out of targets for a little while yet. Them Hessians or Brunswickers or whatever they be show up better to shoot at than Indians do. There—I guess I'm ready again." He had finished his loading, and now he lay beside Whit and they watched the hilltop.

"What held you back?" the other man asked.

"Sick to my stomach. I had to stop."

"Thought that was it. You all right again now?"

"Ayuh."

"Good. They're down in that ditch," he explained, "that they was diggin' there yesterday. You hold still for a minute 'n they'll all raise up to once to let off a volley 'n then you c'n get one. You got t' fire 'fore they do, but you'll have plenty of time. Once they have fired, they scrooch down again."

The cannon went off. Whit was used to it now.

"Here they come!"

Over his front sight, Whit saw them raise up—orderly, regular—but dim through the smoke . . . and he saw their muskets come up. Now they would aim . . . but their heads didn't go down. He couldn't understand that—and he was so taken up with seeing what they would do next that he forgot what he should have been doing himself.

The man next to him fired, and Whit was annoyed because the flash and smoke from his musket made it harder to see. He raised up above it—and he was in time to see the flame of their firing run down the line—the smoke billowed out—and there was the jagged, rattling roar—and he heard the wha-a-ang of the balls fade in back of his head. That sound woke him up! They had fired at him! His left knee swung forward and was a rest for his elbow, his head bent to his gunstock—and through a break in the smoke he saw a man's shoulder—he swung his sights onto it . . . and squeezed off as the bead came down into the notch. He knew he had hit him. He couldn't actually see because of the smoke from his gun. But he was certain enough.

They wanted to shoot, did they? All right, then, let's shoot. He reached round for his pouch and threw a half dozen bullets into his mouth, opened his patch box and took out some of them and folded them into his fingers—and was loading as smoothly and swiftly as he ever had in his life.

This was between him and the men up there on the hill. They had shot at him: he had heard the whang of the musketballs close to his ears. They had shot at him—now he would shoot back.

—he had forgotten the man who lay on the ground next to him; he had no thought for the other men round—

He talked to his rifle. "They want to shoot, do they? Them and their smoothbores! All right, then, you show 'em. You remember old Captain Karr, don't you?—that you used to belong to? He may be dead, but he's got his eye on you. So you better shoot good, or I'll bust you over a rock." This was while he was loading. . . .

—and as he thrust home the ramrod, "Now, then, let's see you shoot!"—and he laid the ramrod aside, and he wriggled about on his belly to get himself set—and he peered through the smoke trying to pick out a mark. . . . He passed up an officer who had only a sword. He was trying for the men who were trying for him.

The next volley was closer. Two yards to his right a ball struck into the ground—and the whining sound of others passing made him half close his eyes.

"They don't do so bad," said the man on his left, "seein' they don't appear t' aim any. I'm goin' t' move up a mite." Bent over and running, he went a little way up the hill, and settled down sideways behind a beech tree.

Whit made up his mind to do the same thing . . . and when the next volley had missed him, he started out and kept going until he saw a pretty good rock that nobody was using, and he got down behind that.

He had forgotten his ramrod.

—and for the first time he swore.

And he started back after it.

A man rose up in front of him, barring his way. He was upset and angry. He was an officer—by his sword and his sash. He said, "Get back in there, damn you"—and drew back his sword.

Whit was wholly disgusted. He spat to one side, and then rubbed his forefinger under his nose. "I'm after my ramrod— down there a step. You want to go fetch it for me? I c'n wait for you here."

"Your what?"

"Ramrod."

"Where is it?"

"Down there."

"Well, then, go get it! Good God, what a fool!" He turned away.

Whit slid down the hill on his heels, picked up the ramrod, and got back to his rock.

He stayed here a long time. It was a gray rock, and smooth to his hand, about two feet high at one end, and sloping off to the right. From the way it went into the ground—not straight up and down, but on more of a slant—it was probably the tip of a boulder. The soil at the base of it was yellow and soft—not the coarse gravel that a granite rock has. These things were different from what they were at home.

This was a good rock; it was a good place to be.

There were plenty of other men round him, but he felt alone.

It would take a cannonball, probably, to knock this rock loose. Stretched out in back of it, with his feet down the hill, he turned on his side when he wanted to load. And there was enough pitch to the hill so that, when he poured, the powder went down all right—he didn't have to raise up. It was as good a place to fight from as there was on the hill.

There was nothing to hurry him, and he took his time. A little crack in the rock on the sloping right side he used for a rest. No one could say it wasn't steady, at any rate—and it was a pretty good height. The thing that bothered him most was that he kept slipping downhill inside of his clothes. It made his breeches bind in the crotch.

He was scared all the time, and he knew that he was, but he wasn't really bad off. There had been one or two hit: one man off to his right, who had flopped around just at first but since then had lain still, and another man more to his left and a little ways up the hill. Whit didn't know who they had been. He hadn't seen Lord—and he didn't know where Joe was.

As for his shooting, he thought he'd done pretty well. Sometimes, of course, he had missed—or he was pretty certain he had—but he figured he had got six of them, and maybe two more. He had got two through the head.

This was a strange thing for him to be doing. But there was no need to think about that. Off and on, he did wonder, though, how long this was supposed to keep up. He was getting wonderfully dry!—his tongue was thickened and foul. And his gun needed swabbing—that was the worst. He knew there was a brook away around to his left. More and more he was thinking that pretty soon he'd go there. He'd got to have water. He would go pretty soon. He could feel how the water would taste in his mouth.

He had decided to go—but he'd got to load first . . . and for the first time, he had trouble. He was uncertain and trembling—both his hands shook—and while he was pouring the powder, he stared and was frightened to see that he was spilling the powder all over the place. So he stopped pouring.

Then he couldn't remember what he was supposed to do next. . . .

He tried hard to remember. He tried as hard as he could. But he had to give it up finally because there was no chance.

The thing to do, so he reasoned, was to leave the gun here. It was no good to him now because he didn't know how to use it.

393

Old Captain Karr had shown him how to use it—back there in the smithy. But that was a long time ago. He would just leave it here. There was nothing else he could do.

He was pleased at the way he had thought this all out. It was clear as could be: lay down the rifle—and then go get the water.

He found he was glad he didn't have to shoot any more.

He started to lay down his rifle, and while he was doing it— he winced all of a sudden and shrank into himself because something was going to hit him. And he was aware of a kind of growling and then a great bursting roar mounting into the air— and he could feel the earth shaking.

Gripping his rifle, he jumped to his feet, looking first right around him, and then up to the top of the hill—where a huge white cloud of smoke was getting bigger and higher.

A man stood up not far away from him and shouted, "That's their amminition! We got 'em now!"—and he began scrambling and clawing his way up the hill.

Other men—all over—the place was thick with them—all moving forward—yelling and shouting—"Here we go, boys!— Here we go!—Here we go—" Whit had to go with them. He started forward—he was going uphill with the rest of them—all kinds of shouting—"By Jesus, we got 'em!"—and a good many just hollering. Whit had his rifle tight in his hand.

The cannon went off and it was pretty close to them. Nobody minded. They didn't holler so much. But they kept a-going.

They were at the top of the hill now. It wasn't so steep. Whit straightened up to see what was ahead. He saw it—a banked-up place made of fresh earth and logs, not very high, and behind that were the Hessians—they stood in line, they held their guns very even and steady; they all had bayonets. Whit didn't try to look at their faces. It was the bayonets that lay ahead now.

He saw Joe Felipe, from among the men just in front of him, go up the bank, swing his musket down like a club—and jump down in amongst them.

Whit followed Joe—he came right in after him. Joe had no gun now. He was bent down and in close. He was working his knife—coming up with it from low on his right.

Two Hessians, side by side, lifted their muskets to thrust down into Joe's back. Joe took the one on the right, going in under the bayonet—and Whit poked his gun muzzle for the other one's face, pulled the trigger—missed fire—and then jammed the bare muzzle on into the face. The man let go his gun and

394

clapped his hands to his face—and as Joe's man went down, Joe was in on this second one, and struck three times with his knife deep into the neck. Whit was afraid Joe would break the blade off.

Whit turned his rifle end over end, and drove with the butt of it for the nearest face that he saw. And again Joe stepped in front of him, still swinging that knife.

Whit turned to his left—saw a thrust coming that he couldn't stop—ducked clear—and fell down. He rolled for the jack boots of the man who'd tried for him, got his arm around one and gathered the other one in—and felt his man coming down. Whit reached for his knife—and then his head seemed to explode. . . .

. . . he knew he'd lost his hold, and he couldn't see anything. He was lying face down. He pushed with his hands and got up onto his knees. He got his eyes open but everything swam so— and he seemed to be swaying and sinking as he would in a swing. He shut his eyes, and tried to get to his feet—and he made it. He stood up on his feet. He had his eyes closed, and he wanted to lie down again. But he opened his eyes—and though he couldn't see far, he made out pretty soon that he stood alone. He stood in the ditch up on top of the hill. There were plenty of other men near him, but there were none standing up. They were lying this way and that. They were mostly all dead. But some of them were not. He saw two sitting up.

Empty-handed, uncertain, Whit stood and looked round—a great pain in his head. He couldn't stand up much longer, he would have to sit down—

. . . there was a man coming toward him; he was close to him now, he was right in front of him—

Whit looked on his face, and knew who he was: that was Joe Felipe's face. Whit could see Joe was asking him something, but there didn't seem to be any way for Whit to tell what it was, and he didn't feel like the effort to recall any words. But he felt friendly toward Joe, and he smiled.

Joe's face got very big and came so close up to Whit's eyes that Joe's nose almost touched him . . . and then Joe's face drew away and got very small. Whit saw these things; he saw they were so—that was all there was to it—he just saw them happen, was all.

And then he knew Joe was bearing him up. Joe's arm was around him—and Whit had his arm up round Joe's neck and Joe had hold of that wrist, Whit could feel that—and he could feel the great, moving strength of Joe . . . who was lugging him off. Whit made his legs go, but his feet just fumbled the ground. Whit felt happy and comfortable except for the pain in his head, and he knew he was all right. He opened his eyes now and then and saw the ground going by underneath.

When Joe laid him down, it made his head hurt so bad that that was all that he knew—only the pain. He dug his fingers into the dirt, and as he writhed onto his side, the pain seemed to let go of him . . . and he lay very still, his breath coming short.

Water struck in his face, and Whit said, "No! No!"

And Joe said, "You all right?"

"Sure, Joe, I'm all right."

"By God, you must be—you know my name, huh? Now set up. I give you a drink." He tried to put his hand under Whit's shoulder, but Whit begged him so not to that Joe gave it up.

"You got your head broke. You be all right. I see 'em before. You got a crack in your head."

"Just leave me lay here."

"Sure. Oh, Whit, what a fight! We beat 'em good, boy! By God, I tell you! Look: I don' know it is you—next to me, I mean. Then when you go down, and try to pull that one down, and get a crack on the head—then I see it is you. I don' know what I said. But I got him, all right. They don' move very quick. Someone else I don' see get t' one you pull down. More fightin', more fightin'—all t' time—all round. Then they start to run, and we get a lot more. They cannot run good—them big coats they got on. And boots, too! They don' get away—just only a few. Bum, we got him, too, I don' know, I think. I got a watch. All the boots that you want. Oh, everybody—everybody got boots! Brandy, too, someone, off an officer. Yes. Oh, t'ere is everyt'ing!—all over t' place. You better get up 'n go get some. I don' know if t'ey share."

"I'm all right, Joe. Le' me stay here."

"You try 'n set up, see?"

"No, Joe, no! Please—"

"Hey! Hold still—wait—"

Whit hadn't moved.

"More shooting, by God!"

Whit heard it, too—and men calling, besides.

"I better go see," said Joe. "You stay right here."

"Sure," said Whit. "Thanks, Joe." And he could feel the thud of Joe's footsteps.

Whit lay there.

. . . at one time he roused up enough to know the brook was near by. He dragged himself to it and drank out of his hand. That took all his strength. The pain still upon him, he fell asleep.

He heard in his sleep someone calling his name—and then he was awake—"Whit—" It was right in front of his face. He put his hand up.

"Whit, you know me? It's Lord."

Whit opened his eyes. It was dark. "Who?"

"Ensign, Whit. Lord. How are you? All right?"

"I been asleep. Ensign? Where'd you come from?"

"I come to get you."

"Night, is it?"

"Yes, Whit. Fightin's all done."

"Oh." Whit hadn't been thinking about it. "Where's Joe?"

"He sent me t' get you."

"He was here—before."

"Ayuh, I know. You want t' try t' set up?"

"Joe all right?"

"No, Whit, he got hurt."

"Oh." Then he asked, "They get Joe, did they?"

"I guess so. Yes, Whit."

"Joe?"

"Ayuh."

"It don't—seem—like they'd ought to. He was 'n awful—strong man."

"He got hit, Whit. Grapeshot—from a cannon. He never knew it."

"Oh. While—while I laid here."

"Ayuh. Some more of 'em come up the road when we thought we was all through. Breyman. We fought 'em awhile—that was when Joe got hit. They had two cannon. We come near gettin' beat. And then Warner showed up with his men—and that done the trick. Joe had told me where you was before he got hit. So I come up to get you. Good thing I remembered, or you'd a laid out all night. Your head much stove up?—or I suppose you don't know."

"It ain't broke, I don't think. I c'n see pretty good."

"How do you feel in your stummick? You looked kind of poorly there, before it began. I didn't know maybe we'd left you behind. How *is* your stummick?"

"I don't know." He held out his hand.

Lord got him up on his feet.

He took a step forward—and he felt himself falling. He seemed to fall a long time. . . .

When he came to, and the motion let up, he knew he was lying down somewhere. He put his hand out to feel of the ground—but it wasn't ground; it was something unnatural— He tried with his left hand—and it fell off into space. That startled him so that he opened his eyes.

It was daylight, all right—and there were high rafters above him. There were people moving about. He heard a man groan . . . and although it cost him a good deal of effort, he figured out finally that he lay on his back on a seat in a church. He didn't know how he had come here.

Using his arms, he tried to pull himself up—and *that* brought the pain back! So that he had to lie back and wait. A great thirst was on him.

He tried again pretty soon . . . and this time he wouldn't give up. He got himself upright, and he hung to the back of the seat— and fought the pain in his head.

A woman—he thought it was—said, "Here, you, lay down"— and took him under the armpits and eased him down where he'd been.

They brought him water to drink.

. . . later on, soup. It tasted all right for the first two or three swallows—but then he lost interest in it.

They took him out of the church sometime during the day. There was a man on each side of him, holding his arms . . . and that part of it ended when they laid him down on a bed. He was in somebody's house.

8

One of the things he remembered about the next few days and nights was that there were two old people often came to his bed. He would open his eyes and see their faces above him— more often the woman, but sometimes the man. The woman had a big, seamy face, and dark-colored, gray hair. Every time that Whit saw it, he knew what was going to happen: she was going to try to pour something into his face. She was determined to drown him with dippers of soup. The man wasn't so bad. Sometimes he wouldn't do anything. He had a thin little face and kept blinking his eyes. Whit wasn't afraid of him. Ensign came once, and stood by the bed. He told Whit he'd located Whit's rifle, and Whit could have it again. But Whit had forgotten he'd lost it. . . .

Even after he got so that he could tell the old woman's footsteps, she always knew somehow that he was awake. The most he ever fooled her was twice in one day.

His head pained him constantly, but more when he moved.

If he could just see Melissa, and take hold of her hand—then he thought he could turn over and go off to sleep. . . .

That old woman, he hated.

A doctor came one day. Whit was helpless, of course, and he didn't know what would happen. But it turned out all right. All the doctor did was to talk for a minute or two—asked Whit about his place and so on—and then for no reason he showed Whit a fishhook he claimed to have fashioned himself—holding it right up close to Whit's eyes and moving it this way and that. Whit thought it looked to be a fair enough fishhook—except the barb was too long. He said, "You got to set that hook hard for that barb to take hold."

The doctor laughed and stood up, and said, "I guess you'll fish again."

And Whit said, "I had figured to"—and the doctor laughed again and went out.

—he had an odd smell to him; Whit didn't know what it was.

The old woman made him take physic that night. Whit had never felt in his life about anyone as he did about her. He knew she was trying to help him, and that made it worse. No one could have been so bound and determined to work a man harm as that terrible woman was to do him some good. He wanted to get well, and he longed to go home. But the first thing he wanted was to get away from her face.

They got him up in a chair after what they said was only a week, and the old man brought him his rifle and put it into his hands—but Whit didn't feel any interest in it, and put it aside.

At the end of another four days that took twice as long as the week, he could walk about pretty well. It jarred his head mightily if he came down on his heels, and it hurt him to chew. They saw this was so, and they loaded him down with spoon victuals—that

399

sloshed about in him and put no strength in his knees. He wanted wild meat—whether he could chew it or not. Deer's liver, he wanted. Or even honest fried pork—maybe with a few streaks of lean in it—he wouldn't have to chew that—not the way Melissa would cook it, it would melt in his mouth.

He told them next morning that he'd got to go home.

They put up quite an argument, and the old woman threatened to go get the doctor again.

But Whit felt so good just at the prospect of leaving that he said, "All right, you go get him. I'll take him along."

She was truly distressed, though. And that made him feel bad. But he knew now that she never would touch him again. Still, she wouldn't give in—and it was the old man brought his things for him.

Whit put them on. They felt heavy, of course, but they felt pretty good, his powderhorns and his bag. He was missing his hat and his knife, but he said nothing of that.

She tried to get him to wait while she fixed him some soup to take with him. But Whit wouldn't have waited for anything now. If he could get only a half a mile from the house—and then lie down by the road—he would be on his way home.

He thanked them both, and he meant it—he meant every word. And when he told the woman his thanks, he spoke straight to her face . . . and he knew while he spoke he was grateful, and he hoped she knew it, too.

She cut him short, though. She just nodded her head and went out of the room.

The old man went with him a little piece up the road.

He said, "I wish't you wouldn't go. You ain't in no kind of shape."

"I'll pick up on the road. I got t' get home."

Not for an instant convinced, the old man merely nodded—as much as to say there was no use his trying further. Then he suddenly lifted his head, and said—not looking at Whit, "Wait! I forgot—" and started back to the house. He turned and called back to Whit, "You stay right still—I'm comin' right back."

Whit stood by the gate, thinking that all this waiting round was using up strength that he was going to need on the road. . . .

Then the old man was back again. He held his hand out toward Whit—and across that dry, wrinkled hand with the fingers curved up, there lay a slender, sharp-pointed knife. Whit stared

400

at it—and knew it: that was Joe Felipe's knife.

"Where'd you get that?"

"That captain," the man said, "time he come t' see you. He left it then for you—and then I forgot. I meant t' clean her up, too, for you—but I guess you c'n do that. You got a whetstone, I seen, in your bag. That there's quite a knife. Kind a narrer, perhaps, but it's awful good steel. B'longed to a friend o' yourn, he said. He didn't say who."

"All right," said Whit. "Thank you." He picked up the knife and slid it into his sheath. He looked up at the man. "Well—good-by. I thank you—and her—like I said before."

"You're more'n welcome. Good-by to you. If you get a good chance to, let us hear you got home."

Whit said, "Ayuh, I will."

"Good luck to you"—and he saw that he'd got to be the one to turn away first—and he nodded and smiled—and he turned away. He started off up the Manchester road.

The old man called after him, "I hope you find that your woman is well!"

Whit wished he'd let go. He turned and waved back and called, "I guess I will"—and that hurt his head. Then he faced to the road again—keeping his eyes on a bend up ahead. If he could get round that bend, he would feel safe.

Although he got round the bend all right, he then had a strong wish to look back over his shoulder—just so as to know that they weren't on his track. But he knew this would be foolish, and so he held on. He'd got to keep his head now. He had a long way to go.

After a little, the road crossed a stream. They had put a good heavy bridge over it, and a stout railing, to boot. They had used sticks of ash for the railings, some of the bark was still on. He set down his rifle, and leaning his elbows on the railing to rest, he looked up the stream, watching the slow-turning eddies. . . .

Slowly, he reached his hand round to his sheath—and drew out Joe Felipe's knife. He took hold of the point between his thumb and forefinger, raised it over his shoulder, and flipped it well up the stream.

Then he picked up his rifle, and started again up the road. He was on his way home.

401

9

Seventeen days, by road, river, and path . . . and he came in the evening to Jonas Moore's house.

There was no one about—not even the dog.

Whit went into the house. The fire was low, but it hadn't been banked, and Jonas's gun was up on its pegs. They'd be back before long. He stood his gun in the corner, and went across to the fireplace to put on a stick. It was getting cold out. The pot had been swung aside from the fire, and he looked down into that . . . and it appeared to have some kind of stew in it. That was an interesting thing. It looked to be venison stew. . . and he put in his finger and stirred it about . . . there was venison in it, all right!— and other things, too. . . .

In twenty minutes or less, he was stretched out by the fire, and full of a warm and rich venison stew. It had had an herb in it he'd never tasted before. And he didn't know now what it was. . . .

Sleep was coming fast toward him—and he let it come . . . he'd surely wake up at the sound of Jonas's voice. . . .

Fifteen miles today. That was the best day he'd had. . . . He was pretty near home now. . . . He had pretty near won. . . .

He would be home tomorrow.

Tomorrow night he would lie with Melissa beside him. All night.

One of the sticks settled down in the fire. He opened one eye just a crack—and closed it again. There was not now any pain in his head. This was Jonas's house that was all around him, the floor that he lay on, the walls, and the roof . . . it was familiar and friendly. . . .

Tomorrow night, home.

It was gray daylight when he wakened next morning after a long, solid sleep—and outside there was rain . . . well, he would go on today in spite of the rain.

Mrs. Moore was moving about at the other end of the room. Jonas, most likely was out in the barn.

Whit said to her, "Mornin'"—and threw back the fur covering that one of them had put over him sometime while he slept. It was gettin' cold now, they were into the fall. The summer had gone—and he'd not seen it go.

"Mornin'," Ida Moore answered. "Well, you slept pretty good."

"Reason I slept good," getting up onto his feet, "was I'd et most of your supper. Set so good on my stummick, my conscience slept, too. Jonas out in the barn, is he?"

"Ayuh."

Whit drew his belt tight. "When 'd you last hear of M'lissa?"

"I heard three days ago they was all right. Most of your hay's in."

"You're sure about that, are you? I mean—about them?"

"'Twas Fred Mason told me."

"Her and the boys?"

"Yes—and the oxen. He didn't mention the dog."

"Oh, she wouldn't come to no harm. She's a good able dog. She might miss me, I s'pose—but that would be all."

"Jen would, you mean."

"I ain't got any other."

"I'll go call Jonas." She stepped to the door.

Whit would be glad to see Jonas coming in through the doorway. But he wouldn't like telling him that he was going straight on.

Mrs. Moore called, and he heard Jonas answer. She came back inside.

"Jonas," she said, "wanted to wake you last night."

Then Jonas came in. "What a man you be! Eat another man's supper 'n lay by his fire—" He stopped. "Hell, you look even more thinner 'n you did layin' down. You didn't get hurt, did you?"

And Jonas kept after him until he found out what had happened. Finally he asked, "Pain you at all?"

"Not now—not a mite."

"Works just as good, I suppose, as it ever did?"

"Better."

"Don't tell me!"

Ida Moore interrupted. "Jonas, you leave him be! Whit, you hungry to eat, are you?"

"Hungry!" Jonas turned on her. "How could he be hungry? He ain't done nothin' but sleep on a gallon of stew!" . . . then he turned back to Whit and just stood there and looked at him—and a slow grin of happiness came over Jonas's face. . . .

Then Jonas said, "Tell you: you come out 'n wash up, 'n she'll fix you your breakfast, 'n then you 'n me c'n get on. I'm goin' with you."

403

Jonas stayed with him a little more than halfway, but then he stopped in the path and said he'd got to turn off—he had to see Jewell, whose house was near by. That was the reason he'd come, he said. Chances were, he'd get over to Whit's place in the morning. He said he guessed Whit could make it the rest of the way.

And Whit said he guessed so. He said he hoped Jewell wouldn't be too surprised to see Jonas—that is, if Jonas should find him home.

"I got an errand," Jonas assured him. "You get along, now. You got six-seven mile yet. I'll be over t'morrow. You tell her that, will you?—when you get round to it." And he put his head down and took his path in the rain.

Whit knew all right how far he had to go—he knew every step of it. And he thought he had enough strength in him to make it—and even have something left over. It wouldn't do to crawl up to the door on all fours.

He was moving forward again. The wind didn't bother him greatly—most of the leaves were still on—and it didn't seem to be blowing as hard as it had been at first. It was the wetness he hated. His leather shirt and his breeches were soft and greasy with water, they were heavy and clung to him. While he kept moving, he didn't feel cold. But he knew he'd got to keep moving; he couldn't stand still.

When he got home he would sit with his face to the fire and then he'd turn round and feel the heat on his back.

He saw little around him: enough of the path as it lay in front of his feet so that he could pick out his footing; and he saw the familiar, wet woods as, without knowing he did it, he glanced ahead and about him against any surprise. Nothing was traveling—not so much as a squirrel. He went alone in the woods and the rain.

He thought of all pleasant things: his mind wandered among them, turning to this one and that as though he were already home . . . and he picked up young Jonas, and knelt with his arm around Gowan, feeling the good, rugged heft of them. These two were his sons. They were glad he was back, but they'd not worried about him. They would tell him of something that was important to them that had happened this morning or yesterday. He would go out to the oxen—and they would turn their heads at his coming, and he would hear the soft rush in their nostrils as he reached out his hand. These would be the things of his homecoming. They were not far ahead. . . .

Her presence was with him. He went forward to her.

Still, anything could have happened in three days and a half; he was no more sure now that she was all right than he had been way back there in Bennington when he had lain sick.

There were three miles to go yet; he knew every step of them.

Bearcamp River, he noted, as he came out on the south bank of it, was perhaps a little bit higher than he might have thought. The wind was much less now, and more out of the north. This storm wouldn't last long.

Crossing the pine plain, he found he couldn't go fast. He was doing all right, though. He could handle it now.

And the rain had stopped altogether before he came to the ridge.

Before starting the uphill, he looked again at the sky. He wasn't sure but what it was getting ready to clear . . . and he stood and gazed at it longer than there was any real need to because it gave him a chance to gather his strength. He knew he was scraping the corn into a pretty small pile on the bare boards of the bin. There was just about a good handful left of it now. Still, he'd seen it empty before, and had lived to fill it again. And he guessed he would this time. Once at the top of the ridge, it would be easy from there. The sky looked much as it had that day in the autumn when he'd first seen his place—when he'd seen the mountain come out, just the top of it—that had been after a rain, this same time of the year. Well—

—and he tackled the ridge. Stubbornly, slowly, he made his way up. Thirty feet at a time—and then stand to rest.

He got to the top of it. But as he stood there, his knees buckled suddenly, and he had to grab hold of a tree and hang on, his cheek up against it and his arms halfway round. Anyone would have laughed who had come on him then. But he didn't go down! And when the dizziness passed, he grinned and was proud of himself. He stood back from the tree trunk, but with that support gone, he had to steady himself by holding the path with eyes . . . but it would be only a moment, and then he could go on. He waited the impulse to go forward again. . . .

There came into being over the sodden, brown track, between the near tree trunks, and on down through the woods, the same strange, growing light that he had known once before. He turned his head slowly, to his left hand, to his right, and the light was now growing stronger among the wet, blackened trees. There were no shadows; the light lived in the air.

He couldn't see the mountain from here—and not for his life could he have got up a tree. He stood in the path, facing the way he would go . . . and he knew that the mountain had come out of the clouds. As he had seen it before, it rode now in the sky. The top of the mountain lay clean to the sun. Standing here in the path, down in under the trees, he could not see the sun—he'd not seen it, for that matter, that time before. What he had seen was the mountain as it stood forth from the clouds, and it had had the sun on it. That was what he saw now—though he looked down the path.

His thin lips were parted in a kind of smile, he swayed just a little, and he went ahead on the path . . . as it turned down through the woods, down the side of the ridge.

The sky pretty well cleared while he was still in the woods— the wind high overhead coming out of the west—and as he came over the wall at the edge of his field, the late afternoon shadows stretched toward him from the shocks. There was smoke from the chimney—but he saw no one about.

Behind and above the house was the mountain. It looked just the same—the blue sky in back of the high granite peak.

He wondered who had got in all his Indian corn. The Masons, he guessed—the stubble was low, and the shocks very neat.

But over his house and his barns, over all of his place he could see, there was the look of September, and that didn't seem right—though every other place he had passed for the last couple of weeks had had that same look to it. Still, he had expected that his own place would look the same as it had when he'd left it . . . back in August, that was.

Halfway through the field, he could stand it no longer. He leaned on his rifle and stood very still—and he called to the house. He gave a sure, even call.

—and after he'd waited, he called again . . . but his voice didn't work so well this time.

She came out of the doorway—stood—and she saw him— and she picked up her skirts, and she came down that hill as though she were a girl running.

—the boys must be all right, or she wouldn't run that way—

406

He let his rifle fall from his hand—and he went forward to meet her, holding his arms out—

He stood there a time with his face bent to her head—and then she drew her head back and looked up at him.

They had that instant together.

... the two boys came pelting down the hill from the barn— but the old dog overtook them, and got to him first. Jen didn't seem to hold it against him that he'd left her behind when he went away—nor did Jonas and Gowan. He'd been right about them— anybody could see there was nothing the matter with them.

A step at a time—while young Jonas told them about a great woodchuck he'd almost hit with a rock—they went up the hill to the house.

Whit missed his rifle as soon as he was inside the house. "There now," he said, "that wan't very bright. I left my rifle layin' down in the field."

Melissa said, "Jonas, you go down there 'n get it." And turning to Whit, "That's all right for him, ain't it?"

"Yes, I don't know why not. You be careful now, Jonas."

Gowan went, too.

"I don't know why I done that." Whit took his leather shirt off. "I'm all finished fightin'—or I hope I am—but I c'n hunt all the same. I didn't figure t' throw it away." He started peeling his linen shirt off. It was dark gray and wet and clung tight to his skin. It would be good to be dry.

Melissa saw what she'd expected: his body was thinner than she'd ever seen. She got him out a new shirt.

"Where'd that come from?" he asked.

"I made it for you while you been away. I made you two others but this one's the best. You want to rub yourself any?"

"No, I ain't cold. This 'n awful brave shirt. Well—I'll put her on. How'd you know while you was makin' it you wouldn't be wastin' your time?"

"That's why I made it: I didn't know. I made some breeches, too."

"You must a kept busy."

"I had plenty of time."

"Short of two months. That ain't a long time."

"Maybe it didn't seem long to you."

"Seemed long enough to me!"

"Whit, you been poorly."

"Well—travelin' 'n all."

"Tell me, Whit, tell me. I got t' know."

"Yes, I d' know but you have. Well, I *was* kind of poorly there a while back."

"A sickness?"

"No. I'm all right. I—well, I got a blow on the head. But she's all mended now."

"I wish you'd tell me 'fore Jonas comes back. That's why I sent him down after your gun."

"Yes. Well, all right—" and he told her about it—enough, anyhow. He left out about Joe.

"This woman took care of you—" Melissa inquired.

Whit sat down on the bench with his back to the fire. "You know I think maybe I'll try them new breeches—if you got 'em handy."

She brought him his breeches. They were a beautiful pair, and he said so. While he was pulling them on, he said, "Well, now you ask about her. She was a beauty. Black hair 'n red cheeks 'n a little slim, narrer waist. . . . I want t' tell you!"

"You need somethin' t' eat," said Melissa. "You're light in the head." She went to get down his bowl from its place on the shelf.

Whit found the trousers were too big in the waist.

Melissa said over her shoulder, "How are they? Too big?"

"No, not a mite—they won't be—in a week."

He turned round and sat down again, this time facing the fire. He guessed now might be the time to tell her about Joe.

"I'd ought to tell you," he said, "about Joe."

There was no sound from Melissa. Whit didn't look round. "I mean Joe Felipe," he said . . . and then he went on. "He was there, too—along with Lord and the rest. Well, what I was going to say about Joe: when I went down—in the fightin', I mean—it was Joe that stood over me. I guess he kep' 'em off. Someone did, anyhow, or else they thought I was dead. It was when I went down I got the blow on the head. Later on it was Joe was the one lugged me off t' th' side of this brook. I never saw him again. He went back to the fightin' soon 's he heard it start up. Lord told me about it. He said Joe was took quick—he never suffered at all. A cannonball done it. Lord give me Joe's knife. On my way home I pitched it int' th' bed of a stream. It seemed a clean place for it— there in the sand. Though I hope nobody steps on it. You understand, do you? I want you to know: I wouldn't be here with

408

you now if it wasn't for Joe. That is all I can do for him, is just tell you that."

Whit heard her go across to the doorway, and he knew that she stood there for some time looking out. . . .

When she came back, she stood at his shoulder—and as she bent down to him, Whit raised up his face, and he saw the tears in her eyes and that there were tears on her cheeks. Her lips were parted and trembling as she bent swiftly to his, and he put his arms up and round the back of her head.

When that was over, Melissa straightened up and smiled down at him—and laughed—and went to get down his bowl that was still up on the shelf.

She filled his bowl while he watched her, and she set it down on the table at his regular place.

But Whit stayed where he was. He said very suddenly, not looking at her, "I'm glad I went away, though it didn't work out that I kept any Indians off you—they'd never have come. Still, I feel better than if I hadn't gone when I'd figured I'd ought to— even though I was wrong."

"Yes," she said quietly, "I understand."

He stood up and turned round.

And though she could see that he wanted to talk, he looked so thin and tired that she said, "You—you better eat, Whit."

"Yes, in a minute. It is on me to talk."

She was concerned for him—more so than before.

He stared straight ahead of him, looking past her, and as though into the dimness at the other end of the room—and his face suddenly gentled because it seemed to please him in some way that he was going to speak. "I am grateful to God," he said, "because you are all right. We are together. That seems the main thing. It did while I was laid up—and it does to me now. And I am glad, too, that I can get back to work. I got a plenty to do— fall plowin', 'n wood, 'n I got t' help in return most of them that helped you. Right now, I am tired, and I'm down and look poor. But I ain't slipped any, I'm sart'n of that. We have been lucky, and I hope it keeps on. And I hope if it don't, we c'n handle that, too—or I hope that I can—I *know* about you.

"Well—I guess I better eat," he said. And when he had sat down, "You know today when I was up there on the hill, the mountain come out up in the sky again the same as that time before—you know what I mean—same as that time when I located here."

"Yes. I know what you mean."

Whit looked up at her. She had seen it. She knew.

He said with a grin, "You come here—"

But young Jonas came in, lugging the rifle, breathless and proud.

Whit said, "Set her there in the corner, 'n then you come here 'n set down. Where'd you leave Gowan?"

"He's comin'."

And Gowan came in. He was out of breath, too—but he'd not been far behind.

Jonas climbed up on the bench beside Whit. And his father swung Gowan up close to his side. Gowan had heft to him—for all he was short. He crowded close to his father.

Whit started to eat. He thought, "It does taste real good." It tasted so good that it almost made him shudder and he could have cried.

He swung round to Jonas. "How're them oxen? I hadn't asked."

Young Jonas was grinning. He bobbed his head. "All right," he said.

Whit looked up at Melissa—just to make sure.

She had been standing there watching all three. . . .

He saw her in happiness.

"Yes," she said, "all right."